T0220399

Beginning DotNetNuke 4.0 Website Creation in C# 2005 with Visual Web Developer 2005 Express

From Novice to Professional

Nick Symmonds

Apress®

Beginning DotNetNuke 4.0 Website Creation in C# 2005 with Visual Web Developer 2005 Express: From Novice to Professional

Copyright © 2006 by Nick Symmonds

ISBN-13 (pbk): 978-1-59059-681-4

ISBN-10 (pbk): 1-59059-681-1

9 8 7 6 5 4 3 2 1

Trademarked names may appear in this book. Rather than use a trademark symbol with every occurrence of a trademarked name, we use the names only in an editorial fashion and to the benefit of the trademark owner, with no intention of infringement of the trademark.

Lead Editor: James Huddleston
Technical Reviewer: Adriano Baglioni
Editorial Board: Steve Anglin, Ewan Buckingham, Gary Cornell, Jason Gilmore, Jonathan Gennick, Jonathan Hassell, James Huddleston, Chris Mills, Matthew Moodie, Dominic Shakeshaft, Jim Sumser, Keir Thomas, Matt Wade
Project Manager: Beth Christmas
Copy Edit Manager: Nicole LeClerc
Copy Editor: Damon Larson
Assistant Production Director: Kari Brooks-Copony
Production Editor: Kelly Winquist
Compositor: Pat Christenson
Proofreaders: Nancy Riddiough, Lori Bring
Indexer: Valerie Haynes Perry
Artist: Kinetic Publishing Services, LLC
Cover Designer: Kurt Krames
Manufacturing Director: Tom Debolski

Distributed to the book trade worldwide by Springer-Verlag New York, Inc., 233 Spring Street, 6th Floor, New York, NY 10013. Phone 1-800-SPRINGER, fax 201-348-4505, e-mail orders-ny@springer-sbm.com, or visit http://www.springeronline.com.

For information on translations, please contact Apress directly at 2560 Ninth Street, Suite 219, Berkeley, CA 94710. Phone 510-549-5930, fax 510-549-5939, e-mail info@apress.com, or visit http://www.apress.com.

The information in this book is distributed on an "as is" basis, without warranty. Although every precaution has been taken in the preparation of this work, neither the author(s) nor Apress shall have any liability to any person or entity with respect to any loss or damage caused or alleged to be caused directly or indirectly by the information contained in this work.

The source code for this book is available to readers at www.apress.com in the Source Code section.

For my daughter, Kate. The world is open to you.

Contents at a Glance

Contents

About the Author

NICK SYMMONDS works for the Integrated System Solutions division of Ingersoll-Rand, developing and integrating security software. He started out his professional life as an electronics technician. While getting his bachelor's degree in electrical engineering from the University of Hartford, he started to gravitate toward programming. Nick has spent quite a few years programming in assembly language, C, C++, and Visual Basic. Recently, he has latched onto .NET like a lamprey and loves digging into the .NET core. Nick has written several articles on programming and has three books currently out: *Internationalization and Localization Using Microsoft .NET* (Apress, 2002), *GDI+ Programming in C# and VB .NET* (Apress, 2002), and *Data Entry and Validation with C# and VB .NET Windows Forms* (Apress, 2003). He lives with his family in the northwest hills of Connecticut and has recently become addicted to golf and road cycling. He also enjoys woodworking, hiking, and exploring the hills on his motorcycle.

About the Technical Reviewer

ADRIANO BAGLIONI got his first taste of computers as a freshman in high school, using BASIC on a PDP-11/70. He pursued his interest in computers at Rensselaer Polytechnic Institute (RPI), where he graduated with a bachelor's degree in computer and systems engineering. He followed that up with a master's degree in computer science, also from RPI. He has worked in the computer industry for 20 years, programming mostly in C and C++. His experience runs the gamut from embedded programming on 8051s to scientific programming on mainframes. He currently works at Veeder-Root, developing software for environmental monitoring equipment.

When it's time to take a break from the computer, Adriano enjoys hiking, biking, and camping with his wife, Carol.

Acknowledgments

As with all books, the result is always a team effort. My thanks go out to Ewan Buckingham for accepting the idea and letting me run with it. Beth Christmas was always there to make sure I did not forget anything and to offer encouragement. My thanks also go out to Jim Huddleston. Jim always kept me on track from the reader's point of view. Damon Larson provided the final set of eyes to make sure everything made sense.

Finally, I would like to thank Adriano Baglioni for his tireless technical review. He was a big help indeed.

Even though this book was a collaboration, the errors remain mine. I would appreciate you letting me know if you find any; you can contact me at nsymmonds@gmail.com.

Introduction

So, here you are at the start of this book. You're wondering why you should buy this book as opposed to the many others on the shelf. You may have noticed that this book isn't as thick as the others. Does that mean it doesn't contain as much information? Well . . . as a matter fact, yes.

This book is about results. It's about getting from point A to point B with as little hassle as possible. I haven't filled this book with ancient history, and I haven't included any in-depth discussions concerning the technology behind .NET and DotNetNuke. What I have included are the basics to get you going. You'll see concise overviews of .NET and DotNetNuke. You'll see how using the latest technology from Microsoft and the open source community can give you a professional web presence.

In short, this book has what you need and nothing you don't. If you're curious, however, I do point you to other information sources to get more in-depth explanations and examples.

Now that you know the thrust of this book, what is it really about? Can it solve all your problems? Can it instantly shave five strokes off your golf game? Will it get you into a smaller pant size? Does it come with a free steak knife? Well . . . no. This book is all about efficiency, not hype.

- It's about programming C#, the powerful mainstream language of .NET.

- It's about getting your business working more efficiently.

- It's about getting a web presence for internal and external use.

- It's about making web portals that you can plug into your web pages.

- It's about making web portlets that you can plug into someone else's portal.

- It's about combining the best and easiest technology from Microsoft and the open source community to give you the fastest route to a web page.

Microsoft Express editions are new for 2005. They were released in early November of 2005 as part of the new Visual Studio 2005 and SQL Server 2005 releases. There are six Express editions:

- Visual C# 2005 Express

- Visual Basic 2005 Express

- Visual C++ 2005 Expresss

- Visual J# 2005 Express

- Visual Web Developer 2005 Express

- SQL Server 2005 Express

They are separated out as different products to make for a smaller install. For this book, you will be using Visual C# 2005 Express and Visual Web Developer (VWD) 2005 Express.

DotNetNuke (DNN) is a product written using ASP.NET. It was recently revised to take advantage of ASP.NET 2.0, which is what VWD is based on. DNN is a framework that sits on top of .NET. It allows you to rapidly develop professional-looking websites. Developing websites rapidly is what this book is all about.

So . . . who am I and who are you? Let's start with me. I'm a software engineer working for a large company doing all kinds of things. I write complex software in C++, C#, VB .NET, and VB 6.0. I also develop web clients for some of our most complicated software. I do this in both the Sun world (JSP, Java, and JavaScript) and in the Microsoft world (.NET). I've been doing this for about 15 years, and I'm still learning a lot and having a blast. I started working with .NET back in the beta days of the first release. I've written three books based on programming in .NET. These books are in both VB .NET and C#. So, I'm well versed in the world of .NET.

Just as important to your success with this book is who you are. You're a person who needs results fast. You're probably not a career web developer. In fact, you may be a novice programmer. You've probably made a few web pages for personal use and want to expand your knowledge. You may be a person who owns or works for a small business and wants to create a web presence. Outsourcing web development can be an expensive thing. For the cost of this book and a little work on your part, you can achieve the results you want.

One nice thing about using the Express editions of Visual Studio is this: even though they are streamlined, they provide a seamless upgrade path to the full version. If you like programming web pages, and you grow beyond the scope of this book, you'll have the ability to take everything you learn and program to the next level.

Oh, by the way . . . did I mention that all the software you need is free? Yes, free. The Express editions are freely downloadable from Microsoft (for a limited time), and DNN is open source.

The only thing you may need to pay for is an upgrade from Windows XP Home Edition to Windows XP Professional (if you want to use IIS).

I hope you enjoy using this book as much as I enjoyed writing it. Let me know how it goes.

CHAPTER 1

■■■

The Basics

This chapter is here to let you know what you need to prepare yourself for web page design. I'll tell you about the level of programming experience you need to get the most out of this book, and I'll also let you know what you need to complete the projects in this book with respect to operating systems, memory, browsers, and so on.

Finally, I'll get into the development environments themselves. Yes, that was plural. In this book, you'll start with the Visual C# 2005 Express (C#) IDE as a way of getting familiar with C#, the programming language used in this book. Later on, you'll graduate to the Visual Web Developer (VWD) 2005 Express IDE and combine it with DotNetNuke.

Note IDE is short for *integrated development environment*. The *integrated* part refers to the ability to edit, debug, and build a project all in one place. In fact, IDEs often allow you to check into and out of code from a source control database. If you ever work in collaboration with other programmers on the same project, you will need source control. For now, you can get away without it.

What You Need to Know

Here is where I need to be truthful about my level of delivery in this book. It is also where you need to know just what is expected of you. There are many things I will not cover in depth simply because I expect that you are already familiar with them. Let's start with what you know.

Programming Experience

So how much programming experience have you had, anyway? Have you dabbled in Visual Basic? Have you created static web pages in HTML? Do you know what "C" is, besides the third letter of the alphabet? If the last three sentences totally rattle you, then this book is probably not for you.

While this is a book about beginning web page design, it's not a book about beginning programming for the totally uninitiated. You will be expected to know certain things, and I will take you through mini-lessons on the things I think you may not know. Here is a list of the things you need to know about programming:

- What the different kinds of loops are

- How to create a function and how to call one

- How to use an editor

- Basic data flow and how to logically structure a program

It does not matter what programming language you are experienced in. It only matters that programming is not totally foreign to you. If you have spent a lot of time creating Visual Basic for Applications (VBA) routines for Excel or Word, you are well prepared for what is to come in this book. If you are a seasoned HTML and JavaScript programmer, you are even better prepared for this book.

Here is something else that I consider really important: you should have no fear of experimentation when it comes to programming. You should be comfortable around computers and be willing to experiment and learn. Often, the programming failures on the way to bug-free software can be more fun and instructive than if you hacked out perfect code to start with. I often find that failures in the form of bugs and lack of knowledge lead me down paths of learning that I never intended to explore in the first place.

Web Experience

Web experience can mean so many things. It can mean anything from reading news sites to shopping on eBay or Amazon. If you are a hacker, it can even mean creating those dastardly pop-up ads that invade our web space.

The fact that you want to create web pages tells me that you have web experience. I bet you have a couple of browsers running—maybe Internet Explorer and Firefox. Here is a list of things that would be helpful as far as basic web knowledge goes:

- Knowing that there are many browsers out there that can show you the same website

- Knowing that quite a few browsers are derived from the same basic browser engine

- Knowing key differences between browsers and why some people prefer one over another

- Knowing something about security in browsers and how to change it

- Knowing what a URL is

- Knowing what an IP address is and how it relates to DNS

- Knowing what HTML is

- Knowing what cookies are and how they are used

- Knowing how web pages are constructed

- Knowing what the Internet is and how you can use it effectively

- Knowing how to detect errors on a web page

Some of these things are rather advanced, I know. I did, after all, say they would be helpful, not required. During the course of this book, I will teach you about these things and more. By the end, you will be as well versed in browser lingo and manipulation as some of the best web designers. After all, isn't that why you're here?

Basic Web Knowledge

Based on the preceding list, here are some things you need to know about the Internet and browsers. I will also tell you briefly how web pages are constructed and how they operate.

First of all, there are many browsers available to you. Any worthwhile one is free. There's more than just Internet Explorer and Netscape. However, these two are the most well known because of the browser wars back in the late 90s. (Sounds like an outer space conflict, doesn't it?) The most common browsers are Internet Explorer (IE), Netscape, Opera, and Firefox. As of this writing, Firefox is gaining incredible ground on IE, and its uniqueness has finally triggered Microsoft to update IE.

Next is the little known fact that many of these browsers are derived from the same basic engine. For instance, Netscape and Mozilla's Firefox are both derived from the same browser layout engine. This engine is called Gecko. The reason I tell you this is because you are much more likely to encounter similarities among Gecko-based browsers than between IE and Gecko-based browsers. In other words, Netscape is far more likely to work like Firefox than IE is. This is a great source of pain that VWD has resolved for you.

So, what are some of the differences between browsers? Well, as someone who spends about 20 percent of each web project developing code that works on both major kinds of browsers (Mozilla-based and IE), I can tell you that there are some major differences and some minor ones. Some of the major ones are as follows:

- Some JavaScript errors kill IE but not Firefox.

- Some HTML tags are interpreted differently by IE and Firefox.

- IE and Firefox have totally different event models.

- IE can run ActiveX programs (a security risk) and Firefox cannot (Firefox wins here).

The following are some of the minor differences you will see:

- Sometimes, different browsers position some tags differently.

- The order of HTML rendering is sometimes different in different browsers, which can make for strange appearances.

- Some style attributes that work in Firefox may not work in IE.

- Some things render faster in one browser than another.

The reason I tell you some of the differences among browsers is to prevent any undue hair loss. However, this may not always be something that can be helped.

There is a bright side to all this, though. Microsoft is very aware of all the browser differences, major and minor. VWD is designed to account for all these differences for you. It will be very rare indeed that you have to discover which browser the client is running and adjust your code path to make allowances. I can guarantee you that in this book, you will not have to worry about any of this. It is helpful, however, to keep this in the back of your mind.

Next, here are some web-related terms you should know, along with their definitions:

- *URL (uniform resource locator)*: This is what you type in the address bar at the top of your browser. You know, like www.something.com.

- *IP address*: An IP address uniquely identifies the device on the Internet. Every computer or device in the world that is connected to the Internet gets an IP address. This makes it possible for your machine to be found among the millions of devices on the Web.

- *Router*: This is a hardware device that steers information from one computer to another. If the router knows that the address you are looking for is in a particular area of the Internet, it will not broadcast your request everywhere. It will direct it only to where it thinks you are looking. By the way, a router with DHCP has the ability to give out IP addresses and hide those addresses from the Internet as a whole. This means that there will be several thousands of computers with the same IP address. No need to worry, the router takes care of this.

- *DNS (domain name system)*: This is the cool thing about the Internet that makes it accessible to the masses. A DNS server keeps a database of friendly names that match up with IP addresses. For example, say you have an IP address of 10.44.33.126. When you type in the corresponding friendly name (say, www.something.com) in the address bar, the DNS matches it with the IP address, and you're able to get to where you want. Domain names are unique, as are IP addresses. Because of this, people will pay literally millions of dollars for a domain name just because it is the same as their company name.

- *Cookies*: These are small files that reside on your hard drive. Most every website drops cookies on your machine when you visit it. These cookies contain information such as when you last visited a site, what page you were on, and so on. Cookies make it seem that a website remembers you, but it's all an illusion. Cookies can also be used maliciously, such as in the case of website hijacking.

- *HTML (HyperText Markup Language)*: Basically, this is a set of elements delimited by tags in the form of <tag> </tag>. Most of the time, these tags come in pairs, and the stuff in between is controlled by the tag. The tags are defined according to standards that are closely followed by all browsers (ha, ha). At least they should be. Reality, however, shows us that some tags are open to different interpretation by different browsers. Sometimes the differences are slight; sometimes they are major. What you need to know is that HTML is what makes a web page what it is. It tells the browser how to render the content.

- *Web server*: This is a computer or set of computers that handle requests from browsers all over the Internet. Web servers return web pages and access databases when necessary. In your case, your computer will be the web server, using IIS (Internet Information Services) to serve up pages in DotNetNuke.

- *Internet*: I know, everyone knows what the Internet is, right? Did you know that at its root it is a collection of a dozen or so computers controlling DNS services and routing base traffic? Most people think the Internet is just there. Look up the history of the Internet sometime. It is very interesting.

Website Construction

Now that you have a basic understanding of the Web, it might be worthwhile to touch on how a website works. Whether you program in C# or Java or ColdFusion, all websites are essentially built the same.

First of all, the initial page of a website is in a directory on a server somewhere. This directory could be several layers within the actual server's directory structure. If this were your website, the web server would consider this the virtual root of your website.

Under this "root" directory, you will find subdirectories containing images (images are not contained in the web page but are referenced by it), other web pages, and server code. This server code manages the business logic and database access for your website. You will also find a directory for the database if you have one. Figure 1-1 shows you a typical website directory structure for a basic website. This was created using VWD.

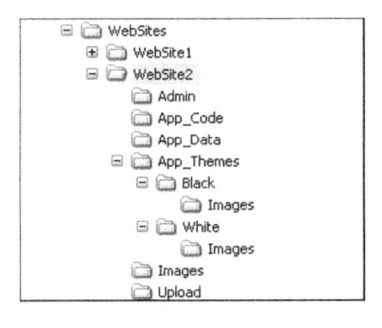

Figure 1-1. *.NET web directory structure*

So here is essentially what happens when a web page is rendered on your machine:

- The browser reads the incoming HTML text. As the text is read, it is parsed, and the screen is rendered.

- The browser renders the HTML tags as they come in. There is no forward referencing of tags.

- As image references are processed, the browser gets the images and displays them.

- Events are fired and various pieces of code are run.

I know this last one is rather nebulous, but this is where a good portion of the book resides. Figure 1-2 shows a small web page. The HTML code behind this page is shown following.

Figure 1-2. *Example of simple HTML code output*

Listing 1-1 shows the HTML code for this simple page.

Listing 1-1. *HTML code for two buttons in a table*

```html
<table width="100%" border="1" bgcolor="green">
  <tr>
    <td width="5%"> </td>
    <td width="20% align="left">
      <input type="button" value="Press me" />
    </td>
    <td width="75% align="left">
      <input type="button" value="No, Press me" />
    </td>
  </tr>
  <tr>
    <td width="5%"> </td>
    <td colspan="2">
      <input type="checkbox" /> check here
    </td>
  </tr>
</table>
```

This is a simple table. The browser runs through the code from top to bottom and renders the tags as they appear. If you are new to HTML, this code will seem like Greek. Do not worry, as VWD will write most of this code for you. You just need to place your buttons and check boxes on your page visually, and VWD will take care of the rest.

HTML Primer

Let's look at the code from Listing 1-1 in a little detail. This small piece of code is pure HTML. It is an example of the most common way to place objects on the screen. In this case, the objects are two buttons and a single check box with some text. As you can see from the code and from Figure 1-2, I have used a table with rows and columns to create cells. These cells divide up the screen real estate into chunks. In these cells are the objects.

First, I have defined a table whose width is 100 percent of the width of the page. I have also defined the background color of this table to be green and to show the border. The vast majority of the time, you will never show the border in any table. I've done it here for debugging purposes and to show you how it looks.

Next, I've defined two rows. These are marked off with <tr>...</tr> tags. The first row contains three cells (akin to columns) that are marked off with <td>...</td> tags. The first cell is 5 percent of the width of the table. It has as its contents just a space. This is defined by , which means *nonbreaking space*. I've used this as a spacer. Using a <td> element as a spacer is very common. The second cell in the first row contains the "Press me" button. Its width is 20 percent of the table width, and the button is left-aligned. The third cell in this row contains the other button. This cell is 75 percent of the table width, and is also left-aligned.

Notice that the widths of all the cells make up 100 percent of the width of the table. You should always try to maintain this.

The second row contains only two cells. However, I need to keep the table balanced. In order to do this, I must span two of the cells in the first row with one of the cells in the second row. First, I make a spacer cell like I did in the first row. The next cell spans two columns as defined by the `<td>` attribute `colspan="2"`. This second cell contains the check box and the associated text.

Viewing Figure 1-2, you can see that the table is balanced and the cells fill up the entire table.

I know that the explanation seems long-winded for a chunk of HTML that is so small. However, if you can understand this little piece of HTML and how it is rendered on your browser, you are a long way toward understanding how web pages really work. Now obviously, there are a ton more HTML tags, and each tag may have several attributes that define how it is rendered. I don't remember all this stuff, and I don't expect you to either. I use a certain percentage of tags in my work and know of most others. If I need in-depth information on how a tag is used or how to display something, I go to the Web. There are a great many websites out there devoted to HTML tag explanations and examples.

When I am surfing, I keep an eye out for new ways to display things. If I see that someone has done something neat, I know that I can do it, too. It usually takes me only a few minutes to find an example or to figure it out myself. If you have a basic understanding and are willing to experiment, you can find out too.

■**Tip** The HTML code for any page is viewable to the user. In IE, you can view the source code by choosing View ➤ Source from the menu at the top. The HTML code will show in a text editor. I do this all the time. You can get some neat pointers this way. Firefox has the same capability, through the menu command View ➤ Page Source.

When a user navigates your website, she may click on menu items or links. What happens behind the scenes is that the web server calls up a new web page from one of the subdirectories under your website. Essentially, all links are references to other pages either on your site or on another site.

One of the major things you need to be aware of during website construction is the use of pictures and drawings. What follows is a small primer on images in web pages.

Images

Images on a page can be either pictures, drawings, or text. Text as a picture, you say? Well, consider the case in which a site developer wants to depict text in a certain font. Your machine is certain to contain many fonts—but what if he wants to use a unique font called, say, "London Taxi"? He can do one of two things. For one, he can download this font to your machine and thereby proliferate this "London Taxi" font all over the world. However, this avenue has its pitfalls, one of which is that your browser may not allow a font to be downloaded to your machine. The better alternative is for him to write the text on his machine and take a picture of it. As far as your surfing goes, you don't see the difference between text and an image—it reads exactly the same.

Anyway, back to images. I said before, when you construct a web page, the image is not part of the page itself. Instead, the image gets rendered at the place inside your page where the image tag is located.

There are different kinds of images available that can be used. They each have different qualities depending on the attributes you need. Table 1-1 explains the common ones.

Table 1-1. *Image Types (Pros and Cons)*

Image Type	Extension	Pros	Cons
Bitmap	.bmp	Format is universal.	File size can be large; does not support transparency.
JPEG	.jpg	File size is small; supports 24-bit color.	Uses lossy compression, in which some data is lost.
TIFF	.tif	Uses lossless compression, so all image data is retained.	File size is large.
GIF	.gif	Uses lossless compress; can contain transparency.	Uses only 256 colors; sometimes involves patent issues.
Animated GIF	.gif	Animates with no extra programming by you.	Same as GIF.

These are the major image formats. Personally, I prefer JPEG and GIF formats. I like JPEG for photographs and I like GIF for all other images. You will not find a graphical browser that does not support these two.

Got a camera? I bet since you want to create a good website, you have a really nice digital camera with 5+ megapixels that shows images in stunning color. Great for the website, eh? Wrong!

How often have you been surfing the Web to come across a site loaded with images, and your computer screams to a grinding halt? Unless the site was really important to you, chances are you left immediately. In fact, studies on load testing have shown that the average person's tolerance for waiting for a website to render is 8 seconds. I have been to web pages that take almost a minute to load at high speed—this was due to many high-resolution images being downloaded to my machine.

If you are taking pictures to include on your website, I suggest that you take them at a low resolution. Think of the size of the picture and how it will be displayed on your web page. Most likely, it will only take up a small space. If this is the case, then "dumb down" your camera to 640×480 resolution and then take the picture. The resulting file size of this picture will be orders of magnitude smaller than a high-quality color-dense photo. Smaller file size means faster rendering speed on your client's browser. Remember the 8 second rule for page rendering (not to be confused with the 5 second rule for food dropped on the floor).

Figure 1-3 shows a low-resolution picture of my bicycle. I originally took the picture at two resolutions: a high resolution, which resulted in a file size of 355 KB; and a low resolution, which resulted in a file size of just 48 KB. The JPEG files themselves are available from this book's download page at www.apress.com. Compare them yourself.

Figure 1-3. *Picture of a bike taken at a low resolution of 640 × 480 pixels*

Most pictures do not take up the whole page. If they only take a small portion of the page, then use a lower resolution. The photos will still look fine.

How a Web Page Works

I've told you a little about how a web page is constructed. Now I will tell you a little about how a web page works. There are several attributes of a web page that make it different from your classic Windows application (you know, applications like Excel, Word, Photoshop, etc.), and I'll discuss these in the following sections.

State

Web pages are stateless. The programs I mentioned previously are stateful. *Stateful* means that the program remembers what you are doing. The program remembers what is on your display and where the data resides. The program knows at all times what you are doing with the data. All Windows programs are stateful.

Stateless refers to the fact that once the program sends the data to the display, it suddenly forgets all about you. In fact, as far as the program is concerned, it never happened. The program has no idea what data it sent and no idea what you are doing with the data. Web programs are stateless. They preserve state for a fraction of a second at best—just long enough to get the data to you.

Why are web programs stateless? It is the nature of the Internet. There is no persistent connection between a web server and a web browser client. In order for a web server to scale to hundreds of thousands of connections per day, there can't be a persistent connection. No server could handle this. Also, the Internet is built to withstand breaks in communication lines. If a line goes down or a router goes bad, the connection can be rerouted via another path. The Internet is error-resistant and self-healing to an extent. There is also so much traffic over the Net that holding a connection open between two computers would take up too much precious bandwidth. The Internet's statelessness allows you to surf to a site and then go have dinner with no harm done and no bandwidth taken.

But how does a site remember you? How are you able to shop online and have the cart constantly updated? This is all an illusion and a great deal of programming.

There are ways to achieve the personalized experience you know from modern-day websites. I am sure you have shopped online, used a shopping cart, and so on. You've probably also come back to some of these sites and they "remember" you. Cool, huh?

The most common way to simulate state is though a session ID. Once you hit a web server and request a page, the server sends the page with a session ID to the browser. Each time you make another call to the web server, the browser sends this session ID back to the server with your request. This session ID is used to track you and what you are doing at the moment. It is also used as a security token to allow you to see some pages and not others, depending upon your login.

Session IDs are often fleeting. For example, with some sites, when you log on and get a session ID, the web server then starts a countdown timer. If you do not get back to the site within a certain timeout period, the session ID will expire and the web server will log you out automatically. You see this a lot with e-commerce sites.

Note You should note that in traditional website development, state management is quite the programming task. However, by using ASP.NET, you are covered. Microsoft has taken all the state management stuff out of the programmer's hands and manages it automatically for you. There are still ways, however, to manage state yourself if needed.

Managing session state is key to providing a rich user experience with your website.

Events

OK, let's say you're on a website and you choose some value from a drop-down list. Or perhaps you move your mouse over a word and a picture pops up or changes. What is going on in these scenarios?

If you are a traditional Windows programmer, you know that whenever you interact with a control like a drop-down box or button, an event is fired. The Windows operating system allows you to catch the event and write code to respond to that event. The same thing can happen in a web application.

There is a difference, though, between how events are handled in web pages and how they're handled in Windows programs. For one thing, with web pages, you get to decide where the event is handled. This is really important for ASP.NET developers like you. ASP.NET allows you to handle the event in the client's browser or back at the server. Figure 1-4 shows a diagram of browser-based event handling (also known as client-side event handling).

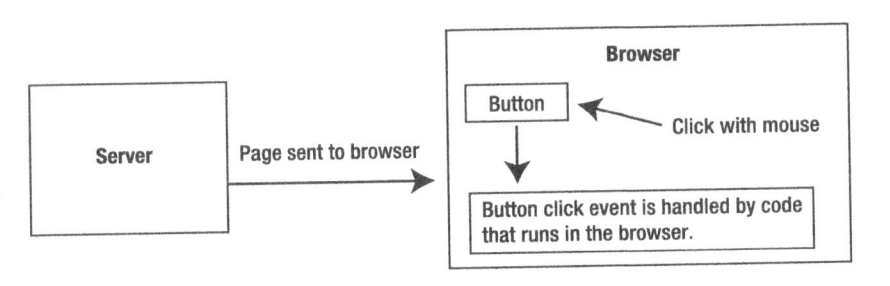

Figure 1-4. *Client-side event handling*

Figure 1-5 shows a diagram depicting events as they are handled on the server.

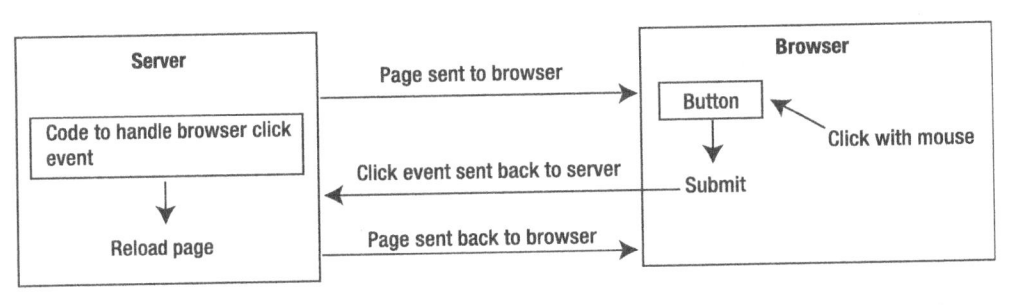

Figure 1-5. *Server-side event processing*

Simply by looking at the number of arrows in the respective diagrams, you can see that the client-side event handling is far simpler than the server-side event handling. If you choose server-side event handling, several things take place before all is said and done:

- The browser detects the click and decides what to do with it.

- The browser submits the request back to the server. This is called a *postback*.

- The server runs some code that handles the event.

- The server renders the page again with any changed data for any fields on the page.

- The server sends the page back to the browser.

- The browser renders the page.

While this often happens in the blink of an eye, it is a lot of work. More to the point, it takes a complete round trip to handle any event. For example, if you caught a "change mouseover" event for several pictures on a page, the round trips to the server could get annoying to the customer. You see, every time you submit the page to the server, it has to render the whole page again and send it back. This results in the familiar flicker you often see on web pages. If you have a dense web page with lots of pictures, these events can really slow down the interaction speed.

As such, it is best to handle simple events on the browser when possible. It makes for a quicker and more realistic experience for the user. However, do not be afraid of using server-side events. ASP.NET makes heavy use of server-side events, and they can be very handy and powerful to program.

Note An advanced method of interaction between the client and the server—called AJAX—is becoming very popular these days. It is a method in which the client can make requests of a server for data without submitting the page. The server can send back data and the client can then update a single field in the page. This is very fast and requires no rerendering of the page. (More on this technique much later in the book.)

Postbacks

I mentioned in the previous section that server-side event handling is done via a postback, or page submittal. Submittals are how the browser sends data back to the server.

You can design a page with several controls. One special control is called a submit button. When this button is pressed in the browser, the page is automatically submitted back to the server. The server can read all the controls on the page and the values of those controls. Once the server has read the control values, it can save the data to a database and perform some business logic based on the values.

When the server is done processing the posted page, it then sends back the same page (with the same or different values) or a different page. Remember this, though: even if nothing changes on the page, the server must rebuild the entire page, values and all, before sending it as HTML back to the browser. While this process may seem wasteful, it has worked for years and is the standard way of doing things.

While postbacks may seem inefficient, web servers such as IIS are very efficient at rendering HTML for web pages. Such web servers use all kinds of memory caching, which speeds up processing to the point that the user won't even notice the flicker, at least on lightweight pages.

What You Need to Have

I have so far explained in general terms what you need to know about programming and websites to continue with the book. This section lets you know what you need in terms of equipment and software.

Hardware

Pretty much any modern-day computer will do. You will need a decent amount of hard drive space to hold the two Express IDEs and any websites you create. About 20 GB free will be OK.

You will need a high-speed Internet connection. A telephone modem will not do, but basic DSL or a cable modem will be fine. You will want to eventually access your computer from other computers to see if your website works.

Software

First on the software list is the operating system. I would recommend the latest from Microsoft, which at the time of this book's publication is Windows Server 2003. I recommend this operating system because it will allow you to upgrade to the full Visual Studio (VS) 2005 edition (complete with source control and more), which you may want to do in the future. Some parts of VS 2005 require Windows Server 2003 as the operating system. However, if you don't have it, you can get away with Windows 2000 Professional or XP Professional just fine for this book.

Note If you're using Windows XP Home Edition, you may want to upgrade to XP Professional with Service Pack 2 (SP2). XP Professional allows you to run IIS, which allows you to better test your web application. However, XP Home will suffice because VWD has its own web server. Chapter 3 deals with installing DotNetNuke on XP Home and XP Professional.

You will need the latest .NET Framework that works with Visual Studio 2005. This framework is available for free from Microsoft. As you load the Express IDEs, it will detect if you have the .NET 2.0 Framework. If not, it will be installed automatically.

If you have an existing framework from version 1.x of .NET on your machine, don't worry. Both frameworks will reside together and can even be run together. There is nothing stopping you from working on .NET 1.x stuff and .NET 2.0 stuff at the same time. Being able to run two versions of the same code at the same time is one part of eliminating DLL hell (explained in Chapter 2). Those of you who are programmers can rejoice. Those who have never experienced DLL hell don't need to worry. Just know that you have avoided something from Microsoft that has plagued us developers since the beginning of time (at least since the 80s, anyway).

Programming Environments

You will be loading two programming environments on your machine: Visual C# 2005 Express and Visual Web Developer 2005 Express.

The reason I'm having you load C# is to help with Chapter 4. C# is the language of choice in this book, and Chapter 4 goes over the basics of C# and how to create Windows programs. This discussion has a twofold purpose: first, to get you familiar with C# and Windows programming; and second, to give you a reference when building web pages. You will find that building a web page that reflects a Windows program is an eye-opening experience. Knowing how a Windows program works gives a great appreciation for the strengths and weaknesses of web development.

C# as a Language

So, why is C# the language of choice for this book? I will list some reasons for you, and then explain in a little more detail.

- C# is a language that is very close in syntax to quite a few others.

- C# allows you to move from C++ and Java easily.

- C# is a very efficient language.

- The C# language is defined by Ecma International and ISO standards.

Before discussing the points in the list, let me give you a bit of history. The first high-level language was the C language. In my beginning programming days, I used C extensively. It was the language of choice for systems programming, and it was platform independent. Those days, "platform independent" meant UNIX or DOS 3.3. (Can you guess my age yet?) I programmed both firmware and software in C. I was able to develop code on my PC and run it on the UNIX box.

After C came C++. It was the turbo-charged, object-oriented version of C. During the object-oriented phase in programming, there was also Delphi (object-oriented Pascal), Eiffel (not seen much these days), and Java (seen everywhere these days).

Java started to gain serious traction in the industry because it ran on every machine. It also had quite a bit of the power of C++ with none of the drawbacks. By drawbacks, I mean memory leaks and pointer arithmetic. Some time after Java became entrenched in the industry, along came Microsoft with .NET and C#.

C# was Microsoft's answer to Java. Microsoft needed an environment that was able to run the .NET code and handle memory management, garbage collection, and so on. Microsoft also needed a flagship language to run in it. This language is C#, which I consider the next generation of C and C++. It is as easy to use as Java and as powerful as C++.

Which brings us to the first point in the preceding list: C# is very close in syntax to other commonly used languages. C# is similar to other mainstream languages such as C and C++ because it descended from them. C# is similar to Java because Java itself was inspired by C++. In fact, C# is much more syntactically similar to Java than to C++. If you are an expert in Java programming, then you are well on your way to being one in C#.

The next point is that C# is an efficient language. Consider its .NET analog, VB .NET. VB .NET requires a lot more wordiness to accomplish the same goals. You will also notice that VB .NET is case insensitive while C# is case sensitive. I also think that the event handling code is better in C# than in VB .NET. OK, this is preference, but this preference is based on my feeling that it is more efficient.

One other thing that I really like about C# is the ability to use unsafe code. This is code that directly addresses the operating system and bypasses all the safety nets that .NET provides. This is not needed very often, but is handy sometimes.

Both Ecma and ISO have released C# language standards. This means that the specification for C# is in the public domain. So what? This is important because it means that someone else can write a C# compiler that compiles code for UNIX. In fact, this is being done right now. The first version of the Mono project (a compiler and environment in which C# code can be run directly on UNIX machines) has been released. There is no emulator involved. Being tied to Microsoft is the biggest detractor to .NET.

One of the things you may like most about C# is that it is very much like JavaScript syntactically. JavaScript is used by ASP.NET for client-side code. Swapping between coding C# and JavaScript is much easier than going between VB .NET and JavaScript. You will feel like you are programming in just one language rather than two.

ASP.NET for Web Development

The second environment you will load is Visual Web Developer 2005 Express Edition. This is where the rubber hits the road, so to speak. VWD is your gateway to creating web pages and sites that will achieve your goals. VWD is not just an IDE—it is an environment in which you can use ASP.NET, HTML, JavaScript, C#, and VB .NET. For this book, the choice of programming languages will be C# for business logic, and ASP.NET and HTML for presentation.

This book is basically about ASP.NET. C# and DotNetNuke are just ways to make developing in ASP.NET easier. If you are not very familiar with ASP.NET, here is the lowdown.

There have always been two major camps for enterprise web development. One comes from Sun Microsystems and the other, of course, is from Microsoft.

Sun gives us the Java/JSP/Servlet/JavaScript development combination. Microsoft gives us the ASP/VB/VBScript development combination. ASP and JSP both give us dynamic content in web pages.

The basic difference comes down to price of development tools and price of the web server. Java-based web pages can be developed for free and run on a free Apache web server. ASP-based web pages have better (but not free) development tools. (However, ASP can be written using just Notepad.) ASP also requires that you use IIS, which is not free.

Along comes ASP.NET from Microsoft with killer development tools that are free (via VWD) and a web server that can be used to test your web page (also free, via VWD). The really nice thing about ASP.NET, though, is that it has fixed all the shortcomings of JAVA/JSP development and classic ASP development.

The DotNetNuke Difference

The last thing you need to load onto your machine is DotNetNuke (DNN). DNN is not an IDE like VWD. Rather, it is a framework of wizards, templates, and code that allows you to create professional web pages in a flash. Working with DNN and VWD will give you all the tools you need for quite a while.

DNN is not a language, and it's not a development environment either. In fact, DNN allows you to program ASP.NET pages in C#, VB .NET, J#, and even COBOL .NET (if you're feeling masochistic).

DNN is a framework that allows you to create websites faster and with more consistency than otherwise. DNN is very popular and is getting more so every day.

So what does DNN bring to the table? While VWD allows you to do everything you need to create a website, DNN is a framework that manages it all for you. A website is not just a page that is shown to a surfer. It is a collection of database tables, back-end logic, administration duties, security concerns, and so on.

DNN allows you to do site hosting if you like. It allows you to manage content and site membership. Although you can do all this development yourself using VWD, using the help of DNN tools makes it much faster and easier.

Web Server

So, where do web pages come from, you ask? I think you are old enough now to know the truth: they come from a web server. A web server is often thought of as a nebulous, high-powered machine that resides somewhere in California. It could be, but in your case it's not. For all the projects in this book, the web server will be your development machine. Perhaps, after you've made your website, you'll want to upload it to one of these high-powered servers. I tell you how to do this in Chapter 10.

There are two web servers you need to worry about. The first is a small test web server that comes with VWD. It is a single-use server that is meant only for displaying web pages as you develop them on your machine. It cannot be used by any other machine. This is cool, as it does not have to be configured, and there is no worrying about how it works. It just does.

The second web server you need to be concerned about is IIS. (As mentioned in the beginning of the chapter, IIS stands for Internet Information Services.) It is Microsoft's web server. It comes on every machine that has Windows 2000 Server or later. However, it needs to be set up and configured to run. You will use IIS to test your websites' deployment and also to do some load testing (for cases when several PCs hit your site at the same time). I will cover IIS in detail in Chapter 3.

Configuring the Browser

For the web pages that you create and display in your browser, you will need to be able to view what you've rendered, run any JavaScript code, and debug any strange behavior. In order to do all this, you will need to configure your browser.

Browser Security

Browser security is where the last decade of security worry has been directed. Everyone these days gets online and browses sites that they shouldn't. Most of the time, this is through no fault of their own, but they are drawn there by mislabeled sites and false advertising.

The browser is a neat tool that can unfortunately let in nasty viruses and other bad surprises—thus the need for browser security.

Here is a list of things you can do to your browser to harden it against malicious attacks:

- Don't allow any cookies.

- Don't allow any JavaScript to run.

- Don't allow any VBScript to run.

- Don't allow any ActiveX components to run.

- Don't allow any ActiveX controls to be downloaded.

- Enable the pop-up blocker.

- Severely restrict Java.

This is just the major stuff. There are a ton of other settings you can enable to make your browser safe—and practically unusable to both you and any outside force. That is the problem with security. How much is enough such that you can still use your browser and not be hamstrung by it? Let's look at some of the settings that affect security in a surfing sense, as well as from a web development perspective.

Cookies

These are files that the browser lets you put on the client's machine. Think of the browser as a window from the outside world into your machine. Yes, you can see out, but others can also see in. There are two things you do not want the outside to do on your machine: one is to run some code that can affect your machine; the other is to drop a file on your machine.

I will cover the code part later. The file part is solved by cookies. Cookies are files that are created and destroyed by the browser itself. You can write some scripting code that runs on a client's browser that tells the browser to create, destroy, or read a cookie. So while people may not be able to send unsolicited files to your machine though the browser, they can tell the browser to drop a cookie.

So what are cookies used for? They are used mainly to keep track of you. If you surf to a website, often it will drop a cookie noting that you have been there. The contents of a cookie might be the last page you visited at that site, or the date of the last movie you rented from that site. A cookie can also contain a username and password. Some sites use cookies to log you back in when you return to a site.

Remember I talked a little about state before? A cookie is essentially a way to remember state. Recall that the web server sends a page to you and then forgets all about you. Since the server cannot remember that you were ever there, the next best thing is to have your computer remember that you were there. As you interact with a website, the cookie is sent back and forth as a memory device.

The bad thing about cookies is that they can be spoofed and stolen. Websites trust the cookies that they leave. If another website changes them, the website that left them will not know that some information in them is false.

So the end result of all this worry is that some people turn off cookies. This effectively gives your computer amnesia every time it visits the same site. Now that there are so many sites that are tailored to the user, it can be really annoying to have to constantly type in the same information every time you visit. However, this is life, and you will find that some clients' machines have cookies disabled.

For this book, however, you will need to allow cookies. To do this in IE 6.0, choose Tools ➤ Internet Options, click the Privacy tab, and set the slider to the Medium setting (as shown in Figure 1-6).

In fact, all the security options mentioned here can be activated in IE 6.0 through the menu option Tools ➤ Internet Options. Firefox can also disable or enable cookies. You can do this by navigating to Tools ➤ Options ➤ Privacy ➤ Cookies.

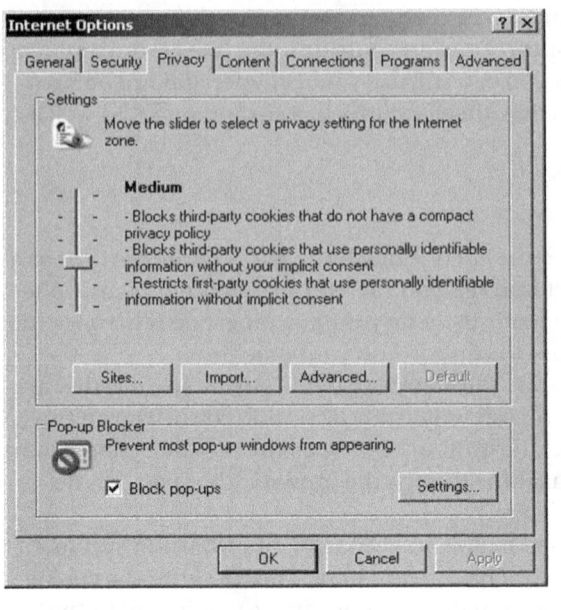

Figure 1-6. *Allowing cookies in IE 6.0*

ActiveX Components

ActiveX components are controls that are able to make full use of your computer's resources. This means, for example, that they can use the GDI (graphics device interface) to perform some really complicated drawing. They can use the file system to read and write files on your hard drive. They can use the operating system to control just about anything on your machine. Note that ActiveX components are available in IE, but not in Firefox.

In effect, an ActiveX component is a control that runs just like any other executable on your machine.

While ActiveX controls give a richer user experience to your web page, I suggest that you not only don't use them, but that you turn them off. Most websites and web clients these days do not use anything that must be downloaded to the client's computer. Most businesses will not allow it. To turn them off in IE 6.0, go to Tools ➤ Internet Options ➤ Security ➤ Custom Level (as show in Figure 1-7).

By the way, do you know that there is a Java analog to the ActiveX component? It is called an applet. An applet is a small Java program that is downloaded to your machine and acts as a helper for the web page. It serves the same purpose as an ActiveX component. Most businesses do not allow applets either.

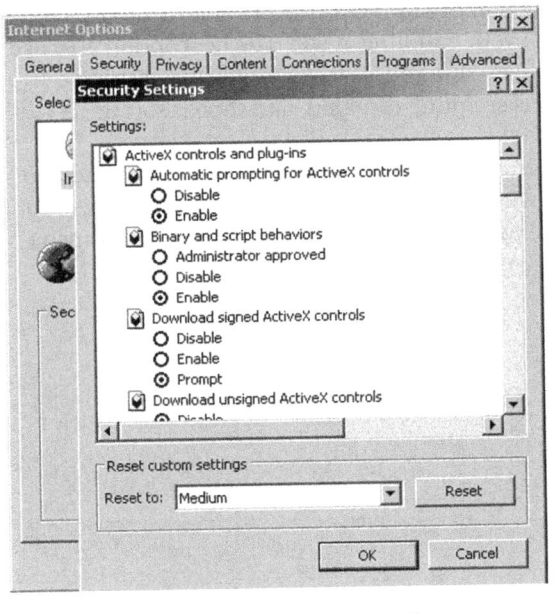

Figure 1-7. *Security for ActiveX controls*

Scripting

Here is something that brought web pages out of the dark ages and into the full user experience you know today. *Scripts* are small functions that run inside your browser. These scripts control how the HTML controls act and react to user input. They allow the dynamic interaction that you get with most websites. Scripts are different from ActiveX controls or applets, as they are controlled by your browser and run in a "sandbox."

Now, you can certainly interact with the user on your website without using scripting, but it's slower and harder. For instance, many HTML controls, such as text boxes or buttons, have events that you can catch and respond to. There are two ways to do this.

The first way is to submit the page to the server, figure out what event was fired, react to the event, and return the page in whatever new state it needs to be in. This can be pretty fast on a small page with few controls, but it can be pretty slow on a very dense page with many HTML elements on it.

The second way is to program event handlers though JavaScript or VBScript. This allows the client browser to handle the event with no posting to the server. No round trip means no delay. There are many things you can do using client-side scripting that does not need any server intervention. I'll explain this in detail in Chapter 12.

ASP.NET has the unique ability to use either client-side scripting or server-side code for event handling. You have the ability to redirect event handling at will. The best option is to use client-side scripting whenever possible, and server-side code when serious business logic is involved. You can even detect when the user has scripting disabled, and then resort to server-side code.

Most businesses allow client-side scripting, so you need to turn it on. Remember how to do this, because you will be testing some code with your browser later in the book, with scripting turned both on and off. You need to be able to work on computers that have scripting on and off. Figure 1-8 shows the security setting for this.

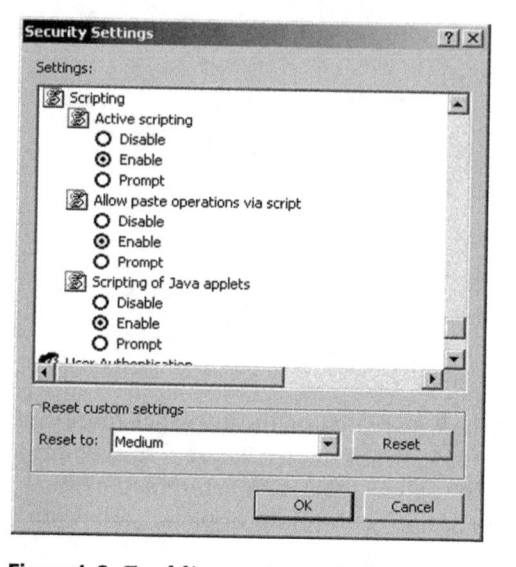

Figure 1-8. *Enabling active scripting*

Debugging

There is one last thing you need to do before starting out in web programming. You've just enabled web scripting; now you need to be able to debug it. VWD works just fine for debugging C# code and any other server-side code—however, it cannot debug code that runs in the browser. IE can. You can allow client-side JavaScript debugging with a tool called Microsoft Script Editor, which comes with Microsoft FrontPage 2003. Figure 1-9 shows how to allow debugging in IE.

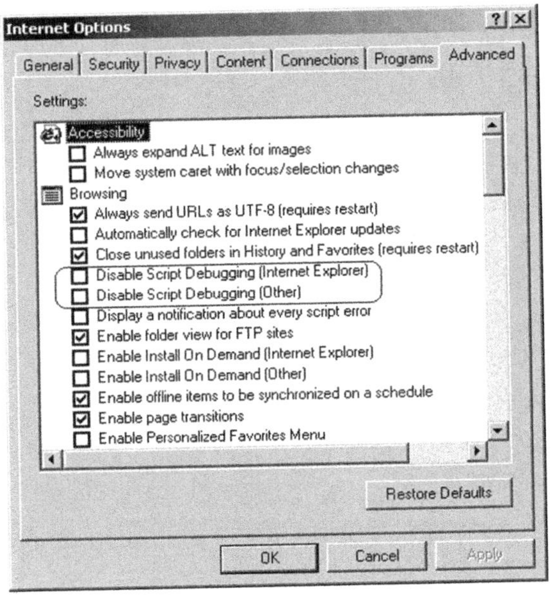

Figure 1-9. *Allowing client-side script debugging*

Note that you need to uncheck these options in the Advanced tab of the Internet Options menu. (This was confusing to me at first.)

If you do not have FrontPage loaded, there are other debugging techniques that I will go over with you in Chapter 12.

Summary

This chapter has covered the basics of what you need in order to effectively use this book. By basics, I mean not only the physical aspects but the conceptual ones as well.

You will need to know something about web pages and maybe a little programming. Mostly, though, you will just need to be willing to experiment with writing code. If you are willing to try out new things, you will go far in creating web pages.

This chapter has also covered the hardware and software necessary for the projects in this book. The hardware is something you most likely already have, and all the software you need is free.

Chapter 2 will explain why the combination of VWD and DNN is the choice for you to create professional web pages in a short amount of time.

CHAPTER 2

■■■

The Express and DotNetNuke Combination

Chapter 1 went through the basics of what you need in terms of a system and software. This chapter tells you why you need it. I'll tell you about some of the history of .NET and some of its major features. I'll also go into some of the background of DotNetNuke (DNN).

You may be thinking that this chapter really has nothing to do with making web pages, and technically you'd be correct. However, some background can increase your understanding of why things are being done they way they are, and what the advantages are. It makes you a more complete programmer.

Microsoft .NET

Microsoft .NET was first released in 2001. Just after the first release, I wrote a book called *Internationalization and Localization Using Microsoft .NET*. I had worked in programming for many years before, and once the .NET Framework was released to the world in beta form, I was all over it.

Before .NET

You see, before .NET, I was writing code in C, C++, and Visual Basic (VB) 5.0/6.0. I loved the power and raw capability of the C language. I loved the object-oriented slant of C++. I loved VB's ease of use and its slick visual development environment.

There were some problems with each of these, however. I disliked how difficult it was to create Windows programs in C. I disliked the nested code and obtuseness of C++. Sure, with C++, I could now write some Windows programs, but not quickly. (Try to find the `main()` function in a Visual C++ program. You'll be hunting for days.)

I also disliked the abstractness of VB. Although writing a Windows program with VB was simplicity in itself, trying to do any complicated drawing presented some pretty stiff barriers. Not to mention that even a Hello World program required quite a few DLLs (dynamic-link libraries) to be included. This made the simplest of VB programs very bloated in size, which was a problem, because these were not the days of 200 GB hard drives and $40 DVD burners. Computers have come a really long way in a few short years.

DLL Hell

There was also something else that all windows programmers were fighting back then. It was known as DLL hell. You may have heard of it. It is still around.

DLLs were invented as a way to save on memory and disk space—quite ingenious, actually. DLLs were useful when you would have a set of functions that could be common to many programs. Instead of linking the same code into many programs, you could make a DLL with common code that could be used by many programs, and not loaded until needed. This greatly reduced the size of all the executables on disk. DLLs could also be loaded into memory, which would also reduce the memory footprint of programs as well.

Sounds good, eh? Well, it was—that is, until the registry and COM (Component Object Model) came along. In order for a COM DLL to be registered, it needed a GUID (globally unique identifier). This is a unique 128-bit number. Your program would be required to use a DLL with a particular GUID. This assured no spoofing of code, and also assured that you got the proper version of the DLL. (As an aside, VB 6.0 is 100 percent COM. All the controls are COM; everything in it is COM.)

There is an unenforceable rule in the world of DLL programming that the signatures of all the functions within a DLL must not change between versions. It is OK to add new functions to a DLL, and you are allowed to change the logic in a function if you like between versions, but it is not OK to delete a function or change a function's name or arguments.

As I said, this is unenforceable, and it was frequently ignored. In fact, Microsoft was just as guilty of this as anyone else. It would not be unusual for two programs from different companies to use the same DLL. When one company wanted to change a function in a common DLL, they would do it—but they wouldn't necessarily bump up the version. Often, they would keep the GUIDs the same so that your unsuspecting program would think it was using the correct DLL, and they would frequently ship the new DLL with the new executable. You would install it on your machine, and all of a sudden your other program that used the same DLL would not work right. This happened frequently, and it is affectionately called DLL hell.

After much hand wringing and debugging, you might find that a function was changed to add a new argument, or perhaps an argument was changed from a long to a short. A difference like this would not show up until you tried to pass in a number greater than 65,535 (the max number for a short). A bug like this would be infuriating to find and fix.

Other Problems

There are some other quite significant problems with using raw languages such as C and C++, and they have to do with memory usage.

These languages allow you to manipulate memory at will. They allow you to allocate and de-allocate memory as you need for buffer space. Often, this results in a very common issue called a memory leak, in which you allocate memory for use and forget to de-allocate it. If you did this in a loop, you would eventually run out of memory. This can be a very sticky bug to find and fix.

The second most common type of memory problem is the buffer overrun. In C, for instance, a string is a denoted by a start position and special character at the end of the string. When iterating through the characters of a string, you are supposed to look for this special end character. Oftentimes, it is easy to go beyond this character and into other memory space without the operating system complaining at all. A few years ago, buffer overruns were a serious security leak in some Microsoft products. Hackers were intentionally exploiting buffer overruns and putting malicious code into unprotected memory space. All it required to get a virus running was a simple instruction pointer redirect.

Another problem is related to threads. A thread is a piece of code that (appears) to run at the same time as other code. Threads are used for printing and other background tasks such as modem communications. Threads are used everywhere in Windows programs.

A thread has to communicate with the program that spawned it. It does this through common variables that are available to the main thread and any worker threads. What do you think happens when two threads tried to change a variable at the same time? Chaos happens. Thread synchronization issues, deadlocks, and race conditions are easy to introduce and very hard to debug. It takes a great deal of knowledge to program threads properly.

What .NET Fixes

I have told you some of the neat aspects of other languages and some of the pitfalls. Depending on what you need to do, I feel the pitfalls outweigh the advantages. The business of testing and debugging code is expensive. However, it is not nearly as expensive as letting a bug escape to the customer.

It is this expense in both time and money that .NET addresses. When .NET was introduced, it offered the following solutions to programming pitfalls:

- *Garbage collection*: No more memory leaks

- *Safe code:* No more buffer overruns

- *Versioned assemblies*: No more DLL hell

- *Complete classes*: Almost no need to call a low-level Windows API directly

- *Common data types*: Ability for multiple programming languages to be used in writing parts of the same program

- *.NET Remoting*: No more COM

- *Reversion to configuration files*: No more using the registry to store settings; XML configuration files in .NET (used to be INI configuration files before Windows 95)

- *Discontinued use of pointers*: No more pointers, which are confusing and a big source of memory leaks

Let's look at some of these in detail.

Garbage Collection

When Java was introduced, it had the great ability to do garbage collection—automatically releasing memory once it was no longer needed.

.NET has a low-level garbage collection thread that gets run every so often. It is low-level so that it does not interfere with any of the horsepower you require from the machine. It runs during your CPU's idle time.

THREADS AND PROCESSING TIME

Windows uses a time-slice threading model. In this model, the operating system takes chunks of time and gives it to threads in round robin order. This time slices are very small, so all threads look as if they are running in real time.

Threads have priority. A low-priority thread is not given any time if a higher-priority one needs it. While this seems unfair, think about how much time is needed to actually perform a task. I am sure you have had many programs running on your machine at the same time. This might include something like a word processor, a streaming audio program, and maybe a mail program, all of which run threads that have both low and high priorities. The computer is so fast that it is able to handle all these threads in round robin order and still have a ton of time and processing power left over for other tasks. Such tasks could include the .NET garbage collector.

To get a sense of how fast the computer is, you can take a look at the Task Manager. To do so, right-click the taskbar and choose Task Manager. Figure 2-1 shows the menu you will get.

Multiple processors and better operating systems can handle this kind of massively multithreaded program, but the normal Windows computer can't.

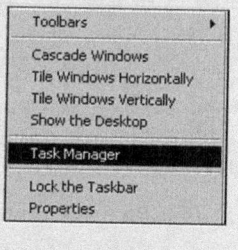

Figure 2-1. *Menu to pull up the Task Manager*

Once you get the Task Manager running, choose the Processes tab and click the CPU table column header. This will organize the entries by CPU time from greatest to least. Note that in Figure 2-2 I have many processes open, but the system idle process takes 99 percent of the computer's time.

You will notice that my computer with all these things running is doing absolutely nothing most of the time. I have hundreds of threads running and all of them take up less than one percent of the computer's time.

There is one thing to note about threads. If you get thread-happy in your program and spin off hundreds of threads, the overhead to manage those threads soon takes up a good portion of the time allotted to your program. There is a certain amount of time needed for things like switching threads, saving thread state, and so on. If you have too many threads, this management time could overwhelm the time allowed for your threads. This does not even take into account thunking. (*Thunking* is a great word, don't you think? Thunking is what happens when a 32-bit program has to step down to a 16-bit program. It largely has to do with memory management. Basically, your program is running along at light speed, and then it goes *thunk*!)

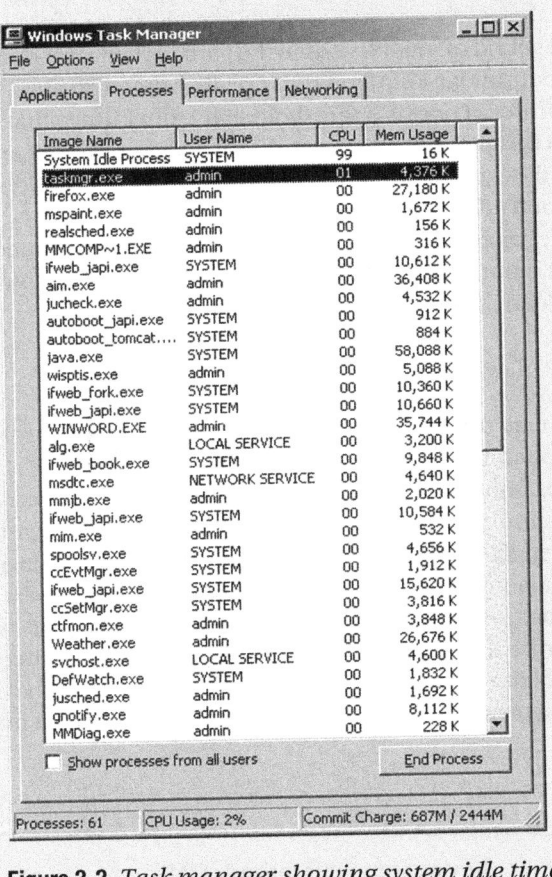

Figure 2-2. *Task manager showing system idle time*

The garbage collection thread walks the heap for any memory that seems to be unclaimed. It also finds thread objects that have stopped and are no longer really connected to anything. Once it finds some memory to be reclaimed, it marks it as such. Your object will then fire an event that you can listen to. This event says "I don't think this is being used anymore. Unless you change a flag, I will delete it the next time I see it." You get a chance to stop the garbage collection by resetting a flag. This process is used just in case you haven't lost connection with an object and you really want it around.

If this flag is not reset, then the next time the thread runs and sees this object, it will de-allocate the memory and delete the object. But that's not all.

Consider a case in which you've instantiated objects 1, 2, 3, and 4. Now, let's say you dispose of objects 2 and 4. This leaves 1 and 3. This also leaves a hole between objects 1 and 3. If you now want to instantiate another object that is slightly larger than object 2, the system will be unable to use the dead space between objects 1 and 3.

In this way, the garbage collector has another job, which is to create contiguous space where there was none. In this case, it would move the contents of object 3's memory to where object 2 was. This will open a contiguous space that's the size of objects 2 and 4. The garbage collector is a neat freak.

You might be asking, why should I get rid of memory when the garbage collector does it for me? Well, for small programs that do not run for long, you don't really need to. Realize, however, that even these days memory is scarce. There is a threshold of memory usage that the garbage collector will tolerate. Beyond this point, it starts running at a higher priority and for longer. Since garbage collection takes time, your program could slow down, and could slow down significantly. Besides, it is just good etiquette to clean up after yourself.

I will teach you about proper object disposal in Chapter 4, when we delve into some C# programming. Don't worry though—it is not terribly geeky or difficult to do. And remember, if you forget, the garbage collector will clean up after you.

Safe Code

Safe code in .NET parlance is called managed code. This is code that is within the control of the .NET memory manager and security apparatus.

As far as the memory manager goes, this means that if you instantiate an object using .NET, then .NET will take care of the memory management of that object, including garbage collection. If you use "unsafe" code, then all bets are off. .NET will not be able to manage this code for you, and you are back to all the potential problems you had before.

The security apparatus I refer to does not mean keeping out the hackers. It means not letting you do anything that will compromise the system. .NET has many rules concerning what you can and can't do. For instance, it will not let you accidentally write into memory that is not yours. It will not let you stuff a 50-character string into a 30-character space. C will be more than happy to let you do this.

Versioned Assemblies

You can still create DLLs in .NET. However, they are not your father's DLLs.

Microsoft realized when designing .NET that memory was no longer the scarce resource it once was. It is no longer necessary to have a single DLL for many executables. To this end, you can now create a DLL for your program that resides in that program's folder on the machine. You can also have the same DLL for another .NET program that resides in that other program's folder on the machine. Start both programs up, and they will both use their own respective DLL. Change one DLL and it will not affect the other program like it used to.

Each program is forced to use the DLL that is assigned to it. It is possible to have two versions of the same DLL in memory at the same time. With one stroke, DLL hell is a thing of the past.

So is the commonality of code lost? No. If you want, you can sign your DLL (for security reasons) and put it into the GAC. But keep in mind that versioning is enforced here, and if you change a DLL and put a new one in the GAC, then both versions will be in there even though both DLLs have exactly the same name.

WHAT IS THE GAC?

The GAC is the global assembly cache. It is a common area to store DLLs that may be used by more than one .NET program. All the .NET Framework is in the GAC.

You can find the GAC using Windows Explorer. In Windows XP, you will find it in C:\WINDOWS\assembly (provided that the .NET Framework is installed on your machine). Open up Windows Explorer and look in there. Figure 2-3 shows my GAC.

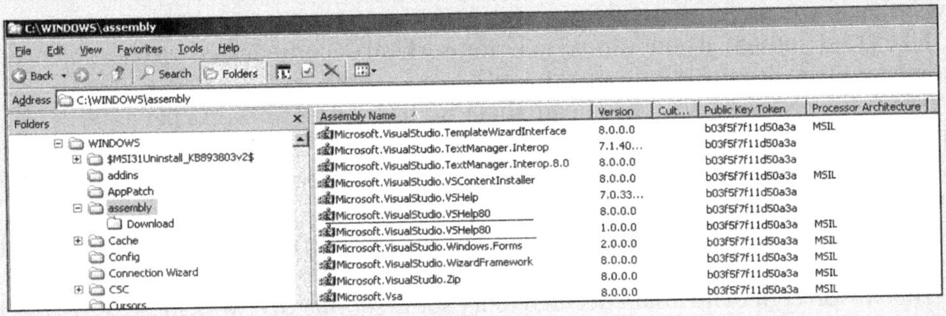

Figure 2-3. *The GAC, showing multiple files with same name*

Notice in this screenshot I have underlined two files in the same directory with the exact same name. Try to give two files the same name in any other directory and you will get an error. These two files are distinguished by their version number and public key token. When you install the .NET Framework onto your machine, it loads an add-in to Windows Explorer that enables it to see the GAC this way. If you were to go to a DOS box and do a DIR command, you would not see anything like what you see in Figure 2-3.

There is one thing to note about putting assemblies in the GAC. .NET allows you to do an XCOPY deployment. It does not need to register anything. If you need to put something in the GAC, then you lose this capability. This is something to remember when considering an install for your program.

Your program will know, for example, that it wants version 2.0.3.4.5 of some DLL, and another program will know it that it wants version 2.0.3.4.6. The point here is that DLLs can no longer be overwritten, and again DLL hell is avoided. This feature is a major reason why I was so anxious for .NET to come along.

By the way, there is a signing process that goes along with your program and the DLL that it uses. This process uses encryption to make sure that the DLL it gets is the one it wants. Microsoft has gone to great lengths to make sure that bad DLLs cannot be introduced onto your system and spoof a DLL that you are trying to use.

Complete Classes

VB suffered from a severe lack of performance. It is a great language and development environment for writing Windows programs that do not require extensive use of system resources—but some of its features are lacking indeed.

One such feature is the drawing capability of VB. To put it bluntly, it is pathetic. Any rendering of complicated shapes becomes impossible in VB without resorting to the Windows API.

The Windows API is unsafe code. In fact, it is downright scary and really complicated. However, if you want to create any kind of usable and professional program in VB, you will need to resort to the Windows API.

I have a book on the Windows API that is a few thousand pages long. It is a few years old and very worn. When I was working heavily in VB, I knew quite a few API commands by heart, and how to use them.

VB is like an overbearing parent. It protects you from the big bad operating system and does not allow you to do anything that might hurt you. However, VB does allow you to make API calls, which become the back door out to the wild world. Using these API calls can crash your system if you are not careful.

Like I said, though, if you wanted to write any kind of complicated system, you needed to become familiar with the Windows API.

Then along comes .NET. I had heard that VB .NET and C# were on a par as far as what they could do. This is true. VB .NET can now do some incredibly complicated drawing and other neat things that it could never do before. .NET allows this because it has wrapped all the API calls you would need in .NET classes and calls.

.NET allows you to dig deep into the Windows API using safe code. You will not get into trouble like you could by using the raw API.

This was so cool to me that I decided to try some serious GDI work in .NET. (GDI is the graphics device interface, and is probably the most common set of raw API calls).

Microsoft has come up with a set of classes called the GDI+. While I was trying this out, I wrote my second book on .NET, called *GDI+ Programming in C# and VB .NET*. This book is all about graphics in .NET and how to use the classes to do some amazing things. I think that I used direct API calls only once or twice throughout all the examples in the book. I was very hard-pressed to find something that the GDI+ classes could not do.

The important point is that .NET has a complete set of classes that allow you to do almost anything you could want to do without needing to go to the API.

Common Data Types

In C, the size of an Integer data type is compiler dependent. Most times, however, it is 4 bytes. In VB 6.0, an Integer is something different altogether. In C, a string is a starting memory position and an end character. In VB, a string is totally different and has a size characteristic to it.

Likewise, if you wanted to write a program in C++, all your code for that program would need to be in C++. There is no way to pass data directly from a part of a program written in VB to one written in C++. You can pass data from VB to a C++ COM DLL using marshaling, but that is very complicated. So you end up having to have your programming team write code using the same language. You have no chance to leverage the talents of your best VB programmer.

.NET enforces a common data type set throughout the framework. It also compiles the code you write to something called intermediate code. This intermediate code ends up being the same regardless of whether you wrote it in C# or VB .NET or even COBOL .NET.

These two things allow you to write a program using assemblies from any of the .NET languages. The VB programmer can write a complicated set of classes in VB, and the C# programmer can pass data back and forth and use the interfaces with no problems. All this is native and requires no extra marshaling of data.

This allows you to use programmers with knowledge in several different languages on the same project. Your VB programmer no longer needs to feel left out of the "real" projects.

.NET Remoting

Ah, remoting! Although Microsoft will deny it, this is where they got rid of DCOM (Distributed COM). It is a way for a client program to talk to a server. It is not the browser/web server combination, but an executable on one machine instantiating and talking to an executable on another machine. These days, this type of client is called a fat client. Unlike the browser, this client can make full use of the client machine's operating system and is in fact operating system dependent.

DCOM was, and is, a nightmare. It is difficult to set up and even more difficult to use properly. It can be slow and it is not firewall-friendly.

DCOM is also dependent upon GUIDs being in synch. Often, if you changed a server, you would change its set of GUIDs. Then the client would no longer recognize the server and couldn't work with it. So, if you changed the server, you would need to recompile the client to work with the new server. You would need to redistribute the new client whenever a new server came along. This could be avoided in C++; but in VB 6.0, you were hosed.

.NET Remoting changed all that. There are two kinds of remoting available to your .NET programs: HTTP remoting using SOAP, and binary remoting.

Binary remoting is the fastest, but it may not be able to pass through firewalls. HTTP remoting is XML serialization, and passes through on port 80. HTTP remoting is much slower than binary remoting. There is a third kind of remoting as well, which is a combination of the two mentioned here. It is HTTP remoting using binary data.

.NET has made changing between remoting types very easy. There is no recompiling of any program. It is just a value change in a configuration XML file.

Remoting is different from DCOM because it uses a leased lifetime for an object. DCOM relies on pinging. If the objects cannot ping each other, then the remote object is destroyed.

Remoting has divorced the tight coupling between the client and the server, which makes updating one part or the other much easier.

Reversion to Configuration Files

A far as .NET is concerned, the registry is a thing of the past. All configuration options and persisted values are kept in XML configuration files.

These configuration files allow your .NET program to be installed on a computer just by copying it to a folder. You then invoke the executable and you are running. Think of this compared to installing something like Microsoft Word.

Back in the DOS days, this was how all programs were installed. Just copy them from one machine to another. Along came Windows 95/98/ME/NT/2000/XP with its much heralded registry. Now we are back to the original method. (I am not the only one who finds this amusing.)

Discontinued Use of Pointers

Ah, pointers. No self-respecting C or C++ programmer would ever admit to not being an expert in pointer arithmetic, right? Single indirection I could handle just fine, but sometimes I would see double and triple indirection in code, and I would just throw up my hands. Some programmers took great joy in producing abstruse C code.

Well, Java came along and changed all that. Java is very object oriented and has no provision for pointers. This alone reduced the amount of bugs by an order of magnitude.

In case you are wondering, here is a little explanation of pointers. A pointer is a reference to a memory location. If you wanted a function to work on a very large string, the efficient thing to do would be to pass a pointer to the string into the function instead of passing in the string itself. The function would then reference the string and work on it. This had the added advantage (or disadvantage) of permitting you to change a variable directly in the calling program. If you were to pass in the whole string, the function would work on a copy of the string, and nothing in the main program would change. While pointers may seem like a cool thing, they are a major source of bugs. The memory referenced by pointers is not protected well. It is very easy to inadvertently change something you should not have access to.

Everything in .NET is an object. .NET does not allow you to pass things by passing pointers. It certainly does not allow you to walk through memory one byte at a time like "C" does with pointers.

.NET is very safe. There is a way, however, to pass a reference to an object into a function. This allows you to use a function to change an object in a calling function. The .NET method of passing a reference is explicit. You must explicitly say that the argument in a function call is a byref argument. Type safety is still enforced in .NET even when passing a variable by reference.

The Evolution of DotNetNuke

Like anything new from Microsoft, .NET came with a whole host of help files and examples. One of the first examples to come out was a starter kit for ASP.NET called IBuySpy. This was a portal application that contained enough code to actually be useful. Microsoft released the code to the world, and the license agreement was such that anyone could release any derivation of it with no fees.

This application caught the eye of an ASP.NET programmer in Canada by the name of Shaun Walker. He took the program and altered it to fit an amateur sports web hosting environment. Along the way, he more than doubled the code—from 11,000 to over 25,000 lines.

The program worked fine for him, so he tried to sell it to the world. When this was not successful, he decided to release it to the open source community as a general purpose web application framework. It took off.

Within three months he had 5,000 registered users, and the product was dubbed DotNetNuke. It was named after an existing open source web portal product called PHP-Nuke.

DNN is free and its licensing scheme is similar to the BSD (Berkeley Software Distribution) license. Basically, you can use it, enhance it—whatever you need. The BSD license gives the most freedom of any licensing scheme.

Currently, DNN has over 40 core programmers and is over 200,000 lines of code. This is truly amazing.

DotNetNuke Features

DNN has many features that allow you to create websites and manage them easily. While VWD 2005 Express does have starter kits for individual websites, DNN goes far beyond this.

Virtualized Websites

DNN allows you to have *virtualized* websites. Many companies have multiple websites. Think of Microsoft. It has www.microsoft.com, http://msdn.com, http://search.microsoft.com, http://hotmail.com, and a few others.

While www.microsoft.com provides a way to get to some of these other websites through the main page, you can also get to these sites directly.

DNN allows you to set up multiple URLs that are accessible and manageable though a single URL. Your company may have one URL for sales, one for the help desk, and another for frequently asked questions. DNN allows you manage all these through a single portal.

Consistent Framework

Whether you are working on Microsoft Word, Excel, or PowerPoint, you can be assured that the menu structure for all three programs will be the same. You can be assured that the look and feel of the three programs is also the same. It is this consistency that makes these programs usable.

The framework in DNN is very consistent when it comes to adding pages, managing content, and so on. You will find that the modules that can be plugged into DNN are also familiar to you. This even extends to the folder structure and the files that are on your hard drive.

This consistent framework just may entice you to create your own module for public use in DNN. Who knows?

Modular Architecture

The framework of DNN is such that a single page can have several sections on it. Each of these sections can contain a module of your choice.

A module is a self-contained program that can run within this space. If you wanted a search engine, a shopping cart, and some text on a single page, you would normally create a single page and include the functionality of all these items on it. DNN allows you to separate the functionality of each item while still displaying a single page to the user. You will find this feature very powerful indeed.

Multilanguage Capabilities

ASP.NET uses the same type of resource files as a C# full-client program. The language resource files are XML files called ResX files.

There are many language packs that you can download and install into your DNN project. Every text string and word in DNN is inside one of these language resource files. All you need to do is download one and log in again using the new language.

It is also a simple matter to show a drop-down list of languages in your application to allow the user to choose his language as well.

Skinning

Skinning is the process through which you define the look and feel of a web page or website in an external file. The program looks to this file before the page renders, and applies this look and feel to the page.

DNN allows you to write and provide skins for your website, and to change them when you want. Also, the flexibility is such that you can even change the look and feel on a page-by-page basis if you want.

Skinning is probably the most used and coolest feature of DNN as a whole.

Membership Management

DNN has several roles that you may apply to your website. It has the ability to create roles such as guest, registered user, administrator, and so on.

When you create a page in DNN, you can specify whether that page is viewable by anyone visiting the website or only by registered users. This is a very powerful feature that is very easy to use. Managing role security without this feature takes quite a bit of work.

Tested Code

While there are many more DNN features not mentioned here, there is one that is perhaps more important than all the rest: proven code.

DNN has been around for a while now, and it has been used by thousands of people in thousands of websites.

DNN is thoroughly tested, and all the kinks have been worked out by testers and users like you. You will be using a product that does what it says and works with no fuss. DNN is a proven product.

Summary

This chapter has provided some information on why the combination of Microsoft .NET and DNN is such a powerful one.

First of all, the complete software package is free. The VWD 2005 Express development environment is free, and the DNN framework is free. This brings professional website development to more non-programmers.

If you are a programmer or manage a programming department, the next advantage is important to you. You can leverage the programming expertise of coders with different language backgrounds. Your website can be written in VB .NET or, as is the case with this book, in C#. Your website can be written in a combination of these languages if you like.

The advantages of DNN enable you to get up and running with a professional website with almost no programming necessary. While this statement usually means "limited functionality," in this case it does not. You will be able to use DNN with VWD to create a website with as little or as much functionality as you like. You can let the pluggable DNN modules do all the work, or you can go into the code and tweak it to your specifications.

The combination is powerful indeed.

CHAPTER 3

■■■

Installation

I could have named this chapter "Fun with Dick and Jane." It has enough pictures to satisfy the most visual of programmers. I count myself among them.

When I perform a new task at work, I document what I do every step of the way. More often than not, a coworker or I will need to perform this task again. A well-documented procedure with lots of pictures always ensures that it gets done the same way again with no missing steps. It may take more time initially, but in the end it saves time.

This chapter will show you how to install the various pieces of software necessary to work with VWD and DNN. I document three different ways (with lots of pictures) to install what you need to get running. Here is a list of what you will be doing:

The XP Home install: This is the simplest install of all. It does not require any upgrade to XP Pro, and it does not require IIS to be installed. This install makes use of the File System server that comes with VWD 2005 Express. There is a caveat to this that I will explain later.

The XP Pro install: This includes the Windows 2000 Server and Windows 2003 Server operating systems. Most people doing this at home will not have these operating systems. This install makes use of the IIS web server, version 5.0 or 6.0, from Microsoft. This is the preferred install.

The "I forgot to install it" install: This is the clean-up install for those of us who forgot to click a check box or two. Mainly, this will show you how to install SQL Server separately from the Express installs.

Note I strongly suggest that if you have Windows XP Home to upgrade to XP Pro so you can use IIS as a web server. While the simple File System web server with VWD works, it has some drawbacks. First of all, it can be a little flakey at times. This is from the DNN guys themselves. I have not experienced this flakiness myself, but be forewarned. The other drawback is that the simple server only accepts internal requests. You will not be able to test your website from outside your computer.

I'll show you how to install the following software:

- VWD 2005 Express Edition

- SQL Server 2005 Express Edition

- SQL Server Management Studio CTP

- DNN application framework

- IIS

- Visual C# 2005 Express Edition

Some of these programs will be installed by default when you install others. For instance, you can elect to install SQL Server 2005 along with the MSDN help when you install either VWD Express or Visual C# Express.

Before I get into the development environment install, I'll spend some time on one of the basics. If you have Windows XP Pro or Windows 2003, you should install IIS. If you have XP Home and do not wish to upgrade to Pro, then skip the next section and go to the "Installing Visual C# Express Edition" section. Otherwise, let's get started.

Installing IIS

If you have Windows XP Pro or 2003 Server operating systems, you should install IIS before starting the VWD and DNN installs. If you only want to use the File System web server that comes with VWD Express, then you can skip this step.

Steps for Installation

IIS is the Microsoft version of a web server. IIS can be used from the smallest local intranet sites all the way up to massive redundant server sites hosting thousands of hits a day.

First of all, you will need to see whether you already have IIS installed. Go to Start ➤ Settings ➤ Control Panel ➤ Add or Remove Programs. Click the Add/Remove Windows Components button. Figure 3-1 shows how the screen should look.

You can see here that I do not have IIS installed at all. I will need to remedy that fact. If you do not have IIS installed, check the IIS box and click Next. A screen will come up and tell you that you need to put in the original Windows XP disk. This is shown in Figure 3-2.

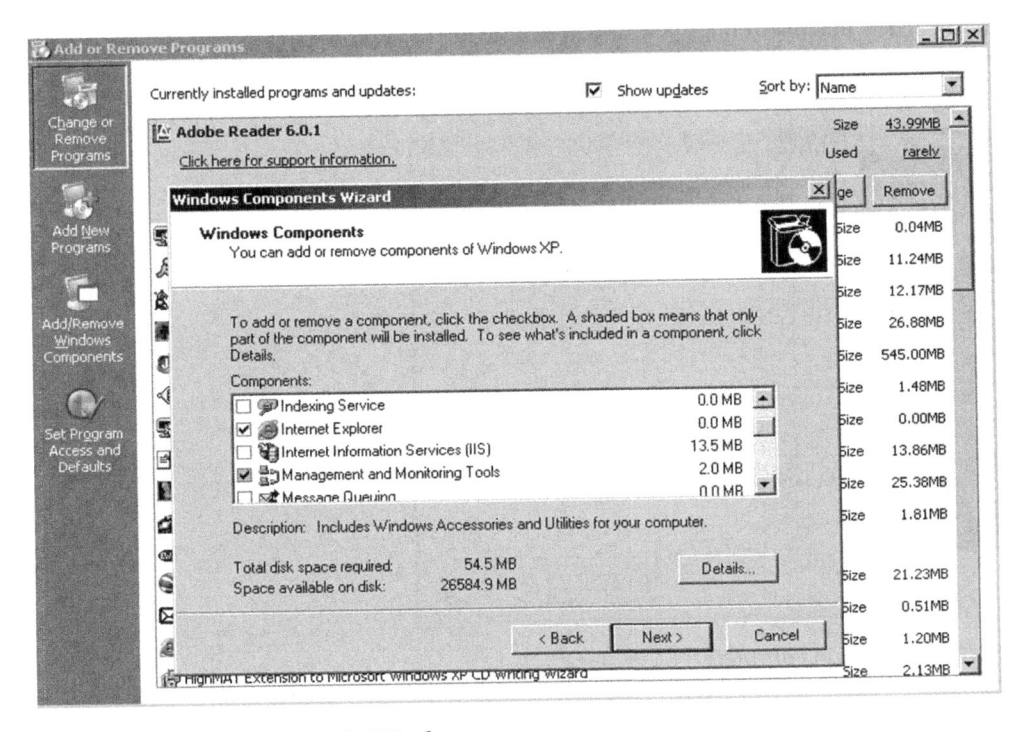

Figure 3-1. *IIS configuration in Windows*

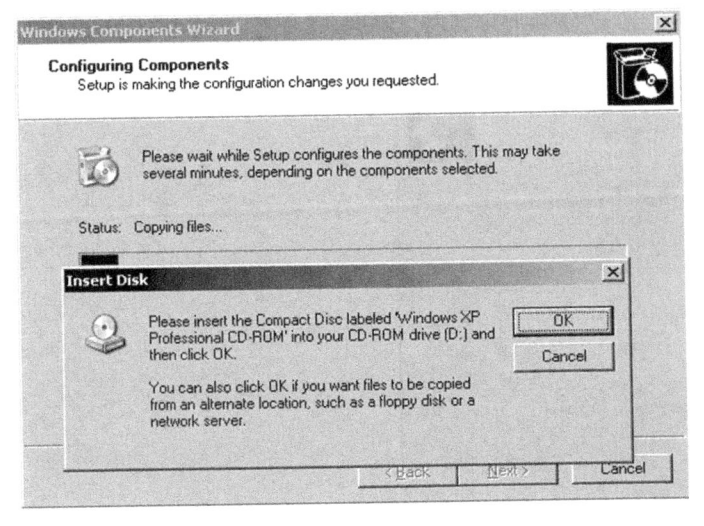

Figure 3-2. *Pop in the Windows XP disk.*

After the disk is inserted, click OK and you should be off and running. When you are done, you should get the Finish screen, as shown in Figure 3-3.

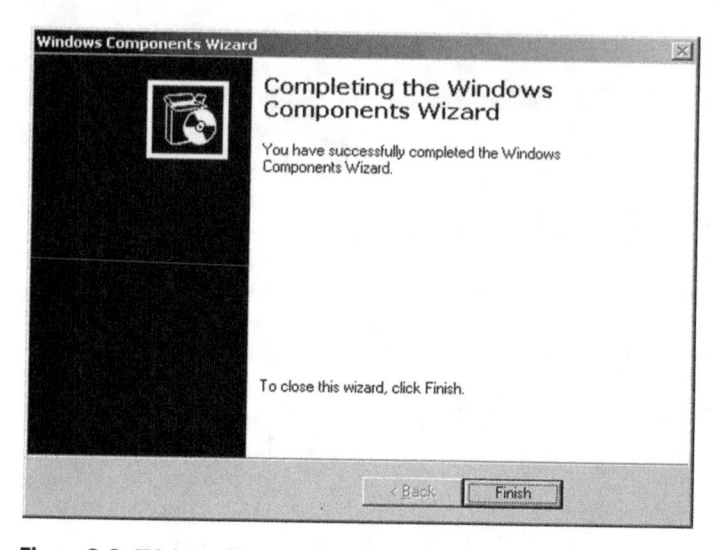

Figure 3-3. *IIS installation complete*

Just to make sure that you have installed IIS, go back to the Add or Remove Programs screen and click the Add/Remove Windows Components button again. Your screen should look like mine, shown in Figure 3-4.

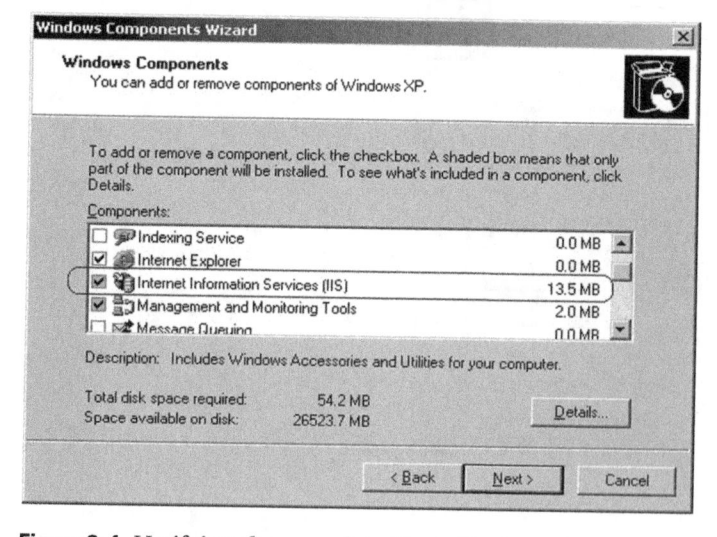

Figure 3-4. *Verifying the completed installation*

Installing Visual C# Express Edition

You will use C# as your language of choice when working with web pages. Installing the Express Edition now is useful for projects later in the book, and is also useful as a learning tool. The help and the projects included can really get you going in a hurry.

Since this is the first Express product you will install, it will notify you that you will need to install the .NET Framework 2.0. This is essential. If you have the .NET Framework 1.1 or below, do not worry. They play well together. If you have installed the .NET Framework 1.2 or *any* beta versions of Express, then read the accompanying sidebar "Beta Version vs. Release Version." It is essential that you not have any beta versions of the 2005 Express Editions or the .NET 2.0 Framework beta installed on your machine.

Start by double-clicking the vcssetup.exe file. Once started, you should get the screen shown in Figure 3-5.

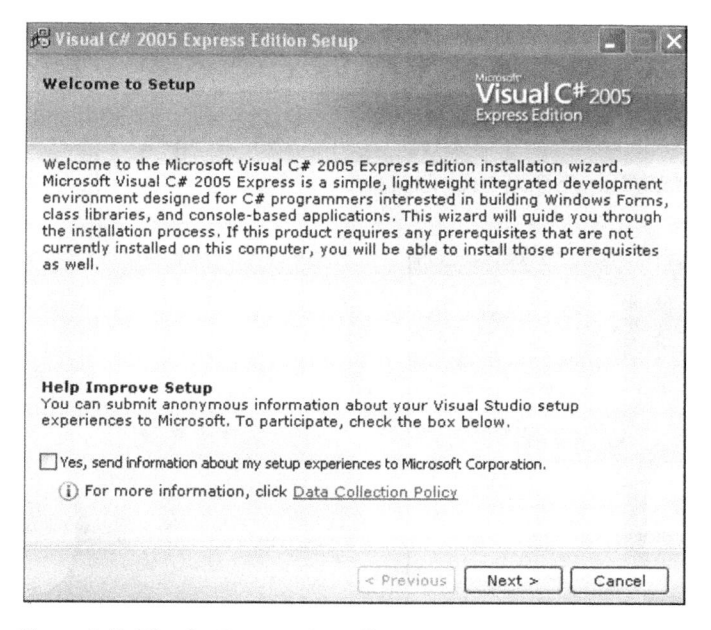

Figure 3-5. *The C# Express install screen*

You can choose to send information to Microsoft. I choose not to myself. Once you accept the license agreement, you will be asked if you want to load MSDN and SQL Server Express as well. Check Yes and continue. This is shown in Figure 3-6.

You will need the SQL Server Express Edition when working with DNN. As I said, if this install is the first of the Express installs, you will get a screen showing that the .NET 2.0 Framework will also be installed. Figure 3-7 shows what will be installed here.

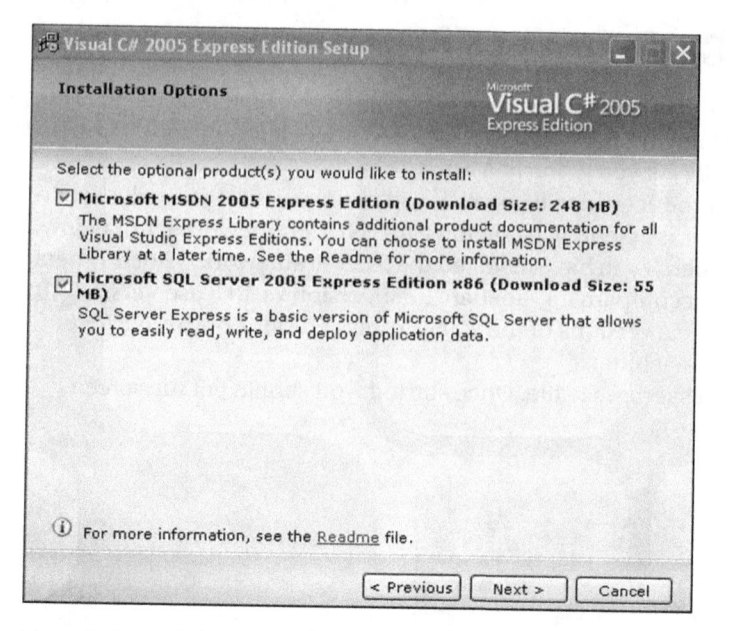

Figure 3-6. *Enabling installation of MSDN and SQL Server Express*

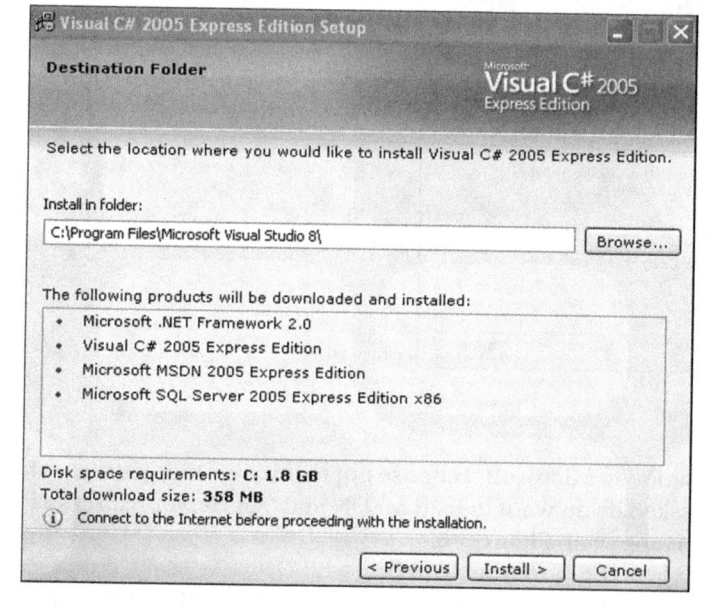

Figure 3-7. *The complete install list*

This install will take a while. Once done, though, you will be halfway to having everything you need to program.

While you are waiting for the install to run, just think about all that money you have saved. All this software is free. If you didn't have the money to spend, think of the opportunity you now have. A world of programming is now open to you.

BETA VERSION VS. RELEASE VERSION

I have installed and uninstalled all this software quite a few times while writing this chapter. Most of the time things went smoothly. The one time it did not go so smoothly was when I tried to uninstall the .NET Framework beta when I had a beta version of Visual Studio 2005 already installed.

The official rules state that you must uninstall all .NET beta products before you even think of installing the release version. Even more importantly, you must uninstall these products before uninstalling the beta version of the .NET 2.0 Framework. What I did wrong was uninstall things in the wrong order. I forgot exactly what I had installed on my test machine and I uninstalled the beta .NET Framework before some aspects of the SQL Server Express beta.

When I went to install the release version, I was able to install everything except SQL Server Express, which always gave me an error. After much searching through my hard drive and the Add or Remove Programs folder, I was still unable to install SQL Server. After a quick Google search, I found that I wasn't the only one with this problem, and that I should hunker down for a night of pain.

I essentially had two problems. One was that one of the uninstalls left some stuff in the registry, and the other was that Windows said I had a previous instance of SQL Server running (even though I knew I did not).

In the end, I prevailed. I did have the help of quite a few blogs, many of which were from Microsoft developers themselves.

So the moral of the story is this: make sure that you uninstall everything .NET development–related *before* you uninstall the .NET 2.0 beta Framework. Life will be so much easier.

Once this is all installed, you will need to register the product. This requires a .NET Passport. Follow the links on the registration page, and you will be led to a Microsoft site where you will get the registration number. Open Visual C# and click Help ➤ Register Product. You will get a page like the one shown in Figure 3-8.

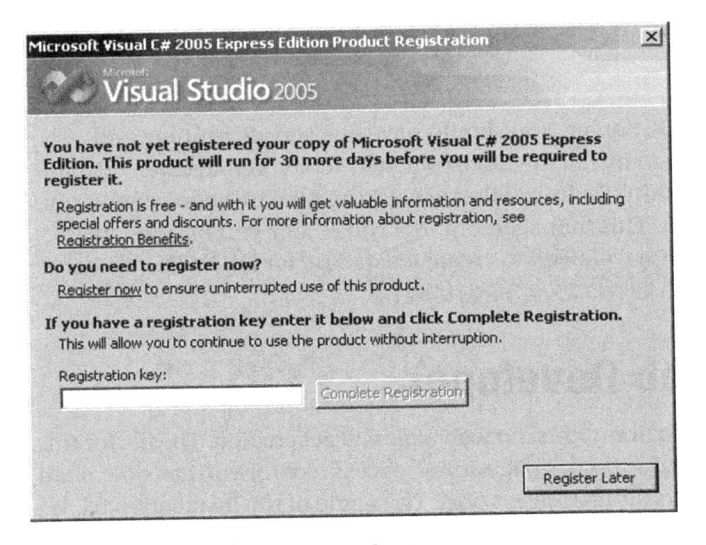

Figure 3-8. *Registering your product*

You will need to do this for VWD as well.

The next thing to do is check if SQL Server installed OK. Click Start ➤ Programs ➤ Microsoft SQL Server 2005 ➤ Configuration Tools ➤ SQL Server Configuration Manager. Once it's open, you should see some services. This is shown in Figure 3-9.

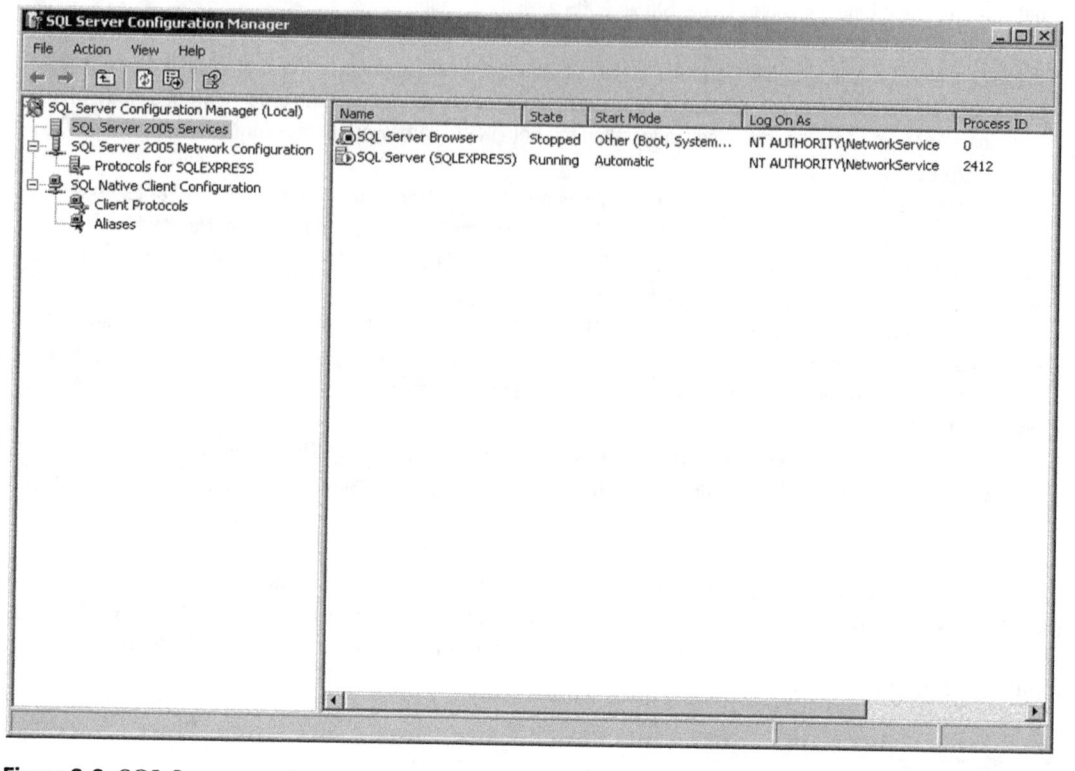

Figure 3-9. *SQL Server services*

Now you know all is well with SQL Server. You should have one service running and another stopped. Now is a good time to install the Microsoft SQL Server Management Studio Express CTP. CTP stands for Community Technical Preview. By the time this book comes out, I am sure it will be a released product. This management tool will enable you to view, create, and manage SQL Server databases. You will need to create a database for DNN. The file name for this management tool install is SQLServer2005_SSMSEE.msi.

Installing Visual Web Developer

VWD is the backbone of this system. Without this, no web page will get created. The file for this install is available for download from this book's page at www.apress.com, or you can download it from http://msdn.microsoft.com/vstudio/express/vwd. The name of the installation file is vwdsetup.exe. Double-click this file and install it. Since you have already installed MSDN and the .NET Framework, VWD is the only product to be downloaded and installed at this time. This is shown in Figure 3-10.

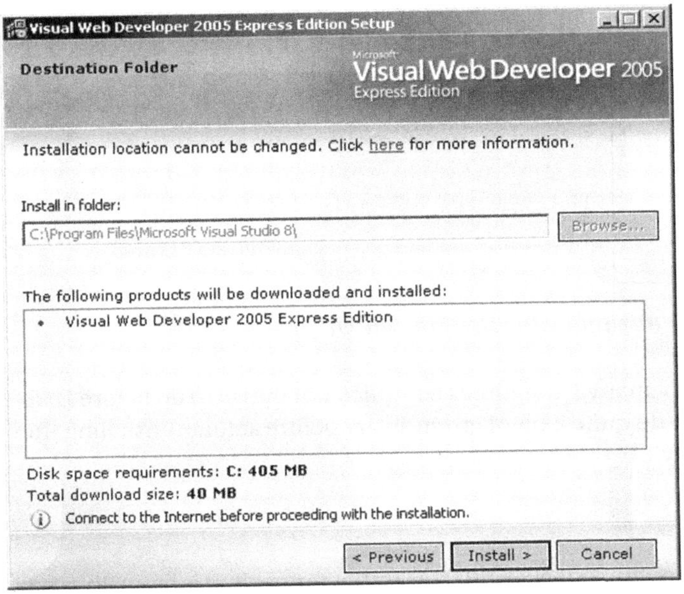

Figure 3-10. *Installing VWD by itself*

Again, like the others, this will take a while. Note that what you are clicking on is a program that gets and installs the proper software. It is not the software itself. This is kind of cool in that you are always guaranteed to install the latest version. If I gave you the whole program to install, who knows how old it would be before you got to install it. At that point, you would need to go look for updates. A real potential mess has been avoided by doing it this way.

After installing, you will need to register this program just like you did with Visual C# Express.

Installing DotNetNuke

DNN does not really have a classic install program like Microsoft Word or even VWD. This makes things a little more involved. There are two ways to install DNN. The first way involves a ZIP file that needs to be extracted to a particular directory. The name of this file (at the time of this writing) is DotNetNuke_4.0.1_Install.zip. Look for a newer version on www.dotnetnuke.com to get the latest.

If you were to use the old install method for DNN version 3.x (do not do this), the directory that you would unzip the file to is called c:\DotNetNuke. After unzipping DNN version 3.x, your directory should look like this one shown in Figure 3-11.

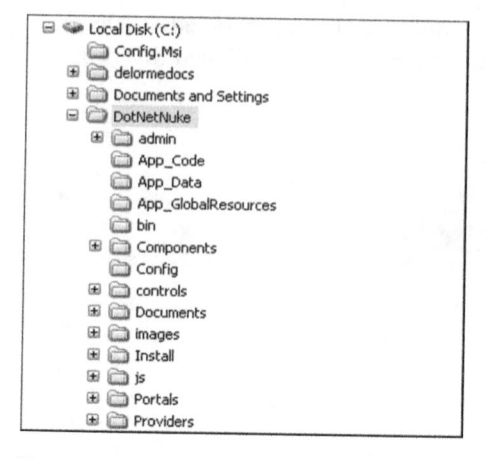

Figure 3-11. *Directory structure after unzipping the DNN install ZIP file*

Unzipping this file is the first of many (sometimes complicated) things to do before DNN is finally installed. You will need to do quite a bit of groundwork before actually installing the DNN product. There is a better way.

A Better Install

Microsoft added a great new feature with ASP.NET 2.0. This is the starter kit. It is basically a way to create an install for an ASP.NET development environment. As you just saw, the versions of DNN before 4.0 needed to be installed by unzipping a file to a directory. Although I have not shown you, you would also need to set up a SQL Server database, set permissions, and so on. While not especially difficult, these steps often lead to errors. The explanation of these steps also always leaves something out. Something shows different on your machine than on mine, and then where do we go?

Starting with DNN version 4.0.0, there is a starter kit for the install. It is on the download page for this book at www.apress.com, as well as on the DNN website. You can even get it from the Microsoft ASP.NET Developer Center. As you can guess, DNN is not the only starter kit out there. Be aware, though, that starter kits are not supported by Microsoft and are technically considered third-party software.

Anyway, back to the DNN install. The name of this install is DotNetNuke_4.x.x_StarterKit.vsi. The xs represent the current minor version and build.

Once you have installed VWD 2005 Express, you can double-click this file and it will install. Figure 3-12 shows the first screen.

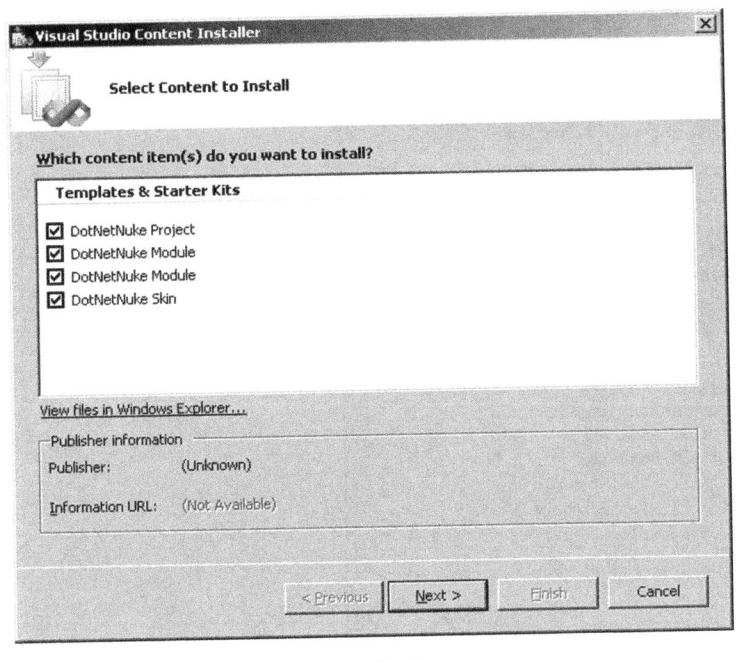

Figure 3-12. *Getting ready to install DNN*

Click Next and the install will start. Before the actual install starts, however, you may see a message like the one shown in Figure 3-13. The install has not been digitally signed yet, so you will need to confirm the install here. By the time you get to use this install, it may be digitally signed and you may not get this screen.

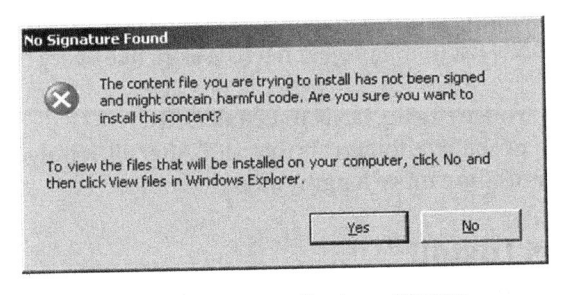

Figure 3-13. *Confirm installation of DNN*

The install of the starter kit happens really fast. The end result of the install will look like Figure 3-14.

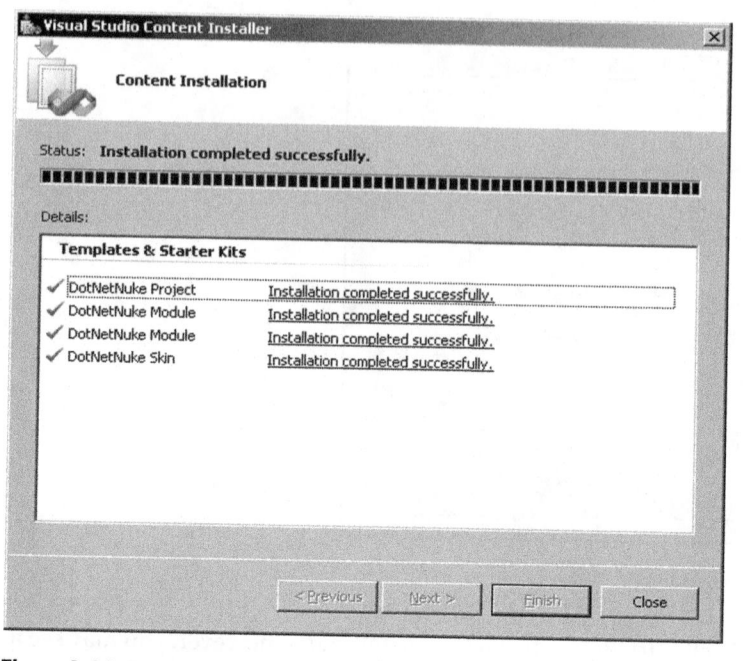

Figure 3-14. *DNN installation complete*

Note what got installed here. You now have a DNN project, which is used to complete the install later, and two modules necessary for the completed install. Note that you also have a DNN skin. I may have mentioned before that skinning is one of the most powerful features of DNN. Since it is a DNN project that will install DNN itself, the project needs a skin, like every other DNN project.

This is kind of like a chicken-and-egg thing. You are using DNN to install DNN.

If you blew though this starter kit install, you probably thought "Is that all?" After all, it only took about 30 seconds to complete. Well, there are some more lengthy steps to come.

Using VWD to Complete the DNN Install

The rest of the install gets done inside the VWD environment. This is where the XP Home install and the XP Pro with IIS installs differ. Start by opening up VWD Express. If this is your first time starting VWD, you may get a message like the one shown in Figure 3-15.

This message may stay up for a few minutes.

Once VWD is up and running, click File ➤ New Website. You should get the same screen as shown in Figure 3-16.

This screen shows several things. First is that you have a DNN web application framework template. This is what you select. Second is that the language is Visual Basic. Do not be alarmed. DNN is written in VB. It is the only language you can create the project in. However, as I said before, you can create code that runs in DNN in any of the .NET languages. For this book, you will be using C#. You will see how this works later.

The third thing to notice here is the location. It is set for File System and has a directory structure deep within the Documents and Settings folder.

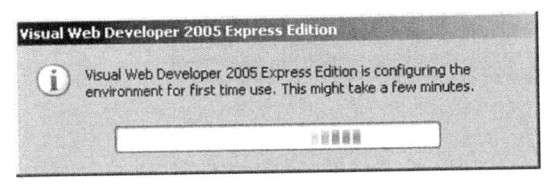

Figure 3-15. *VWD message for first time use*

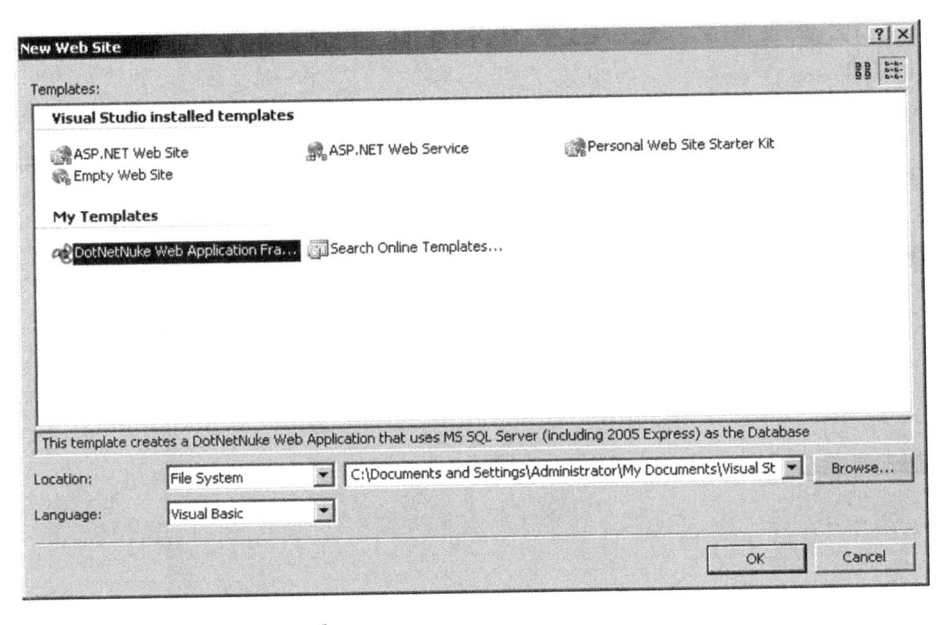

Figure 3-16. *New DNN template*

Local Web Server or IIS

For the location, you can choose File System, HTTP, or FTP. FTP is a file transfer protocol—this option won't be covered in this book.

HTTP is the IIS web server. Choosing this creates the DNN install so that it runs under IIS. As you know, running under IIS requires that you have at least XP Pro installed, and IIS installed as well.

Choosing File System creates the DNN install so that it runs under the debug personal web server that comes with VWD Express. This can be run under XP Home and is free. No need to upgrade here. I will cover both installs for you in the following sections.

Using the Local Web Server

Choose the File System location and change the directory to C:\DotNetNuke. This is easier than digging several layers deep under C:\Document and Settings\.

Your choice should look like Figure 3-17.

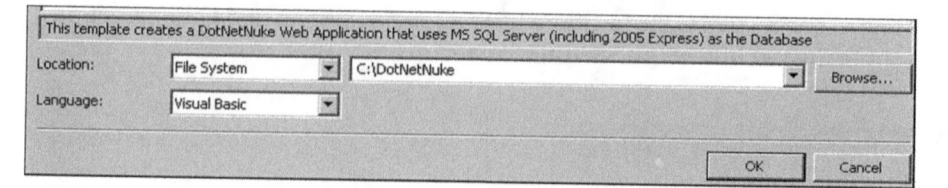

Figure 3-17. *Choosing the local web server*

Press OK and start the process. This process creates a DNN project, and will take a few minutes, so be patient. When all is said and done, your DNN portal install will almost be complete.

Using the IIS Install

If you are using the local web server, you can skip this step.

As shown in Figure 3-16, create a new DNN website. This time, however, you will be using the HTTP location. This is shown in Figure 3-18.

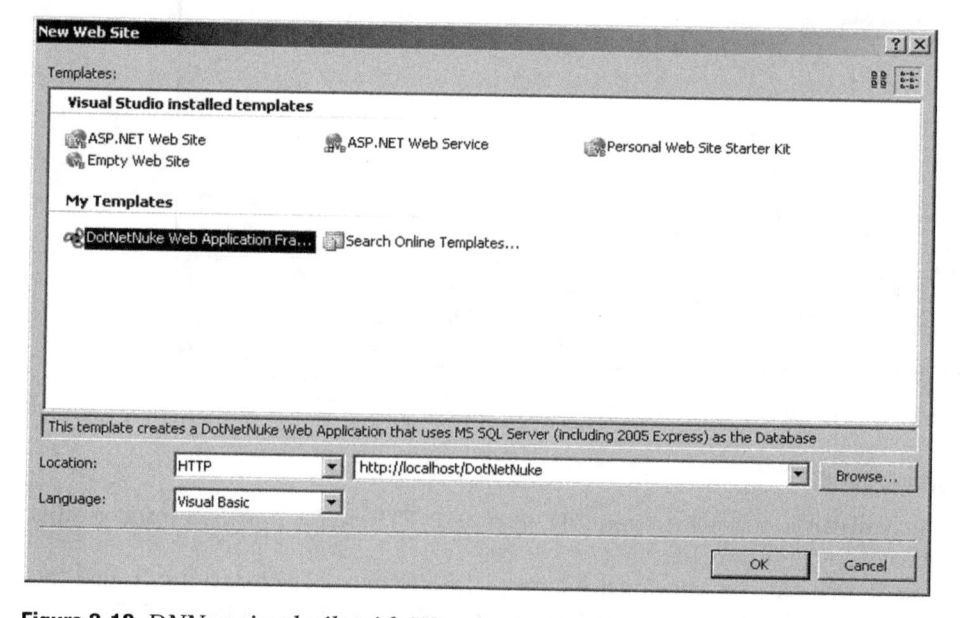

Figure 3-18. *DNN project built with IIS*

Click the Location drop-down menu, and choose the HTTP file server. Instead of a directory for a location, you will be choosing http://localhost/DotNetNuke. The program will live in the C:\Inetpub\wwwroot\DotNetNuke folder. The wwwroot folder is referred to as the virtual root for IIS. This is where IIS stores all the websites it manages.

Once again click OK, and the install will start. When this process finishes, your DNN portal install will almost be complete. Figure 3-19 shows the new directory where the DNN project resides.

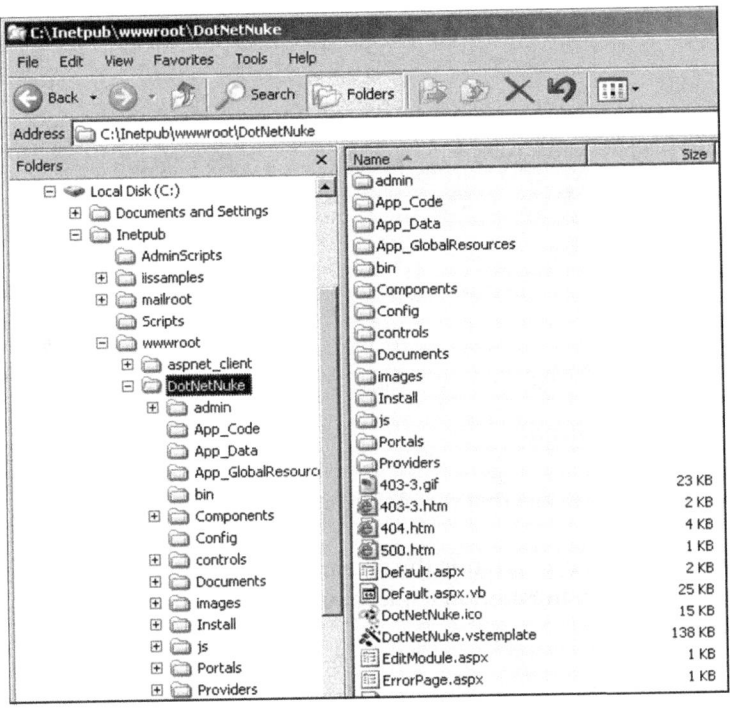

Figure 3-19. *DNN created in virtual root directory of IIS*

Once this step is complete, you will get the screen shown in Figure 3-20 that tells you your DNN web application project is ready.

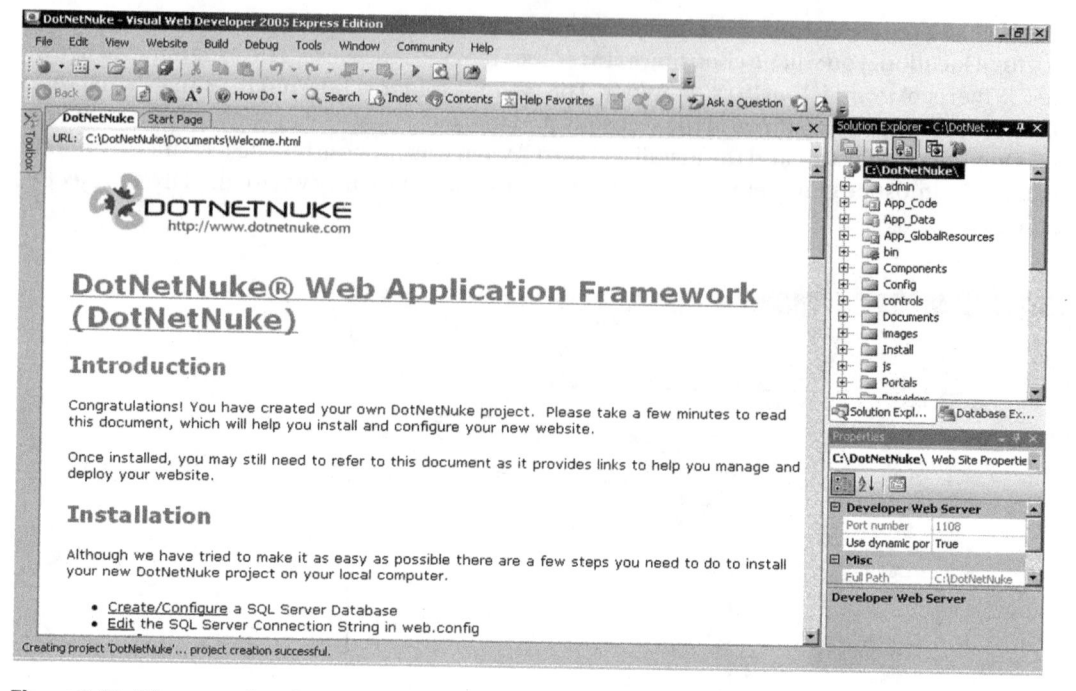

Figure 3-20. *The completed DotNetNuke IIS install*

Read the document shown, and you will see that the install is not quite complete. There are a couple more steps.

The first step (because it is the easiest) is to rename the `release.config` file that is created with this project to `web.config`. Scroll down in Solution Explorer until you see the `release.config` file, as shown in Figure 3-21.

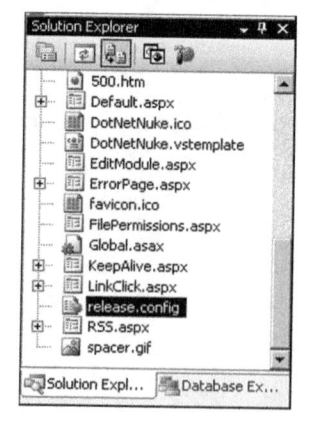

Figure 3-21. *Renaming release.config to web.config*

Right-click this file and rename it `web.config`. If you read the install web page, it says you may need to modify the `web.config` connection string. I have found that this is not needed. In fact, no editing of this file is needed at all.

The next thing to do is to create a database that will be used by your website. Do this under the `App_Data` node in Solution Explorer. Right-click this node and choose Add New Item. This node is shown in Figure 3-22.

Figure 3-22. *Creating a SQL Server database under App_Data*

Figure 3-23 shows the SQL Server database `Database.mdf` being chosen. Choose this and click OK; after some grinding, a database will appear under the `App_Data` node.

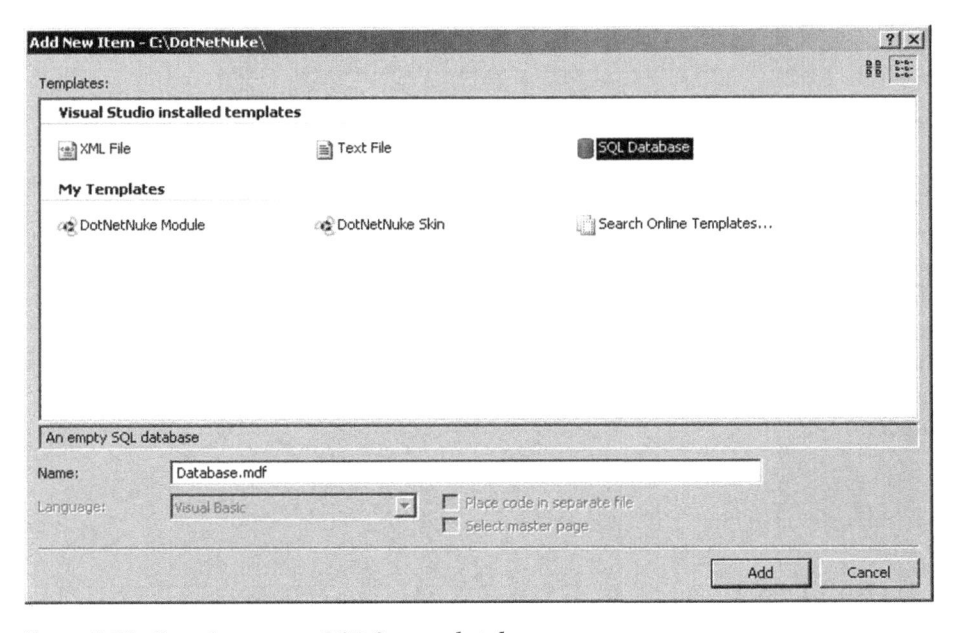

Figure 3-23. *Creating a new SQL Server database*

The last thing to do before compiling the project and creating the actual website is to make sure that the security settings are correct for the website. Since you created the project in C:\DotNetNuke, this is the folder that needs its security adjusted.

If you are using Windows XP Home Edition on your machine, then right-click the C:\DotNetNuke folder and choose Sharing and Security. You'll get the screen shown in Figure 3-24. If you are using IIS as your web server, you will do the same for C:\Inetpub\ wwwroot\DotNetNuke. This folder was shown in Figure 3-19.

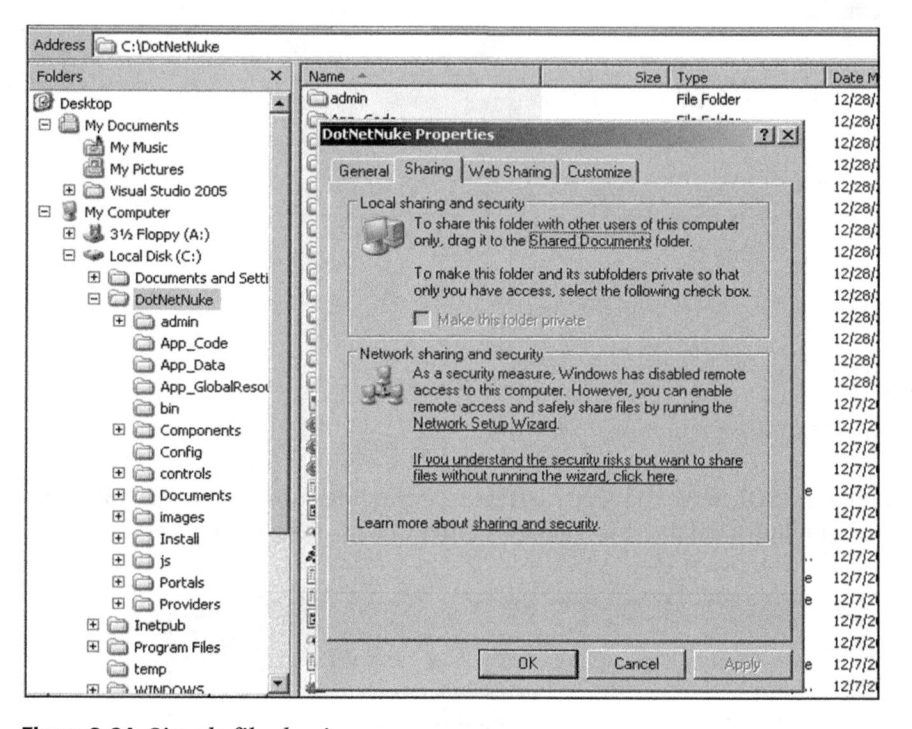

Figure 3-24. *Simple file sharing*

As you can see, there is no way to access any security settings from here. This is frustrating if you don't know why. Close this window and right-click Tools ➤ Folder Options while still in Windows Explorer. Click the View tab and scroll down to the bottom of the Advanced settings window. Figure 3-25 shows this window and the simple file sharing attribute.

Uncheck the simple file sharing attribute and click OK. Next, right-click the C:\DotNetNuke folder again, and choose Sharing and Security. You should now see a security tab like the one shown in Figure 3-26.

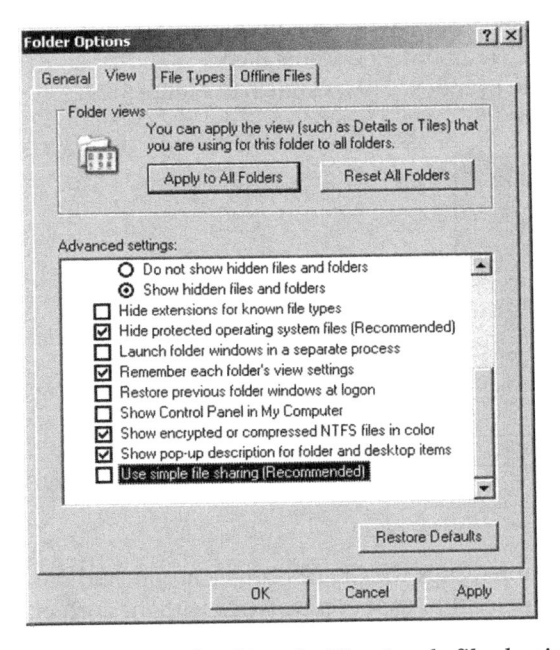

Figure 3-25. *Unchecking the Use simple file sharing option*

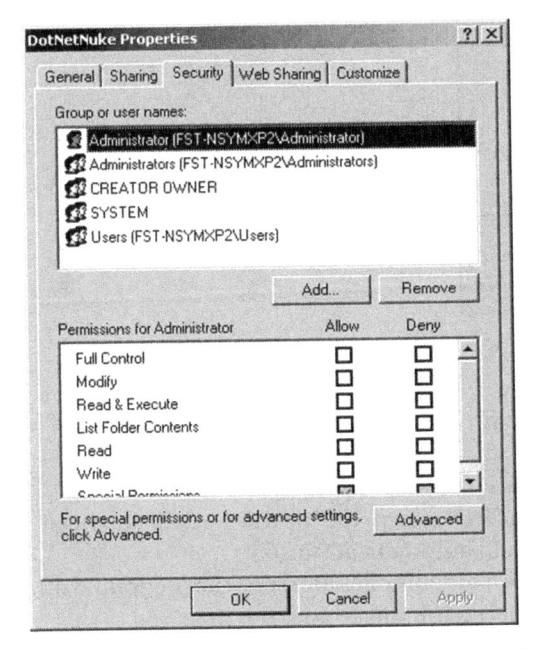

Figure 3-26. *The security tab in the DotNetNuke folders Properties window*

You will need to create a user and give that user access to modify this folder. The user will be the aspnet user that was created when the .NET Framework was installed.

Click the Add button and type **aspnet** into the user box. This is shown in Figure 3-27.

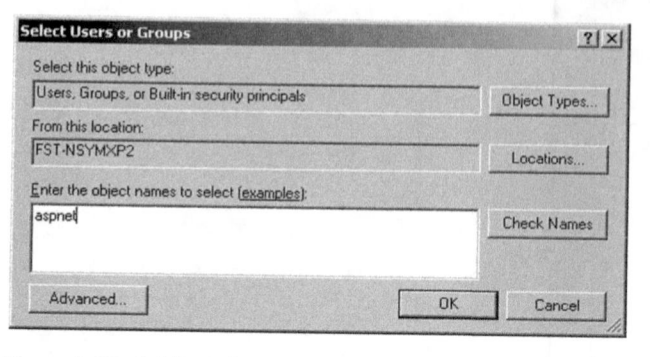

Figure 3-27. *Adding the aspnet user*

How do you know if this is the correct username? Click the Check Names button, and the operating system will find this user for you and replace the "aspnet" you typed with the correct name. Figure 3-28 shows this.

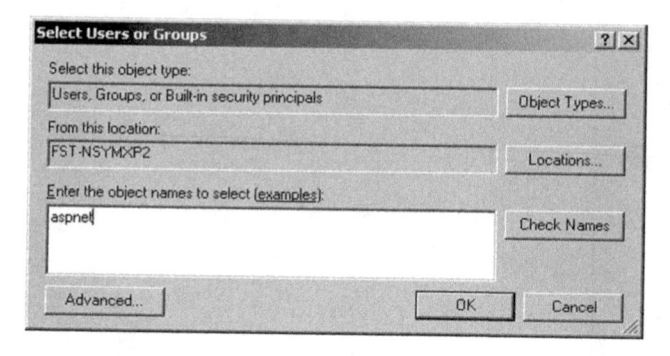

Figure 3-28. *Checking the username*

Press OK to accept this user. Check the modify attribute to give the correct rights to the aspnet user. This is shown in Figure 3-29.

Press OK, and you are done with security for this website.

So now the groundwork has been laid out for a DNN site on the local server. All you need to do now is compile the site, and the program should automatically install.

Get back inside the VWD IDE and press Ctrl+F5. This compiles and runs the program. You can press Ctrl+Alt,O to see the output of the compiler. It is a way to pass the time.

Once the code is compiled, the page that is run will be the install.aspx page. It is this page that truly installs the DNN website and all the modules, skins, and so on. This install page is shown in Figure 3-30.

DotNetNuke Properties
General
Sharing
Security
Web Sharing
Customize
Group or user names:
Administrator (FST-NSYMXP2\Administrator)
Administrators (FST-NSYMXP2\Administrators)
ASP.NET Machine Account (FST-NSYMXP2\ASPNET)
CREATOR OWNER
SYSTEM
Add...
Remove
Permissions for ASP.NET Machine Account
Allow
Deny
Full Control
Modify
Read & Execute
List Folder Contents
Read
Write
For special permissions or for advanced settings, click Advanced.
Advanced
OK
Cancel
Apply

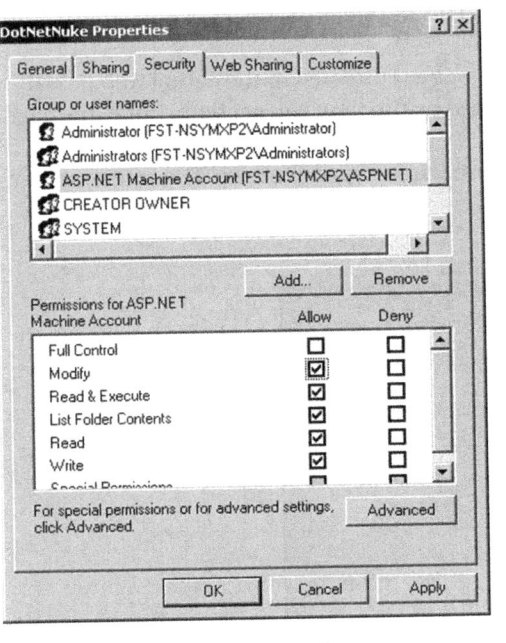

Figure 3-29. *Giving modify rights*

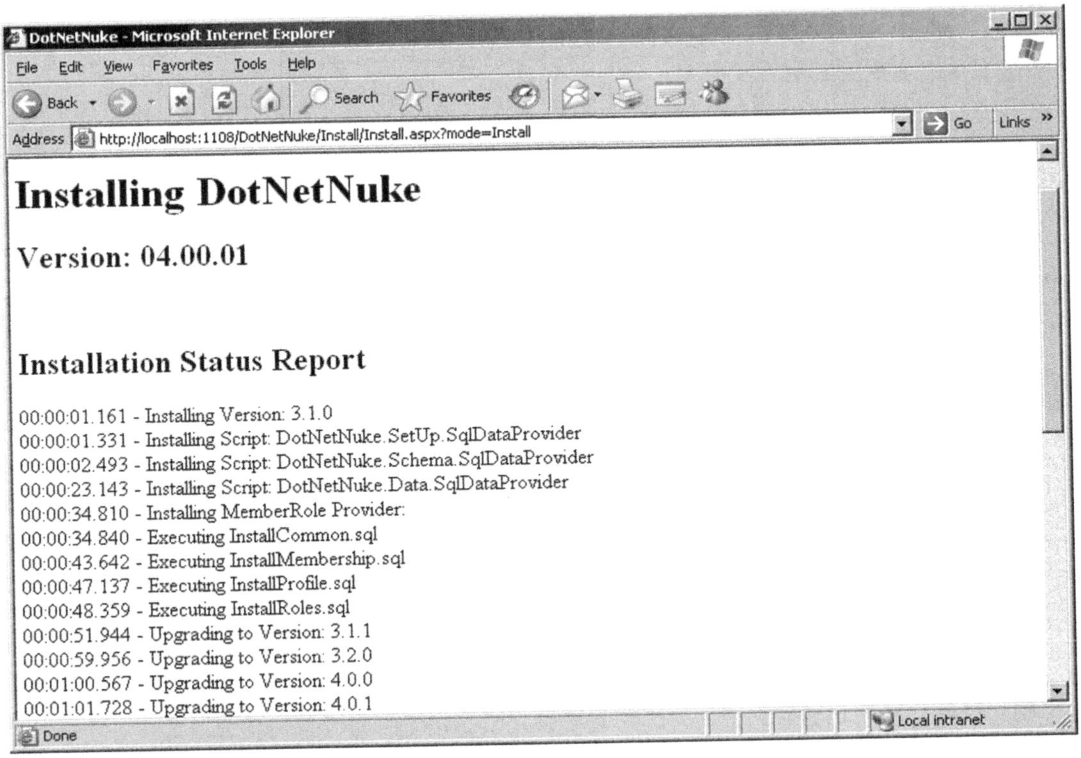

DotNetNuke - Microsoft Internet Explorer
File Edit View Favorites Tools Help
Back
Search
Favorites
Address http://localhost:1108/DotNetNuke/Install/Install.aspx?mode=Install
Go
Links
Installing DotNetNuke
Version: 04.00.01
Installation Status Report
00:00:01.161 - Installing Version: 3.1.0
00:00:01.331 - Installing Script: DotNetNuke.SetUp.SqlDataProvider
00:00:02.493 - Installing Script: DotNetNuke.Schema.SqlDataProvider
00:00:23.143 - Installing Script: DotNetNuke.Data.SqlDataProvider
00:00:34.810 - Installing MemberRole Provider:
00:00:34.840 - Executing InstallCommon.sql
00:00:43.642 - Executing InstallMembership.sql
00:00:47.137 - Executing InstallProfile.sql
00:00:48.359 - Executing InstallRoles.sql
00:00:51.944 - Upgrading to Version: 3.1.1
00:00:59.956 - Upgrading to Version: 3.2.0
00:01:00.567 - Upgrading to Version: 4.0.0
00:01:01.728 - Upgrading to Version: 4.0.1
Done
Local intranet

Figure 3-30. *Installing DNN after compiling*

Scroll down the list and see what was installed. This happens pretty quickly, so there is no waiting around, as during the compile process.

Once the install is complete, you may or may not be redirected to the actual web portal that you just made. This quirk may or may not be fixed by the time you get here, but if this page stays and you do not see the portal, it can be fixed.

Close this page, and while inside the IDE, choose File ➤ Open Website. The screen shown in Figure 3-31 will come up.

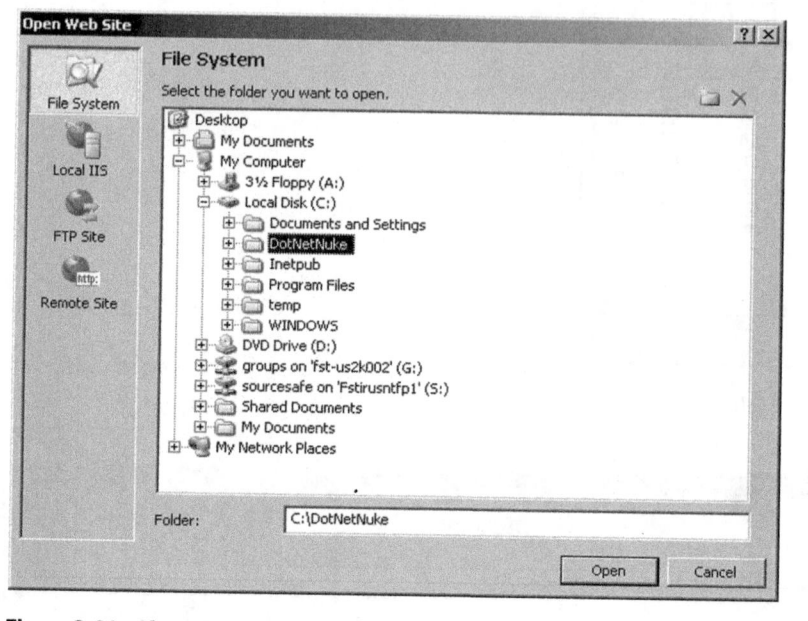

Figure 3-31. *Choosing the website to open*

You will notice that you can open a website from IIS or from the File System, which is the free web server that comes with VWD. You won't be concerned with the FTP site or remote site for now.

Click the File System button and open C:\DotNetNuke. What happens here is that the web server looks for a file called default.aspx inside this directory. You can actually just browse to this file and double-click it using Windows Explorer. You will get the same result.

The web page that comes up will be the same as the one shown in Figure 3-32.

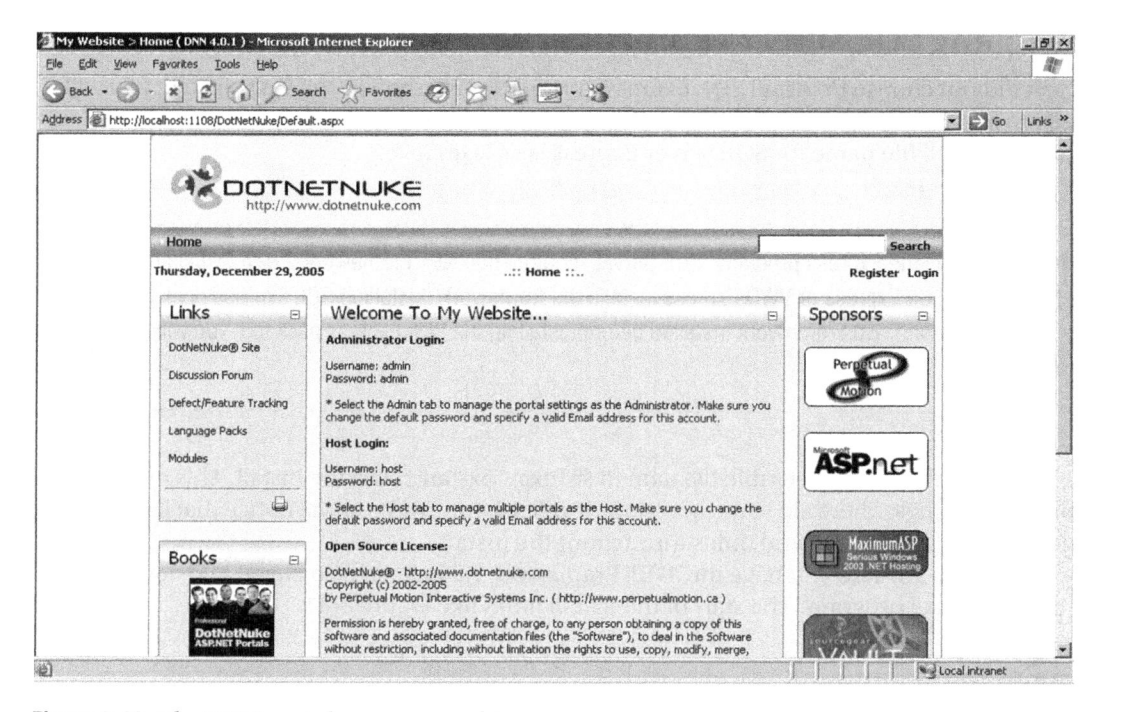

Figure 3-32. *The DNN portal on your machine*

You are done! Now ghost your machine, do it all over again 82 more times, and you will be able to do an install really fast like me.

■**Note** DNN is a huge program and is a heavy load for a small machine. Do not expect the DNN portal to be speedy when you start debugging. It may take a while.

Installing and Configuring SQL Server Express Edition

This is the "Oops I forgot to click this choice!" install.

You cannot run DNN without a database. Installing C# or VWD should have installed SQL Server Express for you. If this did not happen, this is your last-chance install.

A database is required by DNN. The database of choice for this book is SQL Server Express Edition. Like VWD, C#, and DNN, this is also free. It is a large install file, and you can get it from Microsoft at http://msdn.microsoft.com/vstudio/express/sql/default.aspx.

Installing SQL Server Express

If you did not choose to install SQL Express during the C# install or the VWD install, you will need to install it here. If SQL Express was installed, you may skip this step.

The install file name for SQL Server Express is `sqlexpr.exe`.

■**Note** Like all the Express products, SQL Server requires the .NET Framework 2.0 to install and run. Installing Visual C# Express or VWD Express installs the framework. Installing SQL Express does not. If you do not have the .NET 2.0 Framework installed before installing the SQL Express package, you will not be able to install.

Double-click the executable file named `sqlexpr.exe` and start the install. This install does quite a few things. There are some questions it will ask you, and you will notice that it is starting and stopping services several times throughout the install.

Once you are sure you have the .NET Framework 2.0 installed, go ahead and double-click the `sqlexpr.exe` program. The start of the install looks like Figure 3-33.

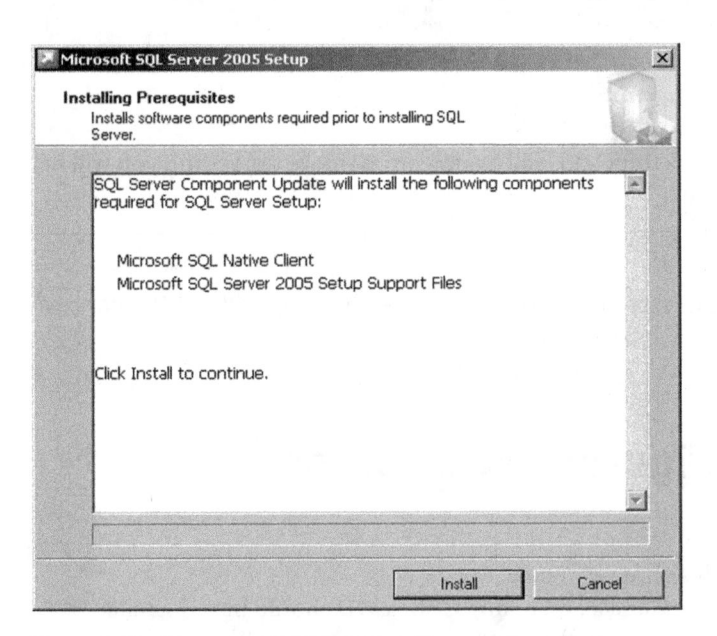

Figure 3-33. *The start of SQL Server Express install*

This tells you that the SQL native client will install, as well as SQL Server. Click the Install button, and the next screen should tell you that these files were installed successfully. This is shown in Figure 3-34.

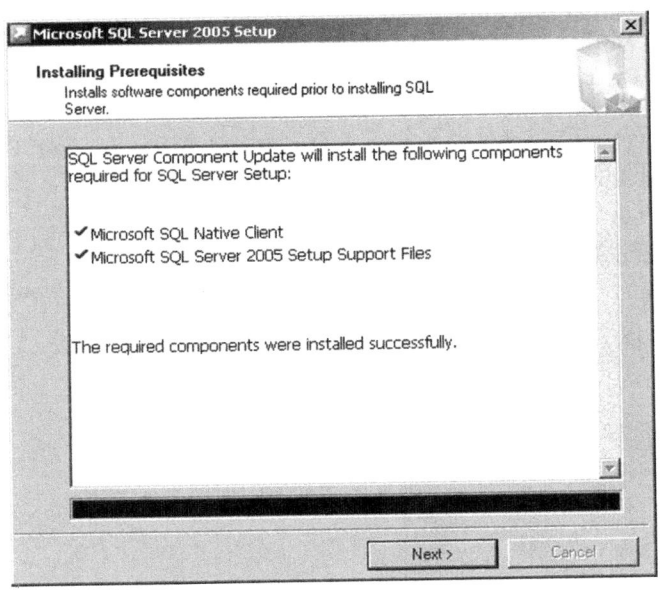

Figure 3-34. *SQL native client installed OK.*

Click Next, and you will come to another screen that starts off the wizard. This is shown in Figure 3-35.

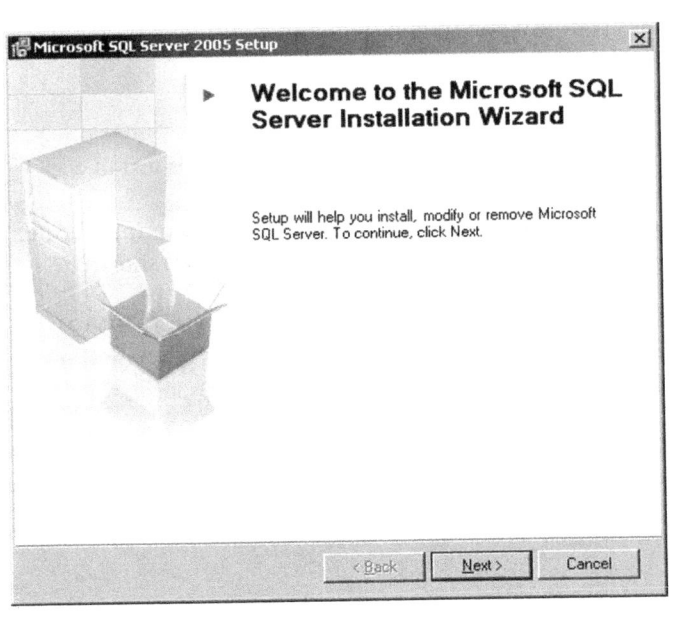

Figure 3-35. *The installation wizard starts.*

Click Next to start this wizard. It will ask you quite a few more questions about how you want to install the basic product. Note that this SQL Server Express install is very user-intensive. If it was installed as part of C# Express or VWD Express, none of this would be asked of you.

The first thing this wizard does is check to see if your system has enough resources and components to complete the install. Figure 3-36 shows this.

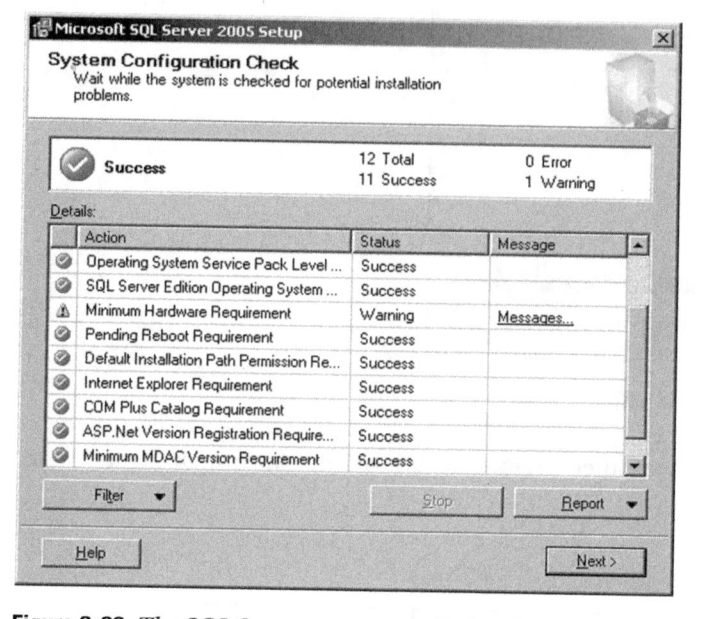

Figure 3-36. *The SQL Server system configuration check*

As you can see here, a simple warning is displayed, which I will ignore. This install was done on a virtual machine, and it has some hardware limitations.

Click Next, and it will ask you some licensing info, such as your name and company. After you enter this information, you will be asked what components to install. This is shown in Figure 3-37.

Just accept the defaults here. You will not need a software development kit. The DNN install will configure SQL Server for you. Click Next, and another window will give you the authentication options for the SQL Server database. This is shown in Figure 3-38.

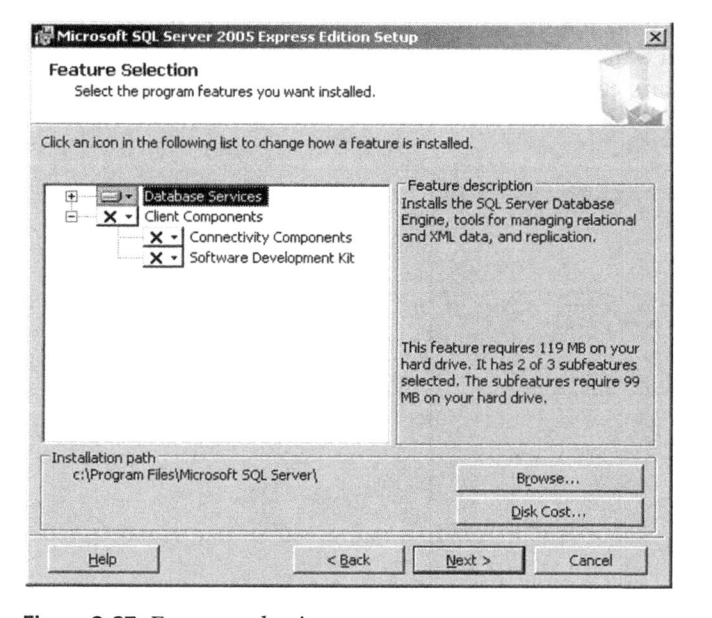

Figure 3-37. *Feature selection*

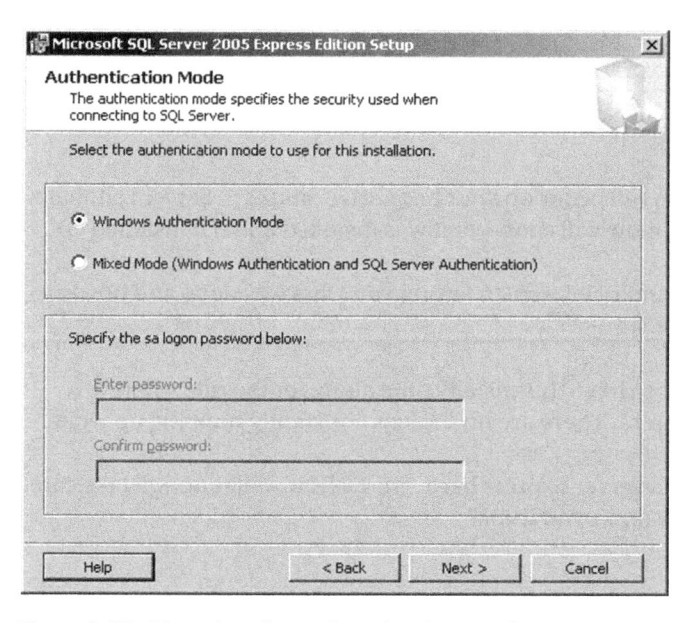

Figure 3-38. *Choosing the authentication mode*

Select Windows Authentication Mode. It is the most secure. Click Next to accept this selection. The next window asks you if you want to send any error reports to Microsoft during the actual install. You can choose not to and click Next again. Figure 3-39 shows the next screen. Click Install.

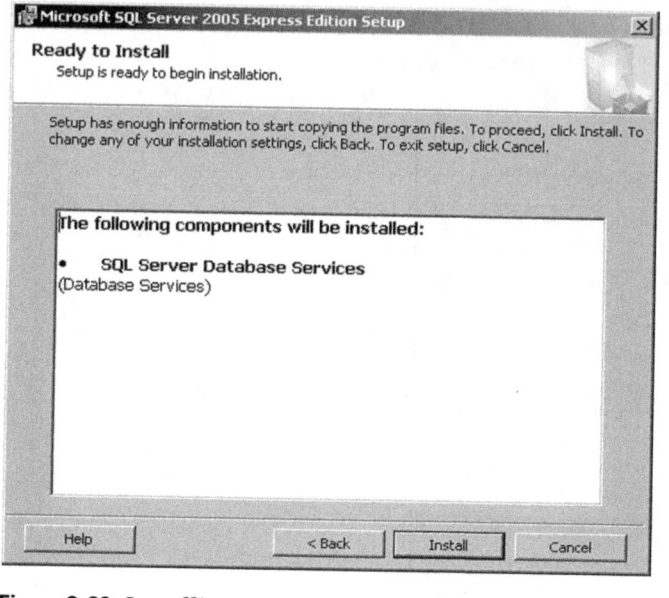

Figure 3-39. *Installing SQL Server Database Services*

When you do this, some grinding will occur on your hard drive, and SQL Server Database Services will be installed. The last window will show what was installed and if it installed OK. This is shown in Figure 3-40.

Click Next and you will get a summary log screen letting you what was done and how successful it was. This is shown in Figure 3-41.

Click Finish, and you are done.

You can see that it would be best to have this install come along for the ride when you install Visual C# Express or VWD Express. There are no screens constantly popping up when it is done that way.

There is no need to configure SQL Server Express here. The DNN installation will take care of everything necessary. Very helpful, don't you think?

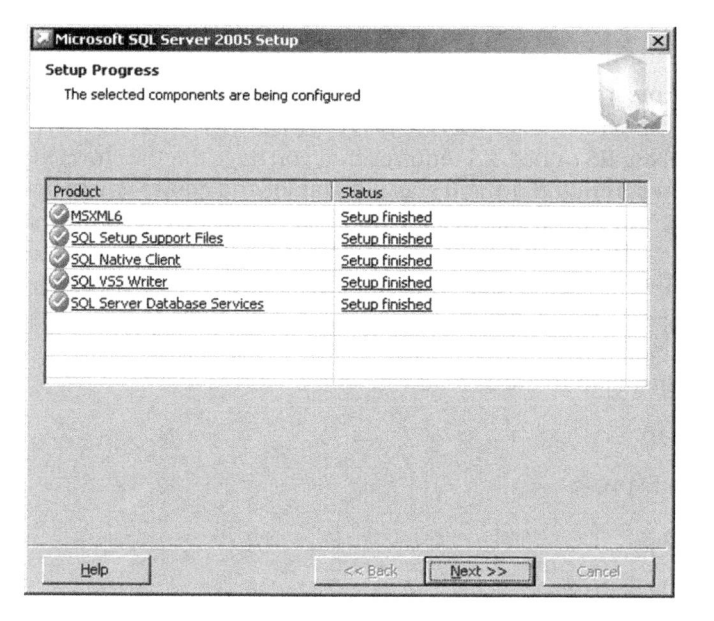

Figure 3-40. *Install finished OK.*

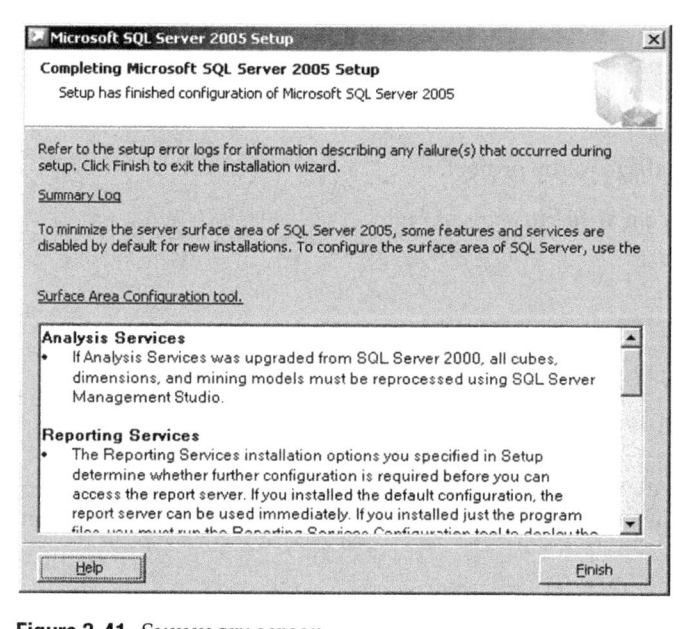

Figure 3-41. *Summary screen*

Summary

This chapter is arguably the most important of the book. There are quite a few steps to go through to get it right. There are quite a few ways to get it wrong.

DNN can be installed using IIS or not. IIS requires that you have the Windows XP Pro (or higher) operating system. I recommend using IIS, as it is stabler and allows you to better test the program you are writing. You will be able to use your PC as a web server and browse to your new website from another PC. This is a big test.

If you have Windows XP Home as an operating system, do not worry. I have shown you how to install the DNN program so that it makes use of the included File System web server that comes with VWD 2005 Express.

Basically, the steps for installation are as follows:

- Install IIS if you need to.

- Install Visual C# 2005 Express.

- Install MSDN Express.

- Install SQL Server 2005 Express.

- Install VWD 2005 Express.

- Install the DNN starter kit.

- Run VWD and start a new project based on the DNN starter kit.

- Give proper security to the DNN website using Windows Explorer.

- Add a SQL Server database to the project.

- Change the `release.config` file to `web.config`.

- Compile the project.

- Install the project.

- Run/debug the project.

I have included as many screenshots as necessary to keep you on the right track at every step of the install.

The next chapter involves working with Visual C# 2005 Express. You will learn the IDE and some C# programming. Some of the code you write in this chapter will be used to create a DNN module later in the book.

CHAPTER 4

■ ■ ■

Basic C#

Chapter 3 dealt with installing the development environment on your machine. You saw how to install the Express versions of SQL Server, VWD, and Visual C#. The level of detail that I went through was precise, because if any installation mistakes are made, it is not so easy to go back and correct them.

If you are like me, you saw the DotNetNuke start page and immediately went poking about. You might have found that you are able to put together a page or two with no programming at all. So why this chapter?

Although it is possible to make websites with no programming, they will be limited indeed. There are only so many free modules, and the ones you pay for may not meet your needs. This is where the programming comes in. C# is the programming language of choice for this book.

I will show you a little of the C# language and the development environment you will be working in. Although you will eventually develop code in VWD Express, the basics of the IDEs are the same.

One of the modules you will be developing later will allow you to punch in and out as an employee. It will show the hours worked that day and week. It will also show who is at work. This is the most basic HR time and attendance (T&A) module that you can have. You will need to write some back-end code to calculate times and such. This will all be done in C#.

You will develop a page in this chapter and the code associated with it to do basic T&A. You will be able to transfer the code to the real module you will build later. Let's get started.

The C# Integrated Development Environment

What can this IDE do? In one word, "Everything you need it to." OK, that was five words, but you get the drift. It can do the following:

- Edit code with syntax highlighting

- Create a design surface for you to build a visual page

- Build the project for you one file at a time, or all at once

- Debug the software you create

- Allow you to step into the software one line at a time, edit a line, and continue where you left off

- Create a deployment package so you can install it somewhere when you are done

- Manage all your projects

- Interface with both local and online help in a context-sensitive manner

- Suggest code for you to insert into your program

I can think of more things, but I will leave it at that. For everything this C# IDE can do, the other IDEs can do the same. In fact, as you know from the installation, the VWD IDE can also act as a small web server.

The Look and Feel

Start up Visual C# and you should get a screen similar to that shown in Figure 4-1.

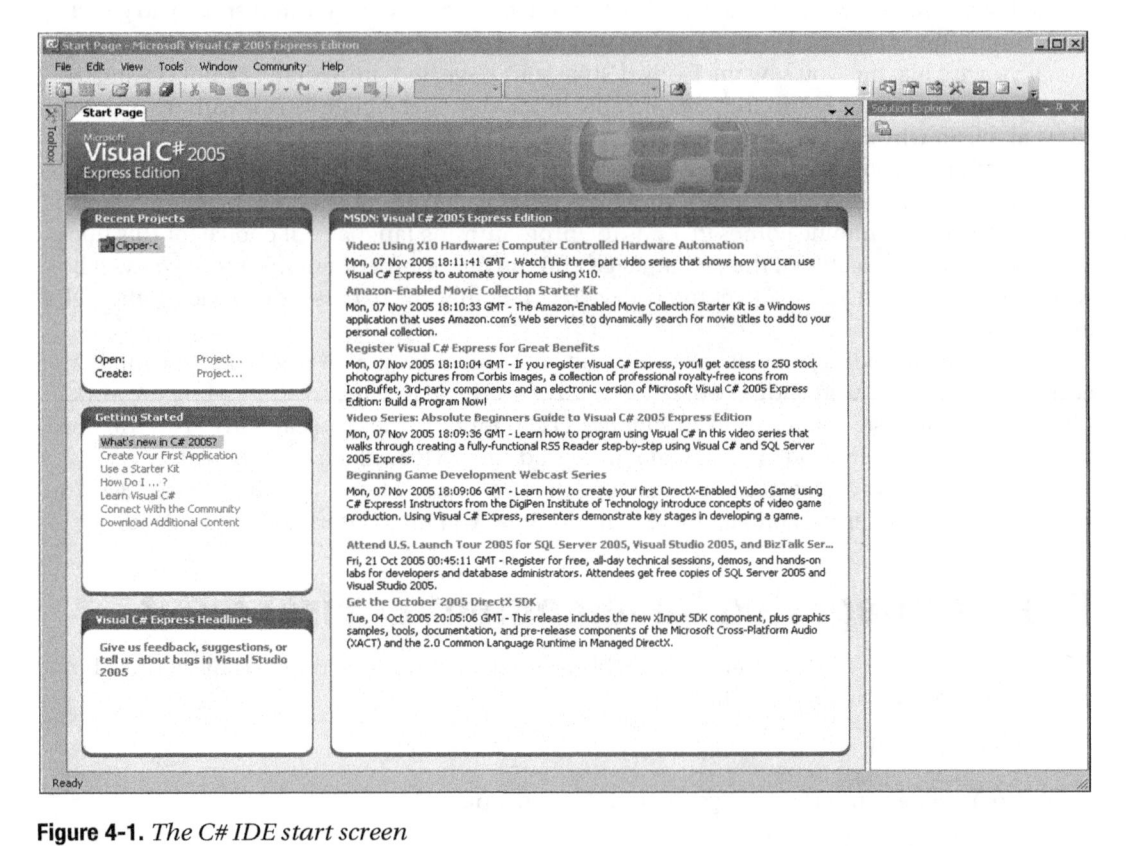

Figure 4-1. *The C# IDE start screen*

You will see a standard menu on top with a toolbar below. Below this, you will see three pinnable panes. The first is the toolbox, which is on the left-hand side and is currently minimized. Run you mouse over it—you will see what looks like a pushpin in the top-right corner of the pane. This is shown in Figure 4-2.

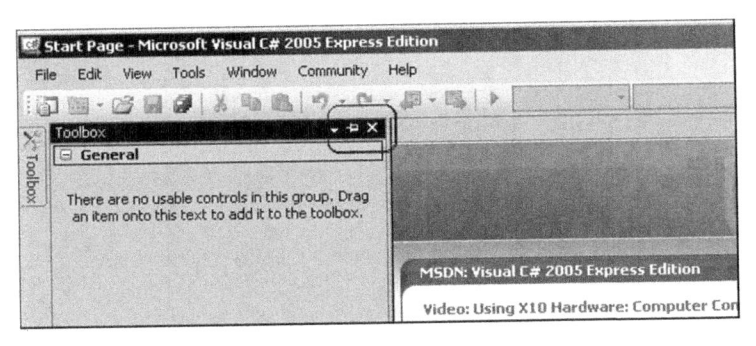

Figure 4-2. *The toolbox pushpin, showing Auto Hide*

Click this pushpin—it will rotate vertically and the toolbox will stay maximized. Note that the Solution Explorer acts this way as well.

This pinnable menu and pane system is a really big help in developing code. Many times you won't need the toolbar or, in some cases, even the Solution Explorer. This feature allows you to maximize the screen space you have for visual screen development or coding.

One last thing to note about the menu system is that it is completely configurable. If you do not like the way it looks, you can move panes around, add new ones, or delete some choices from other toolbars. It is up to you. I would suggest, however, that you use the system as it is for now just to get used to it.

Creating a New Project

The project you will create in this chapter is a simple time sheet. This time sheet will allow you to press a button to punch in and out of work. It will have the following features:

- A button to click that punches you into work at the beginning of your shift

- A button to click that punches you out at the end of the day

- A place that shows how many hours you've worked that day after you punch out

- A grid that shows how many hours you've worked in the current week

The intention of this project is to handle the design work and the business logic so you can bring it over to the Web. In Chapter 7, you will be creating a DNN module that will do this work. All the business logic you create in C# here will be used there.

Starting the Project

The name of this project will be "Punch." Clever, eh?

Open the C# IDE and click the menu option File ➤ New Project. Choose a Windows Application project and name it Punch. This is shown in Figure 4-3.

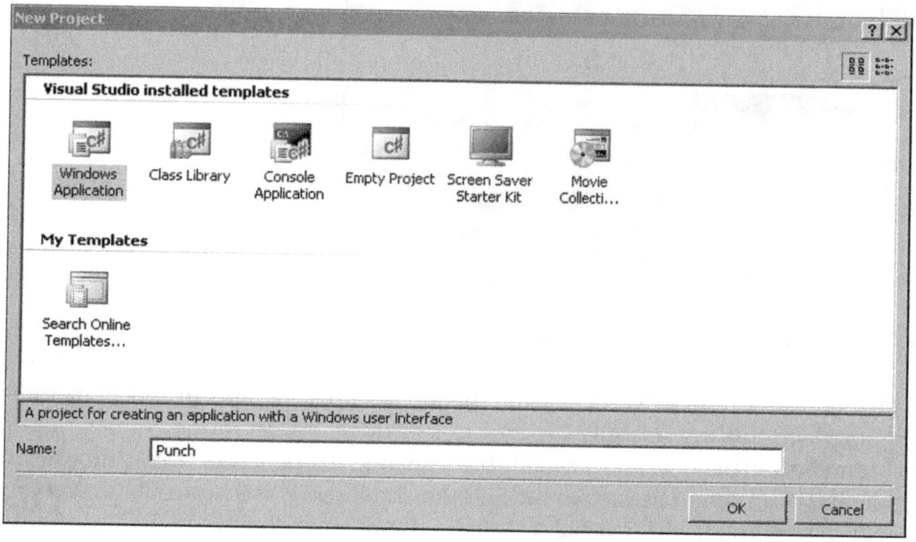

Figure 4-3. *Creating a new project*

Click OK and you will have a project with a single Windows form and a class that runs the code for this form. Unfortunately, the name of the form is "form1" and the name of the code class is "program." This is way too generic, and you should change it.

Inside the Solutions pane, right-click the form1.cs file and select the Properties window. It will show as in Figure 4-4.

Change the file name from form1.cs to punch.cs. Press Enter and you will get the prompt shown in Figure 4-5.

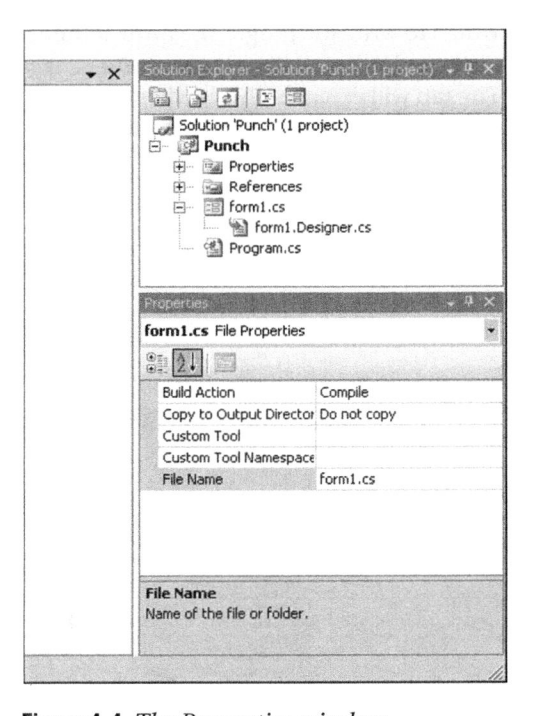

Figure 4-4. *The Properties window*

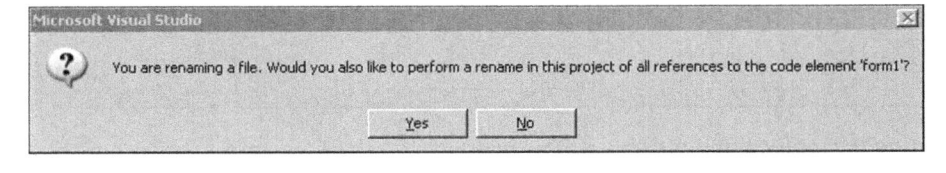

Figure 4-5. *Prompt to propagate changes*

Click Yes here to continue. In previous versions of the C# IDE, the name change did not propagate throughout the project. I used to have to open every file and change every reference myself. This new functionality is a big help.

You now have a single form and a code file with which to write the program. The next thing to do is populate the form with controls so that the user can interact with your program.

Click the form, and then click the Toolbox tab. The tab will expand. This is where you will click the pushpin to force the toolbox to stay open while you are using it. You can see this in Figure 4-6.

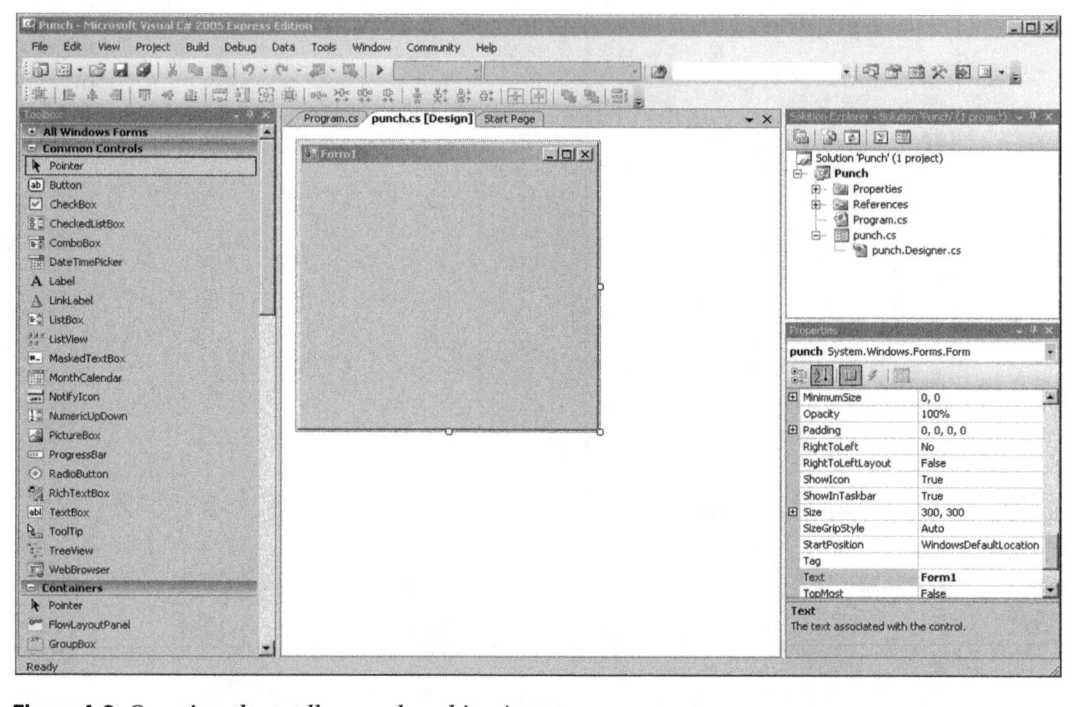

Figure 4-6. *Opening the toolbox and making it stay open*

Notice all the controls that Microsoft gives you for free here. You have common things such as different types of buttons, labels, text fields, and so on. It is possible (and probable) that when you create more Windows applications, you will need some more specialized controls not shown here. There is a wealth of controls available for purchase online. If you feel really comfortable with programming, you can even create new specialized controls out of the ones shown here. If you feel so inclined, I wrote a book on how to write special data input controls, called *Data Entry and Validation with C# and VB .NET Windows Forms*. This book is available from Apress as well.

Project Setup

Before diving into the project, I want to take a break here to explain the setup of a C# solution. The setup of a web solution will be similar. While I am on the topic, I will also show you some aspects of C# and programming itself. This will not be anything too difficult, but it will be about the most complex thing you will see in programming the projects in this book.

The Solution Explorer

The Solution Explorer is the pane shown in the upper right of the screen. It is essentially a list of all the files in your project. This project's solution is shown in Figure 4-7.

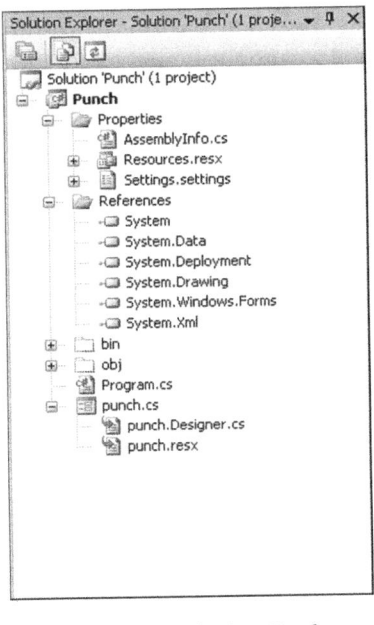

Figure 4-7. *The Solution Explorer window*

My list here is expanded to show some other files. Let's look at what some of these files are.

AssemblyInfo.cs: This file includes information about your project that can be accessed by other programs. This information includes things such as version number and name.

Resources.resx: This file is an XML file that includes localized text you can use in your program. You are not localizing this program, so your text is hard-coded in the class.

Settings.settings: This file has information about user preferences. You can store the last known state of a program in here, and the next time a particular person logs in, the program will return to the state that person left it.

References: The files included under this folder contain the core functionality of .NET. If you write a DLL with some neat methods, you can include it here so you can reference the methods in your program.

Program.cs: This is the most upper-level class that instantiates your Punch class. Basically it starts the program running.

punch.cs: This is the visual form you see on the screen.

punch.Designer.cs: This is the code that Visual C# generates when you place and manipulate controls on your form.

punch.resx: This file contains localized text that relates to your Punch class. It will appear once you add components to your form.

The blank form that you see in Figure 4-6 is the punch.cs file. The code that runs this form is called punch.Designer.cs. This file contains all the code that places controls on the form. It also contains all the code that handles the properties of the form. Double-click the punch.Designer.cs file name in the Solution Explorer and you will see the code shown in Listing 4-1.

Listing 4-1. *Base code for a form*

```
namespace Punch
{
  partial class Punch
  {
    /// <summary>
    /// Required designer variable.
    /// </summary>
    private System.ComponentModel.IContainer components = null;

    /// <summary>
    /// Clean up any resources being used.
    /// </summary>
    /// <param name="disposing">true if managed resources should be
    /// disposed; otherwise, false.</param>
    protected override void Dispose(bool disposing)
    {
      if (disposing && (components != null))
      {
        components.Dispose();
      }
      base.Dispose(disposing);
    }

    #region Windows Form Designer generated code
    #endregion

    private System.Windows.Forms.Button cmdPunch;
    private System.Windows.Forms.Label label1;
    private System.Windows.Forms.TextBox txtHoursToday;
    private System.Windows.Forms.TableLayoutPanel tlp1;
    private System.Windows.Forms.Label label2;
    private System.Windows.Forms.TextBox txtMon;
```

```
    private System.Windows.Forms.ComboBox cmbWeek;
    private System.Windows.Forms.TextBox txtSat;
    private System.Windows.Forms.TextBox txtFri;
    private System.Windows.Forms.Label label7;
    private System.Windows.Forms.Label label5;
    private System.Windows.Forms.TextBox txtSun;
    private System.Windows.Forms.Label label6;
    private System.Windows.Forms.TextBox txtThu;
    private System.Windows.Forms.TextBox txtWed;
    private System.Windows.Forms.TextBox txtTue;
    private System.Windows.Forms.Label label4;
    private System.Windows.Forms.Label label3;
    private System.Windows.Forms.Label label8;
  }
}
```

There are some things to note here. First is the fact that there is a namespace called Punch. A namespace is a way to keep names of controls and methods from conflicting with some other controls or methods that may be named the same. A namespace is like the town part of an address. You may live on 5 Main Street, and I may live on 5 Main Street as well. The way we keep these addresses unique is to define the towns we live in. A namespace allows you to avoid naming conflicts and provide what is called a fully quallified name.

The next thing to note is that you have a class called Punch. It is actually a partial class, but I will get to that later. Writing code in .NET—or any modern language nowadays—means writing object-oriented code. A class is a way of encapsulating a set of funtionality. Functionality could be the visual aspects and code that runs in the background. Everything that has anything to do with this form is encapsulated in this class.

Next you will notice a region called Windows Form Designer generated code. You may click the plus sign next to it to expand and edit this section if you want. I do not recommend this, and neither does Microsoft. Suffice it to say that this section is reserved for the IDE, and this is where it puts code that places the controls on the form.

■**Caution** You may look at the code in the Windows Forms Designer region, but do not change it. The IDE relies on the code here to be exaclty what it put in here. If you change it, you may change the behavior of your form.

Finally, you see a bunch of controls and their names. These are definitions of all the controls you will be placing on this form. You will not have this code yet.

The next file I want you to look at is the file called punch.cs. There are a few ways to see the code in this file. The first and most common way is to double-click the form. This adds what is called an event handler for the form to the code, and the IDE shows the code. The other way is to click the View Code button on the Solution Explorer. This is shown in Figure 4-8.

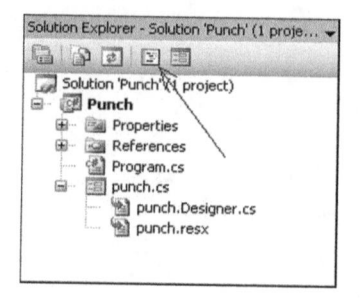

Figure 4-8. *The View Code button*

The code that you will see is shown in Listing 4-2.

Listing 4-2. *Initial code for the Punch class*

```
using System;
using System.Collections.Generic;
using System.ComponentModel;
using System.Data;
using System.Drawing;
using System.Text;
using System.Windows.Forms;

namespace Punch
{
  public partial class Punch : Form
  {
    public Punch()
    {
      InitializeComponent();
    }

    private void Punch_Load(object sender, EventArgs e)
    {

    }
  }
}
```

You will see here that you again have a partial class called Punch within the same Punch namespace that you saw before. You can see from this code and the code in Listing 4-1 that the Punch class is broken up between two files. Hence the word *partial*. You can define part of a class in one file and another part in another file. The reason for doing this is to keep the IDE forms designer–generated code away from the code that you will be writing. It is a way of hiding what you really don't need to see, and prevents some confusion.

I got this code to show up by double-clicking the form. You will see from this piece of code that there is a method called Punch_Load. This is the event handler method that is given to you by the IDE. Since this code is in this file, you are free to edit it as you see fit.

You do not have to add anything to the Page_Load event handler. If you double-click the form to get to the code page, the Page_Load event handler is what you get.

So this is the basic layout of a C# Windows program. As I said before, the layout of a web solution, as far as the files go, is pretty much the same. Now on to the visual layout.

Designing the Form

Designing the form involves knowing what the user will need to see, and laying out the controls correctly. The controls you will need for this form are as follows:

- A button to punch in and out

- A table to see a week's time

- Several labels to view in and out punches

- A drop-down control to choose which week to view

- A label to see daily time

The list that follows instructs you on placing the control on the form. When you are done with the form, it should look like the one shown in Figure 4-9.

1. From the toolbox, click the ComboBox control and place it on the form using your right mouse button. In the Properties window, name it cmbWeek.

2. Choose a button from the toolbox and place it on the form as shown in Figure 4-9. Name this button cmdPunch. Fill in the Text property as Punch In. Make the Font property for this button 14-point bold. You'll use just one button here to do double duty; it punches the user in and out.

3. Choose a label from the toolbox and place it on the form as shown in Figure 4-9. No need to name this label. Fill in the Text property as Hours Worked Today.

4. Below this label, add a text box called txtHoursToday. Change the BorderStyle property to FixedSingle. Change the ReadOnly property to True.

5. Add seven labels to the form, representing the days Sunday through Saturday. There is no need to name these labels. Change the Text property of each label to represent each day of the week, as shown in Figure 4-9.

6. Add seven text boxes to the form below the day-of-week labels, as shown in Figure 4-9. Name the text boxes txtSun, txtMon, txtTue, txtWed, txtThu, txtFri, and txtSat, respectively. Change the BorderStyle of each to FixedSingle. Change the ReadOnly property of each to True.

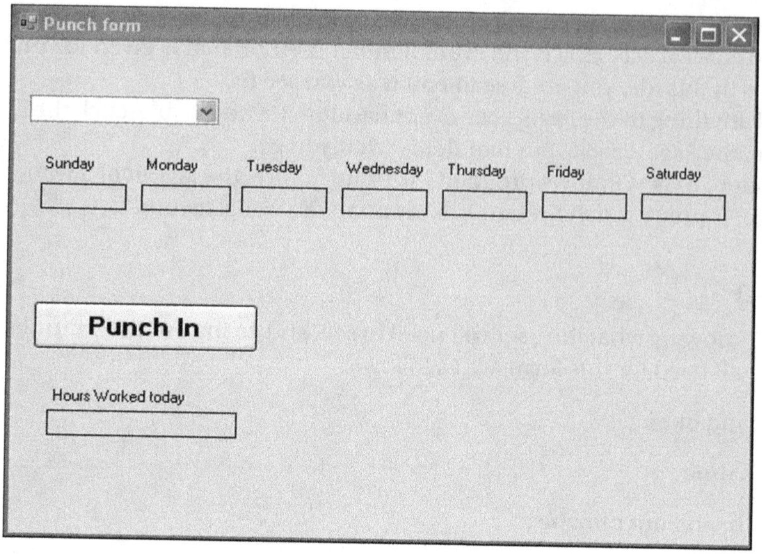

Figure 4-9. *Final layout of controls on the form*

Your final layout should look like that shown in Figure 4-9. You should now have a workable form with absolutely nothing behind it. It is time to add some code to this form.

Adding the Code

There are two events you need to handle in this form. The first is when a user clicks the drop-down box. The second is when the user clicks the Punch button. There are two ways to add the event handlers to this code. The first way is the way I prefer, which involves some hand-coding and a good deal of knowledge about the way the IDE generates code. So, let's get started . . . Just kidding.

The easy way to add event handlers to the code is to double-click the control. So double-click the drop-down box, and you will see a method appear in the punch.cs file. This is the code you will see generated:

```
private void cmbWeek_SelectedIndexChanged(object sender, EventArgs e)
{
}
```

Now whenever someone clicks this control, the code you write inside this method will be run. Next, double-click the Punch button. The code that appears is as follows:

```
private void cmdPunch_Click(object sender, EventArgs e)
{
}
```

Whenever someone clicks the button, the code in this method will run. You can generate event handling methods this way for any control. However, just as an aside, there are many more events that you can handle for these and all other controls. These other events must be wired up manually. You will not be handling any other events in this project.

You are now over the easy part.

A Class in Classes

There are three tenets to object-oriented programming. They are as follows:

- Polymorphism

- Inheritance

- Encapsulation

When it comes to software engineering, nothing is ever a single-syllable word. I think that these three words are meant to confuse the uninitiated, and should be used as ammunition to ask for a raise. Use these three words in a single sentence, and when your boss gives you a quizzical look, ask for a raise.

When I first learned object-oriented programming (OOP) with C++, I spent a lot of time trying to use these words with my colleagues. It soon became apparent that developers never really talked this way. Here is what they actually mean:

Polymorphism: This feature allows you to have the same function for different objects. While the function Circle.Draw() may render a circle, the function Square.Draw() does a completely different thing, even though they both draw a shape.

Inheritance: This feature allows you to have a generic class—for example, one called House. This class could have some basic properties, such as bedrooms, doors, a kitchen, and so on. You could then derive a class—for example, RanchHouse—from House, and it would "inherit" House's properties. You could then add properties that are specific to a RanchHouse—for example, that it has only one floor.

Encapsulation: This feature allows you to store data and functionality inside an object while limiting access to them from outside. This is the OOP feature you will be using most often in this project and other projects in this book. It's often called "data hiding," but one can also "hide" functionality.

The following is a small side project to show you how you will use classes. I will use the IntelliSense feature of the IDE to show how classes work. You can join in the fun . . . or not.

Start a project for a Windows Console Application. This is the simplest application, with virtually no IDE-generated code to get in the way. Name the project "Encapsulation." The Program.cs file should look like Listing 4-3.

Listing 4-3. *Start of the Encapsulation project*

```
using System;
using System.Collections.Generic;
using System.Text;

namespace Encapsulation
{
  class Program
  {
    static void Main(string[] args)
    {
    }
  }
}
```

Not much here, is there? You have a single class called Program. Within this class, you will add another class with some variables that are hidden from the outside, and some that are not. I will show a way to get at these hidden variables later. Listing 4-4 shows the whole Program.cs file with the new class.

Listing 4-4. *The new class, with variables*

```
using System;
using System.Collections.Generic;
using System.Text;

namespace Encapsulation
{
  class Program
  {

    private class DataHiding
    {
      private int mPrivate_integer;
      private string  mPrivate_string;

      public int      mPublic_integer;
      public string   mPublic_string;
```

```
    //This is a constructor.  It is used to initialize the object
    // that is created from this class
    public DataHiding()
    {
      mPrivate_integer = 1;
      mPrivate_string  = "one";
      mPublic_integer  = 2;
      mPublic_string   = "two";
    }

    //Property to get and set the private integer
    public int Private_integer
    {
      get { return mPrivate_integer; }
      set { mPrivate_integer = value; }
    }

    //Property to get and set the private string
    public string Private_string
    {
      get { return mPrivate_string; }
      set { mPrivate_string = value; }
    }

  }

  // This is the method that gets run when the program is started
  static void Main(string[] args)
  {
  }
 }
}
```

The variables that are not allowed to be accessed by any code outside this class are declared Private. The variables that can be accessed outside this class are declared Public. Notice that the variables have an *m* in front of them. I use this convention to let myself know that these variables are internal members of a class and not directly accessible.

Encapsulation

The properties called Private_Integer and Private_String are the ways to get and set the private variables from outside the DataHiding class. These properties allow you to control what values are allowed, and whether or not a variable can be just read, or both read and written.

The best way to see how this all works is to create an object and use the IntelliSense feature of the IDE to tell you the level of accessibility of this class. This will be done inside the Main method. Listing 4-5 shows the Main method with the appropriate code.

Listing 4-5. *Accessing the new class*

```
// This is the method that gets run when the program is started
static void Main(string[] args)
{
  //Create the new object fom the class
  DataHiding dh = new DataHiding();

  //get the public values
  Console.Write(dh.mPublic_integer);
  Console.Write(dh.mPublic_string);

  //get the private values via properties
  Console.Write(dh.Private_integer);
  Console.Write(dh.Private_string);
}
```

The first line of code instantiates (creates) a new object from the DataHiding class. Note that this class was declared private. You can access it here, though, because the Main method is within the Program class and can see all private members within the Program class, including nested classes. The next two lines of code access the public variables of the dh object directly. The last two lines of code access the private variables of the dh object via properties. Figure 4-10 shows what happens when you type the letters "dh" (as in Console.Write(dh.).

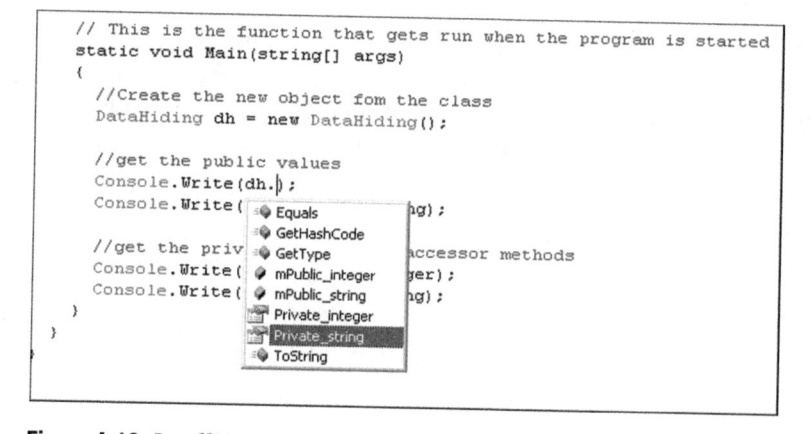

Figure 4-10. *IntelliSense showing what is available*

IntelliSense shows here that you can access the public variables directly, because it shows `mPublic_integer` and `mPublic_string`, but not `mPrivate_integer` and `mPrivate_String`.

IntelliSense also shows that you can access the private variables though the properties `Private_integer` and `Private_string`. This is encapsulation for you!

Tip IntelliSense is fantastic in .NET. It tells you everything you need to know about a method or an object. If you expect a variable to show and IntelliSense does not show it, you know you are doing something wrong.

Polymorphism

Let's use IntelliSense once more to show polymorphism at work. I had you use the `Console.WriteLine` method to output some variables to the screen. The `WriteLine` method of the `Console` object is one of the most "overloaded" methods in .NET. When you were typing it in and you typed the opening parenthesis after `Console.Write`, IntelliSense showed 18 ways to use it. This is shown in Figure 4-11.

```
// This is the function that gets run when the program is started
static void Main(string[] args)
{
    //Create the new object fom the class
    DataHiding dh = new DataHiding();

    //get the public values
    Console.Write(dh.mPublic_integer);
    ▲ 1 of 18 ▼  void Console.Write (bool value) ng);
    value: The value to write.
    //get the private values via accessor methods
    Console.Write(dh.Private_integer);
    Console.Write(dh.Private_string);
}
}
```

Figure 4-11. *Method overloading shown via IntelliSense*

See how IntelliSense shows 18 different ways to use this method? This is because you can write out any of the types that .NET allows, with and without formatting. Outside the `Console` class, it looks like there is only one `Write` method.

Now that I have explained some of what you will see as far as object-oriented programming goes, let's get to the code of this main project.

Back to the Project

Writing code in C# or VB entails some basic knowledge of object-oriented programming. I already told you about classes, namespaces, variables, methods, and properties. There are a few other concepts you need to be aware of before you go on, such as how to use them.

This project is about keeping time on a per-person basis for two weeks. The two weeks in question are last week and this week. The module you will write for the DNN project will encompass as many weeks and as many people as you want.

If you think about the data, you'll find that you need to keep the times that a person punched in and out on a daily basis. To further organize the data, it would be nice to keep this data in a weekly format. So the data you need is as follows:

- Time punched in

- Time punched out

- Day of week

- Week

- Person

Basically, a person has a collection of weeks. Each week has a set of in and out times for each day of that week. Using this design allows you to scale the collections between one and . . . whatever.

This data will enable you to figure the hours worked for any day. There is no need to keep the actual hours worked because there are rules (not included here) that adjust the hours worked based on rounding rules. It is not necessarily true that the total hours worked in a day are continuous from start to end.

The best way to keep and manage this data is with classes. You have seen the class that encompasses the form and its controls. You will need to define your own class that encompasses a person and the time associated with punching in and out. Once you define the proper class, you can scale the program to include as many weeks of data for as many people as you need, with no extra code. I will show you how to do this.

The Private Class

You need a class to hold all the information necessary to run this form. The information you need is the in and out times of each day of the week. Therefore, you will create a WeekPunches class. Go into your punch.cs class file and add a new class. Listing 4-6 shows the complete code for this class. Put this class within the Punch class, near the top.

Listing 4-6. *The new WeekPunch class*

```
private class WeekPunches
{
  #region Class local variables

  private DateTime mMondayStart;
  private DateTime mMondayEnd;
  private DateTime mTuesdayStart;
  private DateTime mTuesdayEnd;
  private DateTime mWednesdayStart;
  private DateTime mWednesdayEnd;
  private DateTime mThursdayStart;
  private DateTime mThursdayEnd;
```

```csharp
private DateTime mFridayStart;
private DateTime mFridayEnd;
private DateTime mSaturdayStart;
private DateTime mSaturdayEnd;
private DateTime mSundayStart;
private DateTime mSundayEnd;

#endregion

#region Accessor Get / Set Methods

public DateTime MondayStart
{
  get { return mMondayStart; }
  set { mMondayStart = value; }
}
public DateTime MondayEnd
{
  get { return mMondayEnd; }
  set { mMondayEnd = value; }
}
public double MondayHours
{
  get { return CalculateHours(mMondayStart, mMondayEnd); }
}

public DateTime TuesdayStart
{
  get { return mTuesdayStart; }
  set { mTuesdayStart = value; }
}
public DateTime TuesdayEnd
{
  get { return mTuesdayEnd; }
  set { mTuesdayEnd = value; }
}
public double TuesdayHours
{
  get { return CalculateHours(mTuesdayStart, mTuesdayEnd); }
}

public DateTime WednesdayStart
{
  get { return mWednesdayStart; }
  set { mWednesdayStart = value; }
}
```

```csharp
    public DateTime WednesdayEnd
    {
      get { return mWednesdayEnd; }
      set { mWednesdayEnd = value; }
    }
    public double WednesdayHours
    {
      get { return CalculateHours(mWednesdayStart, mWednesdayEnd); }
    }


    public DateTime ThursdayStart
    {
      get { return mThursdayStart; }
      set { mThursdayStart = value; }
    }
    public DateTime ThursdayEnd
    {
      get { return mThursdayEnd; }
      set { mThursdayEnd = value; }
    }
    public double ThursdayHours
    {
      get { return CalculateHours(mThursdayStart, mThursdayEnd); }
    }


    public DateTime FridayStart
    {
      get { return mFridayStart; }
      set { mFridayStart = value; }
    }
    public DateTime FridayEnd
    {
      get { return mFridayEnd; }
      set { mFridayEnd = value; }
    }
    public double FridayHours
    {
      get { return CalculateHours(mFridayStart, mFridayEnd); }
    }


    public DateTime SaturdayStart
    {
      get { return mSaturdayStart; }
      set { mSaturdayStart = value; }
    }
```

```csharp
public DateTime SaturdayEnd
{
  get { return mSaturdayEnd; }
  set { mSaturdayEnd = value; }
}
public double SaturdayHours
{
  get { return CalculateHours(mSaturdayStart, mSaturdayEnd); }
}

public DateTime SundayStart
{
  get { return mSundayStart; }
  set { mSundayStart = value; }
}
public DateTime SundayEnd
{
  get { return mSundayEnd; }
  set { mSundayEnd = value; }
}
public double SundayHours
{
  get { return CalculateHours(mSundayStart, mSundayEnd); }
}

#endregion

//This is where you would incorporate some rules such as
//lunch breaks
private double CalculateHours(DateTime Start, DateTime End)
{

  //Check to see if end comes after start
  if (DateTime.Compare(Start, End) < 0)
  {
    TimeSpan diff = End.Subtract(Start);
    return (diff.TotalHours);
  }
  return 0.0;
}
}
```

I know this seems like a lot of complicated code. I will break it down for you, and you will see the logic of it all.

The first thing to note is the list of private variables. When you are working in a class, there is a need to have variables like this and a need to get to those variables. Standard object-oriented programming states "Thou shalt not access variables directly." Seriously.

When you access a variable in a class, you usually do it though a property. For instance, the code snippet that follows shows a private variable and the property to read and write it.

```
private DateTime mThursdayStart;
public DateTime ThursdayStart
{
  get { return mThursdayStart; }
  set { mThursdayStart = value; }
}
```

There is a get accessor to read the variable and a set accessor to write the variable. This not only "hides" the variable, but it also has the advantage of allowing you to validate the data given to you before you write to the variable. This way you can make sure that only valid entries are accepted.

So if you look at the code in Listing 4-6, you will see a pattern of private variables and public properties. There really isn't too much to this.

The last thing to talk about with this class is the "helper" method at the end, called CalculateHours.

Not only can a class hide data, it can also hide functionality. This is also another tenet of object-oriented programming. Only the class itself should be able to directly manipulate its own data. Users of the class should be able to get whatever data out of it they need. In this case, you are storing only punch times. Therefore, you need to calculate hours to present it via a property.

If you look at the CalculateHours method, you will see that it first makes sure that the end time is after the start time. The times that are stored also include date data. This means that, for example, if you punch in at 11 p.m. and out at 3 a.m., this code will work. There is an internal .NET class called TimeSpan that allows you to manipulate time in an easy manner.

Note   I must say that the .NET library is far more complete than the Java library. This CalculateHours method in Java would be at least ten lines longer. You will find that if you want to do something to some data, there is very often a method somewhere in the .NET library that will do it for you.

Other Variables

Now that you have this new self-contained class that can store and manipulate time, how do you use it?

Before I answer this, you will need to add some other variables to the Punch class. These are shown in Listing 4-7.

Listing 4-7. *Punch class variables and placement*

```
namespace Punch
{
  public partial class Punch : Form
  {
    #region Private variables

    private static bool P_IN = false;
    private static bool P_OUT = true;
    private bool mPunchState = P_IN;

    private DateTime mStartPunch;
    private DateTime mEndPunch;

    private ArrayList MyPunches = new ArrayList();

    private class WeekPunches
    {
    ...Code here...
    }

    }

    #endregion
```

I have included not only the variables here, but the placement of them in the Punch class. The variables are within the Private variables region. Note that the WeekPunches class is a private class within the Punch class. This is perfectly valid and is often useful.

So you have a few Boolean variables, a couple of DateTime temporary variables, and an ArrayList. Let's talk about this for a second.

I had you define a WeekPunches class that contained its own data for a week of punches. It also contained a method that manipulated that data to give a result of hours worked for a particular day.

The trick is to use this new class in a way that is reusable for many people for many weeks. This is where the ArrayList comes in.

Collections

The ArrayList is considered a *collection*. As its name suggests, a collection is a group of objects that can be added to and removed from. A collection also allows you to search it and get the object you want. A collection even allows you to iterate though all the objects one by one without explicitly knowing how many objects there are in it.

A collection can be any size and can be cleared of all data at once. In this case, your ArrayList is a collection of WeekPunches objects.

There are many kinds of collections in .NET. I use the ArrayList because it is the most generic and useful. There are some kinds of collections in .NET that only allow unique values in them. This means that if an object is in a collection, you may not add another object that is identical. This is really handy when you are given a list of names, for instance, and you know there are duplicates. Just keep adding names to the collection and it will reject any duplicates. At the end, you have a list of unique names.

As I said before, this project will hold a collection of only two weeks: last week and this week.

The Working Code

I had you double-click the Punch button and the drop-down box to get the event handlers for these controls. Now it is time to add the code.

All programs need some kind of initial conditions set up. After all, how do you get the drop-down box filled with choices? There are two ways.

The first way is to use the Properties pane, which is available to you when you click an object. This is shown in Figure 4-12.

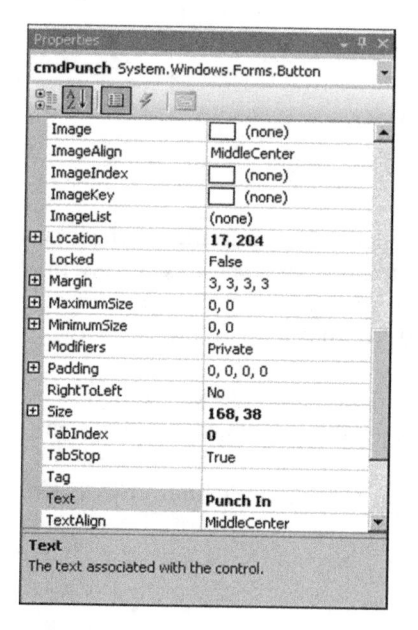

Figure 4-12. *The Properties pane*

Pretty much everything you need to fill in about the control is in here. This is fine for some controls, but there are still some things that cannot be handled this way.

The second way is to enter all the initial conditions via code. This is my preferred way of doing it. It keeps all properties for all forms in the same place and also overrides the Properties pane if anyone inadvertently messes with your control.

You will notice in your punch.cs code that the class is called Punch, and it has a member also called Punch. This Punch member is referred to as a *constructor*. As soon as an object of the class is instantiated (in this case by .NET), the .NET runtime tries to call its constructor. It is in here that you initialize your page.

When I code a constructor, I prefer to call another method that initializes controls. I always call this Init(). This is called just after the InitializeComponents() call. Listing 4-8 shows the initialization code for this program.

Listing 4-8. *The initialization code*

```
private void Init()
{
  FillData();

  cmdPunch.Text = "Punch In";
  cmbWeek.Items.Clear();
  cmbWeek.Items.Add("Last Week");
  cmbWeek.Items.Add("This Week");
  cmbWeek.SelectedIndex = 0;
}
```

You can see from this code that I am filling in the text for the button, and I am also adding the phrases "Last Week" and "This Week" to the drop-down combo box. By the way, this combo box has a collection: the Items collection. Notice that I am clearing all data out of it first, and then adding new objects (in this case, strings) to the collection.

Notice that the last thing I do in this method is set the selected index of the combo box to zero, which is the first selection. Doing this in code is the same as clicking the combo box while the form is running. As you know, clicking the combo box while the program is running causes an event handler to be invoked.

The line cmbWeek.SelectedIndex = 0 will automatically call the method cmbWeek_SelectedIndexChanged(object sender, EventArgs e). Oftentimes you will need to invoke event handlers within your code, and this is one way to do it.

The Fake Database

This Init method calls another method: FillData. This FillData method fills the WeekPunches objects with hard-coded data. Normally you would get this data from a database. I did not want to do this here because it would be too much work for you without the ability to bring the code over to the DNN module you will build later based on this project. Since you would have to rewrite the database code, I decided to wait until you get to the DNN project before getting into that.

Listing 4-9 shows the FillData code.

Listing 4-9. *Filling the collection*

```csharp
private void FillData()
{
  //This takes the place of getting data from a database.
  //We will hard-code last week's data and some of this week's.

  //Create last week
  DateTime LastSunday = DateTime.Now;
  int Days2Subtract = 7 + (int)DateTime.Now.DayOfWeek;
  LastSunday = LastSunday.Subtract(new TimeSpan(
                              Days2Subtract,
                              LastSunday.Hour,
                              LastSunday.Minute,
                              LastSunday.Second,
                              LastSunday.Millisecond));

  WeekPunches LastWeek = new WeekPunches();
  LastWeek.SundayStart = LastSunday;
  LastWeek.SundayEnd = LastSunday;
  LastWeek.MondayStart = LastSunday.Add(new TimeSpan(1,8,0,0,0));
  LastWeek.MondayEnd = LastSunday.Add(new TimeSpan(1,15,0,0,0));
  LastWeek.TuesdayStart = LastSunday.Add(new TimeSpan(2,8,0,0,0));
  LastWeek.TuesdayEnd = LastSunday.Add(new TimeSpan(2,14,0,0,0));
  LastWeek.WednesdayStart = LastSunday.Add(new TimeSpan(3,8,0,0,0));
  LastWeek.WednesdayEnd = LastSunday.Add(new TimeSpan(3,13,0,0,0));
  LastWeek.ThursdayStart = LastSunday.Add(new TimeSpan(4,8,0,0,0));
  LastWeek.ThursdayEnd = LastSunday.Add(new TimeSpan(4,14,20,0,0));
  LastWeek.FridayStart = LastSunday.Add(new TimeSpan(5,8,0,0,0));
  LastWeek.FridayEnd = LastSunday.Add(new TimeSpan(5,15,30,0,0));
  LastWeek.SaturdayStart = LastSunday.Add(new TimeSpan(6,0,0,0,0));
  LastWeek.SaturdayEnd = LastSunday.Add(new TimeSpan(6,0,0,0,0));

  MyPunches.Add(LastWeek);

  //Create this week
  DateTime ThisSunday = DateTime.Now;
  Days2Subtract = (int)DateTime.Now.DayOfWeek;
  ThisSunday = ThisSunday.Subtract(new TimeSpan(
                              Days2Subtract,
                              ThisSunday.Hour,
                              ThisSunday.Minute,
                              ThisSunday.Second,
                              ThisSunday.Millisecond));
```

```csharp
WeekPunches ThisWeek = new WeekPunches();
if (DateTime.Now.DayOfWeek > DayOfWeek.Sunday)
{
  ThisWeek.SundayStart = ThisSunday;
  ThisWeek.SundayEnd = ThisSunday;
}
if (DateTime.Now.DayOfWeek > DayOfWeek.Monday)
{
  ThisWeek.MondayStart = ThisSunday.Add(new TimeSpan(1,7,30,0,0));
  ThisWeek.MondayEnd = ThisSunday.Add(new TimeSpan(1,16,40,0,0));
}
if (DateTime.Now.DayOfWeek > DayOfWeek.Tuesday)
{
  ThisWeek.TuesdayStart = ThisSunday.Add(new TimeSpan(2,8,20,0,0));
  ThisWeek.TuesdayEnd = ThisSunday.Add(new TimeSpan(2,14,50,0,0));
}
if (DateTime.Now.DayOfWeek > DayOfWeek.Wednesday)
{
  ThisWeek.WednesdayStart = ThisSunday.Add(new TimeSpan(3,0,0,0,0));
  ThisWeek.WednesdayEnd = ThisSunday.Add(new TimeSpan(3,0,0,0,0));
}
if (DateTime.Now.DayOfWeek > DayOfWeek.Thursday)
{
  ThisWeek.ThursdayStart = ThisSunday.Add(new TimeSpan(4,0,0,0,0));
  ThisWeek.ThursdayEnd = ThisSunday.Add(new TimeSpan(4,0,0,0,0));
}
if (DateTime.Now.DayOfWeek > DayOfWeek.Friday)
{
  ThisWeek.FridayStart = ThisSunday.Add(new TimeSpan(5,0,0,0,0));
  ThisWeek.FridayEnd = ThisSunday.Add(new TimeSpan(5,0,0,0,0));
}
MyPunches.Add(ThisWeek);


}
```

Let's go over this code so you can understand it. There are some concepts in here that will be very handy. It's not really so hard.

Here is what the FillData method does:

- It fills in time punches for last week. This works no matter when you run it.

- It fills in time for this week's punches up until yesterday. Yesterday is the day before you actually run the program, and it changes on a daily basis.

- It adds last week and this week's WeekPunches objects to the collection.

There is quite a bit of time manipulation in here. The concepts of time and how to manage it will be important later.

Then first thing done in this method is finding last Sunday. This is done by subtracting 7 from today to get to this day last week. At that point, you need to subtract the integer represen-tation of the day of the week to get back to Sunday. So if today is Tuesday, subtract 7 to get to last Tuesday. Since the enumeration for the days of the week starts on Sunday as 0, this means that Tuesday is 2. Subtract 2 from Tuesday of last week and you are at Sunday of last week.

What I also did here was subtract whatever time it is to get to midnight on Sunday of last week. I think the explanation actually took longer then the code.

The next thing I did was instantiate a new WeekPunches object. I then put some start and end times into each day of the week. When I was done, I added the WeekPunches object to the collection using the code MyPunches.Add(LastWeek);.

Next, I instantiated another WeekPunches object that holds this week's time punches. I found this Sunday the same way I found last Sunday, but without subtracting 7 days.

I then added in and out times to this week's WeekPunches, up until today. I did this so that when the project is run and the button is clicked, the time will go into the current day's time slot.

Displaying the Week's Data

So now you have the data for last week and this week. How does it get to the screen? You will need to code a display method. This is shown in Listing 4-10.

Listing 4-10. *Displaying data*

```
private void DisplayWeek(int wk)
{
  txtSun.Text = "";
  txtMon.Text = "";
  txtTue.Text = "";
  txtWed.Text = "";
  txtThu.Text = "";
  txtFri.Text = "";
  txtSat.Text = "";

  WeekPunches Week = (WeekPunches)MyPunches[wk];
  txtSun.Text = Week.SundayHours.ToString("F2");
  txtMon.Text = Week.MondayHours.ToString("F2");
  txtTue.Text = Week.TuesdayHours.ToString("F2");
  txtWed.Text = Week.WednesdayHours.ToString("F2");
  txtThu.Text = Week.ThursdayHours.ToString("F2");
  txtFri.Text = Week.FridayHours.ToString("F2");
  txtSat.Text = Week.SaturdayHours.ToString("F2");
}
```

When you filled in the combo box, you filled in "Last Week" first. The index for this in the Items collection was 0. When you filled in the data, you added last week first to the MyPunches collection. Knowing this relationship, you can just get a reference to the WeekPunches object based on the combo box SelectedIndex property.

Note that I clear the text boxes first. This is to make sure that no old data hangs around between weeks.

Now that you have the DisplayWeek method programmed, you need to call it from somewhere. That place is in the combo box event handler. Here is the code:

```
private void cmbWeek_SelectedIndexChanged(object sender, EventArgs e)
{
  DisplayWeek(cmbWeek.SelectedIndex);
}
```

Punching In and Out

The last thing to do is add some functionality to the Punch button. Since this is a test and you do not want to wait around for time to elapse, I made the Punch Out button add two hours to the time. This allows you to punch in and out quickly and see results. The code is shown in Listing 4-11.

Listing 4-11. *Wiring up the Punch button*

```
private void cmdPunch_Click(object sender, EventArgs e)
{
  if (mPunchState == P_OUT)
  {
    mPunchState = P_IN;
    cmdPunch.Text = "Punch In";
    mEndPunch = DateTime.Today;

    mEndPunch = mEndPunch.Add(new TimeSpan(2, 5, 0));

    txtHoursToday.Text = CalculateHours(mStartPunch, mEndPunch).ToString("F2");

    WeekPunches Week = (WeekPunches)MyPunches[1];
    switch (DateTime.Now.DayOfWeek)
    {
      case DayOfWeek.Sunday:
        Week.SundayStart = mStartPunch;
        Week.SundayEnd = mEndPunch;
        break;
```

```
      case DayOfWeek.Monday:
        Week.MondayStart = mStartPunch;
        Week.MondayEnd = mEndPunch;
        break;
      case DayOfWeek.Tuesday:
        Week.TuesdayStart = mStartPunch;
        Week.TuesdayEnd = mEndPunch;
        break;
      case DayOfWeek.Wednesday:
        Week.WednesdayStart = mStartPunch;
        Week.WednesdayEnd = mEndPunch;
        break;
      case DayOfWeek.Thursday:
        Week.ThursdayStart = mStartPunch;
        Week.ThursdayEnd = mEndPunch;
        break;
      case DayOfWeek.Friday:
        Week.FridayStart = mStartPunch;
        Week.FridayEnd = mEndPunch;
        break;
      case DayOfWeek.Saturday:
        Week.SaturdayStart = mStartPunch;
        Week.SaturdayEnd = mEndPunch;
        break;
    }
    DisplayWeek(cmbWeek.SelectedIndex);
  }
  else
  {
    mPunchState = P_OUT;
    cmdPunch.Text = "Punch Out";
    mStartPunch = DateTime.Today;
  }
}
```

I use the same button to punch in and out. It saves real estate and prevents you from pushing the wrong button. This method notes the state of the punch, and changes the text to "Punch Out" when the user is punched in, and "Punch In" when the user is punched out for the day.

When the user punches out at the end of the day, this method calculates the hours worked and displays it in the label below the button. Also, when the user punches in, this method gets the punches class from this week. It then determines what day it is and saves the in and out punches for today in the class. The last thing it does is call the DisplayWeek method.

Did you catch the CalculateHours method call in here? Remember that you added this method to the WeekPunches class. Well, it so happens that I need to calculate hours outside of the WeekPunches class so that I can display it in the txtHoursToday text field. There are two ways to do this.

The most complicated and coolest way is to create a static CalculateHours method in the WeekPunches class and call it directly from here without instantiating an object. I know this may be gibberish to you, and is a pretty advanced topic. This is why I did not do it here. Instead, I created another CalculateHours method outside of the WeekPunches class to be used here. Lsting 4-12 shows this code.

Listing 4-12. *The CalculateHours method*

```
private double CalculateHours(DateTime Start, DateTime End)
{

  //Check to see if end comes after start
  if (DateTime.Compare(Start, End) < 0)
  {
    TimeSpan diff = End.Subtract(Start);
    return (diff.TotalHours);
  }
  return 0.0;
}
```

There is another reason to repeat this code outside of the WeekPunches class. Remember I told you that calculating hours is not always straightforward and that some rules may be used, such as rounding rules and breaks to calculate actual time worked.

Well, keeping the CalculateHours method in the WeekPunches class separate from this one allows me to change the CalculateHours method in the WeekPunches class without regard to who uses it. This is the method-hiding part of using a class. I can add rules to the class and none of the code that gets hours from this class needs to change. It just gets a different number based on the functionality I change in the internal CalculateHours method.

The CalculateHours method that I use to fill in the txtHoursToday text field will always give me the raw time worked, which is what I want.

Trying the Code

Now is the time to try out the code. If you have typed in the code yourself, I suggest you first compare it to the code from the download.

Press Ctrl+F5 to compile and run the program. You should get a screen like the one shown in Figure 4-13.

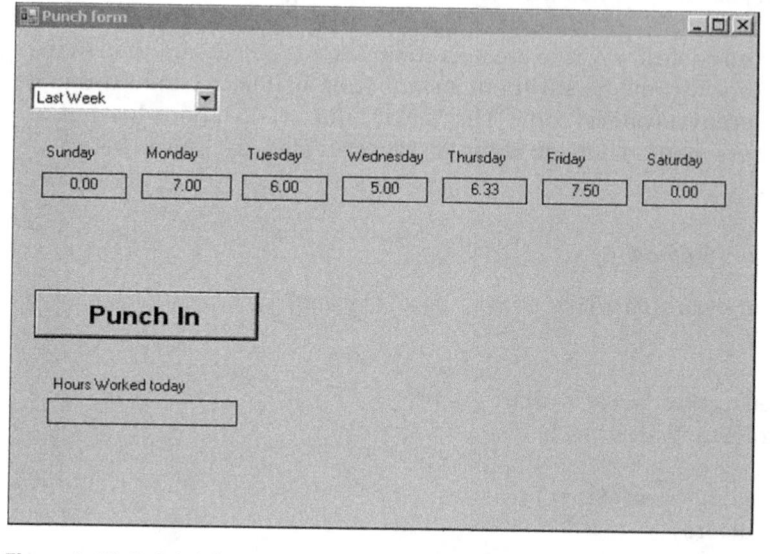

Figure 4-13. *Initial form load showing last week's punches*

Note that the hours are shown for all of last week. Now click the combo box and choose this week. For me, today is a Tuesday, so I show hours for Monday only, as shown in Figure 4-14. Note that I have also punched in.

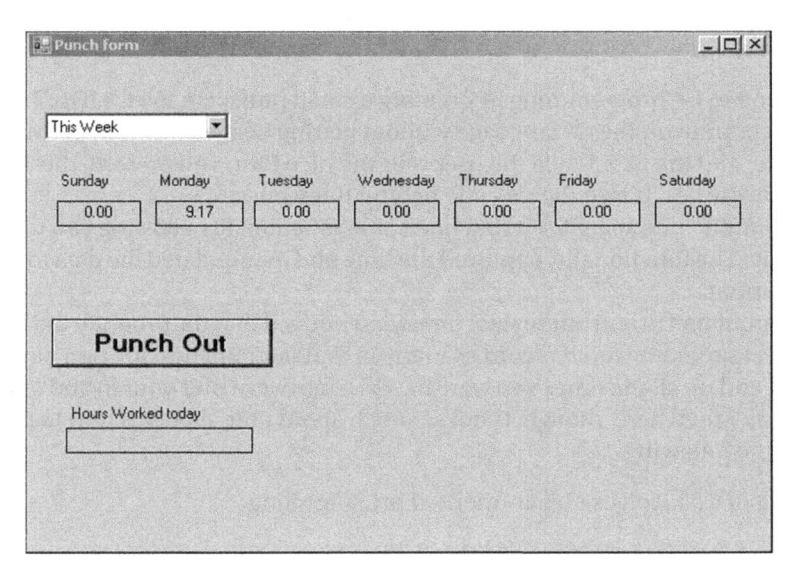

Figure 4-14. *The Punch form showing this week's time totals*

Now punch out, and you should see a screen similar to Figure 4-15.

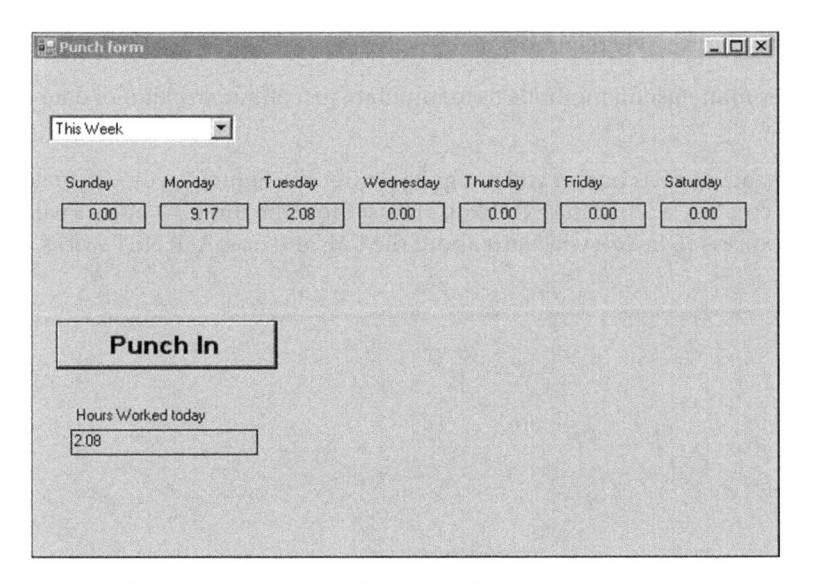

Figure 4-15. *This week's time after punching in and out*

Note that Tuesday now has some hours.

Summary

I have introduced you to C# programming by creating a small project in the C# IDE. This allowed you to concentrate on the C# language without getting bogged down by HTML, JavaScript, ASP code, and the like. While the user sees the nice form you present, this is not where all the complexity lies. It is in the C# code behind the scenes.

You created a simple time sheet form that had some functionality allowing you to punch in and out for the day. The functionality captured the time and manipulated the data to present the time in a nice format.

Of course, you punched in and out several times and noticed that the program did not stop you. A real time sheet program would record as many in and out punches during a day as you want. It would then add up all the times you were in. This one overwrites your in and out times.

What you really learned here, though, is not so much about time sheets as how to program in C#. You learned the following:

- Programming in C# involves object-oriented programming.

- Classes encapsulate data and functionality.

- Instance variables should be accessed by properties.

- There are many collections in .NET that allow you to store groups of information.

- Keeping information in classes and collections allows you to scale the amount of information you want to keep with almost no increase in code.

- .NET provides many useful methods to manipulate just about any kind of data you can think of.

The code you wrote in this chapter will not go to waste. In Chapter 7, you will make use of this code when you create a module in DNN to do almost the same thing. Chapter 5 will get you going in the VWD Express IDE. You will learn about the IDE and how ASP.NET works.

CHAPTER 5

Visual Web Developer

In Chapter 4, you wrote a small program in C# that contained a GUI and some business logic. You performed this task for two reasons. First was to get you familiar with writing in C# with no external distractions such as HTML and the browser getting in the way. The second reason was for you to actually write a piece of code for the DNN project you will create.

The purpose of this chapter is to introduce you to all those other "distractions" that make up the rest of your programming tasks. Although you created a user interface for the C# program, it is not the one you will use. You will use a Web interface that is seen through a browser. This is where VWD 2005 Express comes in.

I often create samples of user interface web pages with the Windows Forms interface provided by Visual C# or VB. It is a very fast and convenient way to whip up some demo screens. Since you've done the same in the last chapter, you know what to shoot for when developing the same GUI in this chapter, but for the Web.

The VWD IDE

I covered the C# IDE in the last chapter. I said that once you knew the C# IDE, you would know how to run the other Express IDEs. While this is true, I will go over the VWD IDE in detail here, in case you missed anything.

The Look and Feel

Start up the VWD 2005 Express program. You will be presented with a screen that has several panes, as shown in Figure 5-1.

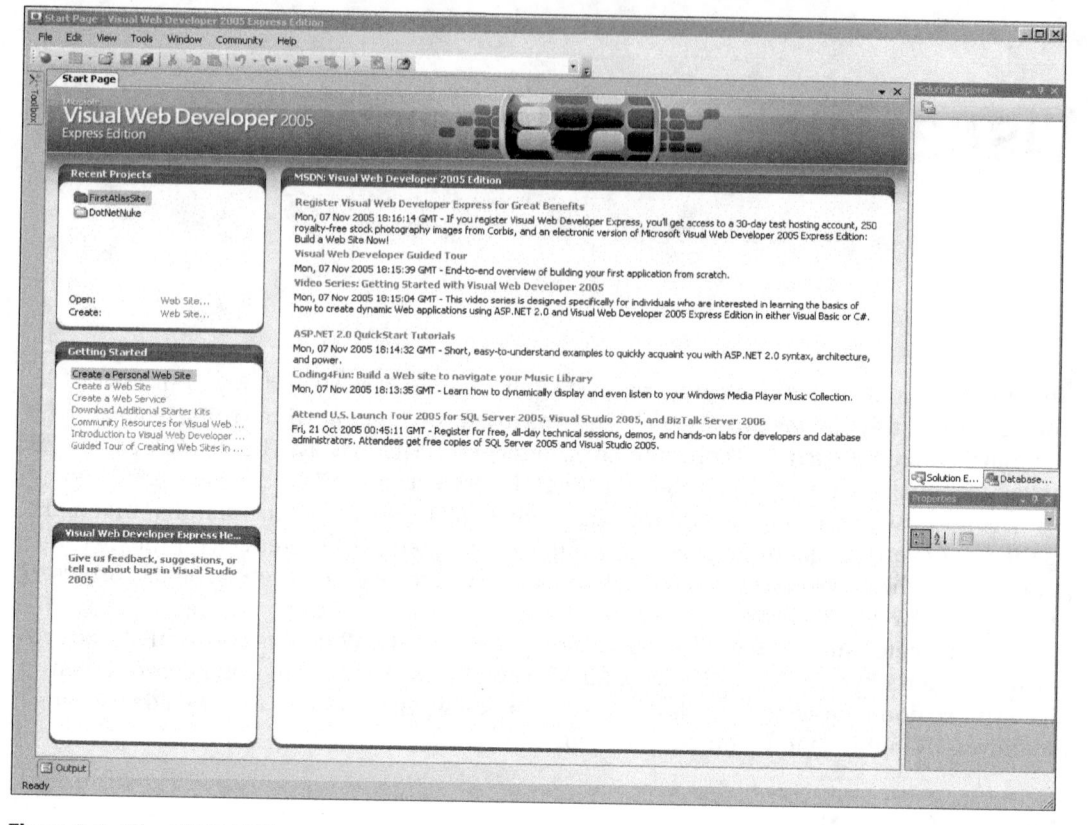

Figure 5-1. *The VWD IDE at startup*

There are several elements to this IDE, which are described in the following list.

- The menu at the top allows you to choose actions to perform or other screens to see.

- The toolbar is just below the menu. Nearly everything in the menu has a corresponding toolbar icon. This toolbar makes it convenient to do repetitive tasks quickly. If the menu choice has an icon next to it, that icon will appear in a toolbar.

- The toolbox menu is on the left-hand side of the screen, running vertically. This menu changes depending on whether you are editing the code or the design. This toolbox menu is currently minimized. If run your mouse over it, it will maximize and give you the ability to leave it open.

- The start page contains a number of interior panes, as follows:

  - The top-left pane of the start page is for launching projects. These can be recent ones or new ones.

  - The middle-left pane is for wizards. These wizards allow you to start new projects based on templates. This page is also used as a base to get you going on tutorials.

  - The bottom-left pane is used as a mechanism to get feedback to Microsoft on this product.

  - The center pane, as you see it here, is used as a news site. Later, the center pane is used to view and edit code and any visual aspects of the pane.

  - The top-right pane is the Solution Explorer. Once you have a solution loaded, this pane will show you a tree indicating the structure of the files in your program.

  - The bottom-right pane is the Properties window. Here you will be able to change properties of different controls in your project.

This list is cursory at best. Not only are there more windows available to you, but there is also much more to say about the panes themselves.

Go to the Getting Started pane and click the Create a Web Site link. In a few seconds, you will have the skeleton of a website. At this point, you can see some of the panes populate. Figure 5-2 shows what you should see.

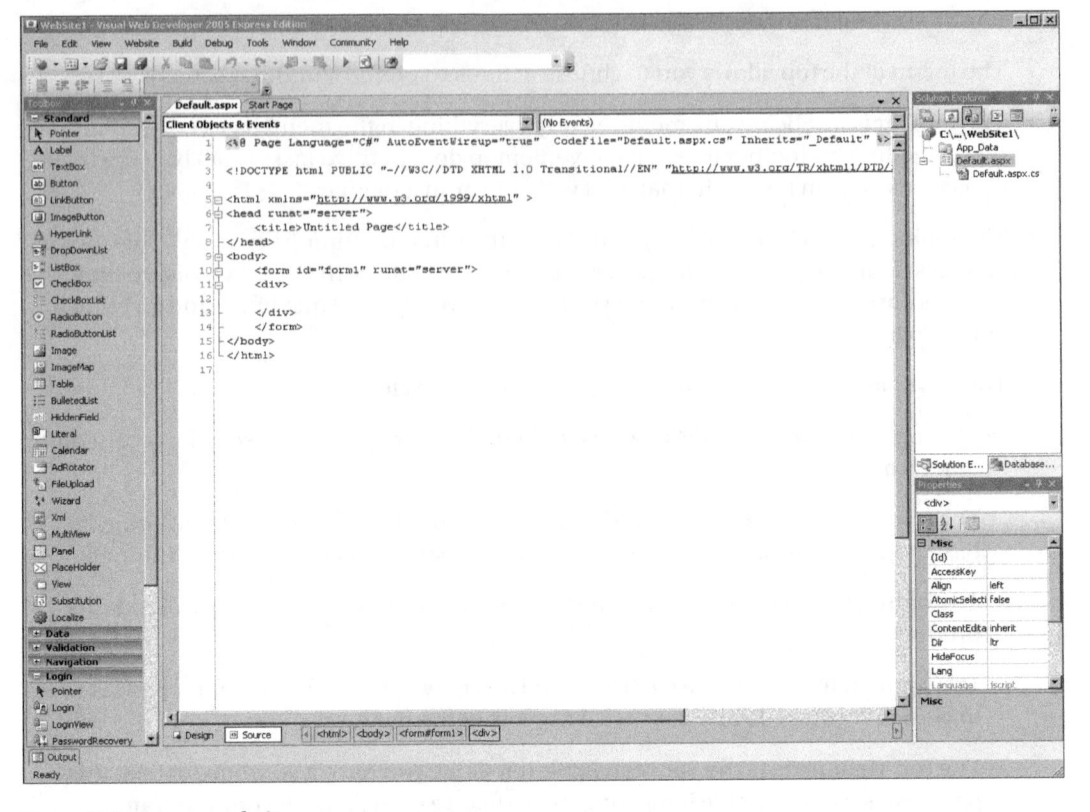

Figure 5-2. *A new website*

Notice that I have expanded the left toolbox pane. I am keeping it open by clicking the pushpin icon in the top right of the pane. This toolbox is now full of controls that can be used on your form. Some of these controls are grouped into subsets, such as Validation, Data, and so on.

The center pane is a tabbed dialog. The tab you see now is the HTML code pane for this project. If you like, you can click the Start Page tab to see that again. I generally click the Start Page tab, and then click the X icon to the right to get rid of the page, since it's unlikely that I'll need it again during this project.

Below this code page you will see some buttons. They are shown in Figure 5-3.

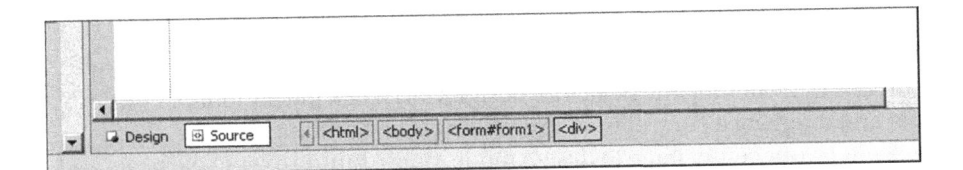

Figure 5-3. *Views on the Code pane*

Clicking the Design button will change the form over to the visual result of this HTML code. Since there is no HTML code that creates anything visible right now, you will see a blank page. Clicking the Source button brings you back to the HTML source code page.

Notice that Figure 5-3 shows some HTML tags next to the Source button. The <div> tag is highlighted. These tags are the ones that represent the level of nesting of the code where your cursor is in the page. Huh? Look closely at Figure 5-4.

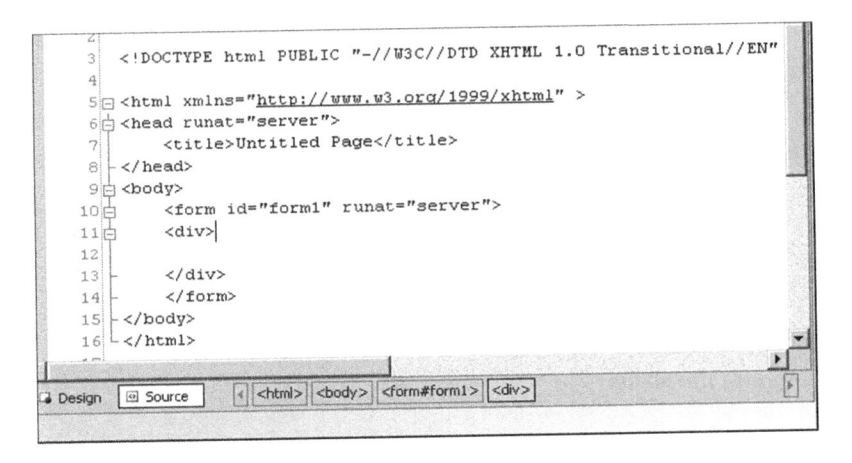

Figure 5-4. *Nested tags*

Notice that the cursor is just after the <div> tag on the code screen. The tags shown next to the Source button show the <div> tag highlighted. It shows that this <div> tag is nested inside a <form> tag, which is nested inside a <body> tag, which is nested inside an <html> tag. If you click one of these tag buttons, you will be able to select the contents of the tag you click. This can be really handy when you've nested so many HTML elements so deep within your code that you don't know where you are. It can also be used as a way to find tags that are missing their accompanying closing or beginning tag. You know that HTML tags come in pairs, right? Well, most of them do, anyway.

Working with Controls

In order for you to see how some of the other panes work, you will need to have something on the page. You do this by switching the page into design view (click the bottom-left button below center pane) and dragging a control from the toolbox onto the designer.

So . . . do that. Switch your center pane to design mode, drag a button over to the page, and drop it anywhere on the page. The chances are that your new button got snapped to the top-left corner of the page, as shown in Figure 5-5.

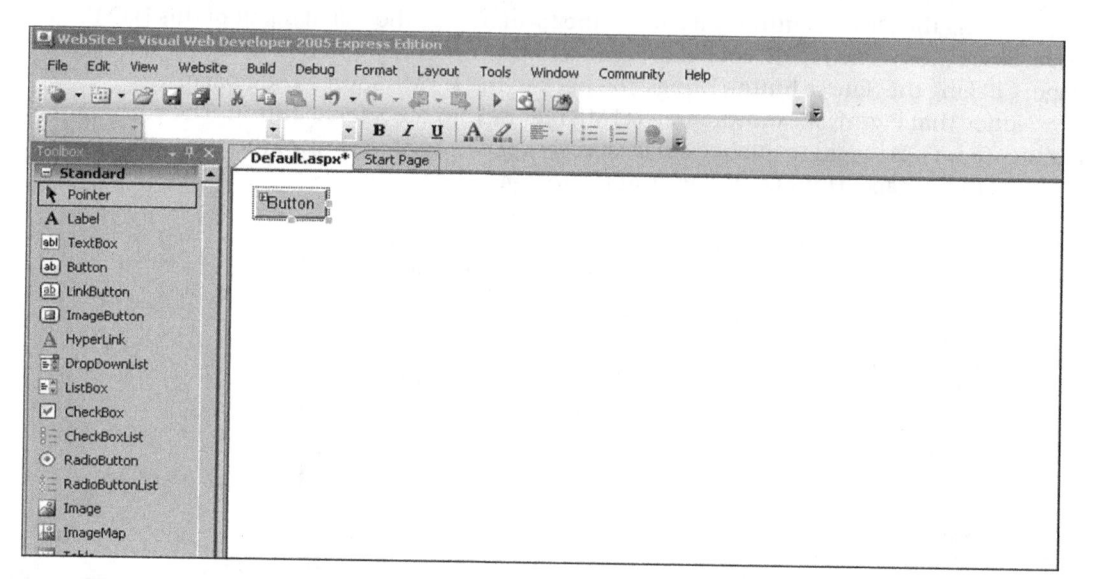

Figure 5-5. *Dragging a button onto the screen*

Before we go any further, I want you to try to drag the button to some other place on the screen. Can't do it, huh? Now add another button to the screen. It will show up right next to the first one with a bit of space between them.

I know what you are thinking . . . "But I thought that you said the VWD IDE and the C# IDE worked the same? Why can't I move the controls where I want them?" Well, the VWD IDE layout will work like the C# layout if you tell it to, but you need to tell it to.

Flow Types

HTML elements can be placed on a page according to several different types of positioning. The main one is flow layout. This is what you see here. Flow layout arranges controls on the page right next to each other according to the order in which you put them on the page.

The type of positioning you will use is absolute positioning. This is what you are used to from creating the user interface in the C# IDE. With this method, you place the controls on the page exactly where you want them. You can drag them around and put them somewhere else later if you like.

The default positioning for VWD is flow layout. I am not sure why, but it is. However, you can change that. If you added the second button, click it and press the Delete key to delete it now.

From the menu, choose Tools ➤ Options, and click the Show All Settings check box. Highlight the CSS positioning node under the HTML Designer tree node. You will see what I've shown in Figure 5-6.

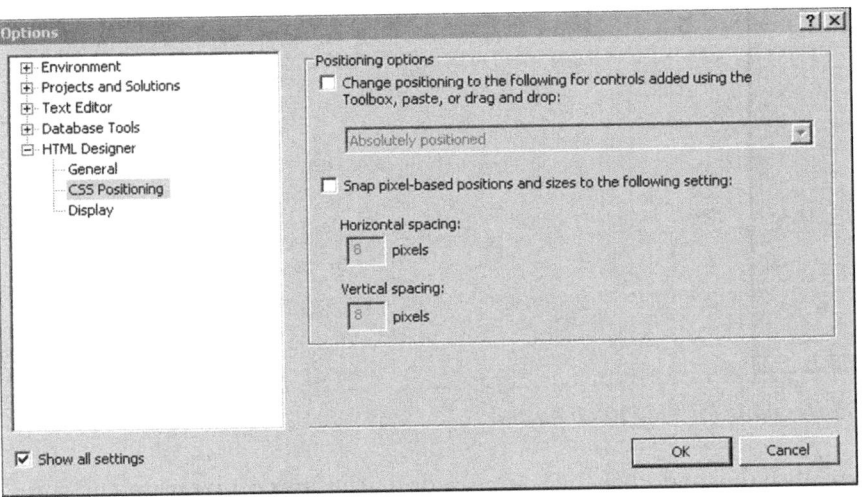

Figure 5-6. *Changing from flow layout to absolute layout*

Check the two check boxes on the right side and click OK. What this does is create an invisible grid on your page, in which each cell is 8×8 pixels wide. Now when you drop or drag a control onto the page, it will snap to a corner of the grid. This allows you to vertically or horizontally align controls on the page.

Try to drag the remaining button around the page. If this does not work, then delete it and add a new one. You should be able to drag it to any position on the page.

Control Properties

Now that you have a control on the page, go to the Properties pane on the right side of the screen and do the following:

- Change the ID of the control to cmdPunch.

- Change the Text property to Punch In.

That's good for now. Your Properties pane for the button should look like the one shown in Figure 5-7.

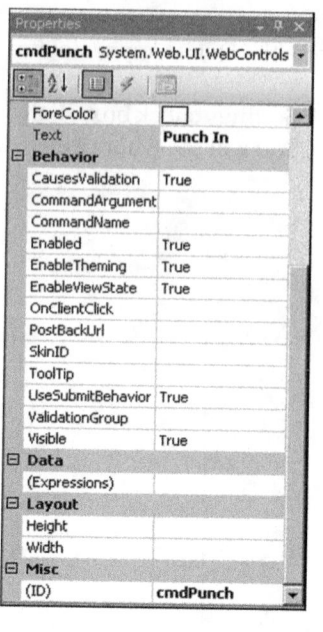

Figure 5-7. *The Properties pane for the Punch button*

To see what actually happened, click the Source button below this center pane, and you should be taken back to the HTML source code for this page. The code between the `<body>` and `</body>` tags has changed. It should read like Listing 5-1.

Listing 5-1. *New button code added*

```
<body>
    <form id="form1" runat="server">
    <div>
          
        <asp:Button ID="cmdPunch" runat="server" Style="z-index: 100;
          left: 224px; position: absolute; top: 240px" Text="Punch In" />
    </div>
    </form>
</body>
```

You see the `<asp:Button...>` tag here. Notice that this button has an absolute left and top position. Its ID has changed, and the text that shows on the button has changed. The browser will interpret this HTML code and render the control just like you see it on the designer page.

The Code-Behind File

So now you know the basics of adding a control to the designer, moving it, and changing some properties. The real power of ASP.NET comes into play when you switch back to the designer and double-click the control. Go ahead and do this. Several things will happen.

Remember in Chapter 4 that when you double-clicked a control, the IDE created an event handler for you? The same happens here. In the C# IDE, the event handler was created in a new file so that the code would be separated from the IDE-generated code. Again, the same happens here.

The new file that is created is called the code-behind file. Take a look at the Solution Explorer now. Yours should look like the one shown in Figure 5-8.

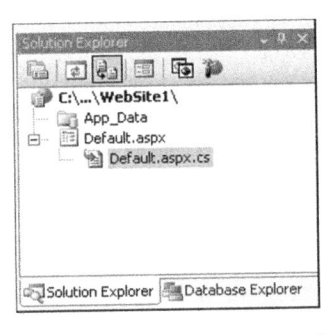

Figure 5-8. *The Solution Explorer*

The first page that shows in your ASP.NET website is called Default.aspx. When you double-click the button, another page is created, called Default.aspx.cs. This is the file that contains the event handling code for the page and anything on the page. This is separation of code and visual design. It is a good thing and is one of the more powerful aspects of ASP.NET.

Note The Default.aspx page is considered the home page of your site. If a user browses to your site and does not specify a page to view, this is the one she sees. You can change this setting, but I suggest you keep it as is. So do not change the name of the Default.aspx file.

Web pages in ASP.NET have an extension of aspx. Since you are using C# as your programming language, the code-behind page has the same name, but with an extension of aspx.cs. If you were using VB .NET as the programming language, you would have an extension of aspx.vb.

So why is the event handling code in another file? Two reasons. The first is to keep the code separate from the design. The second is because it enforces that the event handling code gets run on the server and the HTML code gets sent over to the browser.

CLASSIC WEB DEVELOPMENT

Before VWD Express came along, any web development you wanted to do in the Microsoft world cost you money. In some cases, it cost big money. I did a quick Google search on Visual Studio 2003. The Developer edition costs about $450.00 and the Enterprise edition costs about $950.00. As Yoda would say, "A pretty penny this is."

The alternative to laying out all this money, of course, is getting all your tools for free. And, if you develop in Java, you can. There is a downside to this, though.

I am sure that you have heard of Java and JSP programming. It has been out longer than .NET and probably has far more people programming in it. The advantage to programming in Java is that it can be free. The disadvantage is that you get what you pay for.

First and foremost is the coding language. You have heard of Sun Microsystems. They produce the ubiquitous language called Java. Java is free for downloading. The SDK that includes all the classes you need is also free. The JVM (Java Virtual Machine) is free as well. I'll bet my bottom dollar you have one running on your machine right now.

In order to program with Java, you also need a scripting language to handle any dynamic content in your pages. The most popular is JavaScript. This is followed closely by PHP, Perl, and several others. Fortunately, Internet Explorer will happily run JavaScript, so no worries there.

Let's see. What else do you need?

1. You need a way to write the code. There are many free or low-cost editors out there, including the text editor that comes with Windows.

2. You need a way to compile the code. If you're using Java, JavaScript, and HTML, you can use a compiler called Ant. This is free.

3. You need a way to debug the code. If you get a nice IDE, you can do some debugging. Most likely you will do some "printf"-style debugging. More on this later.

4. You need a web server. You can use an Apache web server with a Tomcat JSP container. (You will soon be able to run ASP.NET code on an Apache server.)

These are the main things you need to develop a website in Java. You also need a great deal of patience, and knowledge on how all these things work and how they work together. The development software may be free, but the knowledge comes at a high price. It takes a long time to learn all this stuff.

There is no such thing that I know of in the Java world that allows you to separate the code from the visual design as completely as you can with ASP.NET. When ASP.NET first came out, this was one of its hallmark features.

For a quick example, here is some JSP code that mixes Java code with HTML:

```
<td width="60%" class="iflxOnTimeWorkrules">
   <center>
   <SELECT style="width: 100%" size=15 name="lstDiff" id="lstDiff" >
      <%
      IflxFieldSetBean EngineList = engines.GetEngines();
      if ( EngineList.getSize() > 0 )
```

Continued

```
    {
       for ( int x=0; x<EngineList.getSize(); x++)
   { %>
               <option value=<%=String.valueOf(x) %>
                   <% String val; %>
                   engid= '<%= EngineList.getValue( x, "engid" ) %>'
                   <% val = EngineList.getValue( x, "engPower" );
                      if(val == " ") val = ""; %>
                   engPower='<%= val %>'
                   <% val = EngineList.getValue( x, "engSize" );
                      if(val == " ") val = ""; %>
                   engSize='<%= val %>'
                   <% val = EngineList.getValue( x, "engType" );
                      if(val == " ") val = ""; %>
                   engType='<%= val %>'
                   <% val = EngineList.getValue( x, "engCylinders" );
                      if(val == " ") val = ""; %>
                   engCylinders='<%= val %>'
                   <% val = EngineList.getValue( x, "engRotation" );
                      if(val == " ") val = ""; %>
                   engRotation='<%= val %>'
                   <% val = EngineList.getValue( x, "engYear" );
                      if(val == " ") val = ""; %>
                   engYear='<%= val %>' >
                   <%= EngineList.getValue( x, "engDescription" ) %>
               </option>
       <% }
       } %>
   </SELECT>
</center>
```

Can you follow this? I can, because I wrote it and I know JSP pretty well. It is messy and inelegant, though.

Many times with JSP, you need to debug using alert statements. These are basically pop-up windows on the screen that you put messages into. For example, if you wanted to find out whether you were running some piece of code, you would put in an alert statement like this: alert("I am running the foorbar function");. This is a form of debugging from decades ago.

The compilation is mostly done by hand using a free program called Ant. Ant stands for "Another Neat Tool."

The biggest problem with programming in JSP is the lack of a fully cohesive IDE. There are many IDEs, but most are not of the caliber of ASP.NET. With ASP.NET, you can do the following:

- Write code with syntax checking and IntelliSense
- Write code in C#, VB, or any other programming language that .NET supports
- Fully debug the code with a powerful, built-in debugger

Continued

- Separate the code from the design with "code-behind"

- Compile any .NET program for debug or release

- Create a release package

- Get superior help

All in all, the ASP.NET experience is friendlier and provides a quicker time to market than traditional JSP programming.

I may have mentioned this before, but here is a little history with ASP. Before ASP.NET, writing ASP involved coding the HTML tags just as you have seen. However, if you wanted any kind of dynamic capability for any of the controls or the page itself, you needed to write script code on the same page as the HTML code. Many times, you would mix the HTML code and the script code together to create the effect you wanted. Other than for very simple pages, this made a mess of your file.

In large organizations, you would have a person responsible for the HTML design and visual aspects of the page, and you would also have a programmer responsible for the code. It became unwieldy for two different people to work on the same section of the page with code intermixed with HTML tags. ASP pages were a nightmare to maintain in this scenario.

I will note here that the current method of JSP programming is still done in this old ASP way. In JSP, there is no analog to the "code-behind" found in ASP.NET.

Server Controls

Now that you've created an event handler for the click event of a button, let's look at the HTML code again. You should have the same code as in Listing 5-2.

Listing 5-2. *HTML code with event handling*

```
<html xmlns="http://www.w3.org/1999/xhtml" >
<head runat="server">
    <title>Untitled Page</title>
</head>
<body>
    <form id="form1" runat="server">
    <div>
          
        <asp:Button ID="cmdPunch" runat="server" Style="z-index: 100;
          left: 224px; position: absolute; top: 240px" Text="Punch In"
          OnClick="cmdPunch_Click" />
    </div>
    </form>
</body>
</html>
```

There is an attribute in the `<head>` tag and the `<asp:Button>` tag. This is the `runat="server"` attribute. This attribute tells the browser that any events that occurs in either the page or this control get sent back to the server for processing. Like anything, this has both advantages and disadvantages.

The disadvantage of sending events back to the server is that it takes time and server bandwidth. The time is taken because the whole page is posted back to the server. The server then processes the call, and must rerender the whole page and send it back to the client. If there is a simple event that requires no business logic or database access, then this takes an unneeded toll on the server's time. Events like this can be handled at the client using JavaScript. With the client handling some events, you use the client's computing power and save the server's computing power for other things.

The advantage, however, is greater in many ways than the disadvantage. The advantage is that you will be able to write code in C# on the server rather than JavaScript on the client. JavaScript is an interpreted language that has little or no enforcement of data types. C# has strict rules concerning data types, and this makes for better code on your part. One other advantage to running the event code on the server is that it is easier to debug. You will have access to all the powerful debugging features that the IDE affords you. Debugging JavaScript is a little more nebulous.

Note It is possible (and in some cases desirable) to write JavaScript event handlers. However, it is not needed for what you are doing in this book, and therefore I will not cover this topic.

So now you know a little history of ASP and the idea behind the "code-behind" aspect of ASP.NET. Let's look at the `Default.aspx.cs` file. Your IDE should look like the one shown in Figure 5-9.

In Figure 5-9, you are looking at the event handler for the button. There are no tools available in the toolbox, and the Properties window is empty because you're not presently looking at any controls. It is possible that you will have a `Page_Load` event handler in here as well. This will have happened if you have double-clicked the empty page.

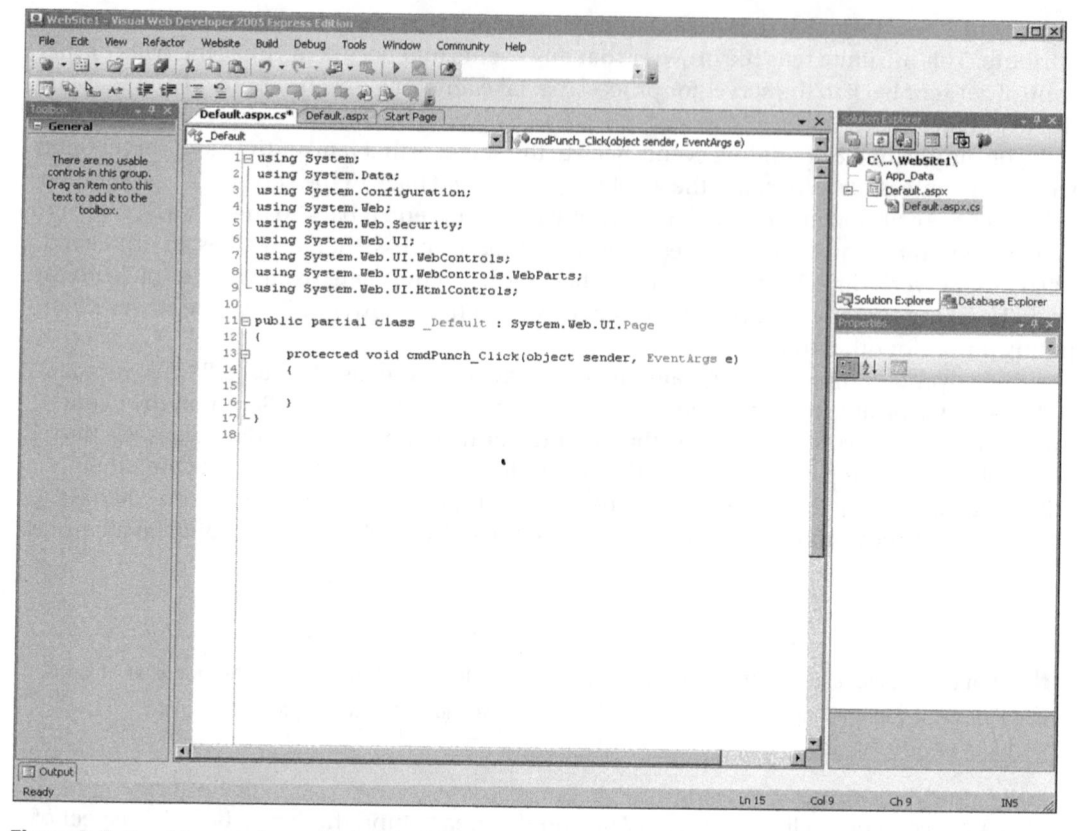

Figure 5-9. *Looking at the code-behind file*

Coding the Event Handler

Now you can add some code to the event handler. Back in Chapter 4, you built a form that had a Punch button on it. One of the tasks of this button event handler was to have the button text change from "Punch In" to "Punch Out" as you click the button. Let's add this part of the code from the Chapter 4 Punch project into this event handler. This is shown in Listing 5-3.

Listing 5-3. *Event handler code*

```
using System;
using System.Data;
using System.Configuration;
using System.Web;
using System.Web.Security;
using System.Web.UI;
using System.Web.UI.WebControls;
using System.Web.UI.WebControls.WebParts;
using System.Web.UI.HtmlControls;
```

```
public partial class _Default : System.Web.UI.Page
{
    private static bool P_IN = false;
    private static bool P_OUT = true;
    private bool mPunchState = P_IN;

    protected void cmdPunch_Click(object sender, EventArgs e)
    {
        if (mPunchState == P_OUT)
        {
            mPunchState = P_IN;
            cmdPunch.Text = "Punch In";
        }
        else
        {
            mPunchState = P_OUT;
            cmdPunch.Text = "Punch Out";
        }
    }
}
```

The IDE added all the DLL references at the top of the page. The additional code is shown in bold in Listing 5-3.

First, I added the class member variables to the class itself. I then added the conditional statements within the event handler. The code that I added is taken verbatim from the Punch project in Chapter 4. I did not add or change anything. I did remove some code from within the event handler, but this was for business logic that you do not need yet.

Now debug the code by pressing F5. The first thing you should see is a message box saying that the Web.config file will be changed to allow debugging. This is shown in Figure 5-10.

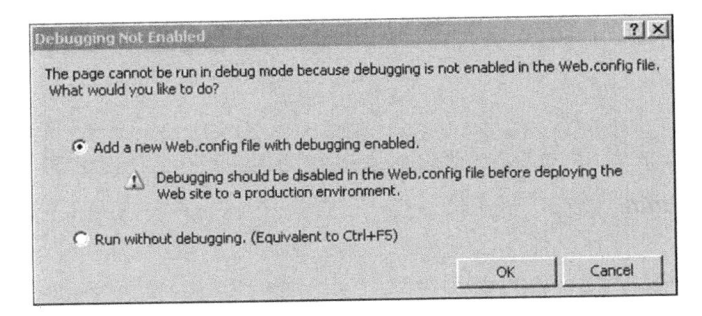

Figure 5-10. *Allowing debugging*

Click OK and the debugging session will begin. The web browser should appear with your single button on the screen. Click the button once, and the text will change from "Punch In" to "Punch Out." Click it again, and according to the code, it should change back.

Nothing happens, right? No matter how many times you click the button, it still says "Punch Out." What is happening here? The code is the same as the C# example, but it does not work in the web page. Let us debug.

A State of Mind

No need to close the web page yet. Go to the IDE and make sure you are looking at the event handler code. Enable a breakpoint by clicking the vertical gray bar to the left of the code. This is sometimes called the gutter. You can see this in Figure 5-11.

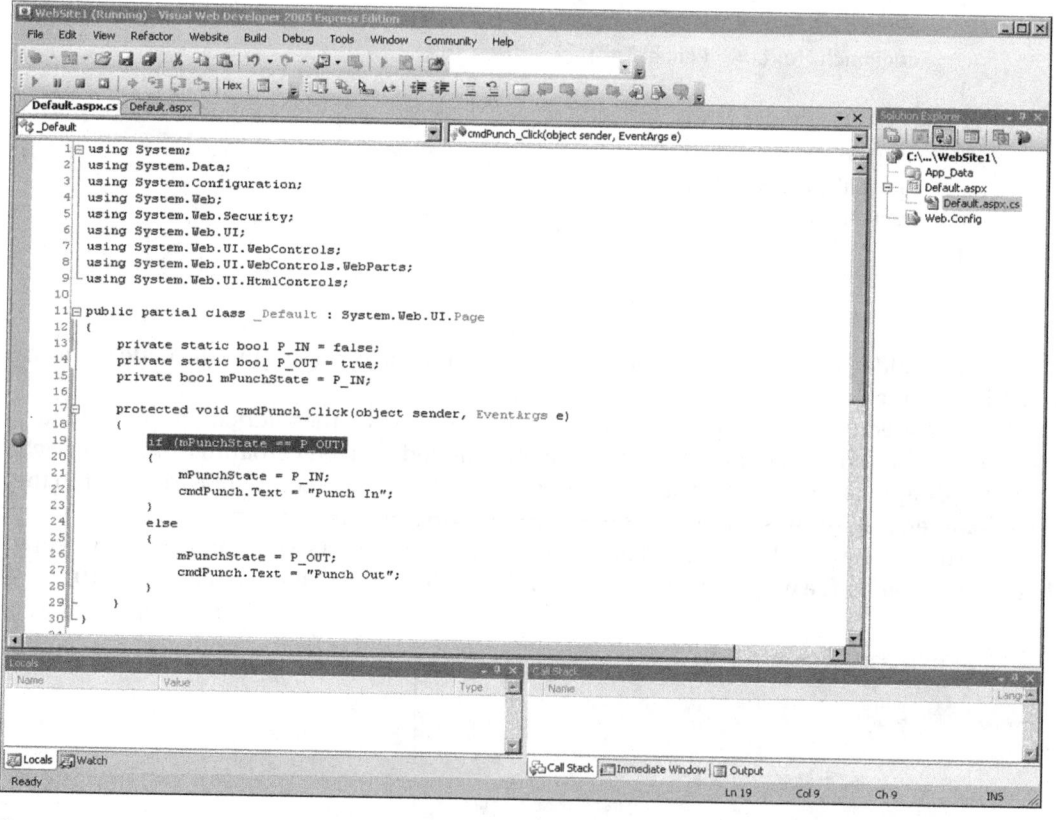

Figure 5-11. *Debugging the C# code-behind*

Now go back to the web page and click the button again. When you do this, the IDE will stop at the breakpoint. Rest your mouse over the mPunchState variable. You will see that its value is false because the value of P_IN is false. Press the F10 key a few times to make sure that you skip over the if block and go into the else block. After you get past the mPunchState = Punch Out statement, rest your mouse cursor over the mPunchState variable again. You will see that it is now equal to true, which is the value of the P_OUT variable.

Press F5 to let the program continue.

Tip Debugging is a powerful feature of .NET. The IDE will let you trace your program line by line and see exactly what is going on. The debugging shown here is the simplest kind, yet is used most often. As you will see in later chapters, the .NET debugger will save you hours of work and frustration.

Now that you've seen the mPunchState variable get changed from false to true, the next time you go into this code, you would expect the if part of the branch to execute and the mPunchState variable to be changed to false. Try it by clicking the button on the web page again.

Let me guess—you got exactly same result as last time. The mPunchState variable was set to false. You can click the button as many times as you like and it will never change. Why?

The reason is one I mentioned before. State is not saved in the world of the Web. Once a page has been sent on its way from the server, all is forgotten. In this case, the object that was created out of the _Default class disappeared. When the button was clicked again, a new object was created out of the _Default class, and the variable mPunchState was reset to P_IN.

There are several ways to fix this particular problem. I will give you the easiest one.

Tip Unfortunately, the easiest route to retain state in a web form is not always the best. In this case, making the mPunchState variable static works, but it has the side effect of being seen and changed by all clients accessing the site. I will show you later how to fix this.

Stop the code from running and add the word static to the mPunchState variable. The code for this class is shown in Listing 5-4. The changed line of code is in bold.

Listing 5-4. *Changing mPunchState to static*

```
public partial class _Default : System.Web.UI.Page
{
    private static bool P_IN = false;
    private static bool P_OUT = true;
    private static bool mPunchState = P_IN;

    protected void cmdPunch_Click(object sender, EventArgs e)
    {
        if (mPunchState == P_OUT)
        {
            mPunchState = P_IN;
            cmdPunch.Text = "Punch In";
        }
        else
        {
            mPunchState = P_OUT;
            cmdPunch.Text = "Punch Out";
        }
    }
}
```

What does this do? A static variable is one that holds its value independently of instances. Now when the mPunchState variable is changed, the change will stick. Try it out. Run the web page again and click the button multiple times. The text will change as expected.

This is the easiest way to keep a variable alive between the time when you send the page to the browser and when the browser does a postback to the server. I will say here that this is not the best way to maintain a value. Unfortunately, the variable maintains its value across browser instances as well. You will change this later.

Managing Session State

A session is created between the client (browser) and the server (web server) when you browse to a site. I said before that a session ID is created and handed to the browser—this session ID is swapped back and forth between the browser and the server whenever the client performs a postback and the server rerenders the page. It is this session ID that tells the server "Hey, it's me again." In ASP.NET, all this is done for you and in the background. This session state is used not only to allow the server to remember values, but also to allow the controls on your page to keep their values between postbacks.

I just showed you one way to get the server to remember values during the session. There are some other ways to get the controls to remember their values during a round trip to the server, as well.

There are two types of state in reference to the HTML page. One is *control state* and the other is *view state*. Control state is a list of properties for controls that must be persisted during round trips. This cannot be easily turned off. The other kind of state management for HTML pages—view state—can be turned on and off as a property for each individual control. This is shown in Figure 5-12.

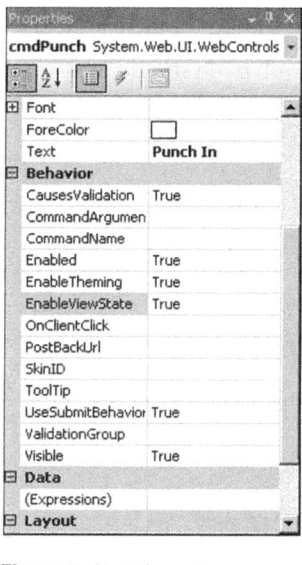

Figure 5-12. *View state property in the Properties pane*

So, why turn off view state at all? Seems like a good thing to keep the values of a control during round trips to the server.

Here is some technical information about view state that is handy to keep in your mind somewhere for the future. View state is sent back and forth as a string. If you have quite a few controls on a page, and these controls have a large amount of information in them, then this string can become the size of a small book. Sending huge amounts of data back and forth can slow a page down dramatically. So the moral of this story is that if you have a dense page, you should determine which controls on your page really need to keep view state. For the projects in this book, keeping view state on for everything is fine.

Before I leave this section, I want to say one more thing about the server controls and events that are sent back to the server.

If an event is sent back to the server, this also means that the page is posted. Posting the page to the server means that view state is saved and sent back and forth during the round trip. As I said already, sending tons of information in view state can be a drag on performance. ASP.NET allows you to catch and handle the event on the page itself. While this is beyond the scope of this book, I would suggest that you learn how to do this. You can easily take care of many simple events that need no help from the server if you catch and handle them in the browser.

Adding More Controls

You should now be a little familiar with ASP.NET and creating a web page. What you have done so far only scratches the surface, though. While you are completing this web page, if there is anything else you need to know, I will stop for a second and explain it to you.

So, you should have a big empty page with only one button on it. This button has some functionality in that the text of the button changes every time you click it. Now it is time to add some more controls and wire them up. The prototype for this page will be the Punch project you did in Chapter 4. Figure 5-13 shows the form detailing how this web page should look.

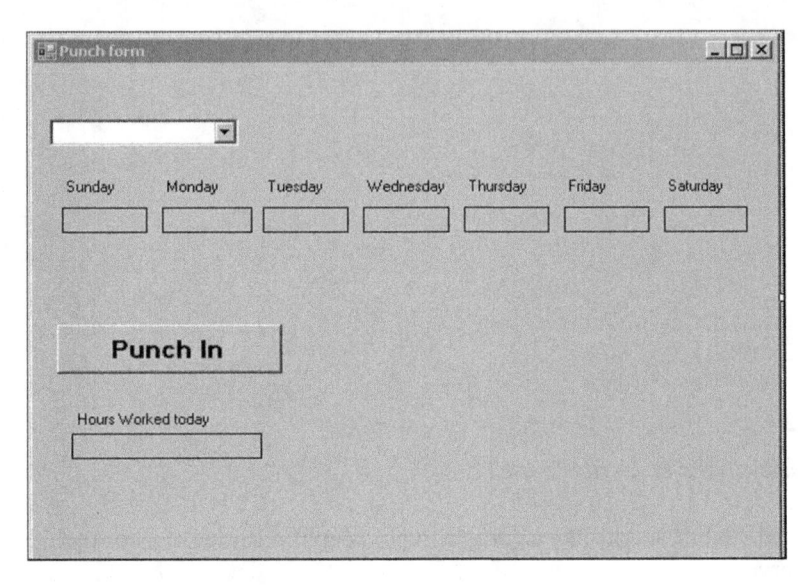

Figure 5-13. *Prototype for the final Punch form*

You will need to add the following server controls to the web page:

- A DropDownList control

- 16 Label controls

- A Button control

Start by adding the DropDownList from the toolbox to the page. Place the control as shown in Figure 5-13. Change the ID of this control to cmbWeek. Next, add a Label control to the page. Using the Properties pane, change this label's width to 80 pixels. Also change the text to read "Sunday."

Now that you have a single label on the page and have changed the width property, you can copy this label six more times and move the copies to where the labels for Sunday through Saturday should be. The copy and paste commands in this IDE are the same as they are in Word. You select the control, press Ctrl+C, click somewhere in the empty page, and press Ctrl+V. You will then see the new control with the width you want. There is no need to name these labels, as they will not be programmatically accessed. You do, however, need to change the text to read each day of the week from left to right (Sunday through Saturday), as shown in Figure 5-13.

Add another label to the page and make the following changes to the properties:

- Change the ID to `txtSun`.

- Change the width to 70 pixels.

- Change the `BorderStyle` to `Inset`.

- Change the `BackColor` to a light gray (#E0E0E0).

Put this new gray label below the label that says "Sunday." You will need one of these for each day of the week.

Tip If you delete the text in a label, the text shows on the screen in design mode as the name of the label. When you copy the label many times on the page, as is done here, you can see the label's ID just by looking at the text shown on the screen.

So, copy this new gray label and paste it back into the form six more times. You will need to rename the IDs of the other six gray labels (`txtMon`, `txtTue`, `txtWed`, `txtThu`, `txtFri`, and `txtSat`, respectively), and place them under their appropriate days of the week.

Create another label and change the text to read "Hours Worked Today." Place this label according to Figure 5-13.

Copy one of the gray labels and place it under this "Hours Worked Today" label. Stretch this new gray label to the same width as the name, which should be about 128 pixels. Change the ID of this label to be `txtHoursToday`.

The New Web Screen

You now have a new screen for the Web that looks like the screen you created for the C# Windows form. Yours should look like the one shown in Figure 5-14.

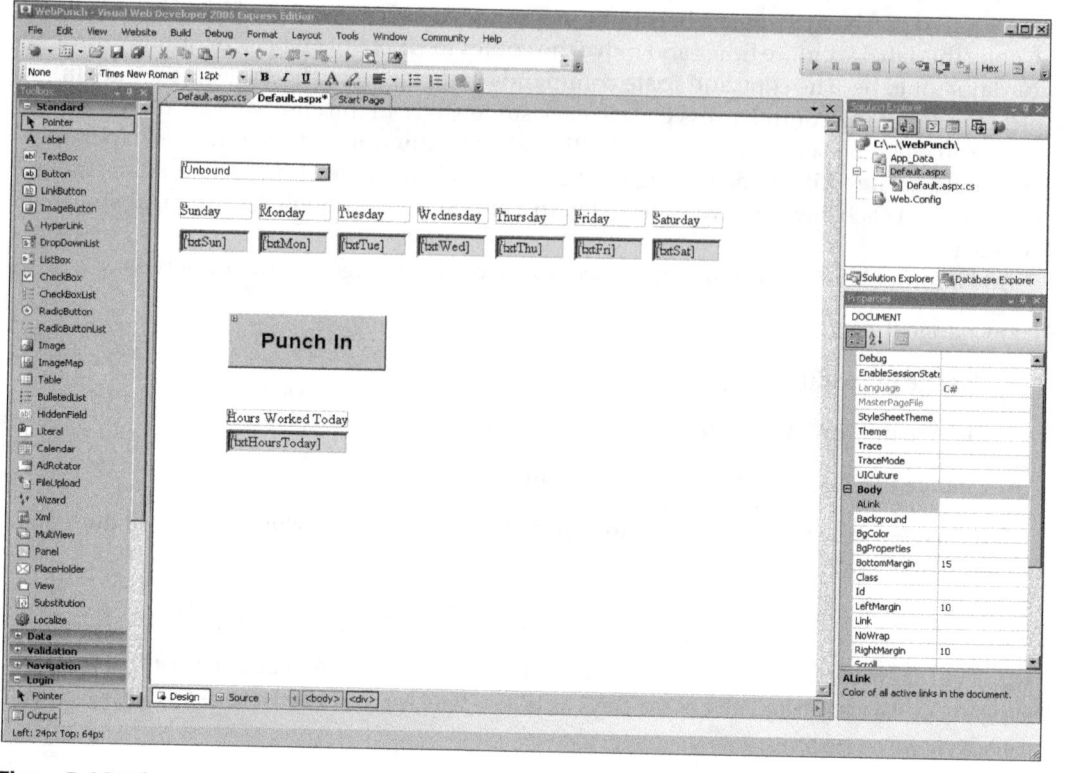

Figure 5-14. *The new WebPunch screen*

Go ahead and press F5 to start the website running. Remember back in Chapter 1 I told you that there are differences between browsers, even though they are supposed to render the HTML code the same? Well, here is one of those differences. Figure 5-15 shows you what you should get when looking at the page with Mozilla Firefox.

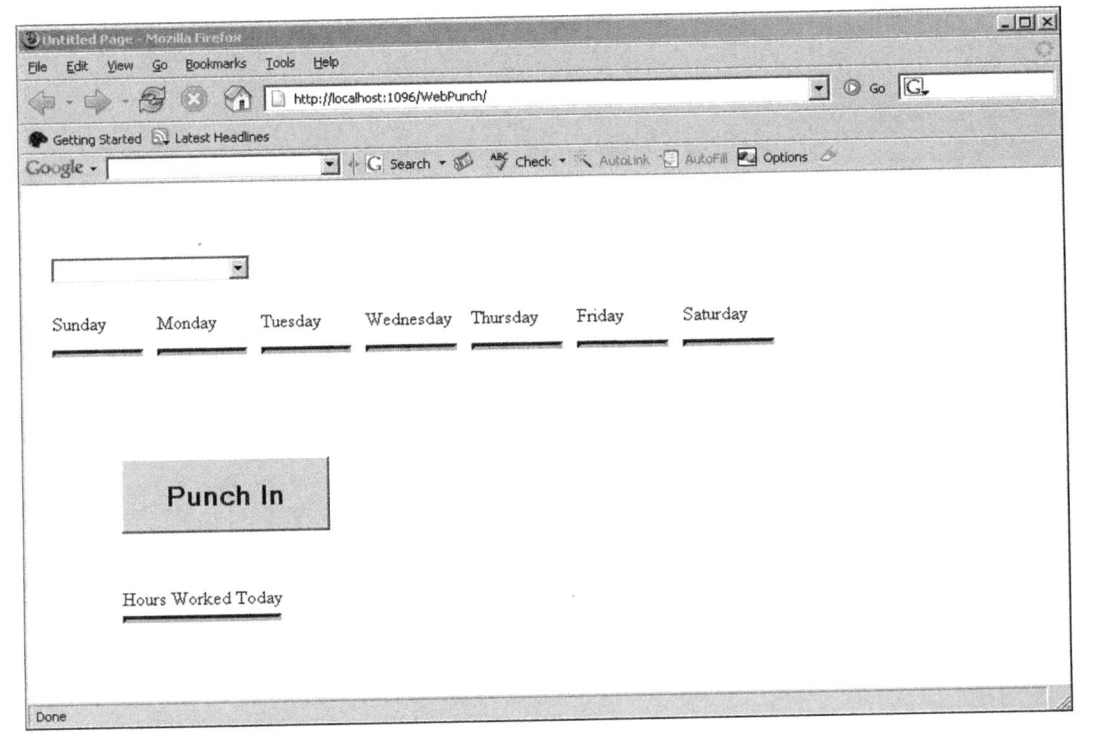

Figure 5-15. *Firefox showing your new page*

Notice that the labels with no text in them are only slivers of their former selves. Figure 5-16 shows what they look like in Internet Explorer.

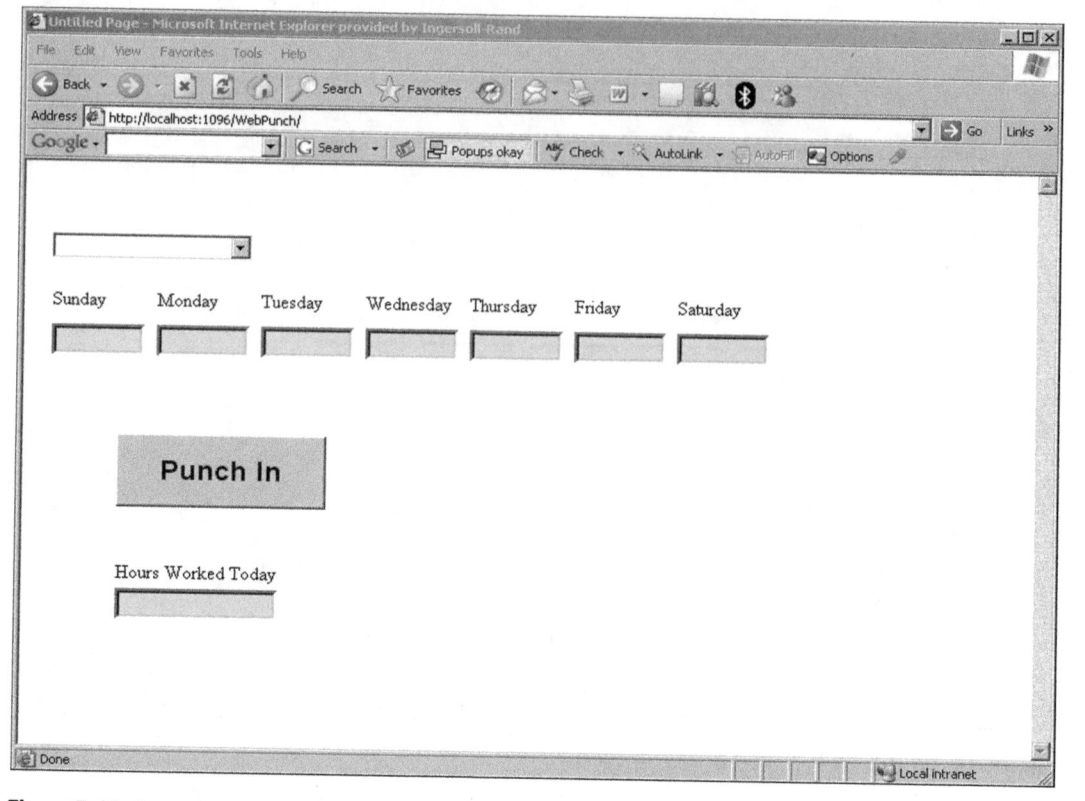

Figure 5-16. *Internet Explorer showing your new page*

Internet Explorer shows it better, don't you think? Here is where you say "Well, everyone uses Internet Explorer, so this is fine." Sorry, that attitude won't do here. You need to test and verify workability with Internet Explorer and at least Firefox. So fix it. After looking at Figure 5-15, what do you think is wrong?

The problem lies in the fact that you gave the control a fixed width, but left the height blank. These controls assume the width and height of their contents if you leave the width and height blank. With no text in it, a label control is nothing high by nothing wide.

For all the gray label controls, make the height 15 pixels. Now run the page again and test in Firefox. You should get what is shown in Figure 5-17.

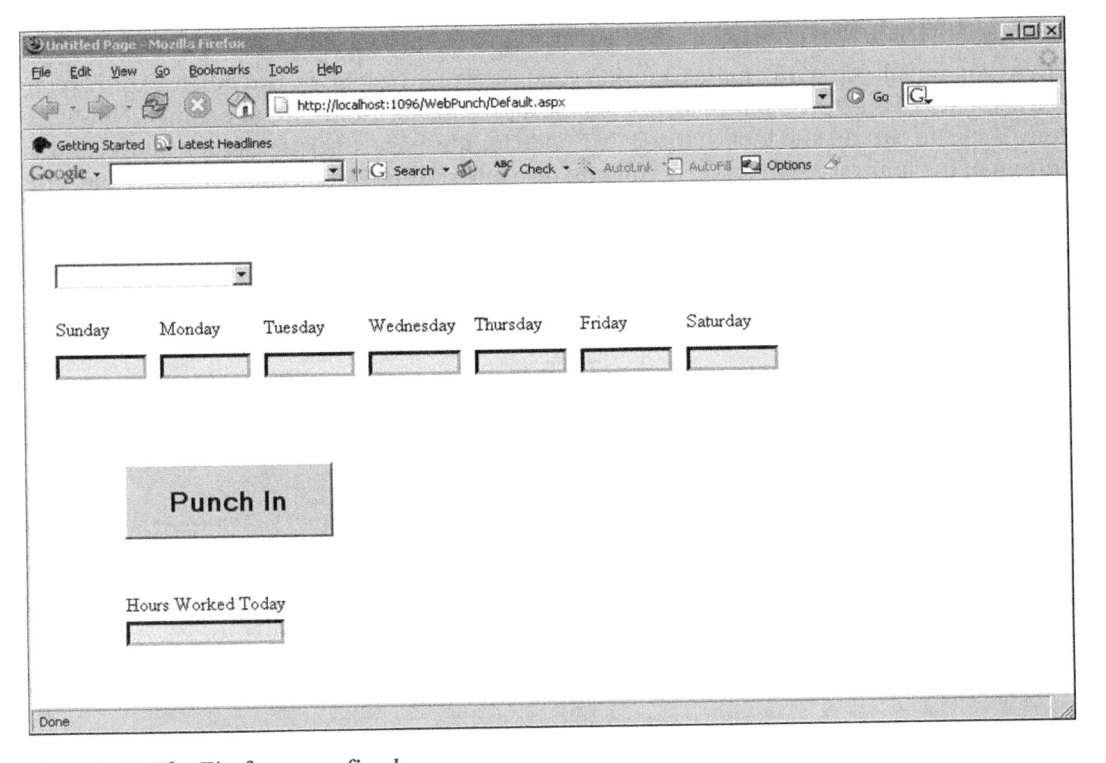

Figure 5-17. *The Firefox page, fixed*

OK, I suppose you want to know how to test the page in different browsers. Normally, the browser that comes up when debugging web pages is the default browser. The default browser is usually the last one you installed, since they all want to be the default. This does not really matter to you, as it is very easy to test in whatever browsers you have on your machine. Just copy the URL from whatever browser comes up and paste it into the other browser you want to test with. The URL is the address line. In the case of my browser, the URL is `http://localhost:1096/WebPunch/Default.aspx`.

I suggest that you have at least Firefox (or Netscape) and IE loaded on your machine. You do not want any surprises.

The HTML Code Page

OK, so you put all this stuff on the page and you tested out the look on two different browsers. You also clicked the Punch button a few times just to make sure it worked as planned. Now let's draw back the curtain and look at the HTML code for this page. Click the Source button at the bottom of the main screen. This gets you into the source code. I won't show you the code, but you can see what the screen looks like in Figure 5-18.

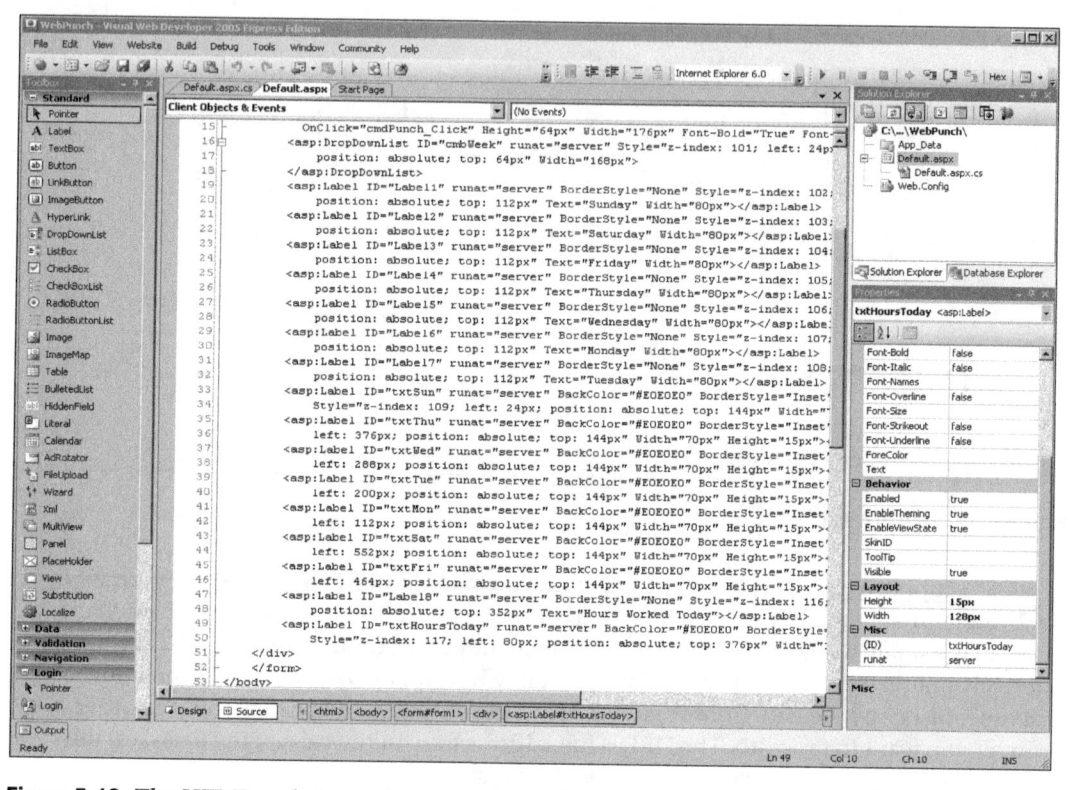

Figure 5-18. *The HTML code to render controls on the page*

If you scroll down and to the right to see all the code, you will probably be aghast at what is there. It seems like such a lot of HTML code. Can you imagine mixing all the C# code inside all this HTML code? What a mess that would be. Lucky for you, the event handling code is all put in the code-behind page `Default.aspx.cs`.

Before you go on, you should take notice of a few things in this HTML code. Listing 5-5 shows one line of HTML code that renders the `txtHoursWorkedToday` label.

Listing 5-5. *Control code*

```
<asp:Label ID="txtHoursToday" runat="server" BackColor="#E0E0E0"
BorderStyle="Inset" Style="z-index: 117; left: 80px;
position: absolute; top: 376px" Width="128px" Height="15px"></asp:Label>
```

The piece of code that says <asp:Label... tells you that this control is an ASP.NET server control. All the ASP.NET server controls have property pages, which you have been filling out. Remember you changed the ID, color, and width, and so on. ASP.NET abstracts the possible attributes of an HTML element to a property page to make it easier and more familiar for you to program. If you look at the Properties page on the lower-right of Figure 5-18, you will see that there is an ID property that matches the attribute in Listing 5-5: ID="txtHoursToday". The width and height properties are contaied in the style attribute of Listing 5-5: Style="z-index: 117; left: 80px; position: absolute; top: 376px" Width="128px" Height="15px". Notice that in this style attribute, the positioning is absolute. You did that as a default for the whole page at the beginning of this chapter. You are able to change positioning on a per-control basis if you want.

Completing the Code-Behind

Now that you have a workable page, you need to add the code that allows a person to punch in and out, and see his hours for the week. You did this in the last chapter, and the code should be virtually the same here.

So, how do you do this? The best way is to take the code from the Punch project in Chapter 4 and put it into the Default.aspx.cs file. There will be a few slight changes to begin with, to handle the differences between a Windows form and a web form. Start by double-clicking the form itself. This takes you to the Page_Load event handler for the form. This event handler will be in the Default.aspx.cs file.

The first thing to add to this C# file is a reference to the .NET collections namespace. This is done by adding the following two lines of code to the top of the page:

```
using System.Collections;
using System.Collections.Generic;
```

The Punch project in Chapter 4 had an Init() function that was called from the constructor when the program began. This Page_Load event handler does the same thing in this case. So add the contents of the Init() function to this Page_Load function. This is shown in the following code:

```
protected void Page_Load(object sender, EventArgs e)
{
  FillData();
```

```
    //cmdPunch and cmbWeek have the attributes "runat=server"  Because of this
    //we can access these controls here and fill in the data.
    cmdPunch.Text = "Punch In";
    cmbWeek.Items.Clear();
    cmbWeek.Items.Add("Last Week");
    cmbWeek.Items.Add("This Week");
    cmbWeek.SelectedIndex = 0;
}
```

If you remember, this function gets called when the program starts. Its job is to fill in the fake data for last week and this week's punches. It also sets some attributes in the controls and selects the last week as the first week to see in the form. All well and good.

Next, you should add the member variables to the _Default class above the Punch_Load function. Listing 5-6 shows the code you need, starting from the definition of the class to the definition of the Page_Load event.

Listing 5-6. *Adding the member variables*

```
public partial class _Default : System.Web.UI.Page
{
  #region Private variables

  private const bool P_IN = false;
  private const bool P_OUT = true;
  private static bool mPunchState = P_IN;

  private DateTime mStartPunch;
  private DateTime mEndPunch;

  private ArrayList MyPunches = new ArrayList();

  private class WeekPunches
  {
    #region Class local variables

    private DateTime mMondayStart;
    private DateTime mMondayEnd;
    private DateTime mTuesdayStart;
    private DateTime mTuesdayEnd;
    private DateTime mWednesdayStart;
    private DateTime mWednesdayEnd;
    private DateTime mThursdayStart;
    private DateTime mThursdayEnd;
    private DateTime mFridayStart;
    private DateTime mFridayEnd;
    private DateTime mSaturdayStart;
    private DateTime mSaturdayEnd;
```

```csharp
private DateTime mSundayStart;
private DateTime mSundayEnd;

#endregion

#region Accessor Get / Set Methods

public DateTime MondayStart
{
  get { return mMondayStart; }
  set { mMondayStart = value; }
}
public DateTime MondayEnd
{
  get { return mMondayEnd; }
  set { mMondayEnd = value; }
}
public double MondayHours
{
  get { return CalculateHours(mMondayStart, mMondayEnd); }
}

public DateTime TuesdayStart
{
  get { return mTuesdayStart; }
  set { mTuesdayStart = value; }
}
public DateTime TuesdayEnd
{
  get { return mTuesdayEnd; }
  set { mTuesdayEnd = value; }
}
public double TuesdayHours
{
  get { return CalculateHours(mTuesdayStart, mTuesdayEnd); }
}

public DateTime WednesdayStart
{
  get { return mWednesdayStart; }
  set { mWednesdayStart = value; }
}
public DateTime WednesdayEnd
{
  get { return mWednesdayEnd; }
  set { mWednesdayEnd = value; }
}
```

```csharp
public double WednesdayHours
{
  get { return CalculateHours(mWednesdayStart, mWednesdayEnd); }
}

public DateTime ThursdayStart
{
  get { return mThursdayStart; }
  set { mThursdayStart = value; }
}
public DateTime ThursdayEnd
{
  get { return mThursdayEnd; }
  set { mThursdayEnd = value; }
}
public double ThursdayHours
{
  get { return CalculateHours(mThursdayStart, mThursdayEnd); }
}

public DateTime FridayStart
{
  get { return mFridayStart; }
  set { mFridayStart = value; }
}
public DateTime FridayEnd
{
  get { return mFridayEnd; }
  set { mFridayEnd = value; }
}
public double FridayHours
{
  get { return CalculateHours(mFridayStart, mFridayEnd); }
}

public DateTime SaturdayStart
{
  get { return mSaturdayStart; }
  set { mSaturdayStart = value; }
}
public DateTime SaturdayEnd
{
  get { return mSaturdayEnd; }
  set { mSaturdayEnd = value; }
}
```

```csharp
public double SaturdayHours
{
  get { return CalculateHours(mSaturdayStart, mSaturdayEnd); }
}

public DateTime SundayStart
{
  get { return mSundayStart; }
  set { mSundayStart = value; }
}
public DateTime SundayEnd
{
  get { return mSundayEnd; }
  set { mSundayEnd = value; }
}
public double SundayHours
{
  get { return CalculateHours(mSundayStart, mSundayEnd); }
}

#endregion

//This is where you would incorporate some rules such as
//lunch breaks
private double CalculateHours(DateTime Start, DateTime End)
{

  //Check to see if end comes after start
  if (DateTime.Compare(Start, End) < 0)
  {
    TimeSpan diff = End.Subtract(Start);
    return (diff.TotalHours);
  }
  return 0.0;
}

}

#endregion
```

The variables mStartPunch and mEndPunch, and the class WeekPunches, are identical to what you pulled out of Chapter 4. No changes here.

Now to add some more functions to the class—here are the functions you will add verbatim from the Chapter 4 Punch project:

- DisplayWeek()

- FillData()

- CalculateHours()

The code is shown in Listing 5-7.

Listing 5-7. *The business logic code*

```
private void DisplayWeek(int wk)
{
  txtSun.Text = "";
  txtMon.Text = "";
  txtTue.Text = "";
  txtWed.Text = "";
  txtThu.Text = "";
  txtFri.Text = "";
  txtSat.Text = "";

  WeekPunches Week = (WeekPunches)MyPunches[wk];
  txtSun.Text = Week.SundayHours.ToString("F2");
  txtMon.Text = Week.MondayHours.ToString("F2");
  txtTue.Text = Week.TuesdayHours.ToString("F2");
  txtWed.Text = Week.WednesdayHours.ToString("F2");
  txtThu.Text = Week.ThursdayHours.ToString("F2");
  txtFri.Text = Week.FridayHours.ToString("F2");
  txtSat.Text = Week.SundayHours.ToString("F2");
}

private void FillData()
{
  //This takes the place of getting data from a database.
  //We will hard code last week's data and some of this week's.

  //Create last week
  DateTime LastSunday = DateTime.Now;
  int Days2Subtract = 7 + (int)DateTime.Now.DayOfWeek;
  LastSunday = LastSunday.Subtract(new TimeSpan(
                              Days2Subtract,
                              LastSunday.Hour,
                              LastSunday.Minute,
                              LastSunday.Second,
                              LastSunday.Millisecond));
```

```
WeekPunches LastWeek = new WeekPunches();
LastWeek.SundayStart = LastSunday;
LastWeek.SundayEnd = LastSunday;
LastWeek.MondayStart = LastSunday.Add(new TimeSpan(1, 8, 0, 0, 0));
LastWeek.MondayEnd = LastSunday.Add(new TimeSpan(1, 15, 0, 0, 0));
LastWeek.TuesdayStart = LastSunday.Add(new TimeSpan(2, 8, 0, 0, 0));
LastWeek.TuesdayEnd = LastSunday.Add(new TimeSpan(2, 14, 0, 0, 0));
LastWeek.WednesdayStart = LastSunday.Add(new TimeSpan(3, 8, 0, 0, 0));
LastWeek.WednesdayEnd = LastSunday.Add(new TimeSpan(3, 13, 0, 0, 0));
LastWeek.ThursdayStart = LastSunday.Add(new TimeSpan(4, 8, 0, 0, 0));
LastWeek.ThursdayEnd = LastSunday.Add(new TimeSpan(4, 14, 20, 0, 0));
LastWeek.FridayStart = LastSunday.Add(new TimeSpan(5, 8, 0, 0, 0));
LastWeek.FridayEnd = LastSunday.Add(new TimeSpan(5, 15, 30, 0, 0));
LastWeek.SaturdayStart = LastSunday.Add(new TimeSpan(6, 0, 0, 0, 0));
LastWeek.SaturdayEnd = LastSunday.Add(new TimeSpan(6, 0, 0, 0, 0));

MyPunches.Add(LastWeek);

//Create this week
DateTime ThisSunday = DateTime.Now;
Days2Subtract = (int)DateTime.Now.DayOfWeek;
ThisSunday = ThisSunday.Subtract(new TimeSpan(
                          Days2Subtract,
                          ThisSunday.Hour,
                          ThisSunday.Minute,
                          ThisSunday.Second,
                          ThisSunday.Millisecond));
WeekPunches ThisWeek = new WeekPunches();
if (DateTime.Now.DayOfWeek > DayOfWeek.Sunday)
{
  ThisWeek.SundayStart = ThisSunday;
  ThisWeek.SundayEnd = ThisSunday;
}
if (DateTime.Now.DayOfWeek > DayOfWeek.Monday)
{
  ThisWeek.MondayStart = ThisSunday.Add(new TimeSpan(1, 7, 30, 0, 0));
  ThisWeek.MondayEnd = ThisSunday.Add(new TimeSpan(1, 16, 40, 0, 0));
}
if (DateTime.Now.DayOfWeek > DayOfWeek.Tuesday)
{
  ThisWeek.TuesdayStart = ThisSunday.Add(new TimeSpan(2, 8, 20, 0, 0));
  ThisWeek.TuesdayEnd = ThisSunday.Add(new TimeSpan(2, 14, 50, 0, 0));
}
if (DateTime.Now.DayOfWeek > DayOfWeek.Wednesday)
```

```
    {
      ThisWeek.WednesdayStart = ThisSunday.Add(new TimeSpan(3, 0, 0, 0, 0));
      ThisWeek.WednesdayEnd = ThisSunday.Add(new TimeSpan(3, 0, 0, 0, 0));
    }
    if (DateTime.Now.DayOfWeek > DayOfWeek.Thursday)
    {
      ThisWeek.ThursdayStart = ThisSunday.Add(new TimeSpan(4, 0, 0, 0, 0));
      ThisWeek.ThursdayEnd = ThisSunday.Add(new TimeSpan(4, 0, 0, 0, 0));
    }
    if (DateTime.Now.DayOfWeek > DayOfWeek.Friday)
    {
      ThisWeek.FridayStart = ThisSunday.Add(new TimeSpan(5, 0, 0, 0, 0));
      ThisWeek.FridayEnd = ThisSunday.Add(new TimeSpan(5, 0, 0, 0, 0));
    }
    MyPunches.Add(ThisWeek);


  }
  private double CalculateHours(DateTime Start, DateTime End)
  {

    //Check to see if end comes after start
    if (DateTime.Compare(Start, End) < 0)
    {
      TimeSpan diff = End.Subtract(Start);
      return (diff.TotalHours);
    }
    return 0.0;
  }
```

Once again, there are no surprises here. This code is identical to what you had in Chapter 4.

There are two more things you need to do. You need to create an event handler for the drop-down combo box, and you need to add some more code to the cmdPunch button's click event handler. Go to the design view of the Default.aspx page and double-click the combo box. You should be taken back to the Default.aspx.cs page, and you should now have an event handler for the combo box. Add a single line of code to display the week program, as shown in the following snippet:

```
protected void cmbWeek_SelectedIndexChanged(object sender, EventArgs e)
{
  DisplayWeek(cmbWeek.SelectedIndex);
}
```

Then change the code in the cmdPunch event handler to reflect what you see in Listing 5-8.

Listing 5-8. *The button click event handler*

```
protected void cmdPunch_Click(object sender, EventArgs e)
{

  if (mPunchState == P_OUT)
  {
    mPunchState = P_IN;
    cmdPunch.Text = "Punch In";
    mEndPunch = DateTime.Today;

    mEndPunch = mEndPunch.Add(new TimeSpan(2, 5, 0));

    txtHoursToday.Text = CalculateHours(mStartPunch, mEndPunch).ToString("F2");

    WeekPunches Week = (WeekPunches)MyPunches[1];
    switch (DateTime.Now.DayOfWeek)
    {
      case DayOfWeek.Sunday:
        Week.SundayStart = mStartPunch;
        Week.SundayEnd = mEndPunch;
        break;
      case DayOfWeek.Monday:
        Week.MondayStart = mStartPunch;
        Week.MondayEnd = mEndPunch;
        break;
      case DayOfWeek.Tuesday:
        Week.TuesdayStart = mStartPunch;
        Week.TuesdayEnd = mEndPunch;
        break;
      case DayOfWeek.Wednesday:
        Week.WednesdayStart = mStartPunch;
        Week.WednesdayEnd = mEndPunch;
        break;
      case DayOfWeek.Thursday:
        Week.ThursdayStart = mStartPunch;
        Week.ThursdayEnd = mEndPunch;
        break;
      case DayOfWeek.Friday:
        Week.FridayStart = mStartPunch;
        Week.FridayEnd = mEndPunch;
        break;
      case DayOfWeek.Saturday:
        Week.SaturdayStart = mStartPunch;
        Week.SaturdayEnd = mEndPunch;
        break;
    }
```

```
      DisplayWeek(cmbWeek.SelectedIndex);
    }
    else
    {
      mPunchState = P_OUT;
      cmdPunch.Text = "Punch Out";
      mStartPunch = DateTime.Today;
    }
  }
}
```

As you saw from Chapter 4, this code handles the logic of where to put the in and out punches for the current day. Now compile the program and run it.

Here are some problems you will see right away:

- The punch times for the days of the week are not filled in for last week.

- Changing the drop-down from last week to this week does nothing.

- Punching in makes the drop-down combo box change back to last week.

- Punching out gives you a weird number of hours.

You may have some other problems, but these are the ones I had, and I expect that you'll have them as well. What went wrong?

Changing State

Don't you think that, if you created this web page exactly like the Windows Forms page, it should work? There is nothing wrong with the logic, as it was tested in Chapter 4.

Personally, I think it should work—but I know it won't, and I know the reasons. It all boils down to state.

The Windows Forms Punch program from Chapter 4 was a monolithic program that was meant to be used by one person at a time. There is no disconnect between the GUI and the business logic. They are one and the same.

A web page is not the same as a Windows Forms program. As I said more than once: when a web page is sent on its way, the server forgets about it. When the page posts back, it is like a whole new start.

You saw how to get by one aspect of this by changing the mPunchState variable to be static. This held its state between round trips, and the button worked as designed.

How about making all the variables you need static? This would work, but would defeat the purpose of doing things in the web page. Static variables hold their values independently of instances of a class. This means that if you punch in using one browser and you have another browser connected, the Punch In button will have same state in both browsers.

What you want is to have each client look at and manipulate its own data. You want this page to be used by many people at the same time. This is what web pages are all about. How do you accomplish this? It is all done with session state.

Remember that I said session state has an ID that is passed back and forth between the browser and the server so that the server can remember you? Well, ASP.NET has a session state capability that is extremely easy to use. Here is the lowdown on session state:

- Session state can be stored in memory on the server, in a database on the server, or on a database on another server (for web farms).

- Session state is a set of key/value pairs that you can make up.

- Session state can store complicated .NET data types if needed.

- Session state has a number of attributes. You can use the timeout attribute to automatically log a person out of a web page.

- Session state in ASP.NET is incredibly easy to use.

Before I get into the code changes for session state, I want you to change the line of code that says this:

```
private ArrayList MyPunches = new ArrayList();
```

to be static like this:

```
private static ArrayList MyPunches = new ArrayList();
```

I know I just got through saying that you want each person to see his or her own data—but think of what this variable is. It is a fake list of punches for last week and this week. Everyone will see the same data anyway in this case.

Now on to the session state. First, remove the static attribute from the mPunchState variable. Next, wrap the contents of the Page_Load function in some session state code, as follows:

```
protected void Page_Load(object sender, EventArgs e)
{
  if (Session["WeekIndex"] == null || cmbWeek.Items.Count ==0 )
  {
    FillData();

    //cmdPunch and cmbWeek have the attributes "runat=server"  Because of this
    //we can access these controls here and fill in the data.
    cmdPunch.Text = "Punch In";
    cmbWeek.Items.Clear();
    cmbWeek.Items.Add("Last Week");
    cmbWeek.Items.Add("This Week");
    cmbWeek.SelectedIndex = 0;

    //Add this function call because in the Web changing the
    //selected index does not fire the selectedindexchanged event.
    DisplayWeek(cmbWeek.SelectedIndex);

  }
```

```
    Session["WeekIndex"] = Server.HtmlEncode(cmbWeek.SelectedIndex.ToString());
}
```

The bold lines are new. What you are doing here is detecting whether this is a new page request. If so, the session variable WeekIndex will be null. If this is the case, do the initialization. At the end of this function, you set the WeekIndex session variable to be the selected index of the drop-down combo box.

Note The default session timeout is 20 minutes. If you do nothing in the page for this timeout interval, then the session is no longer valid and this code will be run again the next time the page is rendered. Timeout can be changed in the Web.config file, but this timeout is fine for now.

Next, you will need to add some session handing to the cmdPunch click event handler. You need to keep track of the in and out punches for this session, and you also need to keep track of the mPunchState. The code is shown following.

```
protected void cmdPunch_Click(object sender, EventArgs e)
{
    //If the session variable is available then
    //refill the mPunchState with the saved value
    if (Session["mPunchState"] != null)
        mPunchState = (bool)Session["mPunchState"];

    //If the session variable is available then
    //refill the mPunchState with the saved value
    if (Session["mStartPunch"] != null)
        mStartPunch = (DateTime)Session["mStartPunch"];

    //If the session variable is available then
    //refill the mPunchState with the saved value
    if (Session["mEndPunch"] != null)
        mEndPunch = (DateTime)Session["mEndPunch"];

    if (mPunchState == P_OUT)
    {
        mPunchState = P_IN;
        cmdPunch.Text = "Punch In";
        mEndPunch = DateTime.Today;

        mEndPunch = mEndPunch.Add(new TimeSpan(2, 5, 0));

        txtHoursToday.Text = CalculateHours(mStartPunch, mEndPunch).ToString("F2");
```

```
WeekPunches Week = (WeekPunches)MyPunches[1];
switch (DateTime.Now.DayOfWeek)
{
  case DayOfWeek.Sunday:
    Week.SundayStart = mStartPunch;
    Week.SundayEnd = mEndPunch;
    break;
  case DayOfWeek.Monday:
    Week.MondayStart = mStartPunch;
    Week.MondayEnd = mEndPunch;
    break;
  case DayOfWeek.Tuesday:
    Week.TuesdayStart = mStartPunch;
    Week.TuesdayEnd = mEndPunch;
    break;
  case DayOfWeek.Wednesday:
    Week.WednesdayStart = mStartPunch;
    Week.WednesdayEnd = mEndPunch;
    break;
  case DayOfWeek.Thursday:
    Week.ThursdayStart = mStartPunch;
    Week.ThursdayEnd = mEndPunch;
    break;
  case DayOfWeek.Friday:
    Week.FridayStart = mStartPunch;
    Week.FridayEnd = mEndPunch;
    break;
  case DayOfWeek.Saturday:
    Week.SaturdayStart = mStartPunch;
    Week.SaturdayEnd = mEndPunch;
    break;
  }
  DisplayWeek(cmbWeek.SelectedIndex);
}
else
{
  mPunchState = P_OUT;
  cmdPunch.Text = "Punch Out";
  mStartPunch = DateTime.Today;
}
//Save the mPuchState variable for use next time through
Session["mPunchState"] = mPunchState;
Session["mStartPunch"] = mStartPunch;
Session["mEndPunch"] = mEndPunch;


}
```

Again, the new code is in bold. What you are doing is getting the saved punch variables from the session object, and when you are done with them, you are saving them back. Very simple.

There is one last thing to do. It involves how events are handled in a web page. Some events, such as button click events, are posted immediately to the server. Other events, such as the SelectedIndexChanged event, are cached in the page and sent to the server when a button is clicked. You do not want this. You want the drop-down box to show new data in the page as soon as you select a new choice. You can do this by setting the AutoPostBack property to true.

That's it. Save the code and run it. You page should start out looking like the one shown in Figure 5-19.

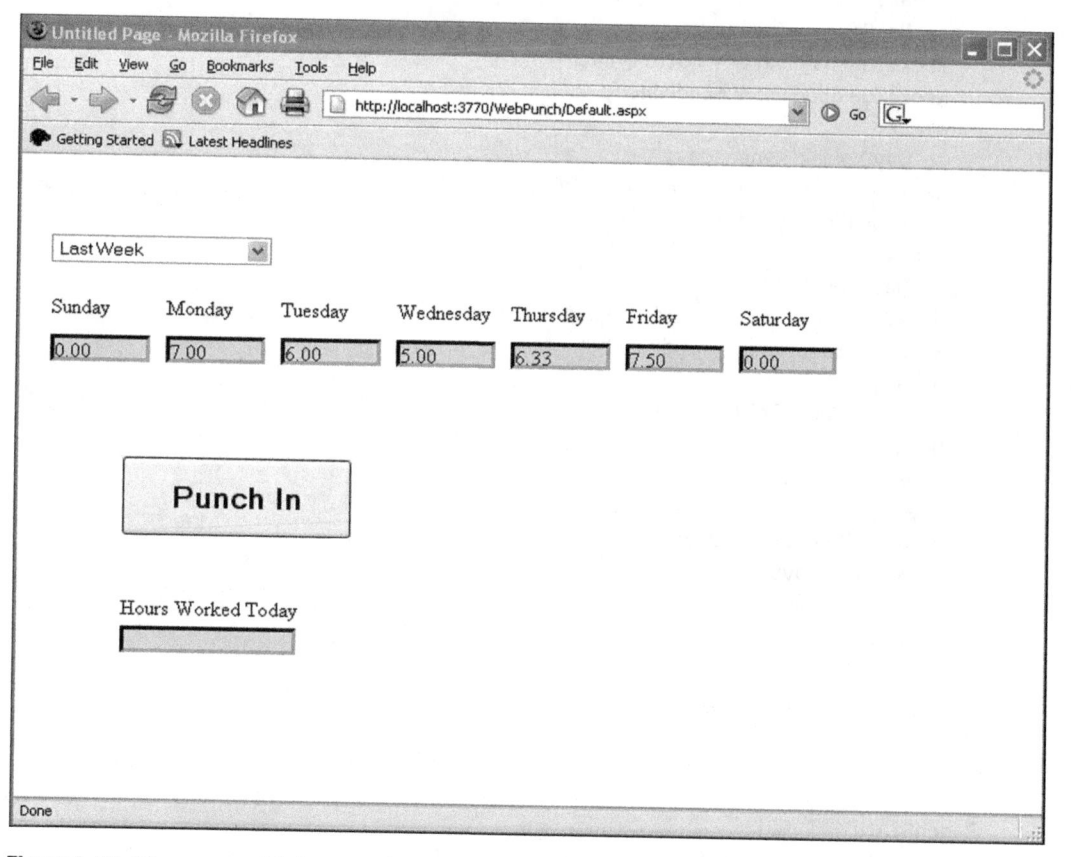

Figure 5-19. *The page with last week showing correctly*

In Figure 5-19, you can see that last week shows correctly. If you change to this week and punch in and out, the correct times will show in the correct places, as well.

BASIC SESSION STATE MANAGEMENT

Session state is an intrinsic object given to you by ASP.NET for every project you make. Session state can be used on a very simple scale, as you are using it here; or you can scale session state to manage thousands of users across dozens of servers in a web farm. It is up to you.

Session state comes with a default configuration. If you want to change any of the session state attributes, you will need to edit the Web.config file that comes with your project. Editing this file is neither hard nor arcane. If you double-click the Web.config file, you will see an XML file. The basic XML text is shown in the following code.

```xml
<?xml version="1.0"?>
<configuration>
  <appSettings/>
  <connectionStrings/>
  <system.web>
    <compilation debug="true"/>
    <authentication mode="Windows"/>
  </system.web>
</configuration>
```

I omitted all the comments from this XML text. Note that the Web.config file currently has debugging set to true.

In order to control session state, you will need to add a new set of tags to this file. Here is an example of the session state timeout being changed from the default of 20 minutes to 10 minutes.

```xml
<?xml version="1.0"?>
<configuration>
  <appSettings/>
  <connectionStrings/>
  <system.web>
    <compilation debug="true"/>
    <authentication mode="Windows"/>

    <sessionState timeout="10">
    </sessionState>

  </system.web>
</configuration>
```

The bold text shows the session state tags. There is plenty of IntelliSense help while you are typing this in. IntelliSense will show you all the attributes that you can change.

Continued

If there is no sessionState defined in the Web.config file, the system uses the default. The default session state object has the following properties:

```
<sessionState
      mode="InProc"
      stateConnectionString="tcpip=127.0.0.1:42424"
      stateNetworkTimeout="10"
      sqlConnectionString="data source=127.0.0.1;Integrated Security=SSPI"
      sqlCommandTimeout="30"
      customProvider=""
      cookieless="UseCookies"
      cookieName="ASP.NET_SessionId"
      timeout="20"
      allowCustomSqlDatabase="false"
      regenerateExpiredSessionId="true"
      partitionResolverType=""
      useHostingIdentity="true">
   <providers>
      <clear />
   </providers>
</sessionState>
```

Summary

This chapter has introduced you to ASP.NET programming. The project in this chapter taught you how to take the code from the Windows Forms program you wrote in Chapter 4 and transfer it here.

While all the code was transferred directly, you saw that it did not work unless some modifications were made. Generally, the modifications involved solving session management issues. Here is a list of what you learned in this chapter:

- Server controls can be thought of and manipulated in the VWD IDE in much the same way as similar controls in the C# IDE.

- ASP.NET separates the design code from the business logic code into separate files. This allows different people to work on different aspects of the same page with no conflicts.

- Each server control sends its events back to the server to be handled in C# code. This allows for stronger data typing and lets you use the full potential of the .NET Framework classes.

- Some minor events are cached in the browser until a major event, such as a button being clicked, happens. This can be overridden with the `AutoPostBack` property of the control.

- Session state is needed to remember values between round trips to and from the server and the browser.

The next chapter will take you back to DotNetNuke. This WebPunch project will eventually be turned into a DNN module for inclusion in your DNN project.

■■■

CHAPTER 6

DotNetNuke Basics

Chapter 5 introduced you to the ASP.NET VWD 2005 Express Edition. You learned about the VWD IDE and how to program in it. You also learned how web programming was different from programming thick clients, such as you did in Chapter 4.

By now, you know that HTML and the event handling code for web controls are separated into two different files. This makes the code much easier to understand and maintain. Most of what you've learned about VWD and programming the Web has come from converting the Chapter 4 Punch project into a WebPunch project. Now that you know how VWD works and have some understanding of web programming, it is time to get back to DotNetNuke.

Note Chapter 5 was important in many respects. Chiefly, it taught you the basics of website programming via ASP.NET. The WebPunch project was significant in that it brought to light many "gotchas" that you will need to remember going forward. While a lot of these "gotchas" are taken care of in DNN, some aren't. I suggest you review the WebPunch project until you understand fully how it works.

A DotNetNuke Review

Let's review a little bit of Chapter 3.

- You installed Visual C# 2005 Express

- You installed VWD 2005 Express

- You installed SQL Server 2005 Express

- You installed DotNetNuke

You found that either you could install IIS if you had the proper operating system, or you could use the personal web server that comes with VWD. The availability of the web server that comes with VWD allows you to do all your development in Windows XP Home Edition, which does not support IIS.

Once you installed DotNetNuke, you compiled the system and got a page similar to the one in Figure 6-1.

Figure 6-1. *The DotNetNuke start page*

What Now?

OK, you now have a page with a bunch of ads on the left and a bunch of ads on the right. The center pane is the one you are interested in right away. It tells you the first thing to do with this new website: change the password.

There are two types of superusers for the DNN system. One is a host and the other is an administrator. Here is the difference:

- DNN has portal capabilities built in. If you want to administer the whole DNN site, including all portals within the site, you need to log in as the host.

- The DNN start page is actually a portal. If you want to administer the settings of this portal, then you need to log in as the administrator.

Hosting many DNN portals for many people is not a simple task, and is beyond the scope of this book. After all, the purpose of this book is to teach you how to create web pages for your own purposes. However, in Chapter 9, I'll teach you how to segment your website functionality into an external website and an internal one, using the DNN portal capabilities.

The cover page of the DNN site you created is actually a website portal. You can either create a new one or edit this one. Since you don't really want to host other sites right now, let's edit this one.

How DotNetNuke Works

DNN is made up of several components. The short list follows:

The container: The container defines the look and feel of the website. You can change colors, fonts, and so on, and they will be carried through to the pages and modules within.

The page: You can have as many pages as you like. Each page is divided into sections called panes.

Panes: There are several areas of the page that are divided into panes. There are five basic panes. There is a top pane, which runs horizontally across the top. There are left, center, and right panes below the top pane. There is a bottom pane, which spans the bottom of the page horizontally.

The menu: You can choose the menu placement either along the top or along the side. You can also choose to have the menu be of fixed width or span the page.

Modules: A module is a self-contained set of code and design features that you put inside a pane. When a module is inside a pane, it takes on the properties of the container, including size, colors, and other look-and-feel aspects.

The WebPunch project you created in the last chapter will become a DNN module. While there are many modules given to you in DNN, and many more that you can buy, it is the ability to construct one of your own that gives you the power to create a truly unique website.

Let's look at the basic site that DNN gives you. Start by logging into the site using the administrator username and the administrator password. Figure 6-2 shows the login process.

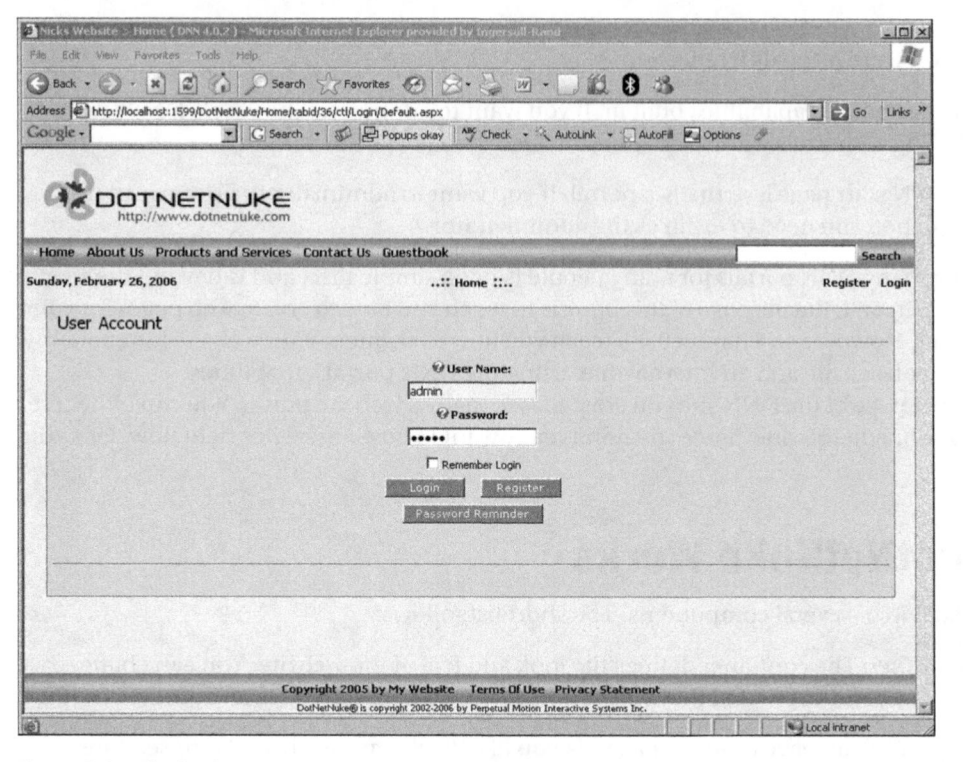

Figure 6-2. *The login page*

This login page is a part of the whole DNN experience. You can have people log in as admin, host, or as a normal user of the site. You can even register on the site. This login page is created by DNN and is included with every website you create.

Once you have logged in, you will see the site in design mode. Figure 6-3 shows the design mode for the basic site.

Notice how the page is laid out. There is a menu along the top. You can see that the top pane has nothing in it. The left pane has two modules in it: some links and a list of books. The right pane has a list of DNN sponsors. The content pane has the My Website page in it. The bottom pane has nothing in it. A blank page with no modules is shown in Figure 6-4.

So, you have seen the main page of DNN and you have seen what a blank page looks like. You also know from looking at the main DNN page that you can put two modules into a single pane. You also know that the panes can be different sizes.

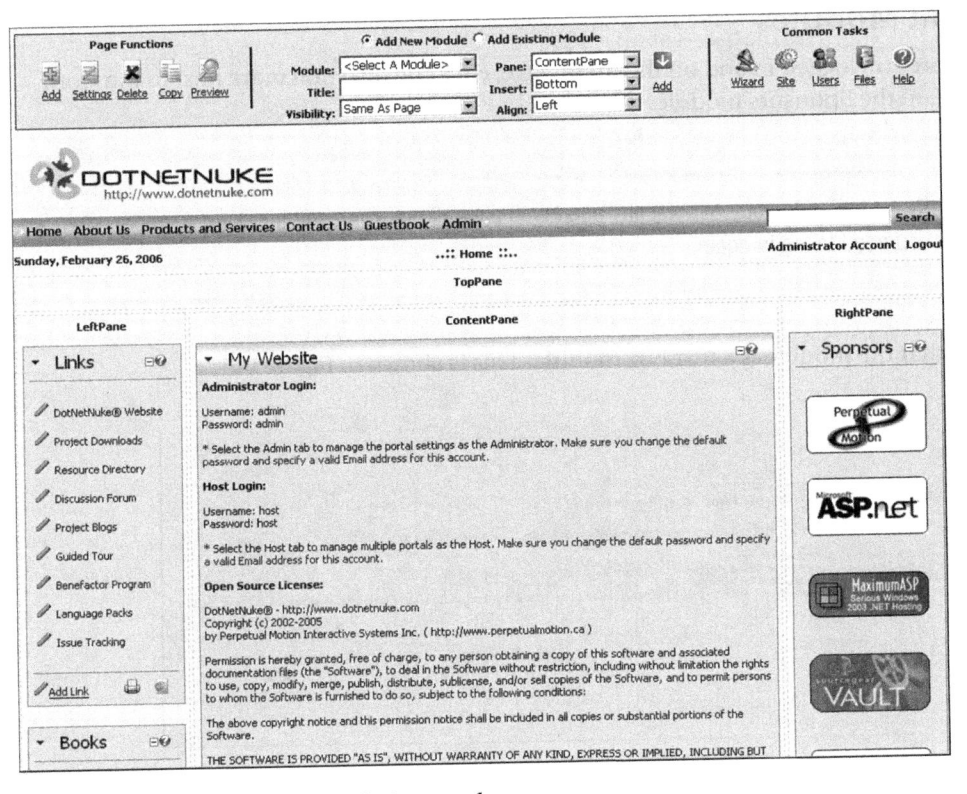

Figure 6-3. *The basic website in design mode*

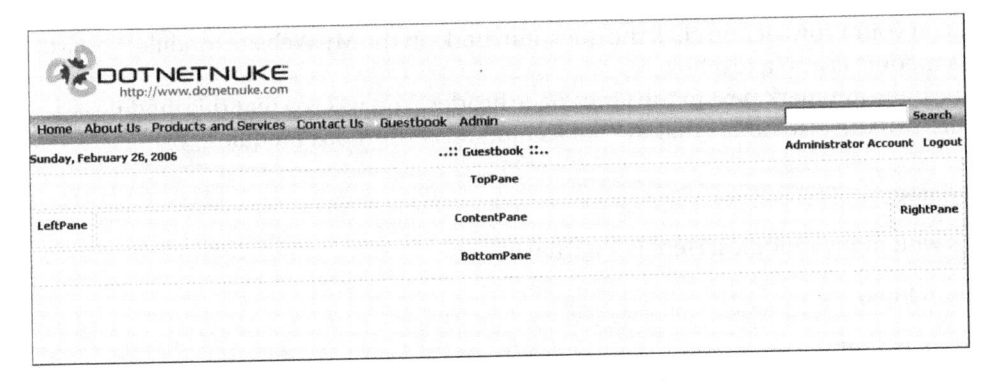

Figure 6-4. *A blank page showing the positions of the blank panes*

A Look at Modules

While you are still logged in and on the main page, click the question mark next to the word "Sponsors" on the Sponsors module.

■**Tip** DotNetNuke has a timeout just like any good web page. If you can't edit the page anymore, chances are good that you need to log in again.

It tells you that the module is a text box module. This is shown in Figure 6-5.

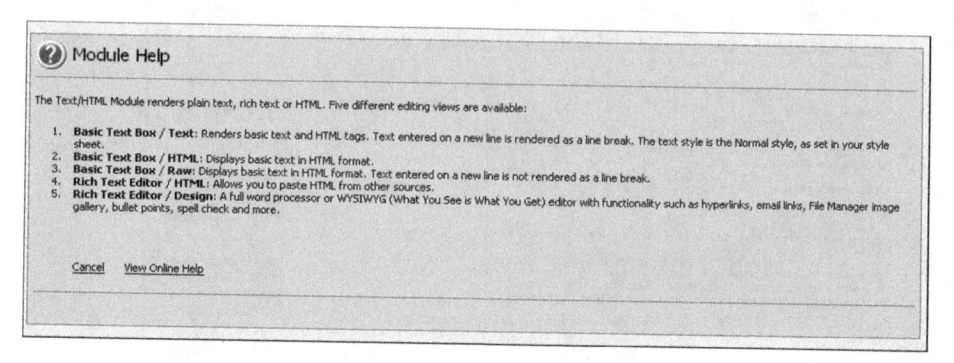

Figure 6-5. *Text box module help*

You can see from this limited help that the text box can be quite full-featured. Click the Back button on your browser and click the question mark on the My Website module. You will see that this module is also a text box.

Click the question mark next to the Links page header. You will see that this module is a links module. You will also notice that the books module is a text box module.

Default Modules

DNN comes with many modules. Here is a partial list:

- Account login

- Announcements

- Banners

- Contacts

- Discussions

- Documents

- Events

- FAQs

- Feedback

- IFrame

- Images

- Links

- New feeds (RSS)

- Search input

- Search result

- Survey

- Text/HTML

- User account

- User-defined table

- Users online

- XML/XSL

If you look at this list and think about it for a minute, you can see that these modules make up about 90 percent of any website you would want to create. For instance, here are some things that a hypothetical website would need:

- An account login module to keep track of users and to allow users access to different pages

- A user account module for people to register for your website

- An announcements module to let users know what is going on at your business

- A contacts module to let users call or e-mail you

- A text/HTML module in several places to contain the content of your website

- A banners module that allows you to show paid advertising

- A search input and results module set to allow users to search your website

Did I miss anything? Probably quite a bit. You get the drift though. This is pretty much a one-stop shop for website creation.

When it comes time to create a website for this DNN project, you will use many of these modules, and I will cover them in detail as needed.

Editing a DNN Site

Let's look at how you can edit a DNN website and what editing capabilities DNN gives you. A quick look at Figure 6-6 shows you an editing bar at the top of the page.

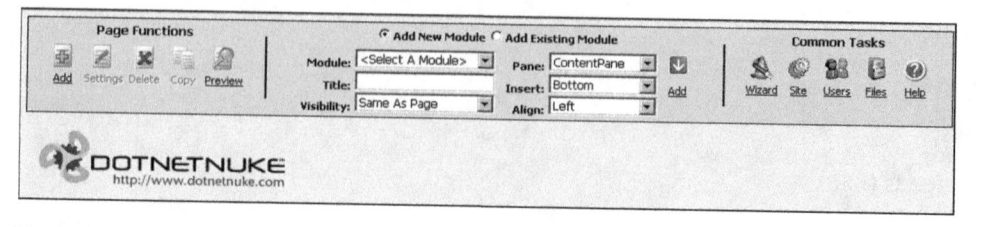

Figure 6-6. *The editing bar*

There are page functions that allow you add, copy, and delete pages in your site. You can also change the settings for whichever page you are on.

The Preview button allows you to see how the page looks to the user while still editing it. Basically, it hides all the editing features of the page temporarily.

The Module section of this editing bar allows you to add modules to a page in different panes. I'll discuss this feature in detail later.

The Common Tasks editing section has a wizard for creating a new site. It also has a Settings button to edit the settings for the site as a whole. The Files button allows you to add files, such as pictures and text files, to the site. For instance, the Sponsors pane on the main page is made up of many pictures with links associated with them. This feature manages those pictures. Click the files button and let's see what pops up. You should see an editing page, like the one shown in Figure 6-7.

Here you can see all the GIF and JPG files associated with this site. You can also change permissions for different classes of people accessing your site. Notice the small toolbar at the top that allows you to add, copy, delete, move, and upload files.

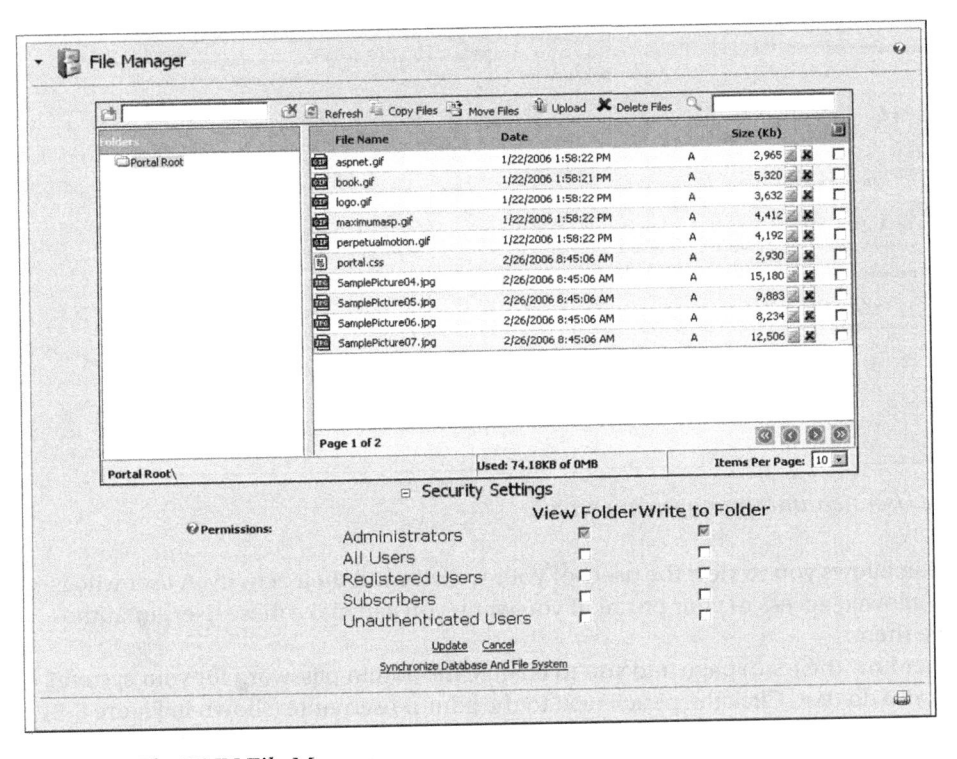

Figure 6-7. *The DNN File Manager*

DNN Users

DNN has several different kinds of users, as shown in Figure 6-7. You already know about the host user and administrator. There are also unauthenticated users (just browsing, thank you) and registered users.

If you want to manage your registered users, click the Users icon in the Common Tasks editing section. The user management screen is shown in Figure 6-8.

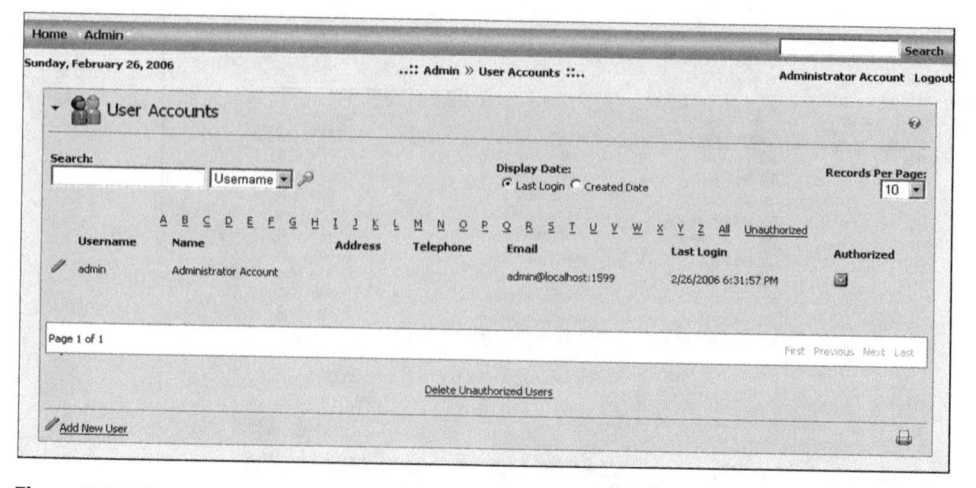

Figure 6-8. *The User Accounts management screen*

This screen allows you to view the users of your website and their activity. A user who is authorized is allowed access to your portal. If you want, you can make these users unauthorized or delete them.

Remember how the main page told you to change the admin password for your system? This is where you do that. Click the pencil next to the admin username (shown in Figure 6-8) and you will be brought to the Edit User Accounts page. The pencil is used throughout DNN to indicate editing capability. Figure 6-9 shows the Edit User Accounts page. Change your password at this time.

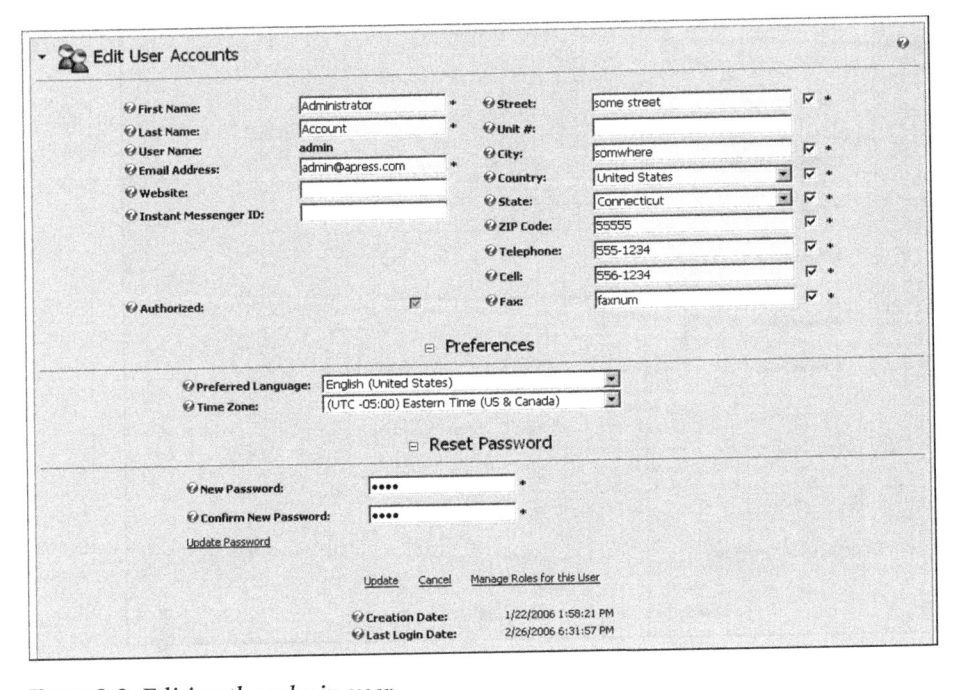

Figure 6-9. *Editing the admin user*

Settings

DNN is constructed such that there is a way to edit the settings of every web page and module. There are settings that can be adjusted for the page as a whole, and there are settings that can be adjusted for individual modules on the page.

Page Settings

Go back to the view of the main page as a whole. Click the Settings icon in the Page Functions section. (You may need to log back in if you have been away from your computer for a while.) This will bring up the Page Management screen (shown in Figure 6-10).

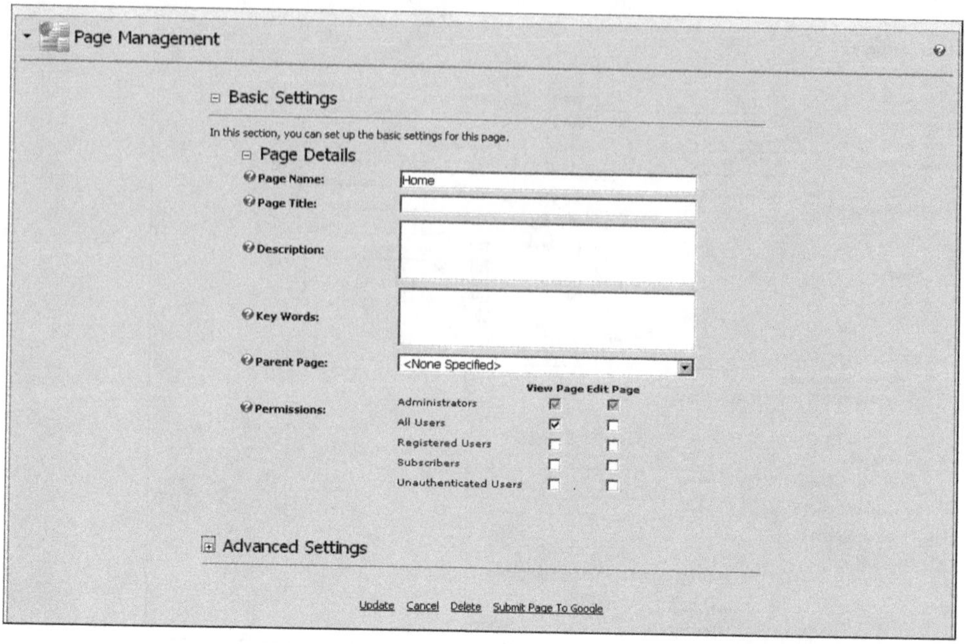

Figure 6-10. *The Page Management screen*

You can see from the permissions that you can allow people to view or edit the page depending on their roles. At the bottom of this page there are several links. These links act like buttons. The Update link updates the settings for this page. The Cancel link cancels the changes you made to this page. The Delete link deletes the page that these settings refer to. Do not delete this page accidentally.

There is one last link at the bottom of the page. This is the Submit Page To Google button. This is very cool because it allows you to tell Google that your page can be added to its list of URLs to crawl. The Key Words section is what Google uses to index your listing. This means that if you add the word *froogelfram* to your list of key words, and someone does a Google search for *froogelfram*, your site will come up.

These are the basic settings for a page. There are also some advanced settings that you can modify. Click the + sign next to the Advanced Settings heading. You should get the same screen as shown in Figure 6-11.

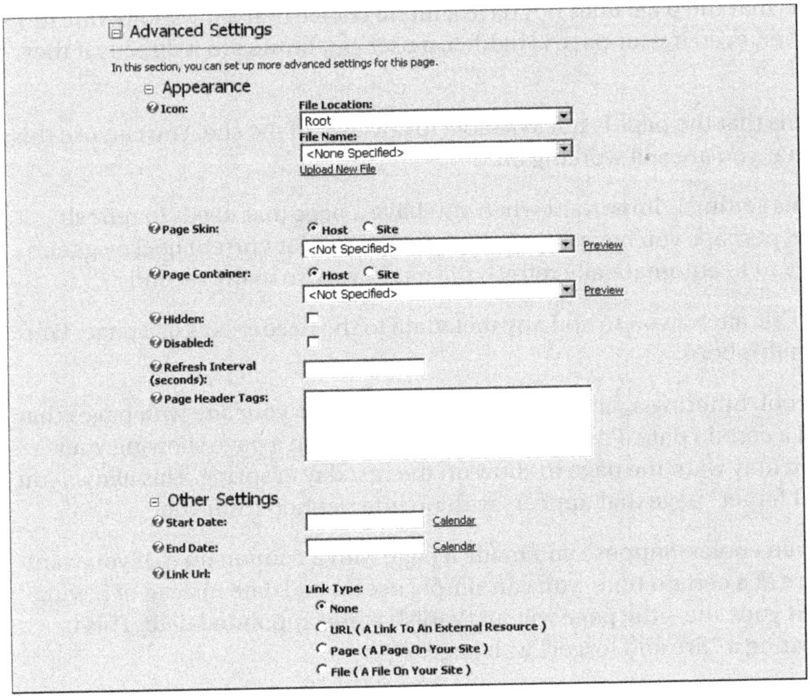

Figure 6-11. *The Advanced Settings page*

Here is a list of the advanced settings and what they mean:

Icon: When you create a page, you get a menu item for that page. This setting allows you to choose an icon for the menu.

Page Skin: A skin defines a certain look for a page. If you click the drop-down box, you will see a variety of skins to choose from. The skin changes the layout and the design of the page.

Page Container: A container frames a module or a set of modules on a page. The container has a look and feel to it that determines how a module will appear. The container you choose will apply to all modules on this page (unless you override it in the module settings).

Hidden: This means that the page does not have a menu choice that allows someone to browse to it. However, even if your page is hidden, a user can browse to it directly if they know the exact URL.

Disabled: This means that the page is not available to any user of the site. You can use this to turn off a page that you are still working on.

Refresh Interval: This setting is important when you have a page that needs to refresh often—for example, perhaps you have a page that gives scores for current hockey games. This setting allows you to automatically refresh the page every so many seconds.

Page Header Tags: This allows you to add any metadata to the header tags of a page. You will not need this in this book.

Start Date: This is cool. Entering a date here allows you to set up your site with pages that will be invalid until a certain date. For instance, you could set up a page showing your spring fashions. You may want the page to show on the first day of spring. This allows you to create a "fire and forget" page that appears with no intervention from you.

End Date: This is even cooler. Suppose you made a page with a coupon on it. If you want the coupon to expire at a certain time, you can simply use an end date instead of having to come back to edit your site—the page will just vanish at the appointed date. This is another case of creating a "fire and forget" web page.

Link URL: If you like, you can specify a page to be a link to another page. Did you ever get one of those pages that say you will be redirected to another page in 15 seconds? These pages use this kind of setting.

Module Settings

Just as there are settings for the page, there are settings for the module you are working on. Since the module is where all the real work gets done, it makes sense that you need to control it somehow. At the bottom-right corner of each module, you will see some icons representing XML, printing, and module settings. The Module Settings icon is shown in Figure 6-12.

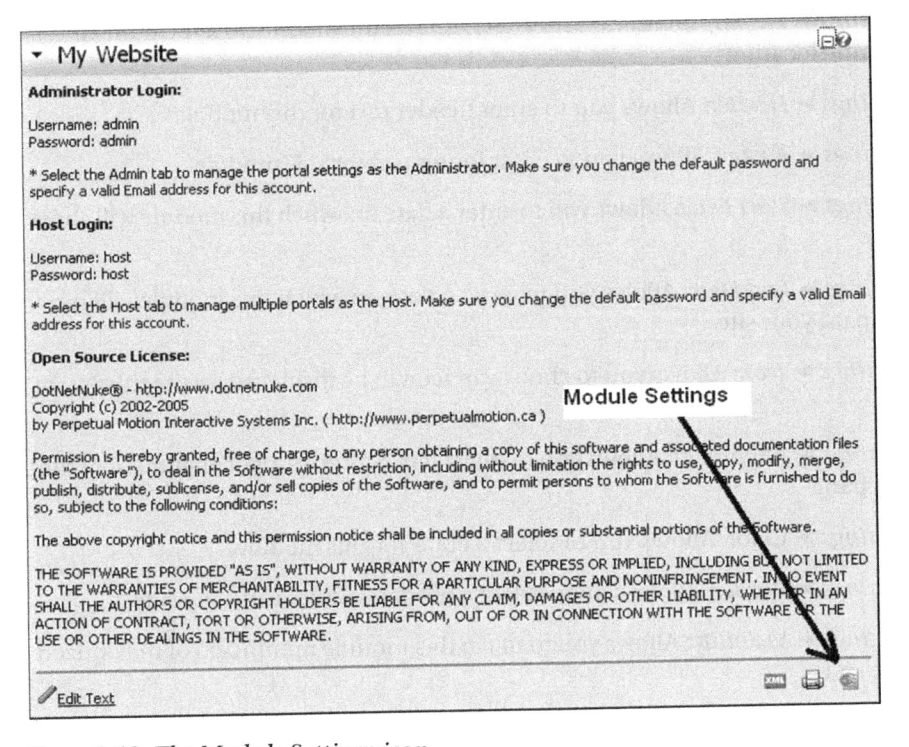

Figure 6-12. *The Module Settings icon*

Click this icon, and you will see a more extensive settings page than you saw with the page settings. Here is a list of the module settings and what they mean:

Basic Settings ➤ Module Title: Changes the title that appears on the title bar for the container of the module

Basic Settings ➤ Permissions: Allows people with certain roles to view or edit this module; these settings can be inherited from the page settings if you want

Advanced Settings ➤ *Display Module on All Pages*: Allows the module to appear on all pages in the same location

Advanced Settings ➤ *Header*: Allows you to enter header text for this module

Advanced Settings ➤ *Footer*: Allows you to enter footer text for this module

Advanced Settings ➤ *Start Date*: Allows you to enter a date on which this module will show up on your site

Advanced Settings ➤ *End Date*: Allows you to enter a date on which this module will no longer show up on your site

Page Basic Settings ➤ *Icon*: Allows you to choose an icon to be displayed on the title bar of this module

Page Basic Settings ➤ *Alignment*: Allows you to select left, center, or right alignment of this module in the pane

Page Basic Settings ➤ *Color*: Allows you to select a color for this module

Page Basic Settings ➤ *Border*: Allows you to select a border width for this module

Page Basic Settings ➤ *Visibility*: Allows you to make this module minimized or maximized when the page starts

Page Basic Settings ➤ *Display Container*: Allows the module to display its container

Page Basic Settings ➤ *Allow Print*: Allows printing of the module contents

Page Basic Settings ➤ *Allow Syndicate*: Allows the module to be an RSS feed (I will cover RSS later)

Page Basic Settings ➤ *Module Container*: Allows you to select a container for the module if one is not already selected

Page Basic Settings ➤ *Cache Time*: Allows you to select the time in seconds that the module is kept in the browser's cache

Page Advanced Settings ➤ *Set as Default Setting*: Allows you to select the page settings for this module to be the default when adding new modules

Page Advanced Settings ➤ *Apply to All Modules*: Applies the settings for this module to all existing modules in the site; this is good for blanket changes

Page Advanced Settings ➤ *Move to Page*: Allows you to select another page to move this module to if you don't want it here anymore

As you can see, there are quite a few ways to make the module specialized or generalized. You now know the basics of adding pages and modules to a site. You also know that you can change settings on a global scale or just for a module.

Before you leave this section, try fooling around a little and changing the settings for the main page.

You are probably wondering about the look and feel of DNN and your site. I have mentioned skins, and that you can change the look and feel if you want. You saw this in the page settings and in the module settings. Notice the menu position in the main page, and also notice that the color is blue. This is shown in Figure 6-13.

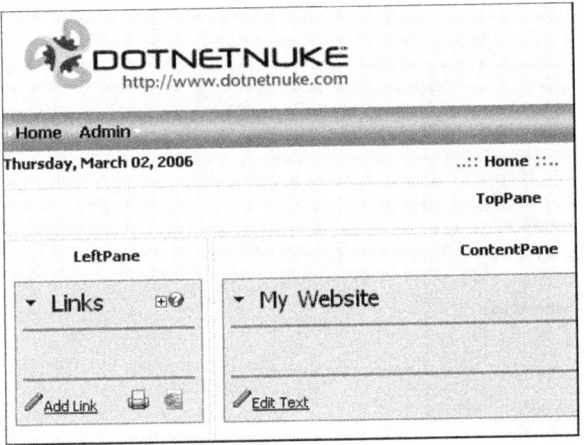

Figure 6-13. *Default menu postion and color*

Now, in the Page Functions icon bar at the top of the page, click the Settings icon to open the Page Settings dialog. Scroll down and select Advanced Settings ➤ Page Skin. You will see that it is set to Not Specified. Click this drop-down box and choose DNN-Green - Vertical Menu - Fixed Width. Scroll down to the bottom of the settings page and click Update. Your main screen should change to look like that shown in Figure 6-14.

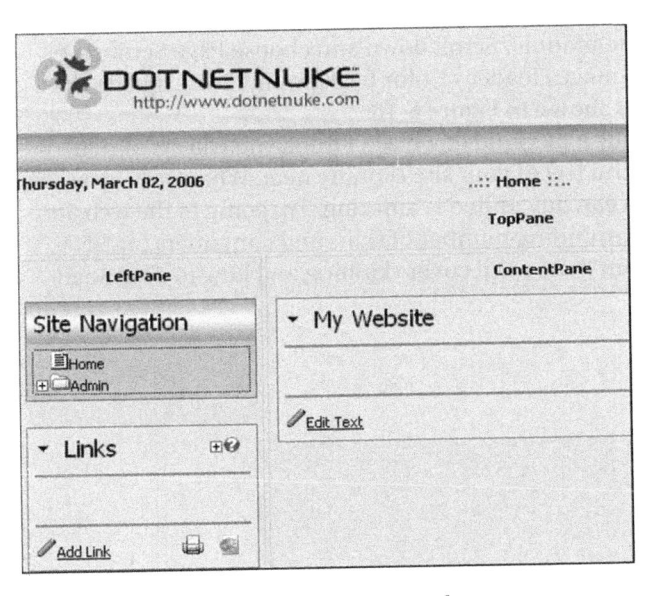

Figure 6-14. *A green page with a vertical menu*

You should now see the menu on the left side laid out vertically instead of horizontally. Notice that the modules have not changed, though.

Now that you've changed the whole page, how about matching the modules? Again, open up the Page Settings dialog and choose Advanced Settings ➤ Page Container. Choose DNN-Green - Image Header - Color Background. Now click Update, and your whole page should look green, as in Figure 6-15.

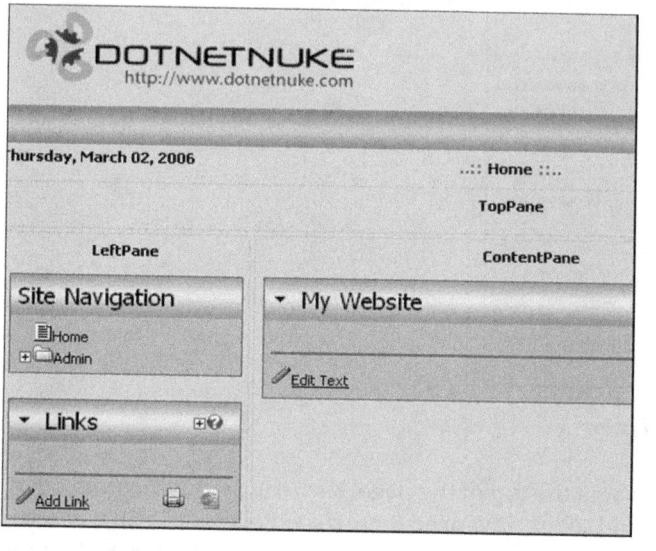

Figure 6-15. *Green all over*

So, you have changed the page settings for every module whose individual look and feel is not specified. You can now drill down into a module and change its settings individually.

Open the settings for the My Website module. Scroll down and choose Page Settings ➤ Module Container. Choose DNN-Red - Image Header - Color Background. Now update the page, and your module should be red, as shown in Figure 6-16.

While this is pretty plain (and actually looks kind of weird), I think you will agree that the fine control you have over the look and feel of your site is pretty neat. What DNN gives you out of the box is good, but what you can buy online is amazing. Try going to the website www.snowcovered.com. This site has an astounding number of skins and containers for DNN. You can buy just about anything you want here. I will cover skinning and how to download new skins in Chapter 9.

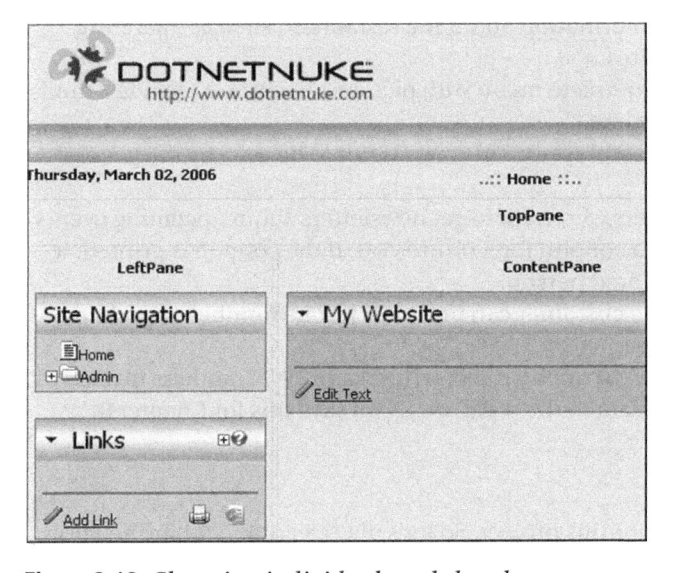

Figure 6-16. *Changing individual module color*

The Project

Now that you know how to work a little with DNN, let's start the major project for the book. This project will be a restaurant website. The site will be set up for both internal use by employees and external use by customers. With DNN, there is no need to have different programs for different functions. The functions can be filtered by permissions. It will have the following pages:

- A main page

- A menu page

- A food inventory page

- A registration page

- A contacts page

- A timekeeping page

Can you guess what is on the last page mentioned here? Yes, it will be the WebPunch project transferred over to a module.

The main page will contain basic information about the restaurant, such as operating hours and links to related specialized sites.

The menu page will be just that: a complete menu with pictures. It will also include a module with specials that will expire after a time.

The food inventory page is for the employees. This page is not to be seen by the general public. It will have printing capability.

The registration page is for customers who want to get newsletters about upcoming events at the restaurant. Also included will be a coupon for a future visit. If the coupon is printed, it will no longer be available to that registered person.

The contacts page will be where the customer can find your phone number or perhaps find a link to e-mail you.

The timekeeping page will be the WebPunch project written as a DNN module. Instead of using dummy data, it will get and save data to the database. I will save this for Chapter 8.

Getting Started

I said that you will use the existing site for this project. So let's play cleanup. Start by deleting the modules on the main page. You can do this by clicking the down arrow next to the module title. Make sure you are logged in first. This is shown in Figure 6-17.

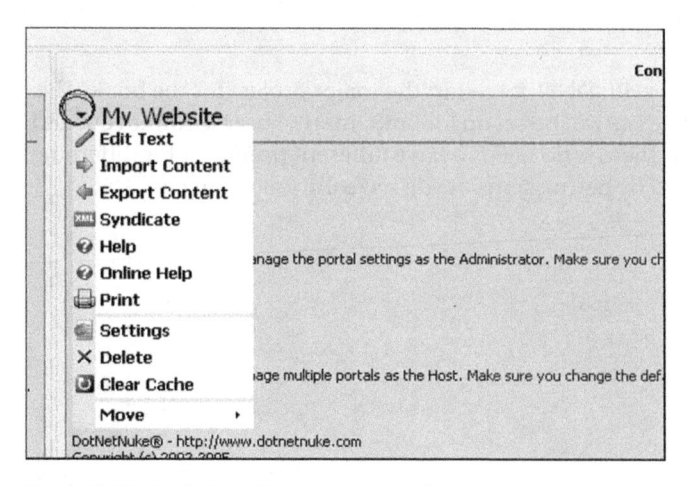

Figure 6-17. *Deleting the current module*

Click the red X to delete this module from the page. Do this for all the modules on the main page.

Your home page should now be blank, with just the empty panes showing. I am not going to have you change the skin for this site, as I kind of like the default one as it is. The other free ones that come with DNN are just variations on a theme anyway. However, if this were a real site, I would invest the time and a little money on researching and purchasing a new skin to get just the right look and feel.

Setting Up the Site

On the menu bar, you will see an Admin button. Run your mouse over it and click Site Settings. Let's change a few things in here. First are the site details (shown in Figure 6-18).

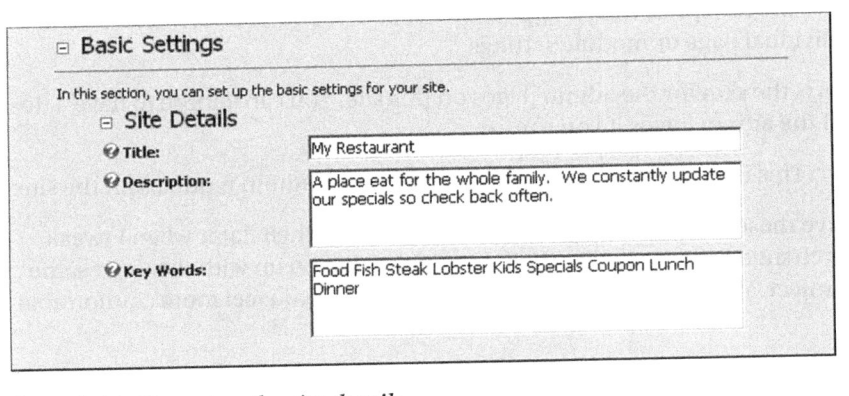

Figure 6-18. *Changing the site details*

First, choose a name and a description for your site. Next, you want to enter some key words that will be used by search engines (these key words are typically things that a person would be likely to type into a search engine). You want your site to come up first in a search engine's list, so you need to think like a consumer here.

The next thing to change is the logo. This is actually one of the first things you should have as a business owner. It can be any kind of picture. Just make sure that its file size isn't too big. Remember that the heavier your site is, the longer it takes to load.

■**Tip** The logo and other graphics you use on your website should have a transparent background. You can do this with transparent GIFs. The logo I use here has a transparent background so that the website's background shows through. You will see later that I use some graphics that do not have a transparent background, and they do not look as good.

The logo file can reside anywhere on your computer. Just click the Upload New File link under the logo heading, and DNN will allow you to find the file. It will then copy it to the appropriate directory.

Included under the Appearance settings on the site settings page are the following settings:

Body Background: This is an image that gets painted on the background of every page, which you can specify depending upon the skin you choose.

Portal Skin: This skin will get applied to all pages of this portal. It can be overridden in the individual page settings.

Portal Container: This container will be applied to all modules on the site. It can be overridden in the individual page or module settings.

Admin Skin: This is the skin for the admin pages on this site. You can choose to have a different skin for all the admin pages if you like.

Admin Container: This is a container that will be applied to all admin modules on the site.

I am going to leave these settings alone for now. I may change them later when I tweak the site. You can also change them if you like. You do not have to end up with the exact same website I do in this project. You can tweak it as you go along and as you feel more comfortable with DNN.

Creating Pages

The first thing you are going to do is create some blank pages for your site. These will essentially be placeholders for links that you want to put on the main page.

Under the Page Functions section of the editing module, click Add. You will be taken to a page management settings page. On this page, you will modify the following settings:

Basic Settings ➤ *Page Details* ➤ *Page Name*: Set the text to "Menu."

Basic Settings ➤ *Page Details* ➤ *Page Title*: Set the text to " Menu."

Basic Settings ➤ *Page Details* ➤ *Description*: Type in an appropriate description here.

Basic Settings ➤ *Page Details* ➤ *Key Words*: Enter a bunch of words that can be used to score hits during a search.

Basic Settings ➤ *Page Details* ➤ *Permissions*: Make sure all users can view this page. You will change this later.

Click Update to get the new page added to your site. The Advanced Settings section can be left alone for now. Once you get all the pages in the site and have them filled out, you will go back and change permissions. These permissions will set the site up to be seen by customers in one way and by employees in another.

Now you have created the menu page. Repeat the steps to create the menu page for four other pages. They are to appear in the following order:

1. Inventory

2. Registration

3. Contacts

4. Time

Your menu should look like the one shown in Figure 6-19.

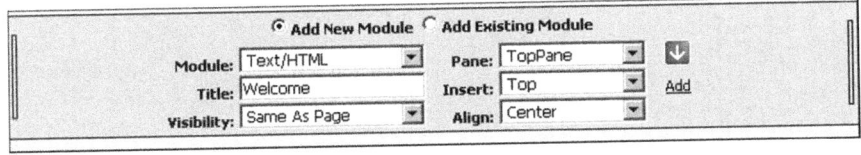

Figure 6-19. *The new menu bar for the site*

By the way, you will be able to find the pictures I use here in the download files for this book, available from the Apress website. Personally, I think the kitchen tools rack is really cool.

Adding Modules to the Home Page

You are going to be adding modules to the home page. You will add an image module, a links module, and a text/HTML module. Let's start with the top pane.

In the Module section of the editing module, you will add a new text module to the top pane. Choose the settings shown in Figure 6-20.

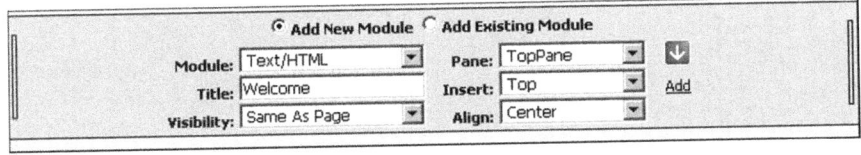

Figure 6-20. *Adding a new module to the page*

Once you click the Add button, the module will be inserted into the top pane of the home page.

Click the Edit Text link, and you will be taken to a rich text editor. This text editor allows you to add text and other word processing elements to the text box. If you like, you can edit the actual HTML code it produces. For now, just add some welcome text to the box. When you are done, your top pane should look like Figure 6-21.

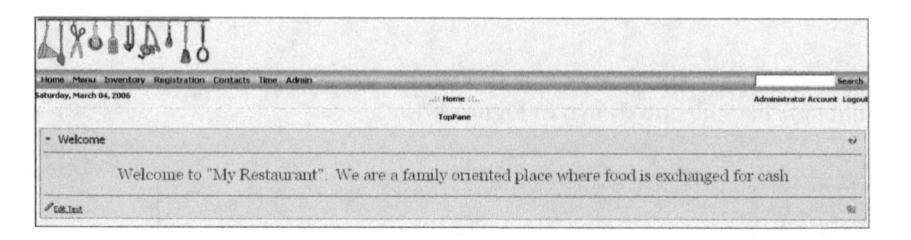

Figure 6-21. *A welcome text module*

The next module to add is the links module, which resides in the left-hand pane. This links module will contain links to other pages in the site, as well as an external URL. This is the reason I wanted to add all the pages before this module. You will be using this module as an alternate menu.

Add the new links module to the left pane similarly to how you added the text module to the top pane. After you add the module, you will need to add four links. The links will be to the following:

- The menu page

- The registration page

- The contacts page

- The DotNetNuke website

Click the Add Link link, and you will be taken to a page where you can add links to pages or URLs. Figure 6-22 shows the complete settings page for the link to the menu page.

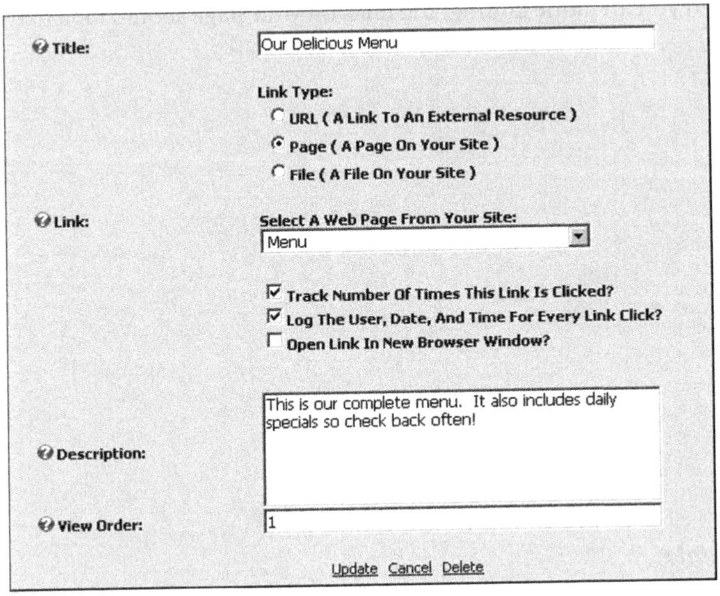

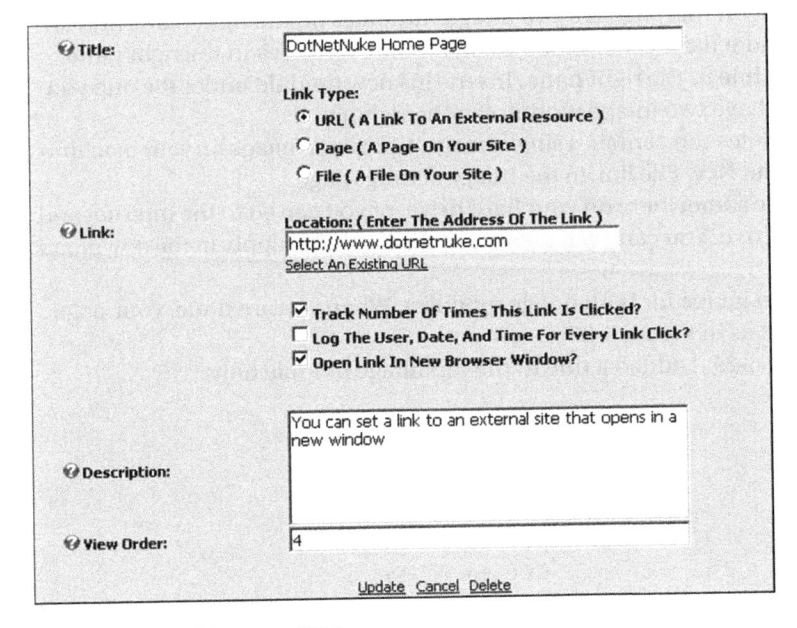

Figure 6-22. *Linking to a page*

Figure 6-23 shows the settings page when you add a link to a site.

Figure 6-23. *Linking to a URL*

Notice the view order. When you are done adding, the links on your page should look like Figure 6-24.

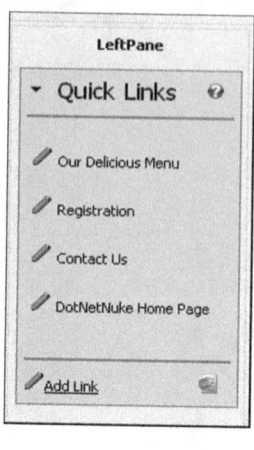

Figure 6-24. *The Quick Links module*

Now, when you click any of the page links, you should be brought to that page of your site. Click the DNN link, and you should get a new window. This was one of the choices made on the settings page (as shown in Figure 6-23). If you click the pencil to the left of the link, you will be able to edit that entry.

The next modules to add on this page are two images modules on the right pane. Add an image module just like you added the other modules. Make sure it resides in the right pane. Now add another image module in the right pane. Insert this new module under the one you just added. You should now have two image modules in the right pane.

Each of these image modules can contain a single image. Choose an image on your machine, and upload it using the Upload New File link in the Image Settings page.

You can choose an image somewhere on your hard drive, or you can go to the Internet and download one to your hard drive. You can even use one of the images I supply in the download files for this book.

Make sure you supply an image for both image modules. When you are done, your page should show the same layout as in Figure 6-25.

As you can see in Figure 6-25, I added a title to the top image module only.

Figure 6-25. *Image modules with content*

The last module to be placed on the page is a text/HTML module. This module gets added inside the content pane. This module is where you will add the meat of the page content.

Add a text/HTML module to the content pane in the same way you added all the other modules to the page.

Edit the text, and you should get a page similar to that shown in Figure 6-26.

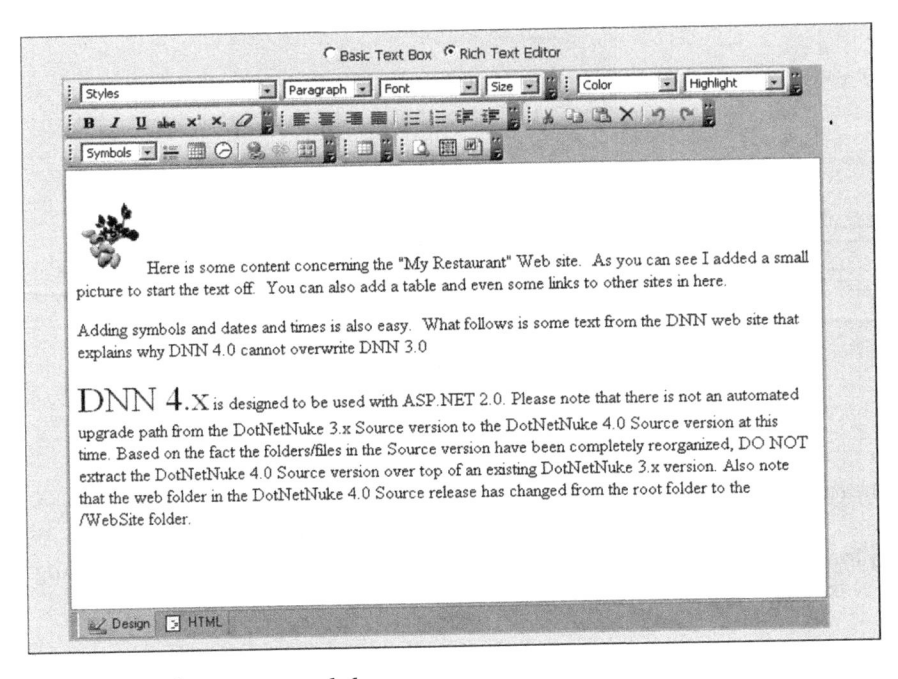

Figure 6-26. *A fancy text module*

Notice that I was able to place a graphic on the page, along with text of different sizes and colors. This rich text editor has some really nice features. You can add dates, times, tables, graphics, and links to a text box. This can make your content look really nice. If you are daring, you can look at the HTML code when you are done adding your content. Just click the HTML button at the bottom of this editor.

Tweaking the Page Settings

There are some attributes of each of these modules that I want turned off. I do not want someone to print the contents of the module and I also do not want people to minimize any module on this page.

Edit the settings of any module on this page. Scroll down the module settings page to the Basic Settings section, and uncheck the Allow Print setting. Also check the radio button labeled Visibility None. These changes will apply to this module.

Scroll down to the Advanced Settings section of this page and check Apply to All Modules. Now update the module. You will find that the changes you made will apply to the other modules of the home page.

You are now done with the home page. Click preview and you should see a page similar to Figure 6-27.

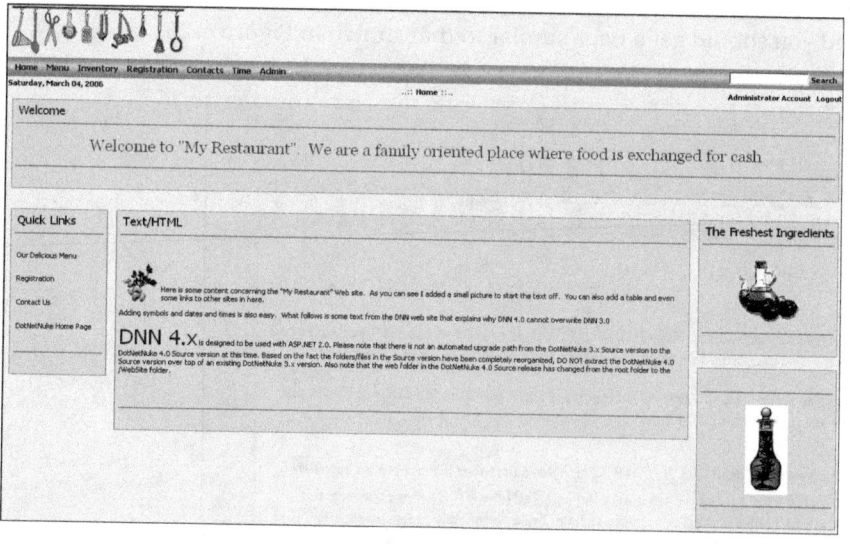

Figure 6-27. *The completed home page*

Your page may look a little different than mine, but by now you should be getting the hang of creating a page. Next you will create the menu page.

Adding Modules to the Menu Page

The menu page should be one whose content can be changed often. It should also be a page where you can export the content to other websites. For instance, there are quite a few sites that collect menus from various restaurants in the area.

Note While I am talking about a restaurant site and a menu page here, do not think this limits you. Suppose you had a real estate site. Your menu page could be a list of choice houses for sale. The construction of websites for many different businesses can follow the same ideas and layout. All you need is a little imagination and some courage to try something. The nice thing about DNN is that if you don't like the module or page you are creating, you can easily change or delete it.

Click the Menu choice on the menu bar. You will need to do this while logged in as the administrator.

The menu page will have only three modules on it, but you'll be adding some more, as follows:

- Add an announcements module to the top pane, and title it "Menu Specials."

- Add a documents module to the left pane, and title it "Recipes."

- Add a text/HTML module to the content pane, and title it "Dinner Menu."

The announcements module allows you to add time-sensitive announcements to the page. For instance, you can run a special that expires on a certain day. Once that day is past, the announcement no longer shows. My announcements module is shown in Figure 6-28.

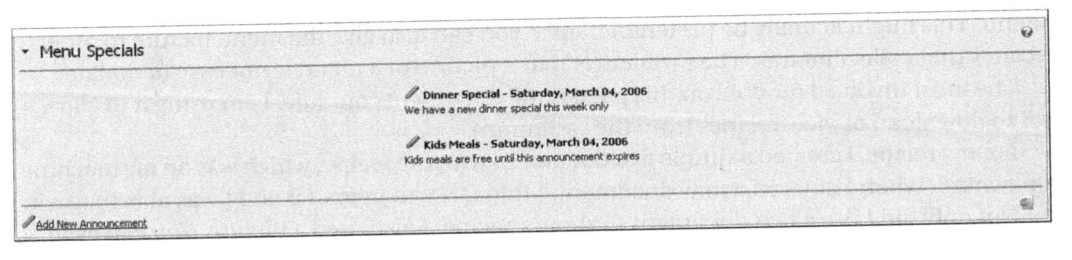

Figure 6-28. *An announcements module*

Both of these announcements expire within a few days of being entered, which makes it a really handy module.

The content pane is where I am showing the menu for the restaurant. Once again, I am using images and various types of text to give it a nice look. Enter some menu items, and perhaps your menu text module will look like mine, shown in Figure 6-29.

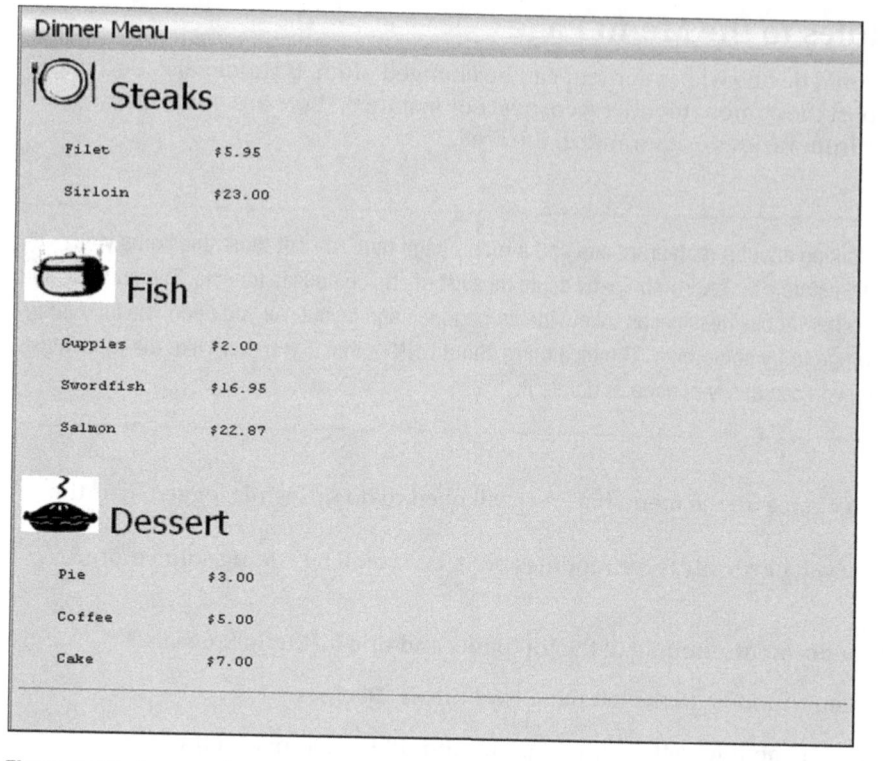

Figure 6-29. *A menu in a text/HTML module*

See how the plate image has a transparent background, while the pot and pie images do not? Which do you think looks better?

If you want, you can replace this text module with an image module and show a picture of a menu. This might actually be preferable, since you can also give the menu picture to other websites that collect menus. The problem is that a picture of a menu is not easy to update.

The most involved module on this page is the documents module. I am using it to allow a user to download or view recipes from the restaurant.

For my recipe, I created a simple text document with the recipe, which was on my machine somewhere. When I entered a new document, I told DNN to upload it and I was able to use it.

Not only did I use a text document to show a recipe, I also used a picture. You can even make a complicated picture with a recipe and an image in the background. This can look really nice as a recipe. The Edit Documents page for my Chicken Chili recipe is shown in Figure 6-30. This is the recipe for which I specified a picture to show in a new window.

Once all the documents are in the module, your menu page should look like that shown in Figure 6-31.

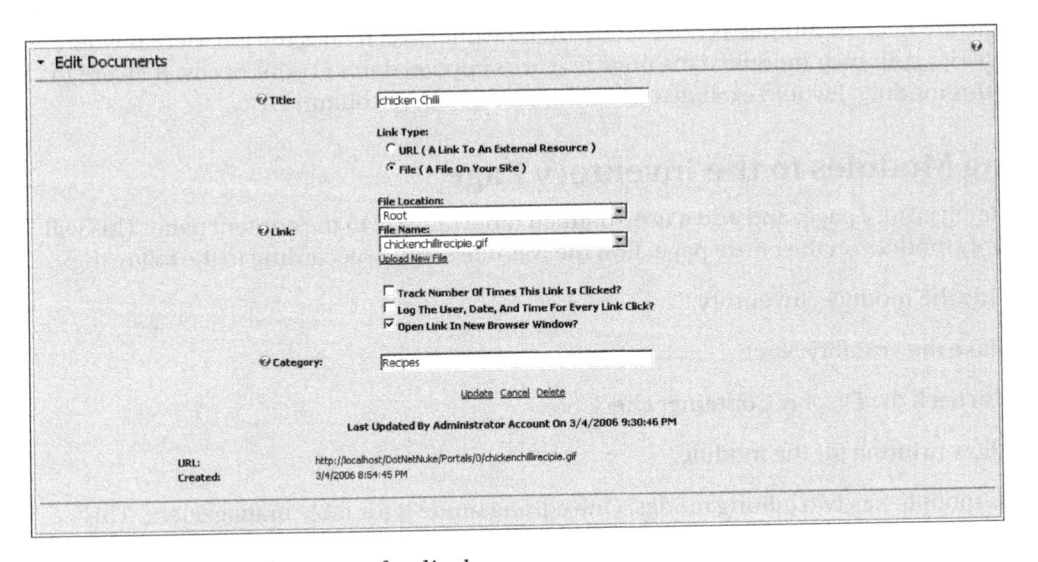

Figure 6-30. *Editing a document for display*

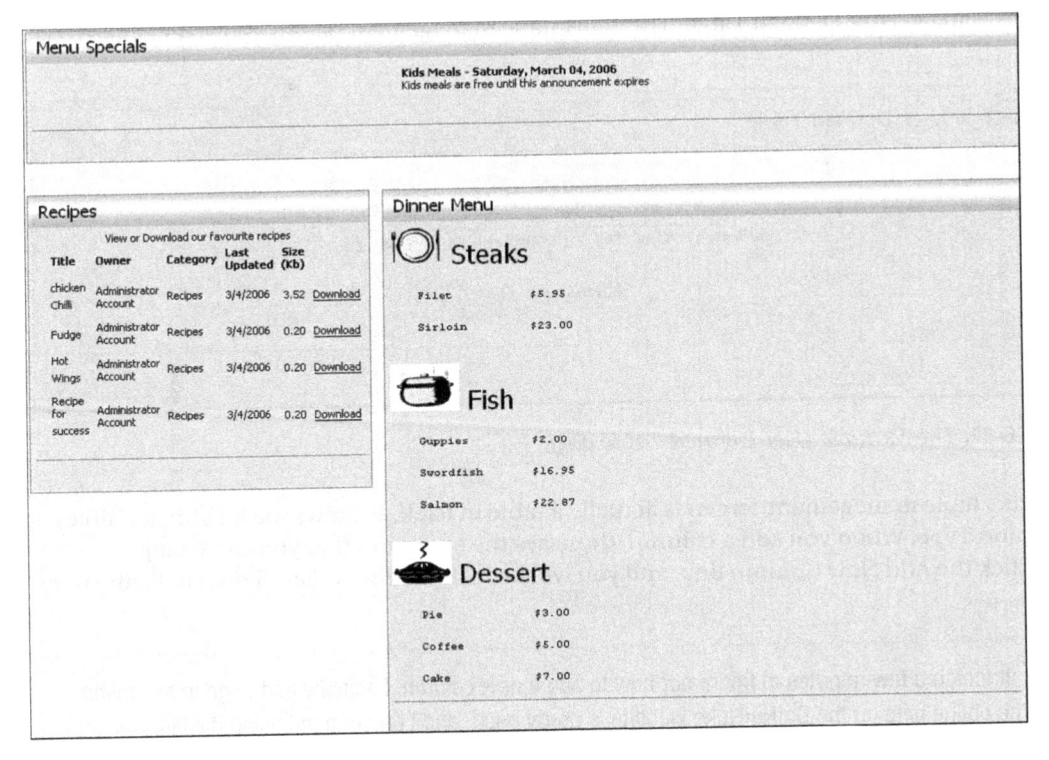

Figure 6-31. *The finished menu page*

While the Recipes module is not exactly what I would like, it does the job. Here is where you can write your own module if the ones that are supplied don't fit your needs. If I were to change this module, I would exclude the Owner and Category columns.

Adding Modules to the Inventory Page

Open the Inventory page, and add a user-defined table module to the content pane. This will be the only module on the entire page. Edit the module settings according to the following:

- Title the module "Inventory."

- Make the visibility None.

- Uncheck the Display Container check box.

- Allow printing for the module.

This module has two editing modes. One editing mode is for table management. This entails adding columns and establishing the initial sort order. The other editing mode is for adding rows to the table. The rows are the actual data.

Start by clicking the down arrow icon next to the "Inventory" title. From this drop-down list, choose Manage User Defined Table. The blank table management page is shown in Figure 6-32.

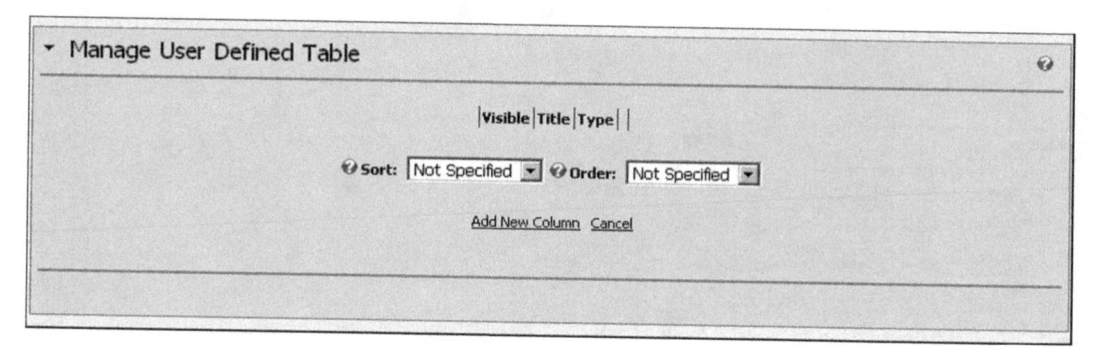

Figure 6-32. *The Manage User Defined Table page*

This table management screen is actually a table in itself. It shows the headings Visible, Title, and Type. When you add a column, these are the attributes that you can change.

Click the Add New Column link, and you will be taken to the screen shown in Figure 6-33.

Tip It took me few minutes to figure out how to add a new column. I actually had to go to the online help. The online help on the DotNetNuke website is pretty good, and I recommend using it whenever you get stumped.

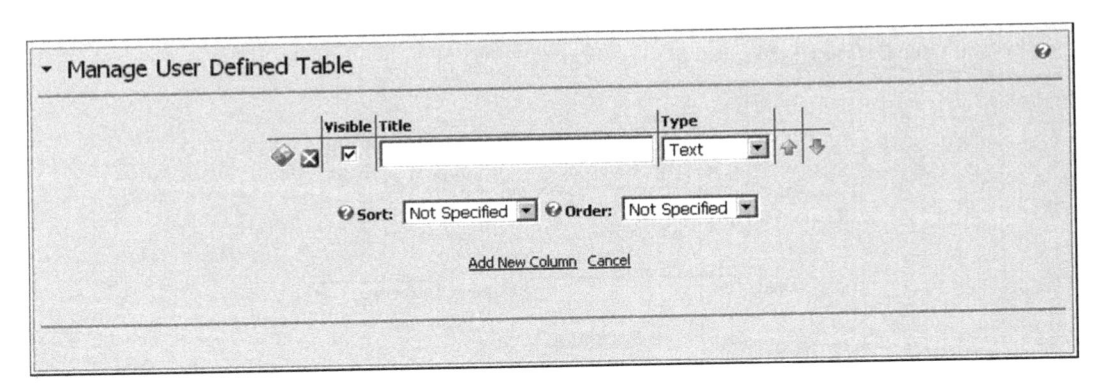

Figure 6-33. *Adding a new column*

The Title is the title of the column. The Type can be Text, Integer, Decimal, Date, or Boolean (true/false).

Checking the Visible check box means that this column can be viewed by anyone. If you uncheck it, the column won't be visible.

The X icon deletes the column, and the floppy disk icon allows you to save it.

Note I have to say here that this module differs from the others in that there is no Update button. When you consider that one of the basic premises of DNN is a consistent look and feel, this module differs enough to require a trip to the help screen.

The columns you'll use for your restaurant inventory page are shown in Table 6-1.

Table 6-1. *Inventory Page Column Titles and Types*

Title	Type
Item	Text
Amount Left	Integer
Minimum Before Reorder	Integer
Reorder	TrueFalse

Once you are done with the columns, your table management screen should look like Figure 6-34.

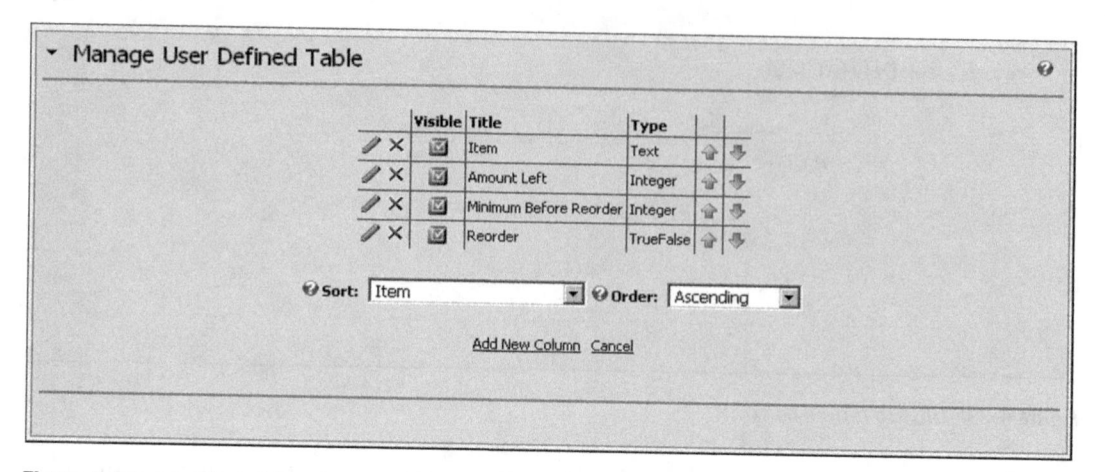

Figure 6-34. *A table, with columns defined*

Click Cancel to exit this page. Next, add some rows so that your table in edit mode looks like Figure 6-35.

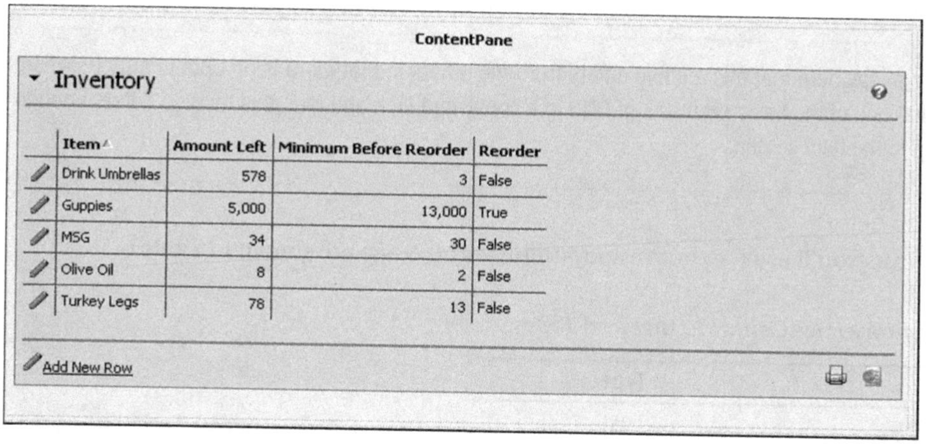

ContentPane

▾ Inventory

	Item⁄	Amount Left	Minimum Before Reorder	Reorder
🖉	Drink Umbrellas	578	3	False
🖉	Guppies	5,000	13,000	True
🖉	MSG	34	30	False
🖉	Olive Oil	8	2	False
🖉	Turkey Legs	78	13	False

🖉 Add New Row

Figure 6-35. *A completed table*

Click the Preview button, and you will see a table on the page as the user would see it. Note that the container is not shown. All you see is a table with no surrounding lines or other icons.

The Inventory Data

The Inventory page will be set up later such that only people with a certain role will be able to edit the rows. This means that the data in here must all be hand-entered. It would be very easy to let a page like this get old and out of date.

The best thing you can do for an inventory is to make the data update automatically. Showing you how to do this is beyond the scope of this book, but I will tell you how it is possible. Here is a brief list of things you will need to do:

1. Look in the DNN database and find the rows and fields that correspond to your user-defined table.

2. Create a meal-ordering page that is used by employees. Each menu item that is ordered has a list of ingredients.

3. The custom meal-ordering module that you create will tally the ingredients for all the orders and adjust the inventory numbers accordingly.

4. This inventory page will show an ever-depleting list of foodstuffs.

While this list may seem simple, it is not easy. You will need to know how to hunt down all the fields you need to change in SQL Server, and you will also have to be well-versed in creating new modules.

You are now done with the Inventory page. Later, you will change the permissions to allow certain people to edit the inventory.

Adding Modules to the Registration Page

The registration page is where a user will administer his account. By *administering*, I mean changing e-mail addresses, changing physical addresses, unregistering, and so on. Account management is not done from here. Account management is done by logging in as an administrator or as a host.

An administrator or host logs in and gets the site management tools at the top of the page. Any other person who logs in will not get this.

Log in as the administrator, open the registration page, and add a user account module to the content pane of this page. Change the settings as follows:

- Title the module "Account Management."

- Make the visibility None.

- Uncheck the Allow Print check box to disable printing for the module.

Depending on what information you want from people who subscribe to your site, you may want to turn off certain mandatory fields. You can do this by unchecking the box next to the field you don't really need. Users will still be able to enter information into this field if they want.

Here is what happens with registration and login:

- The user clicks the Register link, located next to the Login link. (The user can also click the Registration link found on the links module on the main page.)

- The user fills in the required fields in the Account Management module on the registration page.

- The user clicks the Update link at the bottom of the page, and is both registered and logged in.

- The user can click the registration page again, and her information will be filled in automatically. She can then change the info and update it, and also unregister if she likes.

The administrator can log in and click the Users link in the Common Tasks section. This is shown in Figure 6-36.

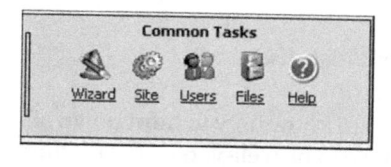

Figure 6-36. *Click the Users link to manage registered users.*

The User Accounts page is shown in Figure 6-37.

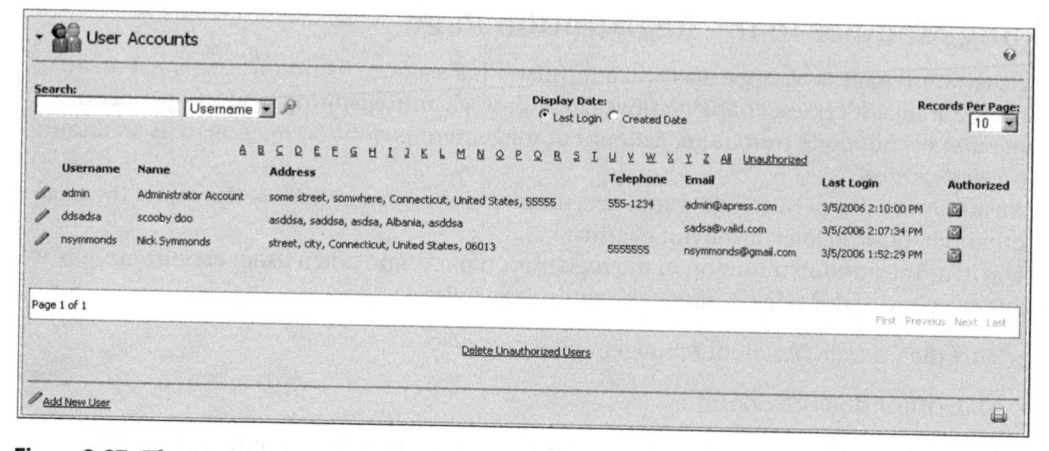

Figure 6-37. *The UserAccounts page*

This page allows you to change roles by editing the user. You can also delete any user here, and add new ones as well.

This page contains a lot of information about the users of your site.

Once you have all the pages and modules set up for the site, you will be changing permissions in each page and module to allow certain actions by users with certain roles.

Once a user has registered with your site, he will need a way to contact you. This is where the contacts page comes in.

Adding Modules to the Contacts Page

Open the contacts page and add a contacts module to the content pane. The settings are as follows:

- Title the module "Contacts."

- Make the visibility None.

- Allow printing for the module.

Add several contacts to the module. When users click the e-mail link, this generates a `mailto` hyperlink. The user will be taken to her e-mail program with your e-mail address in the e-mail's address field.

In addition to having contacts on this page, you will also have some FAQs. Add a FAQ module to the left pane. The settings for this module are as follows:

- Title the module "FAQ."

- Make the visibility None.

- Do not allow printing.

Add some FAQs to this module, such as your operating hours, whether you take credit cards, and so on.

You Contacts page should look something like that shown in Figure 6-38.

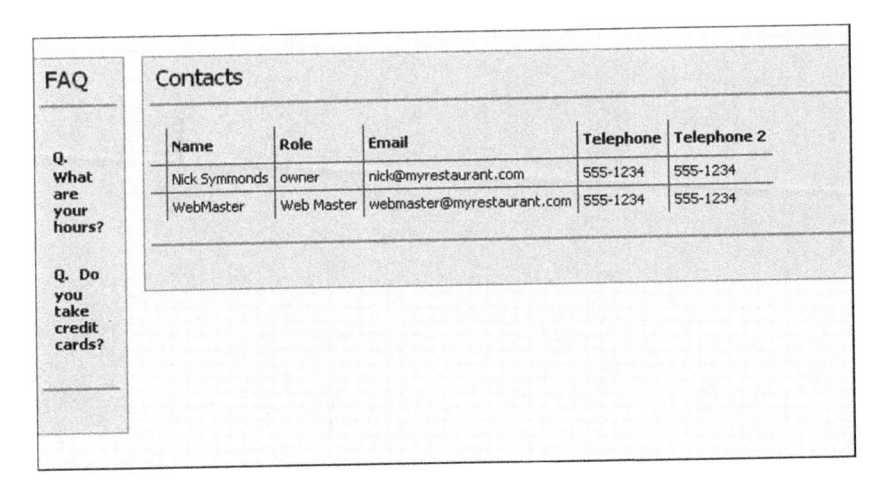

Figure 6-38. *The Contacts page*

There are two more tasks to do before this project is finished. The first is to fill in the Time page. The second is to adjust all the permissions to allow only certain users access to certain pages in the site. These tasks are rather involved, and will be left to subsequent chapters.

Summary

This chapter has taught you how to create your own website using the tools that DNN gives you; you haven't even used any of your new programming skills.

DotNetNuke gives you the ability to control what is on your page, and also to control the settings for the site, pages, and modules.

You saw how to choose a skin for the site and a layout that renders the menu either horizontally or vertically.

DNN is an easy-to-use framework to create websites. There are many good modules that are provided with the DNN install. There are also many modules that you can buy to get just about any functionality you desire.

The true power of DNN comes into play when you create your own modules, which you will do in the next chapter. You will take the WebPunch program and turn it into a module that you can use on the final page of this project.

CHAPTER 7

■■■

Creating a DNN Module

So far, you have been exposed to working with C# in one chapter, web development in another chapter, and creating a DNN website in yet another one.

This chapter combines the work you did in these three previous chapters with the creation of a new DNN module.

You saw in Chapter 6 how DotNetNuke is a powerful framework for creating a website. While this is so for the generic parts of your site, the DNN project you created still lacked some specialized capability. This specialized capability is the ability to have employees of the restaurant clock in and out during the day. This kind of ability enhances your website to be used not only externally for customers, but internally as well.

You are already more than halfway to creating this new module by way of the WebPunch project you did in Chapter 5. The code you created and the web programming skills you learned will be applied in this chapter, where you will be turning the WebPunch project into a DNN module.

Creating the Module

The easiest way to create the module you need is via a two-step process. First, you create the module framework; and second, you edit the module to include the controls and code you need. This section describes the first step: creating the module.

Open the Solution Explorer for your new website. Click the root node of the solution. As you can see from Figure 7-1, this is C:\DotNetNuke.

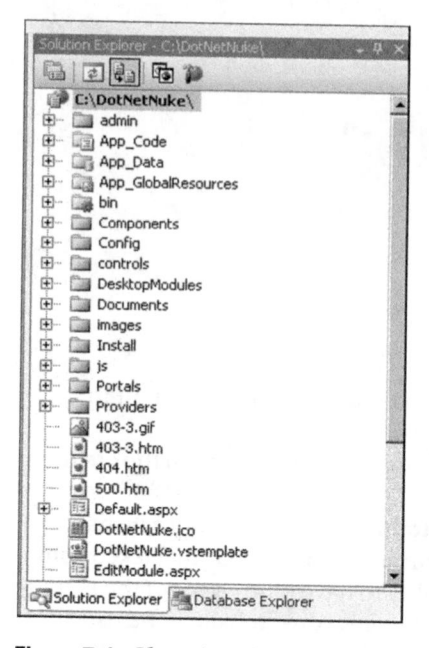

Figure 7-1. *Choosing the root node of your solution*

Right-click the C:\DotNetNuke node and choose Add New Item from the drop-down menu. Choose the DotNetNuke Module template, select Visual C# as the language, and give it the name "TimePunch." This is shown is Figure 7-2.

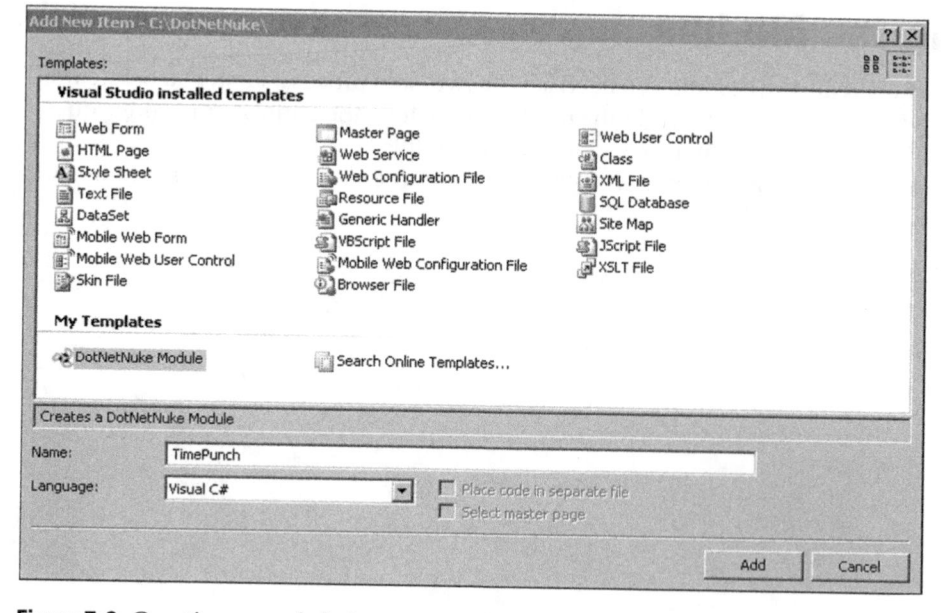

Figure 7-2. *Creating a module from a template*

If you have the nerve . . . click the Add button, and after a few seconds of grinding you should get a nice, friendly web page that tells you to do some file renaming. This is shown in Figure 7-3.

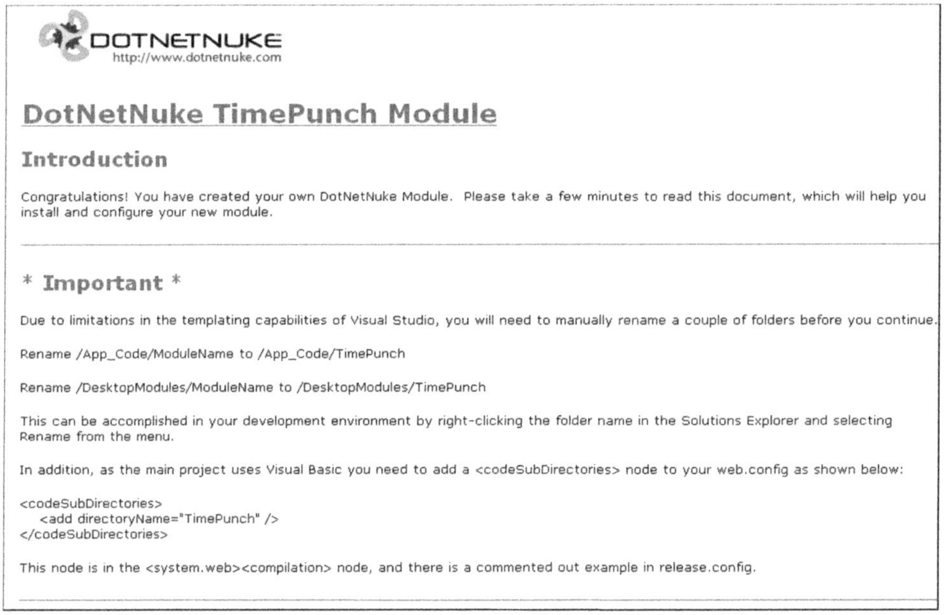

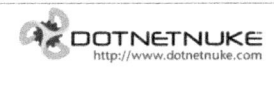

DOTNETNUKE
http://www.dotnetnuke.com
DotNetNuke TimePunch Module
Introduction
Congratulations! You have created your own DotNetNuke Module. Please take a few minutes to read this document, which will help you install and configure your new module.
* Important *
Due to limitations in the templating capabilities of Visual Studio, you will need to manually rename a couple of folders before you continue.
Rename /App_Code/ModuleName to /App_Code/TimePunch
Rename /DesktopModules/ModuleName to /DesktopModules/TimePunch
This can be accomplished in your development environment by right-clicking the folder name in the Solutions Explorer and selecting Rename from the menu.
In addition, as the main project uses Visual Basic you need to add a <codeSubDirectories> node to your web.config as shown below:
<codeSubDirectories>
<add directoryName="TimePunch" />
</codeSubDirectories>
This node is in the <system.web><compilation> node, and there is a commented out example in release.config.

Figure 7-3. *Reminder to rename files*

If you look at the Solution Explorer, you should have two nodes called ModuleName. One is under the `App_Code` directory and the other is under the `DesktopModules` directory (as shown in Figure 7-4).

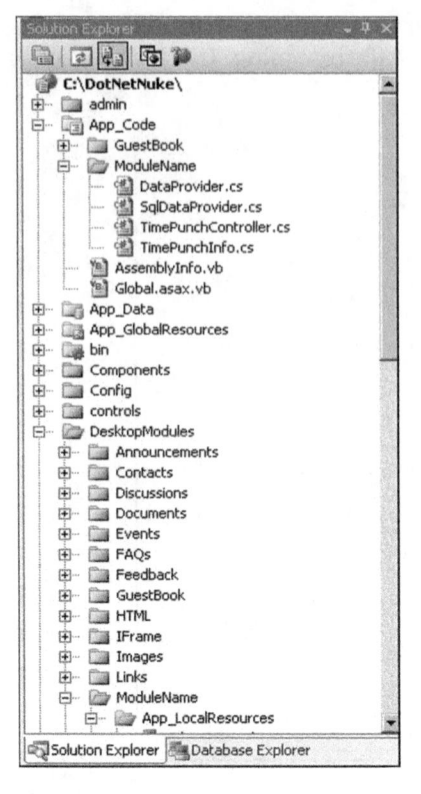

Figure 7-4. *Correct placement of the ModuleName nodes*

Rename both of these "TimePunch."

Since you are writing this module in C# rather than VB, you need to make one other change. In your `web.config` file for this project, you will find the following commented-out XML code:

```
<!-- register your app_code subfolders to generate granular assemblies
during compilation
    <codeSubDirectories>
       <add directoryName="sub-directory name"/>
    </codeSubDirectories>
    -->
```

Remove the comments and change the directory name to `TimePunch`, as shown following:

```
<!-- register your app_code subfolders to generate granular
        assemblies during compilation -->
<codeSubDirectories>
   <add directoryName="TimePunch"/>
</codeSubDirectories>
```

The DNN framework is written in VB. You need to tell VWD that there may be other languages in this subdirectory. This element tells VWD to compile the code in this subdirectory at run time.

It has been estimated that using the module templates to create DNN modules reduces the code you have to write by 70 percent. If you wanted to write a module in DNN 3.x, you needed other tools such as CodeSmith to help write the code for you. Not so any more. One of the tougher tasks was to write the code to set up tables and stored procedures. DNN 4.x writes all this code for you now. You just need to run it.

Creating Tables

Creating the tables requires you to log into your website as the host.

Build your website by clicking the Build ➤ Web Site menu choice. It should build with no errors. Now start the website by pressing Ctrl+F5. Log in as the host of this site.

You should notice a new Host choice on the menu bar. Click this and choose SQL. You should get a blank SQL page like the one shown in Figure 7-5.

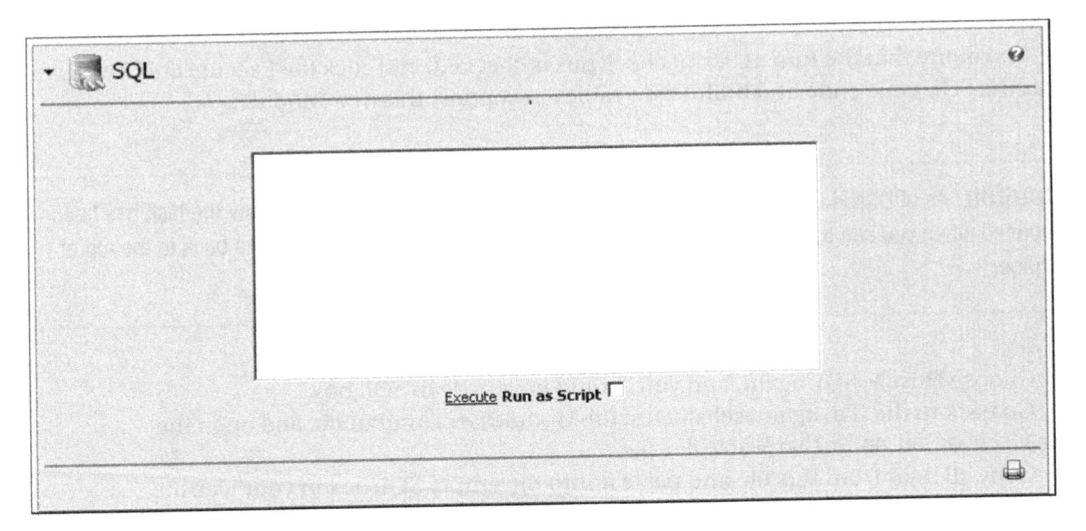

Figure 7-5. *The blank SQL page*

This page is given to you by DNN as a way to execute SQL scripts. The SQL code is also given to you. You just need to find it and copy it in here.

In the Solution Explorer, choose DesktopModules ➤ TimePunch, and double-click the `TimePunch.SqlDataProvider` file. This will open it in the IDE.

If you aren't familiar with SQL table definitions, then this code will be ugly and scary for you. Don't worry, though. It does actually make sense. Since you will make changes to this code later, I will explain it then.

Press Ctrl+A to select all lines in this file, and press Ctrl+C to copy it.

Go back to your SQL page on the website, and press Ctrl+V inside the text window to paste all the code in here. Figure 7-6 shows this.

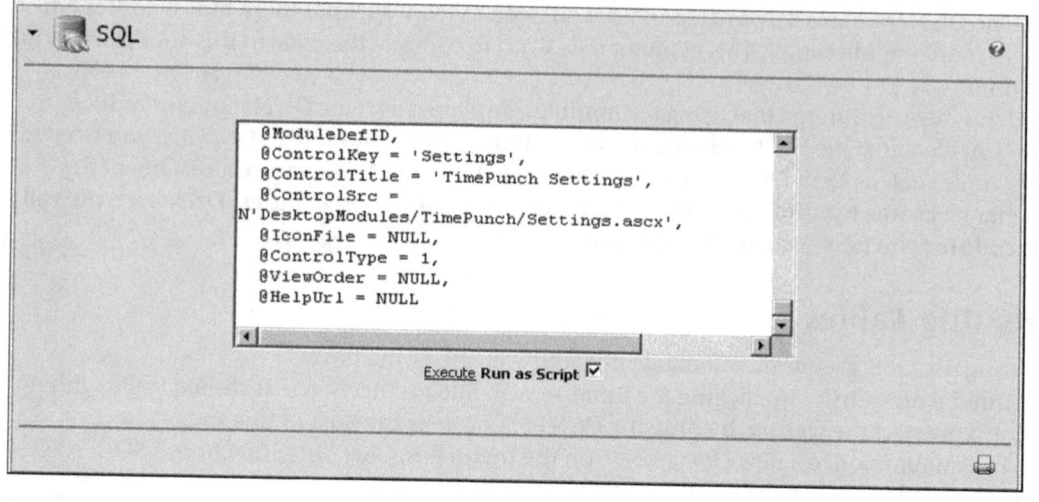

```
    @ModuleDefID,
    @ControlKey = 'Settings',
    @ControlTitle = 'TimePunch Settings',
    @ControlSrc =
N'DesktopModules/TimePunch/Settings.ascx',
    @IconFile = NULL,
    @ControlType = 1,
    @ViewOrder = NULL,
    @HelpUrl = NULL
```

Figure 7-6. *Pasting SQL code into the text window*

Make sure that the Run as Script check box is checked, and click the Execute link. This exe-cutes the SQL table code and builds new tables to support this new module.

■**Caution** As of DNN 4.01, there is no "Completed" message for this task. You know the task has been completed when you see the text in the box "jump." Essentially, the vertical slider goes back to the top of the page.

Choose Host ➤ SQL again, and you should have a clean SQL box.

Go back to the IDE again, select DesktopModules ➤ TimePunch, and open the TimePunch.01.00.00.SqlDataProvider file.

Copy all lines from this file and paste it into the empty SQL box in your website.

Select Run as Script, and execute the SQL code.

Viewing the SQL Results

Now you can go back to your IDE and see what happened. In the Solution Explorer window, click Database Explorer (you may have to double-click the database.mdf file first). Open up the Tables node, and you should see the table YourCompany_TimePunch, as shown in Figure 7-7.

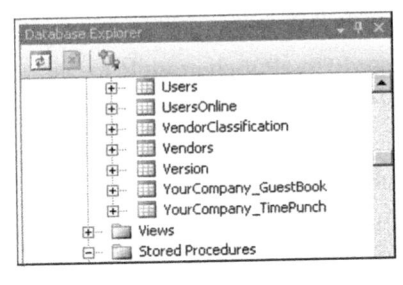

Figure 7-7. *The new table in the Database Explorer*

Scroll down a little more and expand the Stored Procedures node. You should have five new TimePunch stored procedures, as shown in Figure 7-8.

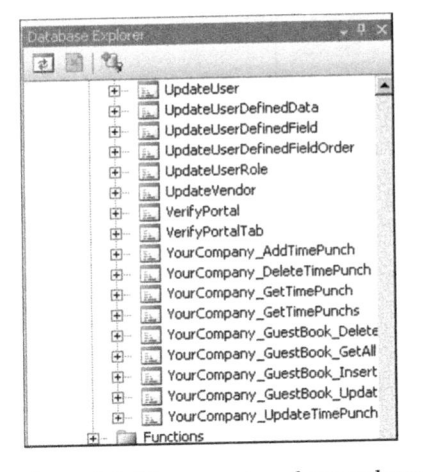

Figure 7-8. *The new stored procedures*

The procedures are as follows:

- YourCompany_AddTimePunch

- YourCompany_DeleteTimePunch

- YourCompany_GetTimePunch

- YourCompany_GetTimePunchs

- YourCompany_UpdateTimePunch

Starting the Module

Click the Time choice from the menu bar. Add the newly created TimePunch module to the content pane. Make the title say "Time." Your website should look like Figure 7-9.

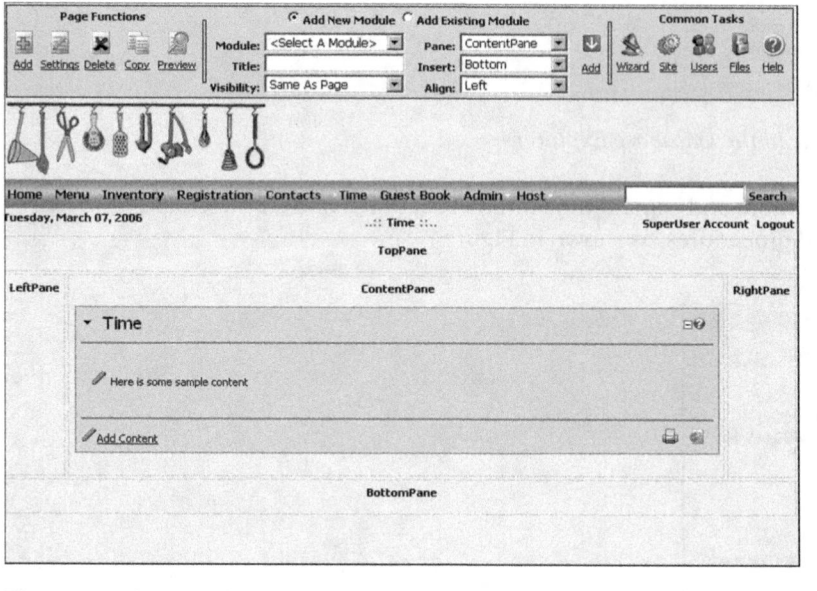

Figure 7-9. *The completed module*

This is amazingly fast for an out-of-the-box solution. Do this a few times, and you should be able to whip up a new module in a couple of minutes.

What Did You Do?

Because this was pretty fast, I did gloss over a few things. You are probably wondering if the next steps are harder or easier than this. After all, you need to add quite a bit of content to this module. Unfortunately, it does get harder and will require some programming, but nothing you have not seen.

In order to understand what you just did, you need to understand the structure of a DNN module.

First of all, a DNN module can be thought of as a small program within the larger web program. It can talk to the mother program, but it is completely self-contained.

Figure 7-10 shows the program structure of a DNN module.

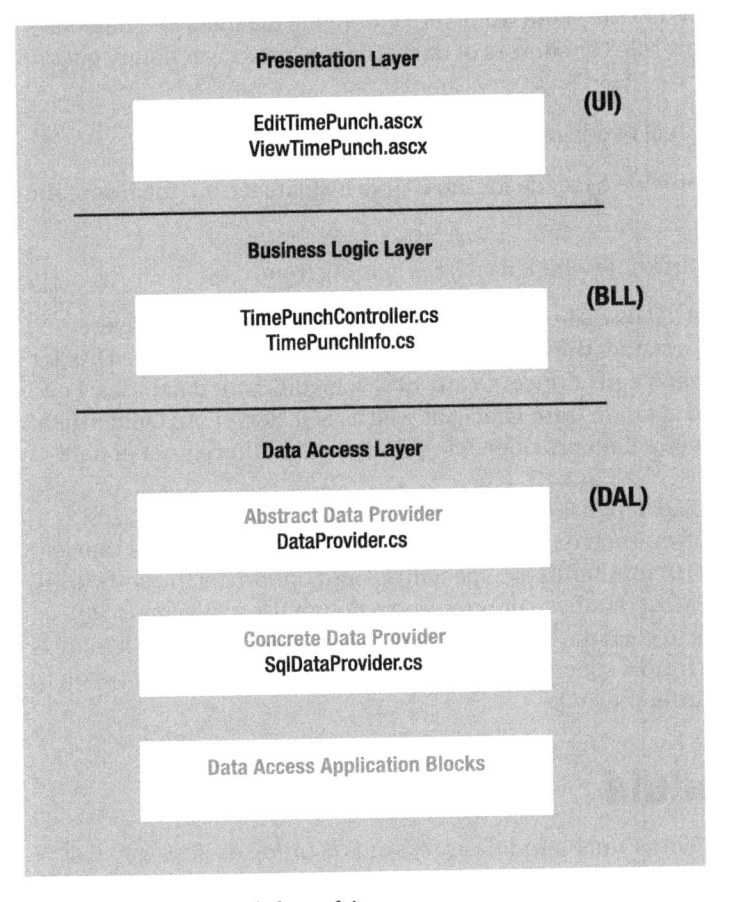

Figure 7-10. *DNN module architecture*

The code for the presentation (UI or GUI) layer is in the DesktopModules ➤ TimePunch section of the Solution Explorer.

The code for the business logic layer (BLL) and the data access layer (DAL) is in the App_Code ➤ TimePunch section of the Solution Explorer.

Figure 7-10 shows the typical n-tier architectural model. In this case, it is really three tiers with some further abstractions in the database layer.

The theory for the GUI layer goes like this:

- Do not put business code in the GUI layer.

- The presentation layer should only include code that the customer will end up seeing.

- It is OK to put validation code in the GUI as long as it is not business validation.

- The GUI should have no idea where its information is coming from.

A good presentation layer can stay the same while the underlying business and database code changes to accommodate new rules or sources of data. The business layer theory goes like this:

- No GUI presentation code shall reside in the business layer.

- The business layer should provide a façade for the GUI to insulate it from the rest of the program.

- The business layer should not know where its data is coming from.

The business layer can change all its code internally without affecting the GUI layer.

The database layer is there to abstract the data from the BLL. The reason that the DAL for DNN can have three layers is so that it can connect to any of several different databases. For instance, DNN can connect to and get data from Oracle as well as SQL Server. An Oracle data provider will need a different concrete data provider, which will need a different set of data access application blocks.

You may have heard that the SQL language is generic and that all modern databases understand it. True enough. However, each database has a subset of SQL commands that is specific to that database. These SQL commands are specialized and optimized to get the best performance out of the database. Most database programmers do not use just generic SQL commands and stored procedures to get data. The emphasis is always on speed, and if there is a better and faster way to get data from a specific database, they will use it. DNN allows you to do this with the different layers within the DAL.

Enhancing the Module

You would have to agree that this TimePunch module as it stands is pretty useless. You will need to make some changes. These changes will be made from the bottom up. Changing the GUI will be the dessert.

The Database Layer

While crawling the Web and looking for examples of module creation in DNN, I found the same theme over and over again. Basically every article said "replace all your existing code with this code shown here." The article would then tell me to fire up DNN and my module would magically appear the same way it looked in the article.

I find this approach useless. You end up with a module that does only what the creators want it to do. To my mind, you need to know what you have and how to change it to meet your needs. A cut-and-replace technique teaches you nothing. Hopefully, my approach will teach you something.

The Database Fields

Before you go about changing anything, let's look at what is needed for saved data. Remember that the WebPunch program did several things:

- It allowed a person to punch in.

- It allowed a person to punch out.

- It showed past data.

The fact that it showed past data for last week and this week is irrelevant to the data. This is a task for the GUI.

It seems to me that you need a table with only three fields for this TimePunch module. These fields are as follows:

- Date and time of day

- Type of punch (in or out)

- Person identifier (same as login name and ID)

You could actually get away without the punch type. You will add it, though, to make enhancing this module easier later. When you boil the functionality of the WebPunch program down to its data, there really is not much here. This is a good thing.

■**Caution** Once you start altering this module, it will not work anymore in your DNN website until you finish all the steps. I suggest you read through the alteration steps thoroughly before starting, so you know what to expect.

Do the following four database-related steps in the order that they're presented, and you won't get into trouble. It involves some SQL code and table setup, all of which will be explained.

Changing the Database Table

Using the Database Explorer in the IDE, scroll down to the YourCompany_TimePunch table. Double-click this table and you should get a table editor in the IDE. This is shown in Figure 7-11.

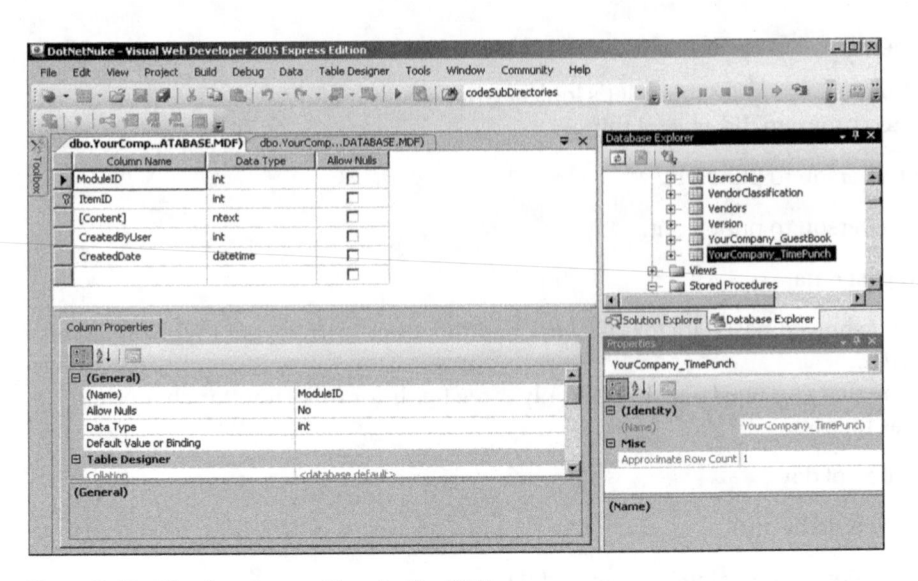

Figure 7-11. *The database editor in the IDE*

I could have you delete this table, add some more code to the SQL page in the website, and execute it—and then you would be done. But where's the learning in that? Using the IDE tools to change a table is easier to me.

In addition to the few data items you need for tracking punches, you also need a couple of identifiers.

DNN allows you to put a module in any pane on any page as many times as you like. You will need to keep track of which module you are working with so that data from one module does not appear in another of the same type. This is accomplished with the ModuleID field. Leave this field alone. (It is OK to allow nulls.)

You will also need an ID that distinguishes one row from another. The ItemID value is automatically incremented when a new row is added. Since this is also the primary key, there cannot be any duplicates of this field. Therefore, every row will be unique, which is what you want.

You will need to change the table as follows:

- Delete the [Content] field.

- Rename the CreatedByUser field to Punch_User, and check the Allow Nulls check box.

- Rename the CreatedDate field to Punch_Date, and check the Allow Nulls check box.

- Add a new field, name it Punch_Type, give it a data type of int, and check the Allow Nulls check box.

Save the table. Your new table definition should look like that shown in Figure 7-12.

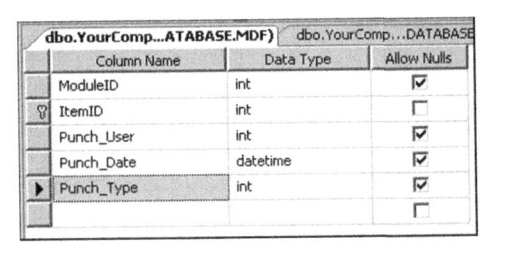

Figure 7-12. *New database definition*

Well, that did it. You've now just broken everything. Don't worry, though, as the next steps will fix things.

Changing the Database Stored Procedures

Modern databases have the capability of running small database-specific programs. These programs are called *stored procedures*.

A stored procedure allows you to offload some of the work of the business and database layers onto the database itself. Stored procedures can do all kinds of validation, perform refer- ential integrity checks, and collate data from many different tables into one data set. (Also, if your database is on another computer, your stored procedures could run on the other com- puter to free up resources.) Without stored procedures, you would need to do all this by hand in your code.

Stored procedures can also be database specific. For example, if you support both Oracle and SQL server databases, the stored procedures for each would have the same names and arguments, but they would be written differently to take advantage of the peculiarities of each database.

DNN makes extensive use of stored procedures and so will you. You already created some back in step 1 when you copied some code to the SQL window and executed it.

Inside the Solution Explorer, click the Stored Procedures folder and choose YourCompany_[xxx]. You will find the five stored procedures here that were mentioned previously:

- `YourCompany_AddTimePunch`

- `YourCompany_DeleteTimePunch`

- `YourCompany_GetTimePunch`

- `YourCompany_GetTimePunchs`

- `YourCompany_UpdateTimePunch`

Note You can change the names of the database and these stored procedures if you like. I kept them as they were so that you could find them easily in the Solution Explorer.

Before you start, here is a greatly oversimplified SQL primer:

- If you want to add a record, use the insert statement.

- If you want to get a record, use the select statement.

- If you want to delete a record, use the delete statement.

- If you want to update a record, use the update statement.

That is SQL in a nutshell.

YourCompany_AddTimePunch

Let's start with adding a time punch to the database. In SQL, adding a row to a table is done with the insert statement.

Double-click the YourCompany_AddTimePunch stored procedure. The code for this will appear in the IDE, as shown in Figure 7-13.

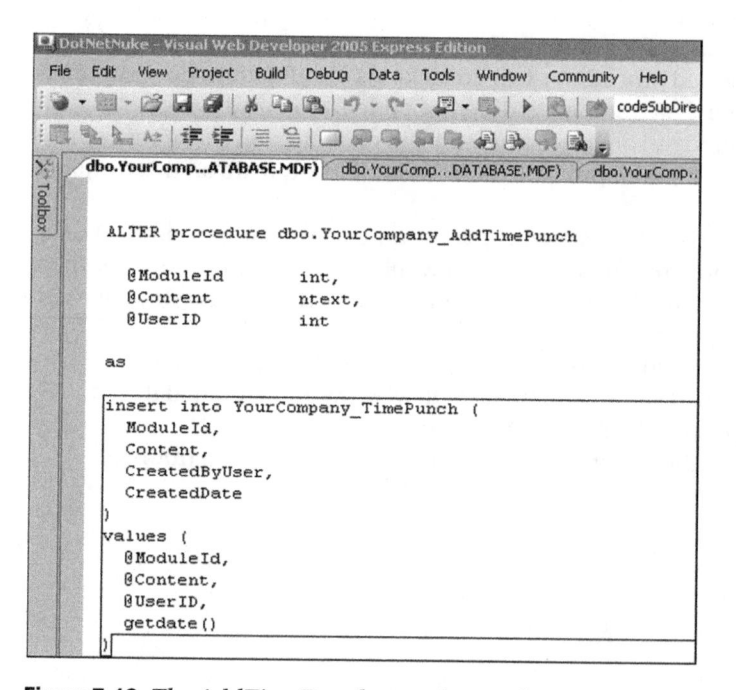

Figure 7-13. *The AddTimePunch stored procedure*

As far as stored procedures go, this one is easy. You can see that it inserts a new row into the YourCompany_TimePunch table. The stored procedure takes three arguments, as shown above the blue box in Figure 7-13.

Note, however, that this stored procedure was created for the database before you altered it. You need to synchronize this procedure with the database fields you now have.

First of all, you no longer have a content field. Second, you have to change the names of some of the other fields. Here is what the new stored procedure should look like:

```
ALTER procedure dbo.YourCompany_AddTimePunch

        @ModuleId       int,
        @PunchType      int,
        @UserID         int

as

insert into YourCompany_TimePunch (
    ModuleId,
    Punch_Type,
    Punch_User,
    Punch_Date
)
values (
    @ModuleId,
    @PunchType,
    @UserID,
    getdate()
)
```

For this code, I have used the new column names. I have also used the capability of the stored procedure to get the date for me, rather than figuring it out myself and passing it as an argument into the procedure. The YourCompany_AddTimePunch function will be called as soon as someone clicks the Punch button on the main screen. There will be no appreciable time lag.

Save the stored procedure. If you get an error while saving the stored procedure, it could be because you forgot to save the changes to the table. If so, go back and save the table, and then come back here and save this stored procedure.

YourCompany_DeleteTimePunch

Open the YourCompany_DeleteTimePunch stored procedure in the IDE. The code for this is as follows:

```
ALTER procedure dbo.YourCompany_DeleteTimePunch

        @ModuleId       int,
        @ItemId         int

as

delete
from    YourCompany_TimePunch
where   ModuleId = @ModuleId
and     ItemId = @ItemId
```

I said that the ItemID field is unique to the database. The ModuleID is unique to your module. The combination of them easily finds the row to delete. You can read this stored procedure and easily understand what it is doing.

You did not change the ItemID or ModuleID names, so this stored procedure stays as it is.

YourCompany_GetTimePunch

Open the YourCompany_GetTimePunch stored procedure in the IDE. The code for this is as follows:

```
ALTER procedure dbo.YourCompany_GetTimePunch

        @ModuleId int,
        @ItemId int

as

select ModuleId,
       ItemId,
       Content,
       CreatedByUser,
       CreatedDate,
       'CreatedByUserName' = Users.FirstName + ' ' + Users.LastName
from YourCompany_TimePunch
inner join Users on YourCompany_TimePunch.CreatedByUser = Users.UserId
where  ModuleId = @ModuleId
and ItemId = @ItemId
```

In SQL, data is retrieved via select statements. What you are doing is selecting which columns from a table will be given back to the calling function. In this case, the stored procedure is taking columns from two tables and combining them before giving back the data. It is doing an inner join, in which it takes the UserID it finds in the TimePunch table and looks inside the Users table for the name that corresponds to this ID. The Users table is where DNN stores its user data. This is cool stuff.

Unfortunately for us, this procedure must be changed, as it references columns that no longer exist. The altered code is shown following, in bold:

```
ALTER procedure dbo.YourCompany_GetTimePunch

  @ModuleId int,
  @ItemId int
```

```
as

select ModuleId,
       ItemId,
       Punch_Type,
       Punch_User,
       Punch_Date,
       'Punch_UserName' = Users.FirstName + ' ' + Users.LastName
from YourCompany_TimePunch
inner join Users on YourCompany_TimePunch.Punch_User = Users.UserId
where  ModuleId = @ModuleId
and ItemId = @ItemId
```

Save this procedure. I kept the code the same; I just changed the names of the columns being used. Is this stuff about stored procedures and SQL starting to make any sense yet? Just think of it as another programming language—one designed to access relational databases.

YourCompany_GetTimePunchs

OK, so you may be asking "What's with the *s* at the end of this stored procedure name?" This does not have the ItemID passed in as an argument. It is also not searching for records based on the ItemID. Since it is the ItemID that makes the row unique, you will get *all* punches for all people entered in through this ModuleID—hence the *s*.

The code for this is as follows:

```
ALTER procedure dbo.YourCompany_GetTimePunchs

    @ModuleId int

as

select ModuleId,
       ItemId,
       Content,
       CreatedByUser,
       CreatedDate,
       'CreatedByUserName' = Users.FirstName + ' ' + Users.LastName
from YourCompany_TimePunch
inner join Users on YourCompany_TimePunch.CreatedByUser = Users.UserId
where  ModuleId = @ModuleId
```

Forgetting for a moment about the wrong field names, you do not want to get all punches for everyone. The TimePunch module will show data only for one person. While the code can get all the punches and troll through them to weed out what you want, it is best to let the database handle this. You need another qualifier to further filter the result. This qualifier will be the UserID. Here is the stored procedure, with the new code in bold:

```
ALTER procedure dbo.YourCompany_GetTimePunchs

    @ModuleId int,
    @UserId int

as

select ModuleId,
       Punch_User,
       Punch_Type,
       Punch_Date,
       'Punch_UserName' = Users.FirstName + ' ' + Users.LastName
from YourCompany_TimePunch
inner join Users on YourCompany_TimePunch.Punch_User = Users.UserId
where  ModuleId = @ModuleId
and Punch_User = @UserId
```

Notice that the extra qualifier with an and logical operator has been added at the end of this SQL statement. The result will now be filtered by the ItemID and the Punch_User value.

Note While this stored procedure will get you what you need, it may still be too generic. Since the time card looks at a week at a time, perhaps it would be best to add another stored procedure that gets punches for a particular user, but during a date span. This further reduces the data you return, and consequently reduces the code you need to write for searching for what you want. I leave this exercise up to you.

Save this stored procedure.

YourCompany_UpdateTimePunch

This is the last stored procedure you will need for this module. In fact, you may not ever use it. This procedure updates an existing record. Right now, the TimePunch screen will not allow you to do that. However, it would be a simple matter to add correction capability to the screen, at which point this procedure comes into play.

Open the YourCompany_UpdateTimePunch stored procedure in the IDE. The code for this is as follows:

```
ALTER procedure dbo.YourCompany_UpdateTimePunch

    @ModuleId       int,
    @ItemId         int,
    @Content        ntext,
    @UserID         int

as

update YourCompany_TimePunch
set    Content       = @Content,
       CreatedByUser = @UserID,
       CreatedDate   = getdate()
where  ModuleId = @ModuleId
and    ItemId = @ItemId
```

The key word in this procedure is the SQL update. Change the code so it looks like the one that follows (the new code is in bold):

```
ALTER procedure dbo.YourCompany_UpdateTimePunch

    @ModuleId       int,
    @ItemId         int,
    @Punch_User     int,
    @Punch_Type     int,
    @Punch_Date     datetime

as

update YourCompany_TimePunch
set    Punch_User    = @Punch_User,
       Punch_Type    = @Punch_Type,
       Punch_Date    = @Punch_Date
where  ModuleId = @ModuleId
and    ItemId = @ItemId
```

Since part of doing a correction is altering the time punched in or out, I did not let the stored procedure automatically figure this one out. The punch time is passed in.

Save this procedure.

Note   The stored procedures as they are used in this module provide a level of abstraction from the database. You will not be using any SQL statements in the code to access the data directly.

Changing the Concrete Data Provider

You are now all done with the database table and the stored procedures. Once you slow down and think about it, you'll realize that this isn't really hard at all.

Now that the stored procedures are changed, it is time to change how they are called. Don't forget, you are still in the database layer (as shown in Figure 7-10).

In the Solution Explorer, scroll back up and open the SqlDataProvider.cs file. This is shown in Figure 7-14.

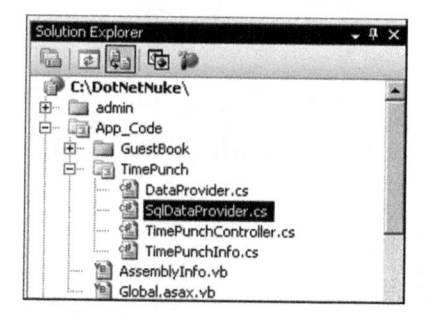

Figure 7-14. *The file containing the database layer section*

This code has methods that call the stored procedures you just modified. Since you modified many of the arguments, you will need to change this file.

The part of the file you need to change is in the Public Methods region. The code is shown in Listing 7-1.

Listing 7-1. *SqlDataProvider code*

```
#region Public Methods

public override void AddTimePunch(int ModuleId, string Content, int UserID)
{
  SqlHelper.ExecuteNonQuery(ConnectionString,
                            GetFullyQualifiedName("AddTimePunch"),
                                                  ModuleId,
                                                  Content,
                                                  UserID);
}
```

```
public override void DeleteTimePunch(int ModuleId, int ItemId)
{
  SqlHelper.ExecuteNonQuery(ConnectionString,
                      GetFullyQualifiedName("DeleteTimePunch"),
                                            ModuleId,
                                            ItemId);
}

public override IDataReader GetTimePunch(int ModuleId, int ItemId)
{
  return (IDataReader)SqlHelper.ExecuteReader(ConnectionString,
                      GetFullyQualifiedName("GetTimePunch"),
                                            ModuleId,
                                            ItemId);
}

public override IDataReader GetTimePunchs(int ModuleId)
{
  return (IDataReader)SqlHelper.ExecuteReader(ConnectionString,
                      GetFullyQualifiedName("GetTimePunchs"),
                                            ModuleId);
}

public override void UpdateTimePunch(int ModuleId, int ItemId,
                               string Content, int UserID)
{
  SqlHelper.ExecuteNonQuery(ConnectionString,
                      GetFullyQualifiedName("UpdateTimePunch"),
                                            ModuleId,
                                            ItemId,
                                            Content,
                                            UserID);
}

#endregion
```

Notice that each of these methods mimics the stored procedures you just edited. Look back at the stored procedures and see what the arguments were. You will need to change the arguments as they are presented here accordingly.

Note Each of these methods calls the GetFullyQualifiedName method. This just adds the prefix YourCompany_ to the table name. If you want to change the table name or the names of the stored procedures, you also need to change this GetFullyQualifiedName to prefix whatever you want. If you ever plan to make a module for distribution, I would suggest using a prefix of your company's real name just to avoid name clashes with other modules.

AddTimePunch

The AddTimePunch method calls the YourCompany_AddTimePunch stored procedure. If you remember, the stored procedure takes the following arguments:

- ItemID as an int

- Punch_Type as an int

- Punch_User as an int

The Punch_Date is calculated by the stored procedure itself.

The argument data types being passed in by the AddTimePunch method are (integer, string, integer). Since you need to pass in all integers, you need to change some data types, as well as the names of the arguments to better reflect what you are passing in. Here is the new AddTimePunch method, which correctly calls the YourCompany_AddTimePunch stored procedure:

```
public override void AddTimePunch(int ModuleId, int PunchType, int PunchUserID)
{
    SqlHelper.ExecuteNonQuery(ConnectionString,
                        GetFullyQualifiedName("AddTimePunch"),
                                    ModuleId,
                                    PunchType,
                                    PunchUserID);
}
```

I changed the content argument being passed into this method from a String to an Integer, and I also changed its name so you know what it means. I also changed the arguments getting passed to the stored procedure.

DeleteTimePunch

The DeleteTimePunch method calls the YourCompany_DeleteTimePunch stored procedure. You will need to look at the stored procedure and see if you need to adjust this method to correctly call it.

Just as you did not change the stored procedure, you do not need to change this method. Leave it as is.

GetTimePunch

The GetTimePunch method calls the YourCompany_GetTimePunch stored procedure. Before you go on, look at the stored procedure and see if you need to adjust this method to correctly call it (the answer follows).

This method, as it stands, gets a punch based on the ItemID and the ModuleID. These two columns make the row unique. If you know the ItemID, then there is no need to change this method. Leave it as is.

GetTimePunchs

This method calls the YourCompany_GetTimePunchs stored procedure. The stored procedure was changed to filter the punches by person. You need to change this method to reflect that. Here is the new GetTimePunchs code:

```
public override IDataReader GetTimePunchs(int ModuleId, int PunchUserID)
{
  return (IDataReader)SqlHelper.ExecuteReader(ConnectionString,
                          GetFullyQualifiedName("GetTimePunchs"),
                                              ModuleId,
                                              PunchUserID);
}
```

All I did here was add the extra qualifier of the PunchUserID. This allows the return of only the punches related to the user I am interested in.

UpdateTimePunch

This method calls the YourCompany_UpdateTimePunch stored procedure. The stored procedure was changed quite a bit to reflect the changes in the table. You need to look at the stored procedure and decide what to change here.

In this case, you are passing in every field. The new code for the UpdateTimePunch method is shown following. Note the changes to the method signature as well as the changes to the argument passed into the stored procedure.

```
public override void UpdateTimePunch(int ModuleId,
                                     int ItemId,
                                     int PunchUser,
                                     int PunchType,
                                     DateTime PunchDate)
{
  SqlHelper.ExecuteNonQuery(ConnectionString,
                          GetFullyQualifiedName("UpdateTimePunch"),
                                              ModuleId,
                                              ItemId,
                                              PunchUser,
                                              PunchType,
                                              PunchDate);
}
```

That is all for this SqlDataProvider.cs file. The next file to change is the one that calls these methods. You will need to make sure that all the arguments are correct. The next file is the abstract data provider.

Changing the Abstract Data Provider

The abstract data provider is the DataProvider.cs file. In the Solution Explorer, scroll up until you find this file. It is shown in Figure 7-15.

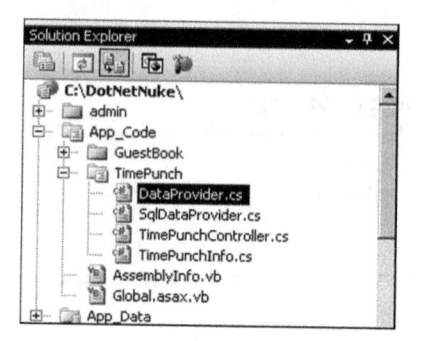

Figure 7-15. *Editing the DataProvider.cs file*

The abstract data provider includes some—you guessed it—abstract methods. These abstract methods are just blueprints for whatever class derives from this one.

The definition of the SqlDataProvider class is this:

```csharp
public class SqlDataProvider : DataProvider
{

    public override void AddTimePunch(int ModuleId, int PunchType, int PunchUserID)
    {
        ...
    }


    public override void DeleteTimePunch(int ModuleId, int ItemId)
    {
        ...
    }


    public override IDataReader GetTimePunch(int ModuleId, int ItemId)
    {
        ...
    }


    public override IDataReader GetTimePunchs(int ModuleId, int PunchUserID)
    {
        ...
    }
```

```
public override void UpdateTimePunch(int ModuleId,
                                     int ItemId,
                                     int PunchUser,
                                     int PunchType,
                                     DateTime PunchDate)
    {
      ...
    }

}
```

This SqlDataProvider class that you just finished editing derives directly from the DataProvider class that you are editing right now. Any abstract methods in the DataProvider class *must* be implemented in the SqlDataProvider class. As you can see, they are implemented using the override modifier. If you were to forget one of these methods, the compiler would complain to you.

If an abstract method in the DataProvider class has a particular signature (name and arguments), then the method that overrides it in the SqlDataProvider class must adhere to it.

Since you changed the overriding methods in the SqlDataProvider class, you must also change the abstract methods in the DataProvider class. The new code for the Abstract Methods region in the DataProvider.cs file is as follows:

```
#region Abstract Methods

public abstract void AddTimePunch(int ModuleId,
                                  int PunchType,
                                  int PunchUserID);
public abstract IDataReader GetTimePunch(int ModuleId,
                                         int ItemId);
public abstract IDataReader GetTimePunchs(int ModuleId,
                                          int PunchUserID);
public abstract void UpdateTimePunch(int ModuleId,
                                     int ItemId,
                                     int PunchUser,
                                     int PunchType,
                                     DateTime PunchDate);
public abstract void DeleteTimePunch(int ModuleId,
                                     int ItemId);


#endregion
```

The abstract methods of the DataProvider.cs file now match the overridden implementations in the SqlDataProvider.cs file.

You are now done with the DAL and you can check that off your list. You can now move up the data chain to the BLL.

The Business Logic Layer

The BLL contains the code that does all the calculations and work for the module. Your TimePunch module is pretty simple as far as any complicated calculations go.

The files you will be editing in this section are TimePunchInfo.cs and TimePunchController.cs.

Editing TimePunchInfo.cs

This file contains a single class that holds the information for any particular time punch record. As such, it needs to have private variables that correspond with the columns in the database table, and public methods that expose those variables.

Let's start with changing the private variables. Here is the section as it stands now:

```
#region Private Members

private int _ModuleId;
private int _ItemId;
private string _Content;
private int _CreatedByUser;
private DateTime _CreatedDate;
private string _CreatedByUserName;

#endregion
```

You need to change the last four variables. The new region is shown following, with the changed lines in bold:

```
#region Private Members

private int       _ModuleId;
private int       _ItemId;
private int       _PunchType;
private int       _PunchUserID;
private DateTime  _PunchDate;
private string    _Punch_UserName;

#endregion
```

Now that the private variables have been changed, you need to change the get/set accessors that read and write these variables. They are in the Public Methods region.

The ModuleId and ItemId properties are fine since the variables did not change data type or name. Here is the new method region for the TimePunchInfo.cs file:

```
#region Public Methods

/// <summary>
/// Gets and sets the Module Id
/// </summary>
```

```csharp
public int ModuleId
{
  get { return _ModuleId;  }
  set { _ModuleId = value; }
}

/// <summary>
/// Gets and sets the Item Id
/// </summary>
public int ItemId
{
  get { return _ItemId; }
  set { _ItemId = value; }
}

/// <summary>
/// gets and sets the punch type
/// </summary>
public int PunchType
{
  get { return _PunchType; }
  set { _PunchType = value; }
}

/// <summary>
/// Gets and sets the User Id who Created/Updated the content
/// </summary>
public int PunchUserID
{
  get { return _PunchUserID; }
  set { _PunchUserID = value; }
}

/// <summary>
/// Gets the User name
/// </summary>
public string Punch_UserName
{
  get { return _Punch_UserName; }
}

/// <summary>
/// Gets and sets the Date when punched
/// </summary>
public DateTime PunchDate
```

```
    {
      get { return _PunchDate; }
      set { _PunchDate = value; }
    }
```

#endregion

Notice something missing? I deleted the set accessor from the Punch_UserName property. The username comes from the DNN Users table during a call to the YourCompany_GetTimePunch stored procedure.

There is no way I can send this name back down the line to the database table, so to avoid confusion on the part of the programmer who uses this class, I deleted it.

Static Methods

Before moving on, I want to explain the Shared/Static Methods region of code located in the DataProvider.cs file This region has a private static variable, a static constructor, and a public static accessor method.

So what is all this static stuff? Well, it means different things depending on how it is used.

The code static DataProvider objProvider = null; means that this variable retains its value across all instances of this class.

The static constructor automatically gets called when you use any public method within the class. This is even more special, because it only gets called once: during the very first call to any public method within this class.

So here is an example of what happens if you have a method that calls the Instance method in this DataProvider class:

```
Public void foobar()
{
    DataProvider.Instance().AddTimePunch(...);
    DataProvider.Instance().AddTimePunch(...);
}
```

The first time I call DataProvider.Instance.AddTimePunch, the DataProvider constructor gets called, which in turn calls the CreateProvider method. This in turn instantiates the objProvider member variable to something meaningful. Finally, the AddTimePunch method gets called in the DataProvider class.

The second time I call DataProvider.Instance.AddTimePunch, the constructor does not get called; instead, the now instantiated objProvider member calls the AddTimePunch method directly.

I am a really big fan of static classes. You will find them littered throughout the .NET Framework.

The next file to edit in the BLL is the TimePunchController.cs file.

Editing TimePunchController.cs

This file acts as the interface to the GUI. It abstracts the business and database layers from the GUI.

Since the methods in here call methods in the DataProvider class, the arguments must match. You will need to change each of the public methods in here. The only things that change, though, are the arguments. Here is the new code from within the Public Methods region of TimePunchController.cs:

```
#region Public Methods

/// -----------------------------------------------------------------------
/// <summary>
/// adds an object to the database
/// </summary>
/// <remarks>
/// </remarks>
/// <param name="objTimePunch">The TimePunchInfo object</param>
/// <history>
/// </history>
/// -----------------------------------------------------------------------
public void AddTimePunch(TimePunchInfo objTimePunch)
{
  DataProvider.Instance().AddTimePunch(objTimePunch.ModuleId,
                                       objTimePunch.PunchType,
                                       objTimePunch.PunchUserID);
}


/// -----------------------------------------------------------------------
/// <summary>
/// deletes an object from the database
/// </summary>
/// <remarks>
/// </remarks>
/// <param name="ModuleId">The Id of the module</param>
/// <param name="ItemId">The Id of the item</param>
/// <history>
/// </history>
/// -----------------------------------------------------------------------
public void DeleteTimePunch(int ModuleId, int ItemId)
{
  DataProvider.Instance().DeleteTimePunch(ModuleId, ItemId);
}


/// -----------------------------------------------------------------------
/// <summary>
/// gets an object from the database
/// </summary>
/// <remarks>
/// </remarks>
/// <param name="moduleId">The Id of the module</param>
/// <param name="ItemId">The Id of the item</param>
```

```
/// <history>
/// </history>
/// ------------------------------------------------------------------
public TimePunchInfo GetTimePunch(int ModuleId, int ItemId)
{
  return CBO.FillObject<TimePunchInfo>(DataProvider.Instance().
                                         GetTimePunch(ModuleId, ItemId));

}


/// ------------------------------------------------------------------
/// <summary>
/// gets an object from the database
/// </summary>
/// <remarks>
/// </remarks>
/// <param name="moduleId">The Id of the module</param>
/// <history>
/// </history>
/// ------------------------------------------------------------------
public List<TimePunchInfo> GetTimePunchs(int ModuleId, int PunchUserID)
{
  return CBO.FillCollection<TimePunchInfo>(DataProvider.Instance().
                                         GetTimePunchs(ModuleId,
                                                     PunchUserID));

}


/// ------------------------------------------------------------------
/// <summary>
/// saves an object to the database
/// </summary>
/// <remarks>
/// </remarks>
/// <param name="objTimePunch">The TimePunchInfo object</param>
/// <history>
/// </history>
/// ------------------------------------------------------------------
public void UpdateTimePunch(TimePunchInfo objTimePunch)
{
  DataProvider.Instance().UpdateTimePunch(objTimePunch.ModuleId,
                                       objTimePunch.ItemId,
                                       objTimePunch.PunchUserID,
                                       objTimePunch.PunchType,
                                       objTimePunch.PunchDate);

}

#endregion
```

Read this code carefully. There is not much in here, but it is important. First of all, several of these methods get passed a TimePunchInfo object. You just finished editing this file. All you are doing is transferring the values from the object into the DataProvider calls. You can see this clearly in the UpdateTimePunch method.

There is a piece of code in here that C++ programmers have been looking for in .NET for quite a while. It has to do with something called generics. It was just introduced in .NET 2.0.

Generics describes a way of creating a class, structure, interface, or method that has a placeholder instead of a specific type for the types they use. While this is way out of the scope of this book, I wanted to bring this to your attention since generics are being used here, in the GetTimePunchs method. Here is the generic call:

```
return CBO.FillCollection<TimePunchInfo>(DataProvider.Instance().
                                GetTimePunchs(ModuleId,
                                        PunchUserID));
```

Notice the construct <TimePunchInfo>. This method call is substituting the type TimePunchInfo as the type of the collection.

Extending the TimePunchController Class

Remember that I said the business layer is where you will do any complicated calculations? Well, you need a complicated calculation.

The time card display will only show hours. The database only stores punch times. You need a function that converts punch times to hours worked. You will be transferring the CalculateHours method from the WebPunch program to here when the time comes.

As a final note for this class, there is a region of code in here called Optional Interfaces. Delete the whole section. You will not be using any importing, exporting, or searching functions in this module. Do not be afraid to delete wizard-generated code if it is unnecessary to your module. Remember that DNN created this as a template, adding in code it considers commonly used. It even labeled the region optional for you. Deleting unnecessary code makes the module easier to maintain.

When you delete this optional content, you will also need to delete the namespace references and the inheritance of the class from ISearchable and IPortable. Delete the following two lines of code:

```
using DotNetNuke.Entities.Modules;
using DotNetNuke.Services.Search;
```

Also change this line:

```
public class TimePunchController : ISearchable, IPortable
```

to read like this:

```
public class TimePunchController :
```

The Presentation Layer

This is the fun part. You are getting near the end, and this is where you will be transferring much of the code from the WebPunch project to this one.

The presentation layer consists of the following files:

- Settings.ascx, Settings.ascx.cs, and Settings.ascx.resx

- EditTimePunch.ascx, EditTimePunch.ascx.cs, and EditTimePunch.ascx.resx

- ViewTimePunch.ascx, ViewTimePunch.ascx.cs, and ViewTimePunch.ascx.resx

Each of these types of files contains the user control design (.ascx), the code behind the user control (.ascx.cs), and the localized resource strings (.ascx.resx). The resource files may not be there initially, but will get created when you add a control to the associated form.

The module is not really a web page, but a user control. A user control is a control that you create by extending a single control or by using a bunch of controls together with code and presenting them as a single control.

A user control (.ascx) does not run by itself, but gets put inside a page (.aspx). Note the difference in file extensions.

Editing the Settings Files

Chapter 6 was all about creating a website that had a few pages with different modules. Every time you added a new page, you adjusted the settings for that page. Every time you added a new module, you adjusted the settings for that module.

These module settings included information concerning content and permissions of the module as it pertains to all pages in which the module appears.

When you used the template to create a DNN module, it added capability to change settings specifically for this module.

Do You Need It?

Figure 7-16 shows the settings page for the FAQ module.

If you look at the settings for all the modules you put on all the pages, you will see a similar setup.

As a test, I commented out huge chunks of code in my presentation layer just to get the website to compile again. Once I got it to compile, I brought up the site and clicked the settings for the TimePunch module. Figure 7-17 shows what it looks like.

Notice the TimePunch Settings section at the bottom of the page. When I saw this, I wondered what settings I would put in here. I then looked in the Solution Explorer at all the modules under the DesktopModules section. More than half did not have any settings page.

Thinking about this, I couldn't find anything I would put in here. So to make things easier, you can delete the TimePunch.Settings files, as follows:

- Delete Settings.ascx.cs.

- Delete Settings.ascx.

- Delete Settings.ascx.resx.

Now when I compile my system, I do not get the TimePunch Settings section. When you eventually compile your system, you will not get it either. That was easy!

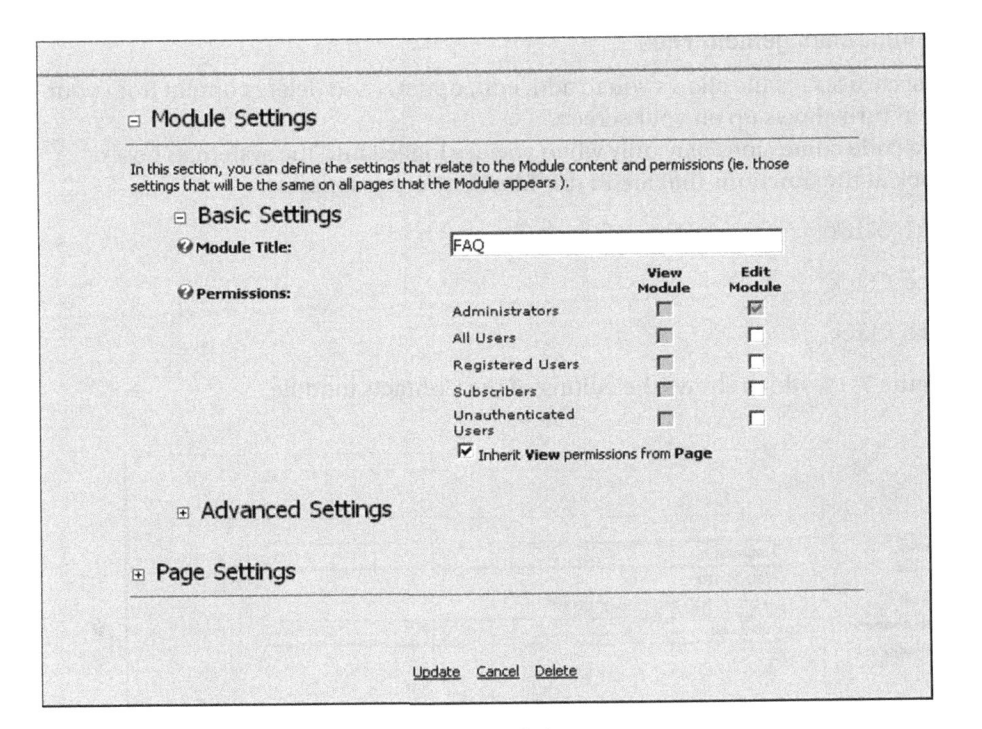

Figure 7-16. *Module settings for the FAQ module*

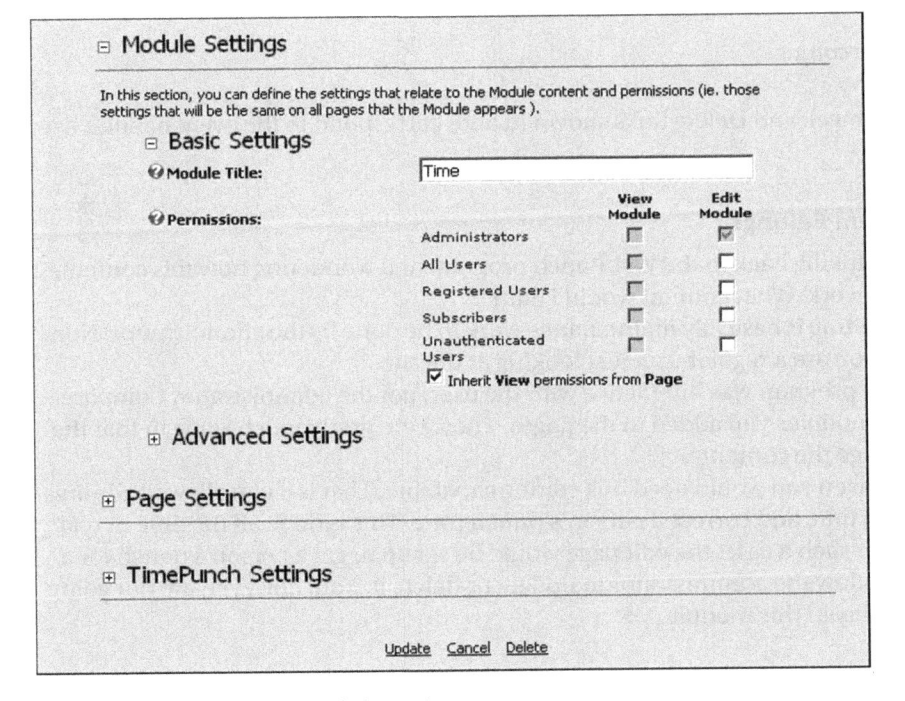

Figure 7-17. *TimePunch module settings*

Editing the Content Management Files

The EditTimePunch.ascx.cs file allows you to add, edit, update, and delete content from your database. This in turn shows up on your screen.

The editing code comes into play only when you are logged into the system as host or admin. Let's look at the functions that are in this file. They are as follows:

- cmdCancel_Click

- cmdDelete_Click

- cmdUpdate_Click

Look at Figure 7-18, which shows the editing of the Contacts module.

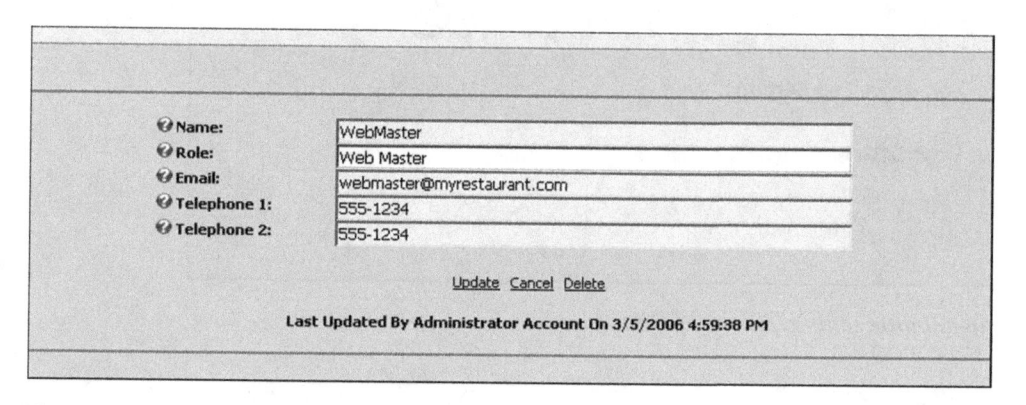

Figure 7-18. *Editing a contact*

The Update, Cancel, and Delete links shown in here correspond to the event handler list just mentioned.

Do You Need Content Editing?

Once again, I am thinking back to the WebPunch program and wondering how this content-editing page would work. What content would I edit?

This content editing is basically maintenance work to be done by the administrator. None of this shows up if you are a regular user just looking at the site.

The WebPunch program was interactive with the user, not the administrator. Compare this with the other modules you added to the pages. They were pretty much static in that the user could not change the content.

There is one reason you would need this editing capability. That is if you allowed administrators to go back in time and correct a person's punch time. This is done all the time in real T&A applications. In such a case, the edit page would be set up to get a person's punch for a particular day and allow the administrator to update or delete it. You, however, are not going to allow this capability in this module.

Tip When all is said and done, feel free to tinker and try allowing editing of previous punch data.

So . . . I'm thinking that this capability isn't needed. However, you cannot get rid of it as easily as deleting the files. Also, you may want it later. So here is what I want you to do.

Edit the `EditTimePunch.ascx` file in source mode. This is the source you should have:

```
<%@ Control Language="C#" Inherits="YourCompany.Modules.TimePunch.EditTimePunch"
  CodeFile="EditTimePunch.ascx.cs" AutoEventWireup="true" %>
<%@ Register TagPrefix="dnn" TagName="Label"
                            Src="~/controls/LabelControl.ascx" %>
<%@ Register TagPrefix="dnn" TagName="TextEditor"
                            Src="~/controls/TextEditor.ascx" %>
<%@ Register TagPrefix="dnn" TagName="Audit"
                            Src="~/controls/ModuleAuditControl.ascx" %>
<table width="650" cellspacing="0" cellpadding="0" border="0" summary="Edit Table">
  <tr valign="top">
    <td class="SubHead" width="125" style="height: 268px">
      <dnn:Label ID="lblContent" runat="server" ControlName="lblContent"
                                        Suffix=":"></dnn:Label>
    </td>
    <td style="height: 268px">
      <dnn:TextEditor ID="txtContent" runat="server" Height="200" Width="500" />
      <asp:RequiredFieldValidator ID="valContent"
        resourcekey="valContent.ErrorMessage"
        ControlToValidate="txtContent" CssClass="NormalRed" Display="Dynamic"
        ErrorMessage="<br>Content is required"
        runat="server" />
    </td>
  </tr>
</table>
<p>
  <asp:LinkButton CssClass="CommandButton" ID="cmdUpdate" OnClick="cmdUpdate_Click"
    resourcekey="cmdUpdate" runat="server" BorderStyle="none" Text="Update">
  </asp:LinkButton> 
  <asp:LinkButton CssClass="CommandButton" ID="cmdCancel" OnClick="cmdCancel_Click"
    resourcekey="cmdCancel" runat="server" BorderStyle="none" Text="Cancel"
    CausesValidation="False">
  </asp:LinkButton> 
  <asp:LinkButton CssClass="CommandButton" ID="cmdDelete" OnClick="cmdDelete_Click"
    resourcekey="cmdDelete" runat="server" BorderStyle="none" Text="Delete"
    CausesValidation="False">
  </asp:LinkButton> 
</p>
<dnn:Audit ID="ctlAudit" runat="server" />
```

Your code may be arranged a little differently, but it is the same code. On this page, you have several DNN controls, including a text editor. This text editor shows on the screen when you are on this page.

I don't really want to get rid of anything on this page, in case I want it later on. What I want to do is disable some controls and let the administrator know that there is nothing to edit on this page. I also only want the Cancel link to show at the bottom of the page.

There is one line of HTML code that I want you to put on this page. It is a `<font>` tag, and it is placed below the `RequiredFieldValidator` control. The code is shown following, with the additional `<font>` tag in bold:

```
...
    <td style="height: 268px">
      <dnn:TextEditor ID="txtContent" runat="server" Height="200" Width="500" />
      <asp:RequiredFieldValidator ID="valContent"
        resourcekey="valContent.ErrorMessage"
        ControlToValidate="txtContent" CssClass="NormalRed" Display="Dynamic"
        ErrorMessage="<br>Content is required"
        runat="server" />
      <font color=red size=5 ><b>There is no content to edit.</b></font>
    </td>
...
```

This is a simple addition to this page, which can easily be removed at a later date if necessary.

Now that you have this page done, you need to edit the code-behind page `EditTimePunch.ascx.cs`. Open this file in the IDE, and do the following:

- Comment out every line in the `cmdDelete_Click` event handler.

- Comment out every line in the `cmdUpdate_Click` event handler.

- Comment out every line in the `Page_Load` event handler.

The `cmdCancel_Click` event handler will stay as it is. You want the user to be able to cancel out of this page.

Add the following bold code to the `Page_Load` event handler:

```
protected void Page_Load(System.Object sender, System.EventArgs e)
{

    cmdUpdate.Visible = false;
    cmdDelete.Visible = false;
    ctlAudit.Visible = false;
    txtContent.Visible = false;
```

```
    //try
    //{
          ...
          ...
          ...
}
```

These four lines of code will make the controls on the page invisible. Although you cannot compile your code right now, your page will look like that shown in Figure 7-19.

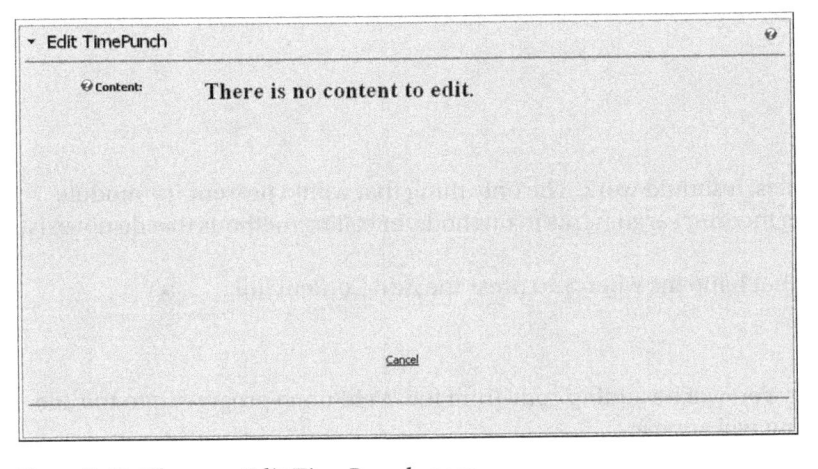

Figure 7-19. *The new Edit TimePunch page*

This should be plain enough. The user can press the Cancel link at the bottom of the page and get back to the main page.

While you did not delete the ASP and C# code files lock, stock, and barrel, you did adjust them so that they fill your needs for now.

The last file to edit is the ViewTimePunch.ascx file.

Editing the Content Display Files

The ViewTimePunch.ascx file will contain most of the code from the WebPunch project. This is the file that shows everything to the user and accepts user input.

The first thing to do here is to comment out all the code in this file. This will allow you to compile the website and see how the TimePunch module looks so far.

Do the following:

- Comment out the code inside the Page_Load event handler (located in the Event Handlers region).

- Comment out the code in the lstContent_ItemDataBound event handler (located in the Event Handlers region).

Since this is the last file you need to edit, commenting out this code should enable the DNN website to compile and run.

Press Ctrl+F5 and see if the module compiles. It should. If it does not, and you cannot easily debug it, I suggest that you take the following code files (available from the Apress website) and replace yours with mine.

- `EditTimePunch.ascx` and `EditTimePunch.ascx.cs`

- `ViewTimePunch.ascx` and `ViewTimePunch.ascx.cs`

- `TimePunchController.cs`

- `TimePunchInfo.cs`

- `DataProvider.cs`

- `SqlDataProvider.cs`

If the module compiles, it should work. The only thing that would prevent the module from compiling is passing incorrect arguments to methods, or calling methods that do not exist anymore.

Figure 7-19 shows what happens when you press the Add Content link.

Adding Content

Now it is time for dessert. You will be adding code from the WebPunch program into this file, and the page that you want will appear.

Open the `ViewTimePunch.ascx` file in source mode. Your screen should look like Figure 7-20.

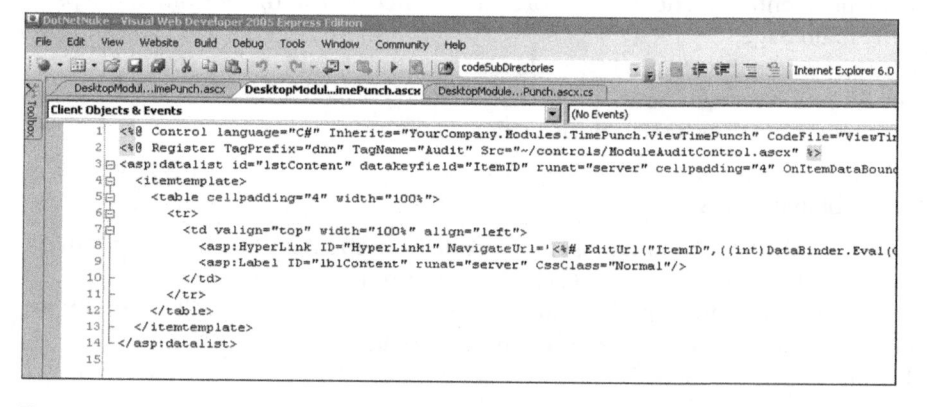

Figure 7-20. *The ViewTimePunch.ascx file, before editing*

Since this page is a control (as evidenced by the first line of code here), there will not be any HTML header or form tags. What you have in here instead is an ASP datalist control. If you are interested in this control, I encourage you to look it up in the help. However, you will not need it, so I won't explain it.

Start up another instance of VWD. You can have as many instances open as you want. In this new instance of VWD, open the WebPunch program. Select everything between the

`<div> </div>` tags, including the tags themselves, and copy this to the clipboard, as shown in Figure 7-21.

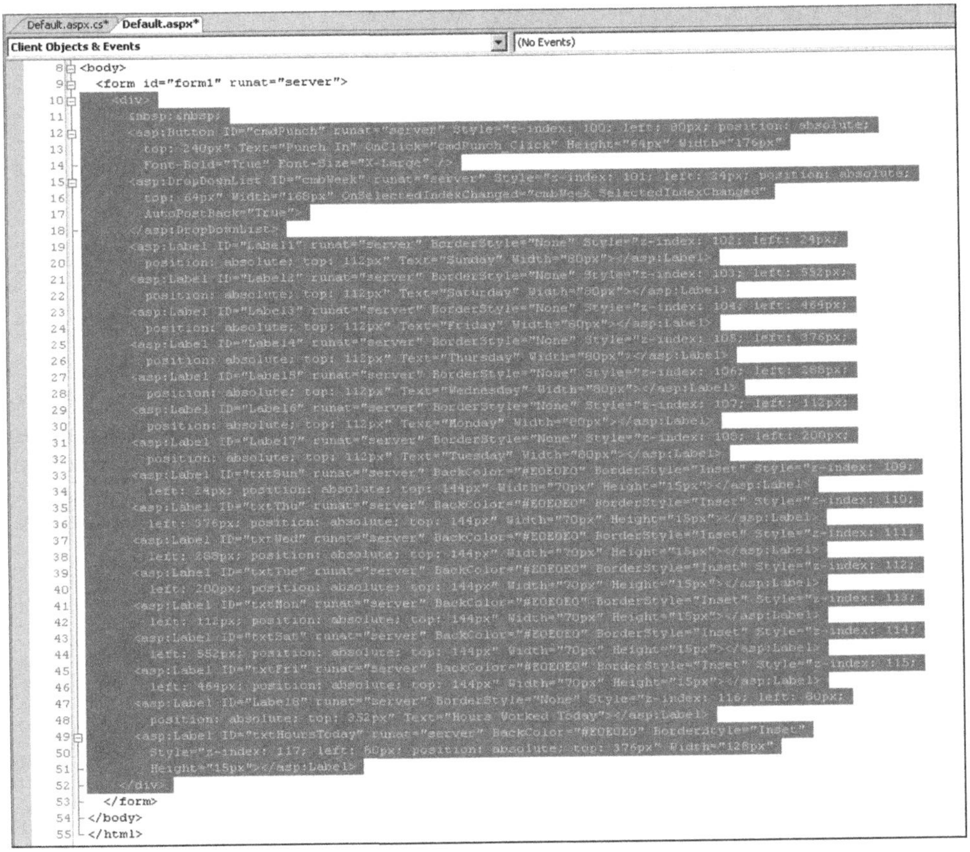

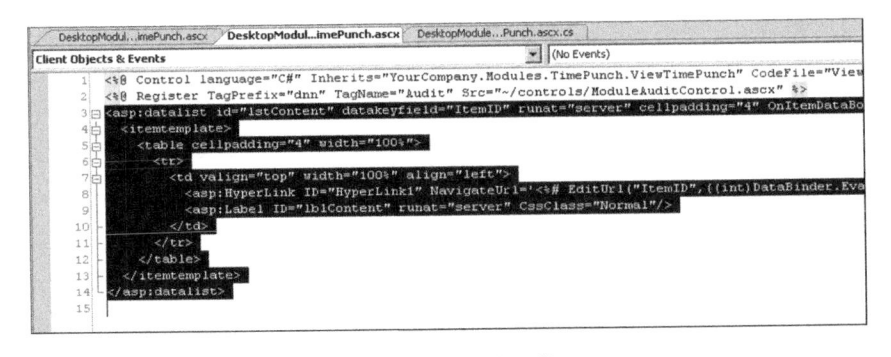

Figure 7-21. *Selecting and copying the WebPunch <div> tag contents to the clipboard*

Now go back to the TimePunch IDE where you have the `ViewTimePunch.ascx` file open in source mode. Select the datalist tags and everything in them, as shown in Figure 7-22.

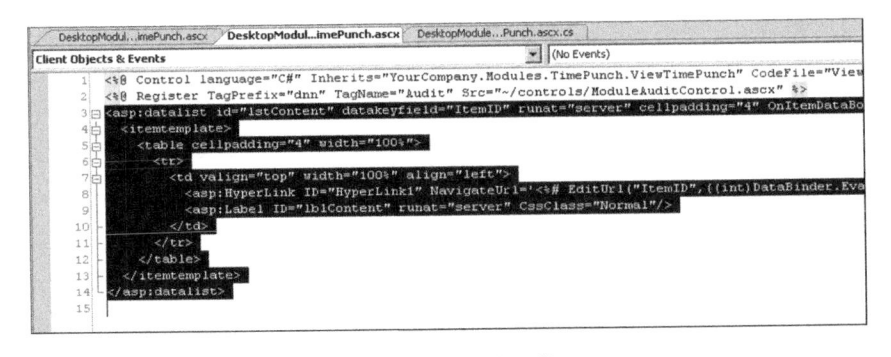

Figure 7-22. *Selecting the ViewTimePunch datalist tags*

Press Ctrl+V to copy the <div> tag information in place of this datalist tag information.

You should now have the design code from the WebPunch program in your TimePunch module.

Inside the ViewTimePunch.ascx.cs C# code file, delete the lstContent_ItemDataBound method. There is no longer any such control to fire this event.

Before you insert the code behind all this design, I want to just stub in the missing event handlers and test the look of the page.

In the ViewTimePunch.ascx.cs file, put the following code:

```
protected void cmdPunch_Click(object sender, EventArgs e)
{
}

protected void cmbWeek_SelectedIndexChanged(object sender, EventArgs e)
{
}
```

Adding this code prevents any compiler errors. Press Ctrl+F5 to build and show the website. Once the website comes up, log in as admin and click the Time menu choice. Your screen should look like the one shown in Figure 7-23.

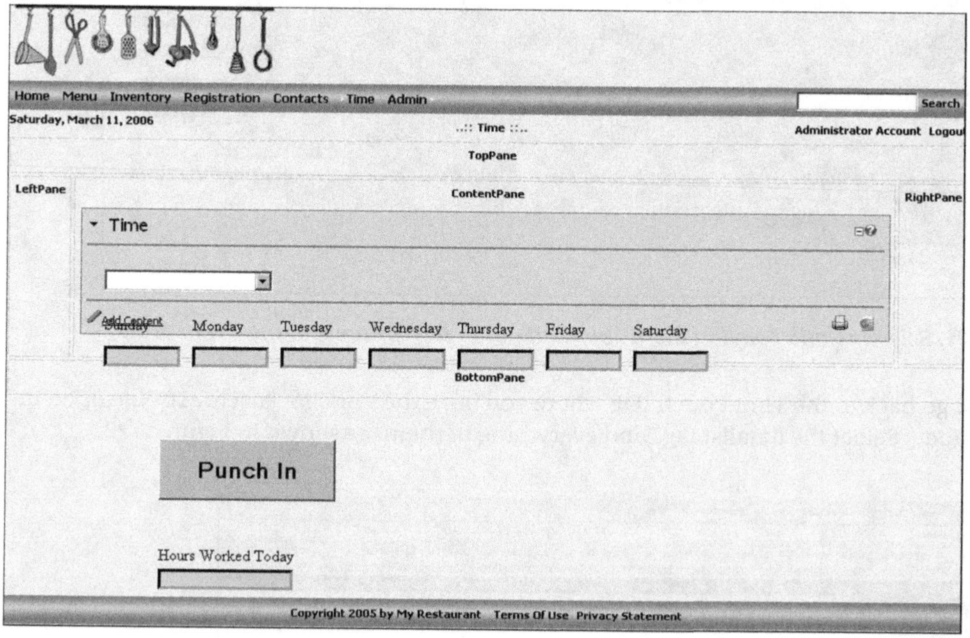

Figure 7-23. *The TimePunch module with WebPunch design code*

Oops! What happened here? Before I tell you, I think you should try to figure it out just from this picture. It looks like the WebPunch controls are not inside the module, but all over the page itself. Resize the browser, and everything moves except these controls. It is almost like they are in a fixed position. Aha! All the controls for the WebPunch program *are* in a fixed position, as evidenced by the position: absolute; style attribute in each control.

I mentioned in a previous chapter that when you are starting to create web pages, it is best to start with absolute positioning. Unfortunately, this has come back to bite you.

The best way to fix this is to use an HTML table within the control and place each of these WebPunch controls within the table's cells.

Creating a Table

An HTML table is a good fit for arranging the controls in the TimePunch module. If it is done right, the controls will move and resize properly according to the control itself.

Now that you've copied all the WebPunch controls over here, I want you to delete them from this page. You will need to add a table and then add the controls one at a time.

Right now, your ViewTimePunch.ascx file should have only these lines in it:

```
<%@ Control Language="C#" Inherits="YourCompany.Modules.TimePunch.ViewTimePunch"
  CodeFile="ViewTimePunch.ascx.cs" AutoEventWireup="true" %>
<%@ Register TagPrefix="dnn" TagName="Audit"
            Src="~/controls/ModuleAuditControl.ascx" %>
```

The table you need will have to have cells to hold each control individually. Since you have six rows of controls, you need at least six rows in the table. By the time you are done, though, you will have added a few more rows just to add some vertical filler space around the Punch button.

There are two ways to add a table to the designer. One is to drag a table control from the toolbox and give it some columns and rows. This has the disadvantage of being a perfect table with an equal number of cells in each row. You do not want this for reasons you will see in a bit. Add the following code to your page:

```
<table id="TimeCard" border=1 width="100%" height="100%">
  <tr width="100%" valign=middle>
  </tr>
</table>
```

This HTML code adds a table whose width and height take up 100 percent of the container. In this case, the container is the module. As the module gets resized, so does the table.

Using a table this way is really the best way to set up a page that can be resized by the user but still keeps the controls relative to each other.

I always start out all tables with a border of 1. This forces the row and column lines to show, and it makes it easier to see how the table is laid out on the page. When I am done, I change the border to 0.

The <tr> tag is a table row. I made this row the same width as its container, which is the table itself. I also made the vertical alignment of controls within this row to be in the middle.

A table row is no good without having some table cells inside of it. So you would think that the table cell tag would be <tc> right? Wrong. It is <td>, which stands for table data.

Add a couple of cells to the table, and you should get the following code:

```
<table id="TimeCard" border=0 width="100%" height="100%">
  <tr width="100%" valign=middle>
    <td  colspan=2>
    </td>
    <td colspan=5>
    </td>
  </tr>
</table>
```

The <td> tags have an attribute called colspan. Remember I said that you do not want an even number of cells in each row of this table? In fact, the maximum number of cells you need in any row is seven. This corresponds to the number of days in a week.

I have two cells in this row, so I make the width of the first cell equal to the width of two cells. I then make the width of the next cell equal to the width of five cells. Now these two cells take up the same space as the seven cells.

The row I will have you put below this one will have seven sets of <td> tags whose total width will be equal to 100 percent of the width of the table. Here is how the table code will look:

```
<table id="TimeCard" border=0 width="100%" height="100%">
  <tr width="100%" valign=middle>
    <td  colspan=2>
    </td>
    <td colspan=5>
    </td>
  </tr>
  <tr width="100%" align=center valign=middle>
    <td  valign=middle width="14%">
    <%-- Sunday label --%>
    </td>
    <td  valign=middle width="14%">
    <%--Monday label --%>
   </td>
    <td  valign=middle width="14%">
    <%--Tuesday label --%>
    </td>
    <td  valign=middle width="14%">
    <%--Wednesday label --%>
    </td>
    <td  valign=middle width="14%">
    <%--Thursday label --%>
    </td>
    <td  valign=middle width="14%">
```

```
<%--Friday label --%>
</td>
<td  valign=middle width="16%">
<%--Saturday label --%>
</td>
</tr>
...
</table>
```

This table now has two rows in it. Each row is the same width as the table as a whole. The second row has seven cells in it. If you add up the width of each cell, you will get 100 percent. The top row has two cells in it. The first cell spans two of the seven cells below it, and the second cell spans five.

Tip   I have found through hard experience to always make sure that the widths of all your tables, rows, and cells add up to 100 percent. Different browsers render the HTML slightly differently. For instance, if you have a table of 90 percent, Firefox 1.5 will rerender that table at 90 percent of itself every time you post back. This means that your table will get smaller and smaller with each round trip. Internet Explorer does not do this.

So now that you have a little knowledge of how a table is constructed, I will show you the code for the whole table, with the controls from the WebPunch program added in. I made some changes to the controls, which I will explain afterward. Listing 7-2 shows the complete table code.

Listing 7-2. *Complete HTML code to render the time card table*

```
<%@ Control Language="C#" Inherits="YourCompany.Modules.TimePunch.ViewTimePunch"
  CodeFile="ViewTimePunch.ascx.cs" AutoEventWireup="true" %>
<%@ Register TagPrefix="dnn" TagName="Audit"
        Src="~/controls/ModuleAuditControl.ascx" %>

<table id="TimeCard" border=0 width="100%" height="100%">
  <tr width="100%" valign=middle>
    <td  colspan=2>
      <asp:DropDownList ID="cmbWeek" runat="server" Width="100%"
                        OnSelectedIndexChanged="cmbWeek_SelectedIndexChanged"
                        AutoPostBack="True">
    </asp:DropDownList>
    <br /><br />
    </td>
    <td colspan=5>
       
    </td>
  </tr>
  <tr width="100%" align=center valign=middle>
```

```
    <td  valign=middle width="14%">
    <%-- Sunday label --%>
      <asp:Label ID="Label1" runat="server" BorderStyle="None"
                Text="Sunday" Width="80%"></asp:Label>
    </td>
    <td  valign=middle width="14%">
    <%--Monday label --%>
      <asp:Label ID="Label6" runat="server" BorderStyle="None"
                Text="Monday" Width="80%"></asp:Label>
  </td>
    <td  valign=middle width="14%">
    <%--Tuesday label --%>
      <asp:Label ID="Label7" runat="server" BorderStyle="None"
                Text="Tuesday" Width="80%"></asp:Label>
    </td>
    <td  valign=middle width="14%">
    <%--Wednesday label --%>
      <asp:Label ID="Label5" runat="server" BorderStyle="None"
                Text="Wednesday" Width="80%"></asp:Label>
    </td>
    <td  valign=middle width="14%">
    <%--Thursday label --%>
      <asp:Label ID="Label4" runat="server" BorderStyle="None"
                Text="Thursday" Width="80%"></asp:Label>
    </td>
    <td  valign=middle width="14%">
    <%--Friday label --%>
      <asp:Label ID="Label3" runat="server" BorderStyle="None"
                Text="Friday" Width="80%"></asp:Label>
    </td>
    <td  valign=middle width="16%">
    <%--Saturday label --%>
      <asp:Label ID="Label2" runat="server" BorderStyle="None"
                Text="Saturday" Width="80%"></asp:Label>
    </td>
</tr>
<tr width="100%" align=center valign=middle>
    <td  valign=middle width="14%">
    <%-- Sunday value --%>
      <asp:TextBox ID="txtSun" runat="server" BackColor="#E0E0E0" Enabled=false
                  BorderStyle="Inset" Width="80%"></asp:TextBox>
    </td>
    <td  valign=middle width="14%">
    <%--Monday value --%>
      <asp:TextBox ID="txtMon" runat="server" BackColor="#E0E0E0" Enabled=false
                  BorderStyle="Inset" Width="80%" ></asp:TextBox>
    </td>
```

```
      <td  valign=middle width="14%">
      <%--Tuesday value --%>
        <asp:TextBox ID="txtTue" runat="server" BackColor="#E0E0E0" Enabled=false
                    BorderStyle="Inset" Width="80%" ></asp:TextBox>
      </td>
      <td  valign=middle width="14%">
      <%--Wednesday value --%>
        <asp:TextBox ID="txtWed" runat="server" BackColor="#E0E0E0" Enabled=false
                    BorderStyle="Inset" Width="80%" ></asp:TextBox>
      </td>
      <td  valign=middle width="14%">
      <%--Thursday value --%>
        <asp:TextBox ID="txtThu" runat="server" BackColor="#E0E0E0" Enabled=false
                    BorderStyle="Inset" Width="80%" ></asp:TextBox>
      </td>
      <td  valign=middle width="14%">
      <%--Friday value --%>
        <asp:TextBox ID="txtFri" runat="server" BackColor="#E0E0E0" Enabled=false
                    BorderStyle="Inset" Width="80%" ></asp:TextBox>
      </td>
      <td  valign=middle width="16%">
      <%--Saturday value --%>
        <asp:TextBox ID="txtSat" runat="server" BackColor="#E0E0E0" Enabled=false
                    BorderStyle="Inset" Width="80%" ></asp:TextBox>
      </td>
    </tr>
    <tr height="1%">
      <%--Filler row to give vertical space --%>
      <td colspan=7>
         
      </td>
    </tr>
    <tr>
      <td colspan=2>
        <asp:Button ID="cmdPunch" runat="server" Text="Punch In"
                    OnClick="cmdPunch_Click" Height="64px" Width="100%"
                    Font-Bold="True" Font-Size="X-Large" />
      </td>
      <td colspan=5>
         
      </td>
    </tr>
    <tr height="1%">
     <%--Filler row to give vertical space --%>
     <td colspan=7>
         
      </td>
```

```
      </tr>
      <tr height="1%">
      <%--Hours worked label --%>
      <td colspan=2>
          <asp:Label ID="Label8" runat="server" BorderStyle="None"
                     Text="Hours Worked Today">
          </asp:Label>
        </td>
        <td colspan=5>
           
        </td>
      </tr>
      <tr height="1%">
      <%--Hours worked --%>
      <td colspan=2>
          <asp:TextBox ID="txtHoursToday" runat="server" Enabled=false
                       BackColor="#E0E0E0" BorderStyle="Inset" Width="80%" >
          </asp:TextBox>
        </td>
        <td colspan=5>
           
        </td>
      </tr>
</table>
```

This is a ton of code compared to the HTML code in the WebPunch project. Almost all of this code is formatting code.

There are some things I changed concerning the controls as I brought them in from the WebPunch project. They are as follows:

- Each control in the WebPunch project had a fixed width in pixels. I changed that to be a relative width of 80 percent of the cell width.

- Each control in the WebPunch project had a style attribute denoting the absolute position in the page. Since you are using a table and its cells to position the controls, this style attribute is not needed.

- The label controls that had the hours worked for the days of the week were changed from labels to text boxes. This was done because, once again, Firefox works differently from Internet Explorer. A label with no text in it shows up with a width of 0 in Firefox even though there is an explicit width attribute set. Internet Explorer does not function this way. Since the controls need to work the same way in both browsers, I decided to use disabled text boxes. They are disabled to prevent someone from entering a value in them.

Enter the code from Listing 7-2 or use the code provided on the Apress website. If your browser is open to your TimePunch module, press Ctrl+F5 to update the browser. Your screen should now look like mine, shown in Figure 7-24.

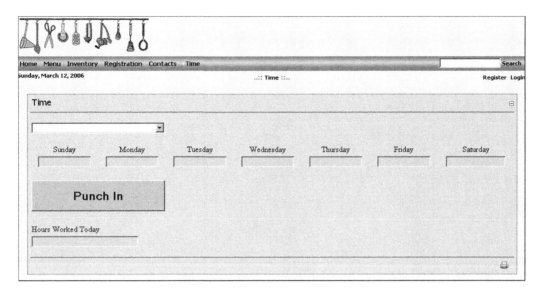

Figure 7-24. *A correctly formatted time card*

Pretty cool, don't you think? If you resize the web page, the controls inside the TimePunch module will resize as well.

The next thing on the list is to add the code to get this control working. If you remember, the WebPunch program had fake data. You will need to change this to store and retrieve real data for real people. Let's take a break—you will start this process in the next chapter.

Summary

This chapter has been all about creating a DNN module. Believe me when I tell you that this is a whole lot easier in DNN 4.x than it was in DNN 3.x.

While you were creating the module, you learned something about the architecture of a DNN module. You learned that it is basically a small program in itself. It includes a presentation layer, a business layer, and a database layer. It conforms to the classic n-tier design.

After creating the module from the template, you changed the database and business layer code to reflect the data that you will need. You also deleted some code that you did not need.

At the end of the chapter, you added the controls from the WebPunch program and formatted them inside an HTML table.

The next chapter will involve adding the code to the presentation layer and the business layer to get the whole thing working. You will also get rid of the fake data you used in the Web-Punch project and use a real database.

CHAPTER 8

■ ■ ■

Finishing the DotNetNuke Module

The last chapter ended with you having created the DNN TimePunch module. You changed the database to include the columns needed. You also changed the database layer code, the business layer code, and the presentation layer code.

At the end of the chapter, you had a visually working module with all the controls necessary on the page. However, there was no code behind the controls to get, save, and display any data.

This chapter will fill in that code. Hopefully, you'll be able to use most of the code from the WebPunch program from Chapter 6 to fill in what you need.

Setting Up the Code Transfer

Since you want to transfer some code from the WebPunch project over to the DNN module, it will be best to have both projects open at once. VWD allows you to do this.

Open the DNN project in one instance of VWD, and open the WebPunch project in another instance.

The first thing that the WebPunch program did was get data and fill in the appropriate controls. The FillData method in the WebPunch program filled objects with fake data. You need real data.

Note As you start transferring code over from the WebPunch project, you will be changing it somewhat. For instance, you now have a real data store and do not need to fake any values. You will also be moving the code around somewhat. In the WebPunch project, all the display and business logic was in the same file. You will make proper use of the presentation, business, and data layers that DNN gives you.

Here is a list of the code that you have to transfer:

The WeekPunches *class*: This class holds punches for a week of time. It also has some functionality in it in that it can calculate hours based on the dates and times it holds.

The Page_Load *event handler*: The code in here initializes the page and sets up the current session. It calls two other methods: FillData and DisplayWeek.

The FillData *method*: This method fills two WeekPunches objects with fake data and saves them in a collection. You need to change this to get real data.

The DisplayWeek *method*: This method gets the WeekPunches object from the MyPunches collection based upon the week passed in. It fills in the time card's Sunday through Saturday text boxes according to the hours saved for each day.

The cmdPunch_Click *event handler*: This method determines if the user is punching in or out. It saves the punch times in a session variable. It also calls the DisplayWeek method to output the punch results to the screen.

The CalculateHours *method*: This method takes a start and end time and calculates the timespan between them in hours.

The cmbWeek_SelectedIndexChanged *event handler*: This method reads the index of the combo box and displays the weekly punches based on the week chosen. It calls the DisplayWeek method.

These six parts of the code do not seem like much. However, the placement of the code in the TimePunch module and the fact that you now have a real database require considerable consideration.

The CalculateHours Method

This method is simple and needs no adjusting. However, this method is considered business logic. As such, it belongs in the TimePunchController.cs file.

Copy the CalculateHours method from the WebPunch project's default.aspx.cs file into the TimePunch project's TimePunchController.cs file. Put it inside the Public Methods region of code.

The WeekPunches Class

Copy the WeekPunches class from the WebPunch project into the TimePunchController.cs file. The WebPunch project had this class labeled as private, and it was also embedded within the Default class definition.

When you copy the WeekPunches class over, you will need to label it as public, and it should not be inside the TimePunchController class. The following code shows this:

```
using System.Configuration;
using System.Data;
using System.Xml;
```

```
using System.Web;
using DotNetNuke;
using DotNetNuke.Common;
using DotNetNuke.Common.Utilities;

namespace YourCompany.Modules.TimePunch
{
  /// -------------------------------------------------------------
  ///<summary>
  /// The Controller class for the TimePunch
  /// </summary>
  /// <remarks>
  /// </remarks>
  /// <history>
  /// </history>
  /// -------------------------------------------------------------
  ///

  public class WeekPunches
  {
      ...
  }

  public class TimePunchController
  {
      ...
  }
```

While you're at it, you also need to move the MyPunches ArrayList object. This object is labeled as private and static within the WebPunch program's _Default class definition.

When you move it over, you will need to put it inside the TimePunchController class definition as private. It should not be static. Also add an enum to denote punch types. The code is as follows:

```
  public class TimePunchController
  {

    private ArrayList MyPunches = new ArrayList();
    private enum PunchType
    {
      PUNCH_IN,
      PUNCH_OUT
    };

    #region Constructors
```

```
public TimePunchController()
{
}


#endregion

#region Public Methods


public ArrayList PunchArray
{
  get { return MyPunches; }
}
...
}
```

Notice the property, called PunchArray, I added at the bottom. Since the MyPunches collection is part of the TimeController class and is private, it needs a property to read it.

The MyPunches object was made non-static because, now that you have a real module with real people logging in and out, you do not want to keep this information around between users. (Remember that there was no one logging into the WebPunch project and there was no data storage.)

Once you have added the WeekPunches class to this file, you will need to add one more method to it. Add the following method to the WeekPunches class:

```
public double TodaysHours
{
  get
  {
    switch (DateTime.Now.DayOfWeek)
    {
      case DayOfWeek.Sunday:
        return CalculateHours(SundayStart, SundayEnd);
      case DayOfWeek.Monday:
        return CalculateHours(MondayStart, MondayEnd);
      case DayOfWeek.Tuesday:
        return CalculateHours(TuesdayStart, TuesdayEnd);
      case DayOfWeek.Wednesday:
        return CalculateHours(WednesdayStart, WednesdayEnd);
      case DayOfWeek.Thursday:
        return CalculateHours(ThursdayStart, ThursdayEnd);
      case DayOfWeek.Friday:
        return CalculateHours(FridayStart, FridayEnd);
      case DayOfWeek.Saturday:
        return CalculateHours(SaturdayStart, SaturdayEnd);
    }
```

```
    return 0.0;
  }
}
```

This method will figure out what day it is and calculate the hours for the first-in and last-out punch for this day. This method will be used in the ViewTimePunch file.

The FillData Method

Copy the FillData method from the WebPunch project and put it in the TimePunchController class.

This method filled the WeekPunches object with fake data for last week and this week. However, now that you have a real database, you need to fill the WeekPunches objects with real data. The new FillData method should look like that shown in Listing 8-1.

Listing 8-1. *The new FillData method*

```
public void FillData(int ModuleId, int PunchUserID)
{
  //Set up a collection of TimePunchInfo objects
  List<TimePunchInfo> colTimePunchs;

  //Get the content from the TimePunch table
  colTimePunchs = GetTimePunchs(ModuleId, PunchUserID);

  //Reset the MyPunches array list
  MyPunches.Clear();

  //Create last week
  DateTime LastSunday = DateTime.Now;
  int Days2Subtract = 7 + (int)DateTime.Now.DayOfWeek;
  LastSunday = LastSunday.Subtract(new TimeSpan(
                            Days2Subtract,
                            LastSunday.Hour,
                            LastSunday.Minute,
                            LastSunday.Second,
                            LastSunday.Millisecond));

  WeekPunches LastWeek = new WeekPunches();

  //We now have a list of punches for this person forever.
  // (This is where a list of punches for a time span would be handy)
  // (Also most programs like this would archive data so there would
  // only be about 1 yr worth in here anyway.)
  LastWeek.SundayStart    = GetPunch(PunchType.PUNCH_IN,
                            LastSunday, colTimePunchs);
  LastWeek.SundayEnd      = GetPunch(PunchType.PUNCH_OUT,
                            LastSunday, colTimePunchs);
```

```
LastWeek.MondayStart      = GetPunch(PunchType.PUNCH_IN,
                                      LastSunday.AddDays(1), colTimePunchs);
LastWeek.MondayEnd        = GetPunch(PunchType.PUNCH_OUT,
                                      LastSunday.AddDays(1), colTimePunchs);
LastWeek.TuesdayStart     = GetPunch(PunchType.PUNCH_IN,
                                      LastSunday.AddDays(2), colTimePunchs);
LastWeek.TuesdayEnd       = GetPunch(PunchType.PUNCH_OUT,
                                      LastSunday.AddDays(2), colTimePunchs);
LastWeek.WednesdayStart   = GetPunch(PunchType.PUNCH_IN,
                                      LastSunday.AddDays(3), colTimePunchs);
LastWeek.WednesdayEnd     = GetPunch(PunchType.PUNCH_OUT,
                                      LastSunday.AddDays(3), colTimePunchs);
LastWeek.ThursdayStart    = GetPunch(PunchType.PUNCH_IN,
                                      LastSunday.AddDays(4), colTimePunchs);
LastWeek.ThursdayEnd      = GetPunch(PunchType.PUNCH_OUT,
                                      LastSunday.AddDays(4), colTimePunchs);
LastWeek.FridayStart      = GetPunch(PunchType.PUNCH_IN,
                                      LastSunday.AddDays(5), colTimePunchs);
LastWeek.FridayEnd        = GetPunch(PunchType.PUNCH_OUT,
                                      LastSunday.AddDays(5), colTimePunchs);
LastWeek.SaturdayStart    = GetPunch(PunchType.PUNCH_IN,
                                      LastSunday.AddDays(6), colTimePunchs);
LastWeek.SaturdayEnd      = GetPunch(PunchType.PUNCH_OUT,
                                      LastSunday.AddDays(6), colTimePunchs);


MyPunches.Add(LastWeek);


//Create this week
DateTime ThisSunday = DateTime.Now;
Days2Subtract = (int)DateTime.Now.DayOfWeek;
ThisSunday = ThisSunday.Subtract(new TimeSpan(
                                 Days2Subtract,
                                 ThisSunday.Hour,
                                 ThisSunday.Minute,
                                 ThisSunday.Second,
                                 ThisSunday.Millisecond));
WeekPunches ThisWeek      = new WeekPunches();
ThisWeek.SundayStart      = GetPunch(PunchType.PUNCH_IN,
                                     ThisSunday, colTimePunchs);
ThisWeek.SundayEnd        = GetPunch(PunchType.PUNCH_OUT,
                                     ThisSunday, colTimePunchs);
ThisWeek.MondayStart      = GetPunch(PunchType.PUNCH_IN,
                                     ThisSunday.AddDays(1), colTimePunchs);
ThisWeek.MondayEnd        = GetPunch(PunchType.PUNCH_OUT,
                                     ThisSunday.AddDays(1), colTimePunchs);
ThisWeek.TuesdayStart     = GetPunch(PunchType.PUNCH_IN,
                                     ThisSunday.AddDays(2), colTimePunchs);
```

```
    ThisWeek.TuesdayEnd     = GetPunch(PunchType.PUNCH_OUT,
                                  ThisSunday.AddDays(2), colTimePunchs);
    ThisWeek.WednesdayStart = GetPunch(PunchType.PUNCH_IN,
                                  ThisSunday.AddDays(3), colTimePunchs);
    ThisWeek.WednesdayEnd   = GetPunch(PunchType.PUNCH_OUT,
                                  ThisSunday.AddDays(3), colTimePunchs);
    ThisWeek.ThursdayStart  = GetPunch(PunchType.PUNCH_IN,
                                  ThisSunday.AddDays(4), colTimePunchs);
    ThisWeek.ThursdayEnd    = GetPunch(PunchType.PUNCH_OUT,
                                  ThisSunday.AddDays(4), colTimePunchs);
    ThisWeek.FridayStart    = GetPunch(PunchType.PUNCH_IN,
                                  ThisSunday.AddDays(5), colTimePunchs);
    ThisWeek.FridayEnd      = GetPunch(PunchType.PUNCH_OUT,
                                  ThisSunday.AddDays(5), colTimePunchs);
    ThisWeek.SaturdayStart  = GetPunch(PunchType.PUNCH_IN,
                                  ThisSunday.AddDays(6), colTimePunchs);
    ThisWeek.SaturdayEnd    = GetPunch(PunchType.PUNCH_OUT,
                                  ThisSunday.AddDays(6), colTimePunchs);

    MyPunches.Add(ThisWeek);
}
```

There are some noteworthy changes in here. First of all, you no longer just make up data. The first few lines get all the punches from the database for a particular user (I will talk about this process in a minute). Once the data is obtained, the method then extracts the start and end punches for each day, and fills in the WeekPunches object. Once the objects for last week and this week are filled in, they get added to the MyPunches collection. This part is pretty much how it happened in the original version of the FillData method from the WebPunch project.

Getting the Data

As you can see from the first two lines of code in this method, getting the data from the database was pure magic.

This level of business layer logic has no idea where the data comes from. This is abstraction at its best. The lower layers of code can change to get data from a subterranean rock for all this method cares. Nothing changes here.

There is something that does go on here in this data retrieval process that you need to know about, though. It affects how the TimePunchInfo class is defined and how the stored procedures are defined as well.

■**Caution** Do not skip this section. Some of the code in the last chapter has some author-introduced errors. They will be fixed in here. Just because a program compiles doesn't mean it will work. These are errors that most people will make.

The colTimePunchs variable is a collection of TimePunchInfo objects. Absolutely nowhere in any of this TimePunch code will you find a method that takes the individual fields from the database records and fills in a TimePunchInfo object. In fact, you won't even find anywhere that a TimePunchInfo object is actually instantiated. How does this happen?

If you trace the code and view the GetTimePunchs method in the TimePunchController class, you see that it calls a FillCollection method. This method is a generic, and it is here where the magic happens.

There is a .NET interface that reads data from a relational database. It is called the IDataReader interface. You will find this reference in the DataProvider.cs file.

The FillCollection method is set up to use the IDataReader interface to read data from the database using the YourCompany_GetTimePunchs stored procedure. Hence the name of the GetTimePunchs method as the stored procedure. This FillCollection method then fills in the TimePunchInfo object according to the data it reads.

There is only one way that a TimePunchInfo object can be filled automatically with data from fields in a record. Can you guess what it is?

The TimePunchInfo class *must* have properties that have the exact same name as the columns in the database. In addition, the properties *must* have both a set and a get accessor.

Here are the TimePunchInfo properties that you programmed in Chapter 7:

- ModuleID: Has get and set accessors

- ItemID: Has get and set accessors

- PunchType: Has get and set accessors

- PunchUserID: Has get and set accessors

- Punch_UserName: Has only a get accessor

- PunchDate: Has get and set accessors

Here are the database columns:

- ModuleID

- ItemID

- Punch_Type

- Punch_User

- Punch_Date

If you were to get done with all the code for the program, it would compile. If you were to run the program, you would get nothing. The TimePunchInfo class must be changed so that the properties have the same names as the database columns. The new code is shown following:

```
public class TimePunchInfo
{

    #region Private Members
```

```csharp
private int        _ModuleId;
private int        _ItemId;
private int        _PunchType;
private int        _PunchUserID;
private DateTime   _PunchDate;
private string     _Punch_UserName;

#endregion

#region Constructors

// initialization
public TimePunchInfo()
{
}

#endregion

#region Public Methods

/// <summary>
/// Gets and sets the Module Id
/// </summary>
public int ModuleId
{
  get { return _ModuleId;  }
  set { _ModuleId = value; }
}

/// <summary>
/// Gets and sets the Item Id
/// </summary>
public int ItemId
{
  get { return _ItemId; }
  set { _ItemId = value; }
}

/// <summary>
/// Gets and sets the punch type
/// </summary>
public int Punch_Type
{
  get { return _PunchType; }
  set { _PunchType = value; }
}
```

```csharp
/// <summary>
/// Gets and sets the User ID who created/updated the content
/// </summary>
public int Punch_User
{
  get { return _PunchUserID; }
  set { _PunchUserID = value; }
}

/// <summary>
/// Gets the user name
/// </summary>
public string Punch_UserName
{
  get { return _Punch_UserName; }
  set { _Punch_UserName = value; }
}

/// <summary>
/// Gets and sets the date when punched
/// </summary>
public DateTime Punch_Date
{
  get { return _PunchDate; }
  set { _PunchDate = value; }
}

#endregion

  }
}
```

Here is the GetTimePunchs stored procedure as you programmed it in Chapter 7:

```sql
ALTER procedure dbo.YourCompany_GetTimePunchs
      @ModuleId int,
      @UserId int
as
select ModuleId,
       Punch_User,
       Punch_Type,
       Punch_Date,
       'Punch_UserName' = Users.FirstName + ' ' + Users.LastName
from YourCompany_TimePunch
inner join Users on YourCompany_TimePunch.Punch_User = Users.UserId
where  ModuleId = @ModuleId
and Punch_User = @UserId
```

The stored procedure creates a new field called Punch_UserName. The TimePunchInfo class has a property called Punch_UserName. However, this will never get set because it is missing a set accessor.

You will need to add a set accessor to the Punch_UserName property in the TimePunchInfo class.

There is one last thing I want you to change regarding this GetPunchs code path. I want you to add the ItemID as part of the result set returned by the GetTimePunchs stored procedure. This allows the TimePunchInfo.ItemId value to be filled, and it will allow you to delete a particular row in the database at a later time if you want to. Here is the new GetTimePunchs stored procedure, with the extra code in bold:

```
ALTER procedure dbo.YourCompany_GetTimePunchs
    @ModuleId int,
    @UserId int
as
select ModuleId,
       ItemID,
       Punch_User,
       Punch_Type,
       Punch_Date,
       'Punch_UserName' = Users.FirstName + ' ' + Users.LastName
from YourCompany_TimePunch
inner join Users on YourCompany_TimePunch.Punch_User = Users.UserId
where  ModuleId = @ModuleId
and Punch_User = @UserId
```

Unless you have all the column names correct throughout the code path, the magic of the IDataReader and the generic FillCollection method will not work.

Is this all that is affected? Unfortunately, no.

Since you changed the properties in the TimePunchInfo class, you need to change any methods that use those properties.

The TimePunchController.AddTimePunch method now needs to change. The method is shown following, with new code in bold:

```
    public void AddTimePunch(TimePunchInfo objTimePunch)
    {
      DataProvider.Instance().AddTimePunch(objTimePunch.ModuleId,
                                objTimePunch.Punch_Type,
                                objTimePunch.Punch_User);
    }
```

By the same token, the TimePunchController.UpdateTimePunch method also needs to change. The method is shown following, with the new code in bold:

```
    public void UpdateTimePunch(TimePunchInfo objTimePunch)
    {
      DataProvider.Instance().UpdateTimePunch(objTimePunch.ModuleId,
                                objTimePunch.ItemId,
                                objTimePunch.Punch_User,
```

```
                                      objTimePunch.Punch_Type,
                                      objTimePunch.Punch_Date);
}
```

That's it for correcting the mistakes you made before.

Parsing the Data

The FillData method calls a help method named GetPunch. You will need to add this new method to the TimePunchController class. The code is shown here.

```
//This method will troll the collection looking for the earliest punch
//of the day if the punch type is punch_in. It will look for the latest
//punch of the day if the punch type is punch_out.
private DateTime GetPunch(PunchType pt, DateTime dt,
                          List<TimePunchInfo> TimePunchs)
{
  DateTime BaseTime = DateTime.MaxValue;
  bool found = false;

  //Set to min or max if punch in or out
  if (pt == PunchType.PUNCH_IN)
    BaseTime = DateTime.MaxValue;
  else
    BaseTime = DateTime.MinValue;

  foreach (TimePunchInfo tpi in TimePunchs)
  {
    if ((PunchType)tpi.Punch_Type == pt)
    {
      if (dt.ToShortDateString() == tpi.Punch_Date.ToShortDateString())
      {
        found = true;
        if (pt == PunchType.PUNCH_IN && tpi.Punch_Date <= BaseTime)
          BaseTime = tpi.Punch_Date;

        if (pt == PunchType.PUNCH_OUT && tpi.Punch_Date >= BaseTime)
          BaseTime = tpi.Punch_Date;
      }
    }
  }

  if (found)
    return BaseTime;
  else
    return DateTime.MinValue;
}
```

This method may look more complicated than it needs to be. After all, its purpose is to extract a start punch or an end punch from the passed-in collection. There is something to think about here, though.

The WebPunch program from Chapter 6 and the Punch program from Chapter 5 both suffered from the same problem. They both allowed you to punch in and out multiple times during the day, but the start time would always be reset to the latest start time. This is the problem with fake data and the lack of persistence.

You want to be able to allow the user to punch in and out multiple times during the day (for instance, lunch). All these punches will be saved to the database. When you get the punches for the day, you want to calculate the *total* time for the day between the first time someone punches in and the last time they punch out.

If the PunchType is PUNCH_IN, then this method will search for the earliest punch time for that day. If the PunchType is set for PUNCH_OUT, then this method will search for the latest punch time for that day. If no punch is found, then it returns a default minimum time.

The last thing to note in this TimePunchController.cs file is the constructor. Make sure that it is empty. The code is as follows:

```
#region Constructors

public TimePunchController()
{
}

#endregion
```

Initial State

The WebPunch program never had any data persistence. Because of this, every time it was started, its initial state was that of a person being punched out. You could punch in with the WebPunch program, kill it, and restart it, and you would need to punch in again.

Now that you have a proper program with a database store, you have the ability to start up in a known state. After all, this DNN project allows many different people to log in and out during the day. If you logged into a computer to punch in, and someone else logged into the same computer to look at something else, the next time you logged in, you would be punching in again, instead of punching out as you intended. The program must remember your state between logins. In this case, you can infer the state based on the last time you punched, which is stored in the database. Add the following code to the TimePunchController class. It gets the state from the database.

```
public int GetPunchState(int ModuleId, int PunchUserID)
{
  int retval = 1;  //punch OUT state
  DateTime LastPunch = DateTime.MinValue;

  //Set up a collection of TimePunchInfo objects
  List<TimePunchInfo> colTimePunchs;
```

```
    //Get the content from the TimePunch table
    colTimePunchs = GetTimePunchs(ModuleId, PunchUserID);
    foreach (TimePunchInfo tpi in colTimePunchs)
    {
     if (DateTime.Today.ToShortDateString() == tpi.Punch_Date.ToShortDateString())
      {
        if (tpi.Punch_Date >= LastPunch)
        {
          LastPunch = tpi.Punch_Date;
          retval = tpi.Punch_Type;
        }
      }
    }
    return retval;
}
```

This method gets the punches for a person and iterates through them to find the last punch of the day. It then takes the punch type for that punch and sends it back to the calling method.

This method will be called from the ViewTimePunch.ascx.cs file.

Editing the ViewTimePunch Code

The rest of the code that you will need to transfer or edit is in the ViewTimePunch.ascx.cs file. So far, you have made all the changes to the database layer and the business layers of this module. Now is the time to connect the visual with the background.

Member Variables

Copy over the Private Variables region from the WebPunch project, and put it in the ViewTimePunch class. This is shown in the following code:

```
#region Private Variables

private const bool P_IN = false;
private const bool P_OUT = true;
private bool mPunchState = P_IN;

private DateTime mStartPunch;
private DateTime mEndPunch;

private static ArrayList MyPunches = new ArrayList();

private class WeekPunches

#endregion
```

The MyPunches collection is now in the TimePunchController class. Delete it from here. The WeekPunches class is in the TimePunchController.cs file. Delete it from here.

The TimePunchController class is now your business layer logic. As such, you need a reference to it here that does not disappear between round trips to the server. Add the following reference to the Private Variables region:

```
private static TimePunchController TimePunchs = null;
```

Later on, you will also delete the start and end punch variables. I will let you know when that time comes.

The DisplayWeek Method

This method displays hours from a punch collection in the appropriate text boxes. You will need to copy this function over from the WebPunch program and change a couple of lines of code. The new DisplayWeek method is shown following, with the changes in bold:

```
private void DisplayWeek(int wk)
{
  TimePunchs.FillData(ModuleId, this.UserId);
  WeekPunches Week = (WeekPunches)TimePunchs.PunchArray[wk];

  txtSun.Text = "";
  txtMon.Text = "";
  txtTue.Text = "";
  txtWed.Text = "";
  txtThu.Text = "";
  txtFri.Text = "";
  txtSat.Text = "";

  //Show the hours worked today in the text box
  txtHoursToday.Text = Week.TodaysHours.ToString("F2");

  txtSun.Text = Week.SundayHours.ToString("F2");
  txtMon.Text = Week.MondayHours.ToString("F2");
  txtTue.Text = Week.TuesdayHours.ToString("F2");
  txtWed.Text = Week.WednesdayHours.ToString("F2");
  txtThu.Text = Week.ThursdayHours.ToString("F2");
  txtFri.Text = Week.FridayHours.ToString("F2");
  txtSat.Text = Week.SundayHours.ToString("F2");
}
```

This method now calls the FillData method to get the data. It then gets a reference to the week's data and fills in the text boxes. The text box below the punch button is filled in here rather than in the button event handler. Since this method displays data, it seemed the best place to put it.

The Combo Box Event Handler

This one is easy. No difference from the WebPunch project. Here it is:

```
protected void cmbWeek_SelectedIndexChanged(object sender, EventArgs e)
{
  DisplayWeek(cmbWeek.SelectedIndex);
}
```

The Punch Button Event Handler

I could tell you to copy over the code from the WebPunch program, but the edits you'll make afterward are so extensive that you may just as well program it from scratch.

This method handled the punch state, saving it in a session variable. It also saved the start and end punches in session variables as well.

Last, it displayed the punch hours for the day in the text box below the button. That job is now taken over by the DisplayWeek method, which cuts out almost 40 lines of code from this method.

Since the data is retrieved from the database, there is no need to save it in memory any longer. This is a much better way of handling the punch times. The code for the cmdPunch_Click event handler is as follows:

```
protected void cmdPunch_Click(object sender, EventArgs e)
{
  //If the session variable is available then
  //refill the mPunchState with the saved value
  if (this.Session["mPunchState"] != null)
    mPunchState = (bool)this.Session["mPunchState"];

  if (mPunchState == P_OUT)
  {
    mPunchState = P_IN;
    cmdPunch.Text = "Punch In";

    //Save the out punch time
    TimePunchInfo tpi = new TimePunchInfo();
    tpi.ModuleId = ModuleId;
    tpi.Punch_User = this.UserId;
    tpi.Punch_Type = 1;
    TimePunchs.AddTimePunch(tpi);

    DisplayWeek(cmbWeek.SelectedIndex);
  }
}
```

```
  else
  {
    mPunchState = P_OUT;
    cmdPunch.Text = "Punch Out";

    //Save the in punch time
    TimePunchInfo tpi = new TimePunchInfo();
    tpi.ModuleId = ModuleId;
    tpi.Punch_User = this.UserId;
    tpi.Punch_Type = 0;
    TimePunchs.AddTimePunch(tpi);
  }
  //Save the mPuchState variable for use next time through
  this.Session["mPunchState"] = mPunchState;
}
```

I told you what was deleted; now let's see what was added. The punch is added to the database with the following chunk of code from the cmdPunch_Click method when mPunchState equals PUNCH_IN.

```
    //Save the out punch time
    TimePunchInfo tpi = new TimePunchInfo();
    tpi.ModuleId = ModuleId;
    tpi.Punch_User = this.UserId;
    tpi.Punch_Type = 1;
    TimePunchs.AddTimePunch(tpi);
```

The same piece of code was added to the punch out part of this method.

You can see that a new TimePunchInfo object is instantiated and passed into the AddTimePunch method of the business layer. Eventually, the YourCompany_AddTimePunch stored procedure is called, and the data gets in the database.

Remember that when I added the stored procedure, I had the stored procedure calculate the punch date. As you can see from this method, I do not need to send the date down. As soon as a person punches in or out, the punch information is added to the database with no time lag. Thus, there is no need to store any punch times in this class.

This cmdPunch_Click event handler is much simpler and cleaner than it was in the Web-Punch program.

Tip You can make this method even cleaner by refactoring out the code that saves the punch. I encourage you to look up this process in the help file. The IDE has some cool built-in refactoring capabilities.

Before moving on, I want to talk about the last line of code in this method. It saves the punch state in the session state object. This is what you did in the WebPunch program. The difference here, however, is that you do not want to use your own state object. You want to use the one that is given to you by the DNN program. That is why you use the this.session object.

This DNN session object gets cleared whenever someone logs out of the system. If you used your own session object, it would hang around between logins, and the session variables for one person would bleed into another's.

The Page _Load Event Handler

This method needs to initialize the module when the person first logs in. One of the things you need to do here is retrieve the punch state from the database and store it in the this.session object.

Copy the Page_Load code from the WebPunch program into the ViewTimePunch class. You will need to add some code after the copy. The complete method is shown following, with the new code in bold:

```
protected void Page_Load(System.Object sender, System.EventArgs e)
{
  if (this.Session["WeekIndex"] == null || cmbWeek.Items.Count == 0)
  {
    //Get the business layer going
    TimePunchs = new TimePunchController();

    //cmdPunch and cmbWeek have the attributes "runat=server"  Because of
    //this we can access these controls here and fill in the data.
    cmbWeek.Items.Clear();
    cmbWeek.Items.Add("Last Week");
    cmbWeek.Items.Add("This Week");
    cmbWeek.SelectedIndex = 0;

    //Add this function call because in the Web changing the
    //selected index does not fire the selectedindexchanged event.
    DisplayWeek(cmbWeek.SelectedIndex);

    //Get the punch state from the database and save it in the session
    //state for fast retrieval. The punch state is whatever the last punch
    //was for the day for this person
    if (TimePunchs.GetPunchState(ModuleId, this.UserId) == 0)
    {
      //Person is currently punched in
      cmdPunch.Text = "Punch Out";
      mPunchState = P_OUT;
    }
```

```
    else
    {
      //Person is currently punched out
      cmdPunch.Text = "Punch In";
      mPunchState = P_IN;
    }
    //Save the mPuchState variable for use next time through
    this.Session["mPunchState"] = mPunchState;

    //If no one is logged in, then disable the button and drop-down
    if(this.UserId == -1)
    {
      cmdPunch.Text = "Disabled.  No log in";
      cmdPunch.Enabled = false;
      cmbWeek.Enabled = false;
    }
  }
  this.Session["WeekIndex"] = Server.HtmlEncode(cmbWeek.SelectedIndex.
                                                 ToString());
}
```

Now that I look at all the bold code, I guess this method is pretty much all new.

You can see where I instantiate the TimePunchs object. Remember that the DisplayWeek method gets the data from the database, so there is no need to call the FillData method here.

The large block of bold code is where I get the punch state from the database and save it in the this.session object.

No One Is Logged In

Now that this module will be in a real program, you need to account for the case when someone calls up this page, but no one is logged in. In this case, you do not want to show anything, and you do not want the person to punch.

The way to do this is to detect the this.UserId variable. If it is –1, then you need to disable the punch button and the combo box and let people know that they cannot use this module. The following piece of code from the Page_Load event handler does this:

```
//If no one is logged in, then disable the button and drop-down
if(this.UserId == -1)
{
  cmdPunch.Text = "Disabled.  No log in";
  cmdPunch.Enabled = false;
  cmbWeek.Enabled = false;
}
```

When you compile the code and test it, try this scenario out.

Last Edit

The last thing you need to do to this page is delete the DisplayAudit method from this ViewTimePunch class. The control is not around anymore, so this code is not needed.

You can also delete the mStartPunch and mEndPunch variables from the class.

Testing It All Out

Compile and run the code. Try looking at the Time page without logging in. You should get a screen like Figure 8-1.

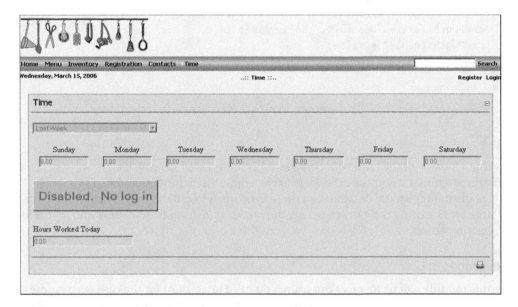

Figure 8-1. *The Time page when no one is logged in*

This is a last resort, really. The next chapter will take you through setting all the permissions of the pages, which will remove this Time menu choice from the menu bar if no one is logged in.

Now log in as the administrator. Since I have been playing with this for a few days, I have some data. My page is shown in Figure 8-2.

Try punching in, then log out, then log back in as admin—the TimePunch module button should say Punch Out.

Looking at the Data

Did you know that you can look at the database table and jam new rows in there for testing? You can also change values if you want.

In the Database Explorer, scroll down to the YourCompany_TimePunch table, and right-click it. This is shown in Figure 8-3.

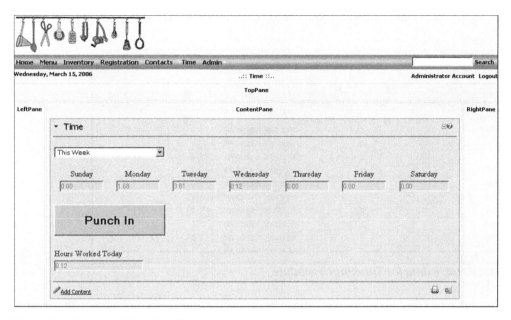

Figure 8-2. *Time card for the admin user*

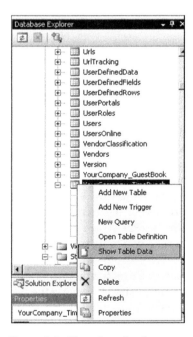

Figure 8-3. *Showing the data*

Click Show Table Data, and you should see the table in your IDE, as shown in Figure 8-4.

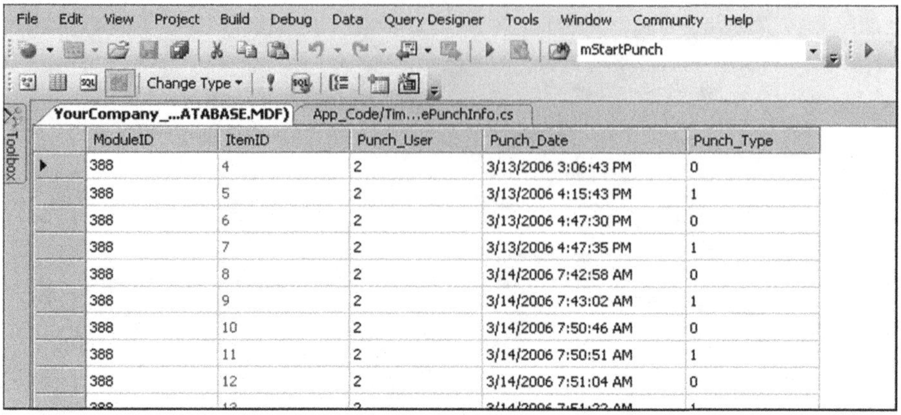

Figure 8-4. *The table data for TimePunch module*

Notice how the ItemID is monotonically increasing. See how the punch type is alternating between 0 and 1.

Notice also that the module ID is the same for all. You can add another module of this TimePunch type to the same page or a different page, and use both at the same time. The rows will be differentiated by different module IDs.

Summary

This chapter has discussed wiring up the TimePunch module from the presentation layer all the way down to the database itself.

Admittedly, some of the concepts are a little difficult to understand, but if you take the time to read and trace the code as it is running, you will see how it all fits together.

It was apparent while copying code from the WebPunch project that the presence of a real database forced you to change quite a bit of the code. There is no longer any fake data, and as such there is no longer any need for some of the state variables you were saving.

I took you through the IDataReader interface and how it works inside a generic class. Because you are using the IDataReader interface, you saw that the TimePunchInfo properties needed to have the same names as the database columns. This forced you to fix some of the code you wrote in the last chapter.

You also found that since this TimePunch module is now a part of a much larger program, it needs to take this into consideration and play nice. This was accomplished by saving the punch state in the database and retrieving it upon entry into the page. You added code to disable the page when the user is not logged in.

Chapter 9 will take you though the next steps in completing this project for real use.

CHAPTER 9

■ ■ ■

DNN Permissions and Portals

Chapters 7 and 8 were all about creating a new module for DNN. This module mimicked a web page called WebPunch that you created in Chapter 6.

This new module allows a user to punch in and out of work while inside the web page. This module is like a mini-application, but it cannot run on its own; it needs to run inside a page on your DNN site.

The final module works well and can handle initial states as well as remember a user's punch state between logins. Once you plugged it into a page, you were essentially done.

The last thing you need to do with this project is to make it usable as both an external and internal site.

Permissions

The TimePunch module is currently available to anyone who browses to your website. Since it doesn't work for users who aren't logged in, it would be better if it didn't show for them at all.

There are two ways to accomplish this. One is through role permissions and the other is through access via a portal. This section will deal with permissions.

Let's look at the security roles in the DNN system and what they do.

The Host Role

This is the big Kahuna of roles. The host can administer anything on any page in any portal connected with this site. In Chapter 7, you logged in as host to create the tables for the Time-Punch project. Other than that, since you have not done any work with portals yet, you have not needed to log into the site using this role. The host can do the following tasks:

- Adjust the host settings.

- Manage portals.

- Add/delete/edit modules for the site as a whole.

- Manage files on the site.

- Add/delete/edit vendors for the site as a whole. This is used to manage vendors who advertise on your site.

- Run SQL scripts. You used this to create the TimePunch module.

- Adjust schedules. Schedules are repetitive tasks performed by DNN, such as purging log buffers. You can adjust schedules to help performance and scalability.

- Manage languages in your site. DNN is multilingual and you can upload language packs.

- Manage search settings for the DNN search engine.

- Manage user-defined lists of things within DNN. Such lists might be ZIP codes or countries.

- Manage superusers (the host and admin logins) within your DNN site.

- Upload and delete skins and containers for your site.

You will not need most of the items in this list for the projects in this book. However, if you ever get into building websites and perhaps opening a virtual store, these settings will come into play. Let's take a quick look at the host settings capability.

Host Settings

Log in as the host for your website. Click Host ➤ Host Settings. You should get a screen like the one shown in Figure 9-1.

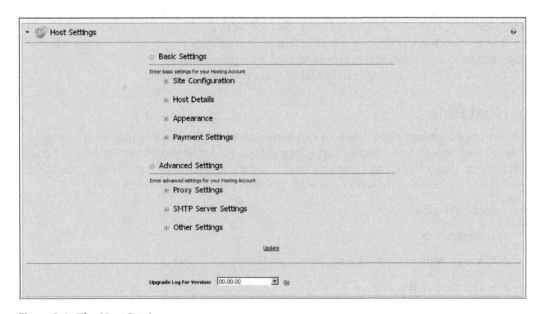

Figure 9-1. *The Host Settings page*

You see that there are several major areas that you can apply settings to. The Site Configuration section gives some information about the versions of software you are working with.

Expand Host Details, and you should get something similar to Figure 9-2.

Figure 9-2. *The Host Details section*

The only portal you have is the one you are working on now, which is the one that was given to you upon installation of DNN. Later in this chapter, you will add a new portal to better segment tasks.

The host title can be whatever you want. When you finally download your site to an ISP for hosting, you can change the hosting URL to be wherever your site resides.

If anyone wants to contact you for support, your e-mail address can be changed in the Host Email field.

Appearance Settings

This is something you will probably use quite a bit in the future. The Appearance section is where you can upload new skins and containers.

So far, you only have the skins that came with the DNN installation. These skins are pretty much all the same, except for their color. While it is nice that these skins were provided for you, they are not very inspiring. As I have said before, you can go online and search for "DNN skins," and find some pretty amazing-looking skins out there. The process of uploading skins and containers is something I will cover in Chapter 10.

Figure 9-3 shows the settings page for choosing and uploading skins.

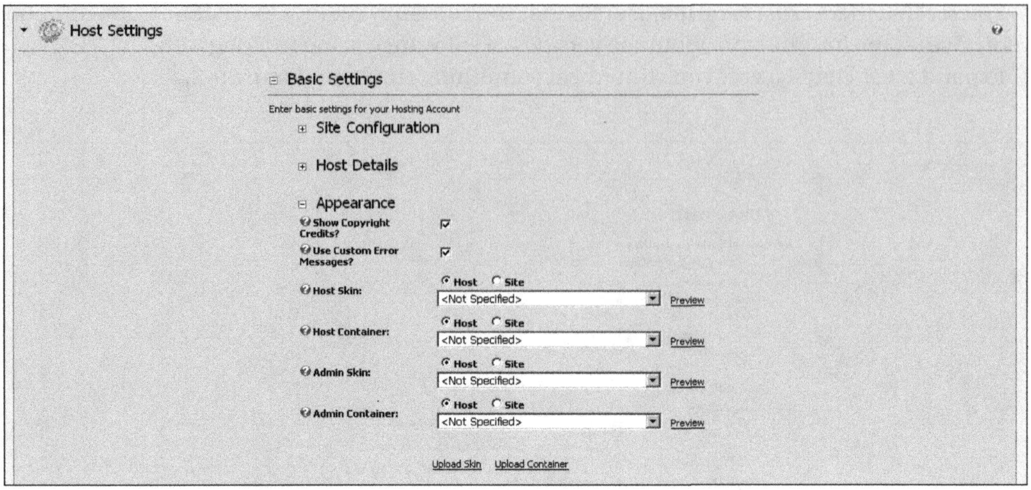

Figure 9-3. *Choosing and uploading skins*

Payment Options

These settings go along with the portal settings. DNN allows you to create and manage multiple child portals off the main one. If you are charging money for hosting portals, you want some way to get paid for it. Figure 9-4 shows the portal-hosting payment settings.

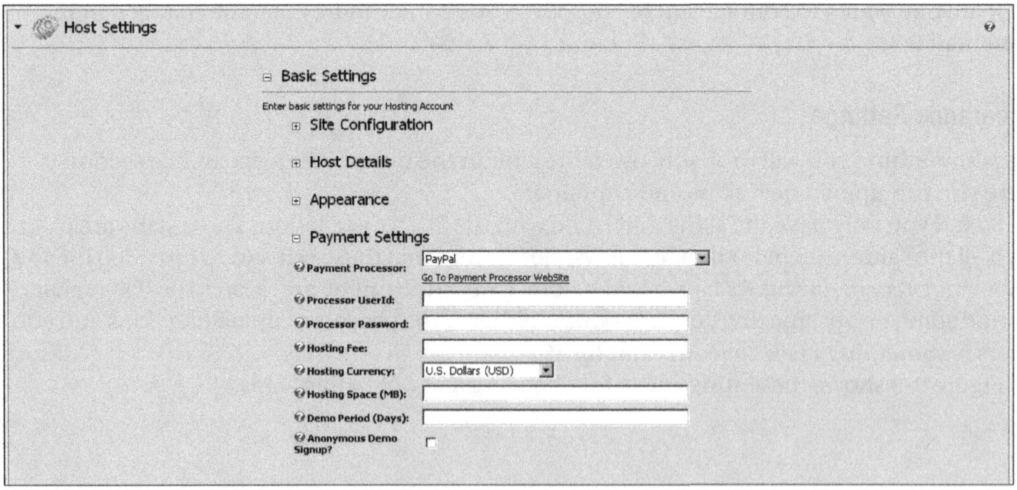

Figure 9-4. *The hosting payment settings*

There are a number of ways to get paid online, with PayPal being the biggest, of course. You can use these settings to allow a trial period for the portal and to charge a hosting fee.

Portal administrators can renew their hosting on the Administrator ➤ Site Settings page.

Advanced Settings

The Advanced Settings page allows you to set up proxies, mail server settings, and other miscellaneous settings for the site as a whole.

Here are the advanced settings in detail:

Proxy Settings: Very often, you need a proxy to process some outgoing web request. An example of an outgoing web request would be from an RSS feed module on one of your pages.

SMTP Settings: These settings refer to setting up an SMTP (Simple Mail Transfer Protocol) mail server to handle all the e-mail for your system. When you sign up for an ISP to host your website, the ISP will provide you with these settings.

Other Settings: These are some miscellaneous settings that affect such things as account timeouts and auto-unlocking of accounts. You can also change site log settings, as well as other things.

You will not really need to touch any of these settings. While I did not cover all the capabilities of the host, I think that just clicking things and seeing what you can do will give you an idea of how flexible DNN is for managing a website. Figure 9-5 shows these advanced settings options from the host login.

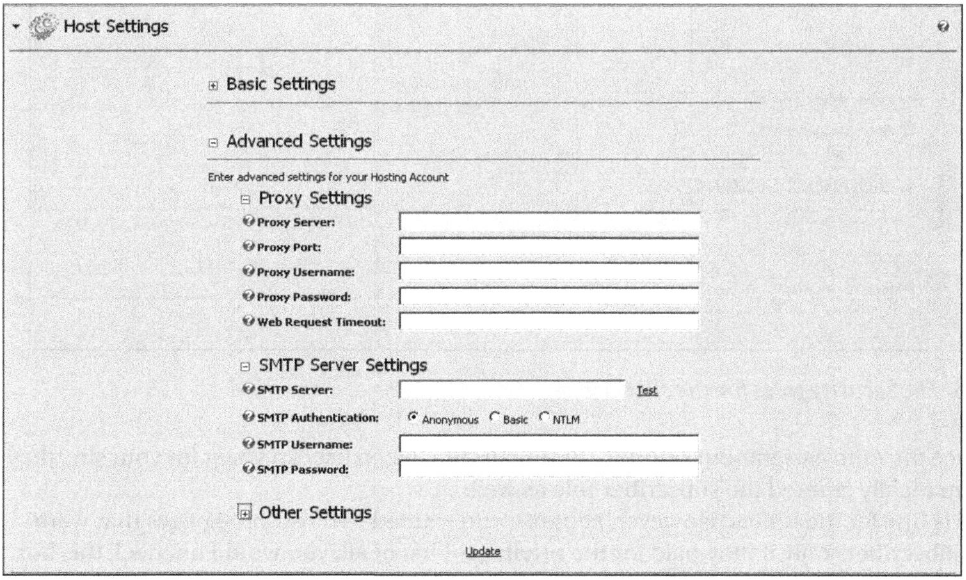

Figure 9-5. *The advanced host settings*

The role of the host is a powerful one indeed.

Before getting into the role of the administrator, I want to cover the other roles that come with the system.

The Registered User

When a user registers to your site, he is then able to log in. If a user can log into a portal as a registered user, he can view and do some things that he would not be able to as a casual browser.

Any user who registers to the site is automatically given the registered user role. You will use this role to hide pages from or expose pages to the user, depending on whether he's logged in or not.

The Subscriber

DNN gives you the ability to allow certain pages to be seen only by subscribers of the site. Figure 9-6 shows the Edit Security Roles page for the subscriber.

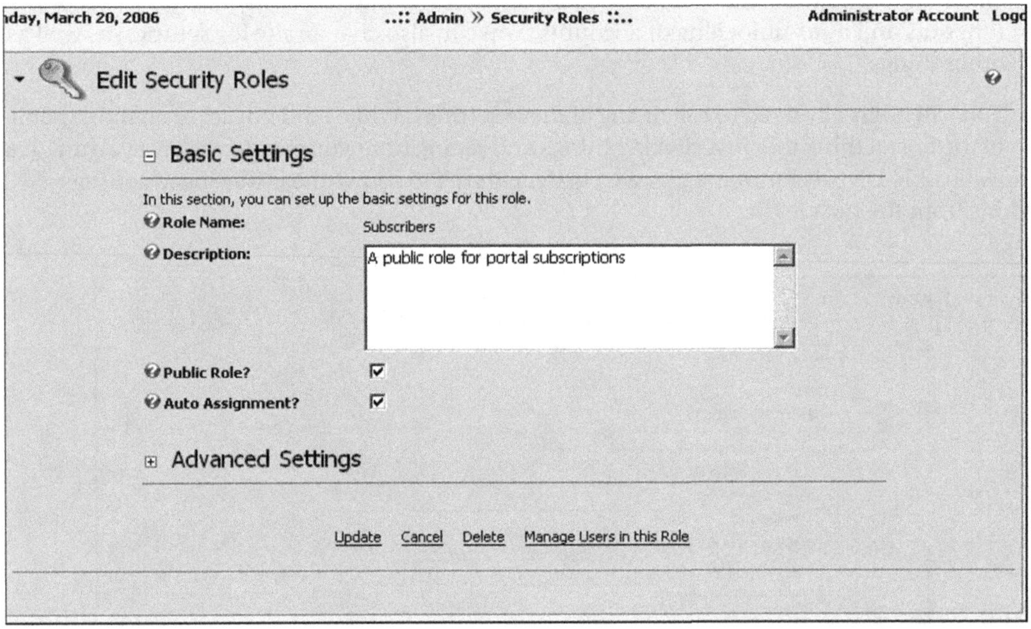

Figure 9-6. *The security roles for the subscriber*

Notice the Auto Assignment setting? This means that when users register for your site, they are automatically granted the subscriber role as well.

This is fine for most sites. However, suppose you wanted to have some pages that were seen by subscribers only if they paid for the privilege? First of all, you would uncheck this box. This way, when users register on your site, they won't automatically be subscribers.

Next, you would open the Advanced Settings section of the settings page shown in Figure 9-6, and fill in the necessary fields for billing subscribers.

Now that users are not automatically subscribers, they need to know how to become one.

Note Web hosting and e-commerce is out of scope for this book. If you want to know more, I suggest reading *Beginning ASP.NET 2.0 E-Commerce in C# 2005: From Novice to Professional*, by Cristian Darie and Karli Watson (Apress, 2005).

I have created a registered user for my site who is not a subscriber. (While not logged in, you can register a person using the link next to the Login link.) If I log in to the site and click the Registration quick link on the main page, I will be taken to the registration page. Figure 9-7 shows the Membership Services section of this page expanded.

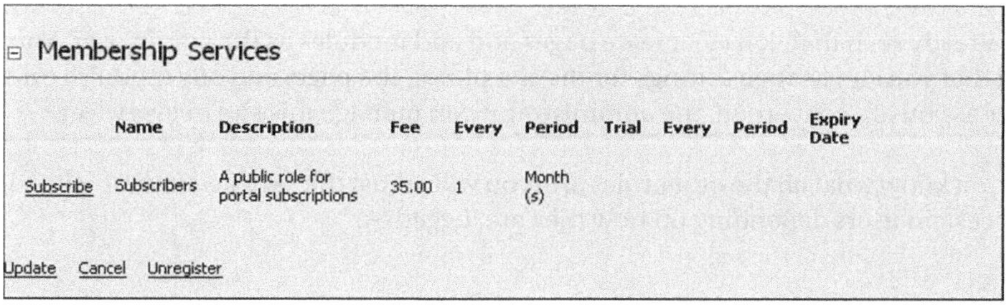

	Name	Description	Fee	Every	Period	Trial	Every	Period	Expiry Date
Subscribe	Subscribers	A public role for portal subscriptions	35.00	1	Month (s)				

Update   Cancel   Unregister

Figure 9-7. *The Membership Services section*

As you can see, as a registered user I can subscribe for $35.00 per month. If I do this, I will have access to pages not otherwise available to me. I will show you how to allow pages for different roles a little later.

All Users

Anyone who browses to this site is considered an *all user* member. This user does not need to be logged in.

Normally when you create a page, the default permission is for it to be viewed by everyone who browses to the page. While this may be fine for some sites, it is obviously not fine for your restaurant site.

Even though you disabled the Time page from doing anything for casual browsers, it would be best if it did not show at all. In a little bit, you will change the permissions for this page to exclude all users.

Unauthenticated Users

This one is a little tricky. Just as you can create pages that can only be viewed by registered users, you can also create pages that can be viewed and edited by unauthenticated users. Unauthenticated users are those who have not yet logged into your portal.

This setting is included in the page and module settings. You will not find a specific role for this user in the Security Roles list. By default, when a user is registered, she also becomes an authenticated user, and will no longer see the page that was specifically created for unauthenticated users.

There are many websites out there that show different pages to prospective customers than those who are logged in. You can think of an unauthenticated user as the reverse of a registered user.

The Administrator Role

This is the role that you will most likely be logging into the system as. Most of the time you will have a just a single portal, and any work you need done to set up pages should be done as an administrator.

You have already seen that you can create pages and add modules as the admin user. You have also seen that you can change settings for the site portal, the page, and any modules on the page. As far as you are concerned, the administrator can manage this site in every way necessary.

Now that you know what all the other roles are, you will adjust the "My Restaurant" site to show pages to certain users depending on how they are logged in.

Managing the Website

You will be creating roles and managing users so that certain aspects of the website show for certain users. The security roles you will use are as follows:

- Administrator

- Registered user

- All users

- Unauthenticated users

- Employees

Wait a sec. I did not list "employees" as a security role—you will have to create this role.

A New Role

Log in as administrator and click Admin ➤ Security Roles. Your screen should look like Figure 9-8.

There is an Add New Role link at the bottom of the page. Click this and you will be taken to the Edit Security Role screen. Fill in this page as shown in Figure 9-9.

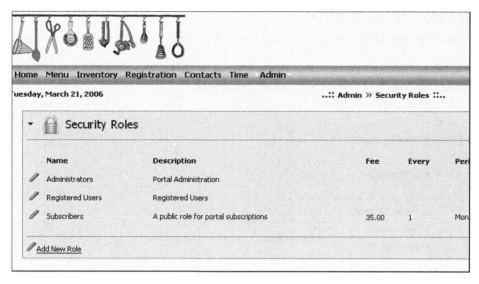

Figure 9-8. *The Security Roles screen*

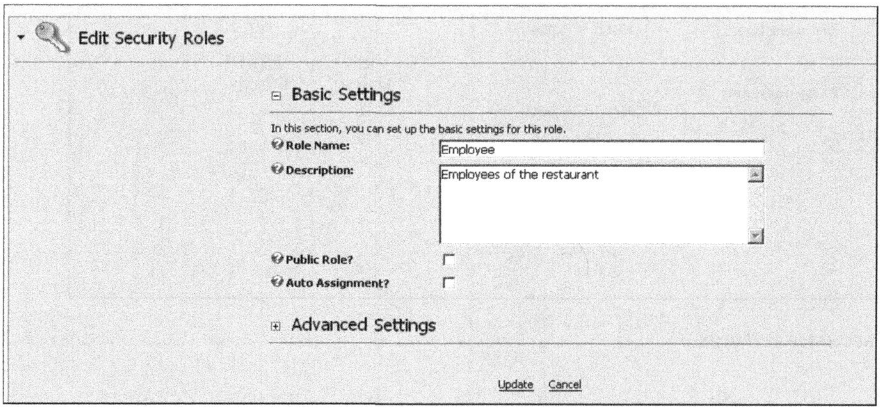

Figure 9-9. *Adding a new role*

You do not want anyone who registers on the site to automatically get this role. There would be no point in that. You also do not want any registered users to be able to assign this role to themselves. Making this role public would allow that. Instead, you want this role to be private so that only administrators can assign this role to users.

There are no advanced settings for this role, so click Update, and your new role will be created.

Now that you have all the security roles you need, let's go back and adjust the permissions for the pages in this site.

Adjusting Page Permissions

Make sure you are still logged in as administrator. Most of the pages in this portal will be open to all users.

Navigate to the home page and open the page settings. Your page should now show the new employee security role you just created, as in Figure 9-10.

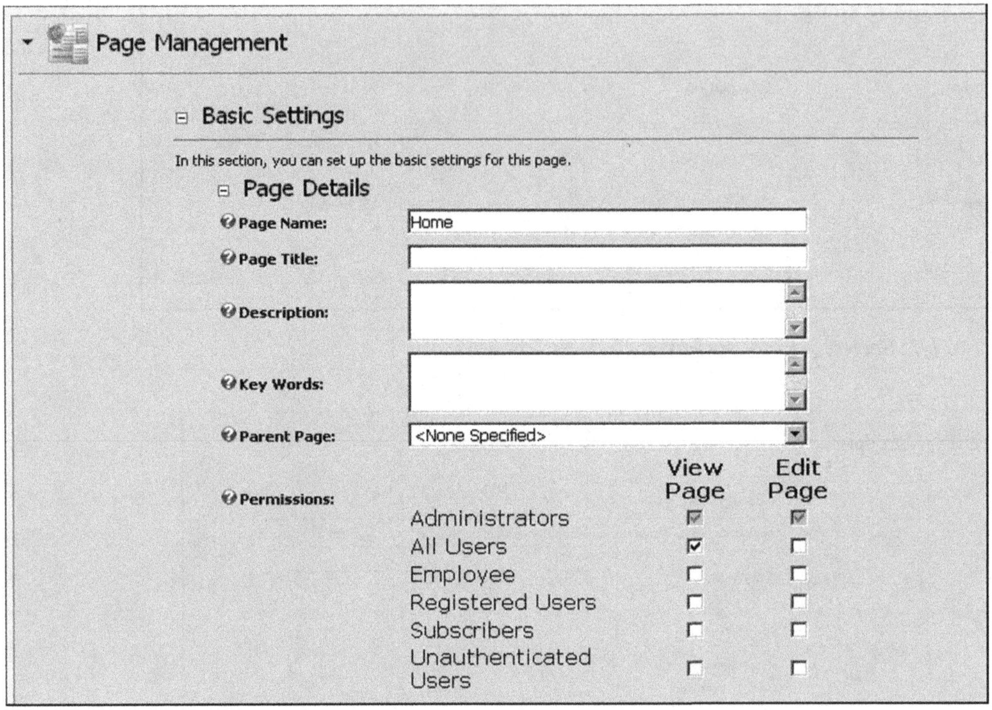

Figure 9-10. *Page security settings*

This home page is something you want all users to see. The permissions for this page are fine as is. The following pages need to have their permissions set up like this one:

- Home

- Menu

- Contacts

You want everyone to see all these pages when they browse to the site.

Open the registration page and make sure that the Registered Users box under View Page is the only one checked. The registration page you created is really intended to manage a user's password and such. There is nothing to manage if no one is logged in.

Click Update and log out. Figure 9-11 shows the menu bar and home page as you have them so far.

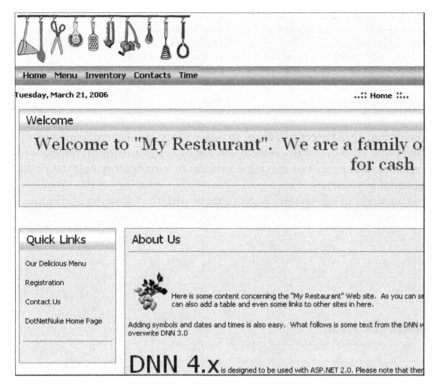

Figure 9-11. *The menu bar with no registration menu choice*

You can see that there is no registration choice on the menu bar anymore. However, if you look at the Quick Links module, you will see a link to the registration page. Click this and you will be asked to log in.

You can see from the menu bar that there are two other pages you need to hide. They are Inventory and Time.

Log back in as administrator and change the settings for these two pages such that only employees can view them (administrators will always be able to view and edit every page).

Now when you log out, you should have only Home, Menu, and Contacts on the menu bar.

Testing the Permissions

OK, so you have configured the pages such that certain users with certain roles get to see the page. Let's test how it all works.

First of all, log out of the portal and you should only see the Home, Menu, and Contacts choices, as shown in Figure 9-12.

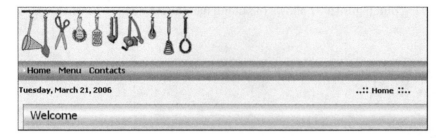

Figure 9-12. *The unregistered users view*

This is the view that unregistered users will have. In order to test the system, you need to add some users. The first thing I did to test the system was log in as administrator, navigate to the registration page, and uncheck every box there. I wanted as few mandatory fields as possible to fill in when I registered new users.

Now let's register some users in the system. Register them with the following usernames:

- Cust_1

- Cust_2

- Emp_1

- Emp_2

Figure 9-13 shows how this is done.

*Note: Membership to this portal is Public. Once your account information has been submitted, you will be immediately granted access to the portal environment. All fields marked with an asterisk (*) are required.				
First Name:	c	*	Street:	
Last Name:	1	*	Unit #:	
User Name:	Cust_1	*	City:	
Password:	••••	*	Country:	<Not Specified>
Confirm:	••••	*	Region:	
Email Address:	c1@something.com	*	Postal Code:	
Website:			Telephone:	
Instant Messenger ID:			Cell:	
			Fax:	

Figure 9-13. *Registering test users*

These four users should be enough to get the point across. Once you have them registered, log in as each one in turn, and see what pages they have access to. The menu bar for each customer should look like Figure 9-14.

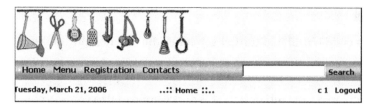

Figure 9-14. *The menu bar for test users*

You can see that Cust_1 is logged in and can now see the registration page.

Log in as administrator and click Admin ➤ User Accounts. Once you're in, edit the Emp_1 account. At the bottom of the Edit User Accounts page, there is a link called Manage Roles for this User. Click this and you will be brought to the Manage Roles for User section, as shown in Figure 9-15.

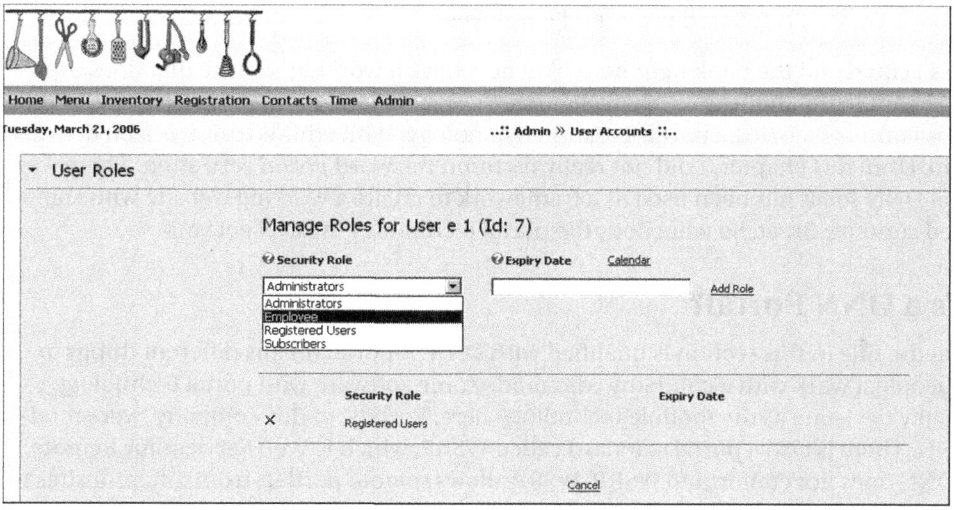

Figure 9-15. *Screen to manage user roles*

As shown in Figure 9-15, click the Security Role drop-down and choose the Employee role. Once you do this, click the Add Role link, and this user will now become an employee. Do this for Emp_2 as well.

Log out and back in as each of the test users in turn. You should see the Inventory and Time pages for the employees, and the registration page for the customers.

This is pretty cool, if I do say so myself. You can see that managing roles is a good way to enable access to parts of the website for different users.

There is a better way, though. You can combine security roles with portals to create a website that truly separates the Internet from the intranet.

Managing Portals

This section deals with creating a child portal that further separates the functionality of the website.

Let's look at what you've done so far with this website.

- You installed DNN, which created a default portal. This portal appeared to you as a complete website.

- You added pages to the site and existing modules to those pages.

- You created a new module for employees to punch in and out of work.

- You added a new page to hold this module and tested it under various conditions.

- You added a new security role to enable filtering of pages based on who was logged in.

- You changed permissions on a page-by-page basis to make the site appear properly to casual browsers, registered users, and employees.

I guess I could end the book right here. You now have a working website that does everything you set out to do. But wait . . . there's more!

DNN is famous for being a portal-creation technology. While this is true, it is a bit of a misconception. Until this chapter, I did not really mention the word *portal* very often. There was no need to. DNN so far has been used as a framework to create a working website with some customized content. Great. So what does the portal technology in DNN get you?

What Is a DNN Portal?

Notice that the title in this section is qualified with *DNN*. A portal means different things to different people. I work with a company who made some software with portal technology that's actually the same as the module technology here. Portals, to this company, were modules to DNN. There is also a portal standard called WSRP, which is Web Services for Remote Portlets. DNN does not conform to WSRP. WSRP allows remote portlets from different sites to run inside a portal via SOAP (Simple Object Access Protocol) calls.

Generally, though, a portal is a website that allows you to create other websites managed by the main one. There are two major kinds of portals. Here are their definitions, according to Wikipedia (http://en.wikipedia.org/wiki/Portal):

Enterprise portals: A framework for integrating information, applications, and processes across organizational boundaries.

Web portal: A kind of Content Management System website, password protected to allow site administrators to edit text, images, and other content as and when necessary. This allows easy updating of the website content without the need to learn programming code.

So far in this book, I think we have come close to the second definition. You have used DNN as a content management system. You have been able to create pages and manage users with no programming involved (once you got the TimePunch module created, that is).

Since you will be having both customers and employees using this website, however, I think you need to come closer to the first definition. The best solution for this website is to create a portal for Internet use and a portal for *intranet* use.

I work at a company that has a web presence to the outside world. In fact, my company owns several other companies. Each of these other companies' websites is actually a portal off the main company's website. We also have an intranet website that is available only to employees when they are connected to the internal network. This intranet is also a portal off the main website.

So why a portal rather than another website that can be accessed through a link from the main site? Table 9-1 outlines the reasons.

Table 9-1. *Separate Sites vs. Portals*

Separate Site	Portal
You cannot manage a separate site from the main one. You would need to have separate superuser rights to manage a separate website.	A DNN portal allows you to manage all child portals with the host user.
You generally cannot have a single login when you link from one site to another. You must log into the second site separately.	A portal allows you to have a single login for the system as a whole. If you log into the main portal, you can go to a child portal and still be logged in.
A separate website shares no common attributes with the main one. Different websites cannot share modules.	A DNN child portal can inherit the same skins and themes as the main portal. This means that users get the same look and feel as they navigate between what looks like one website and another. In reality, they are two different portals sharing the same skin.

Child vs. Parent

There are two kinds of portals that you can create in DNN. The first kind is a parent portal. This is what you have right now. A parent portal has a unique URL. For instance, my URL for the site is `http://localhost:1599/DotNetNuke/Default.aspx`. If you are using the debug web server that comes with VWD, then yours should be very similar.

When you create a new parent portal, you will be asked to give it a new URL.

■**Caution** Do not attempt to create another parent portal.

If you had your DNN website hosted at an ISP, you would have purchased a domain name for your site. Creating a new parent portal requires that you purchase a new domain name and have your host map the domain name to the IP address of your new account. If you create a new parent portal without having all the DNS mappings in place, you may not be able to access your new portal.

What you want is a main portal that is the face of the company (this is what you have now) and a child portal for every section you want to separate.

A child portal has the same URL, but has an extension of the sub-portal name. Here is an fictitious example of a website with a main portal and some child portals:

`Mysite.com`: This is the main portal.

`Mysite.com/finance`: This is the finance child portal.

`Mysite.com/marketing`: This is the marketing child portal.

`Mysite.com/employee`: This is the employee child portal.

Hopefully, this makes it clear for you. What you want to do now is create the last example: the employee child portal.

Creating the Portal

Log into your site using the host account. Click Host ➤ Portals. You should come up with a screen like mine, as shown in Figure 9-16.

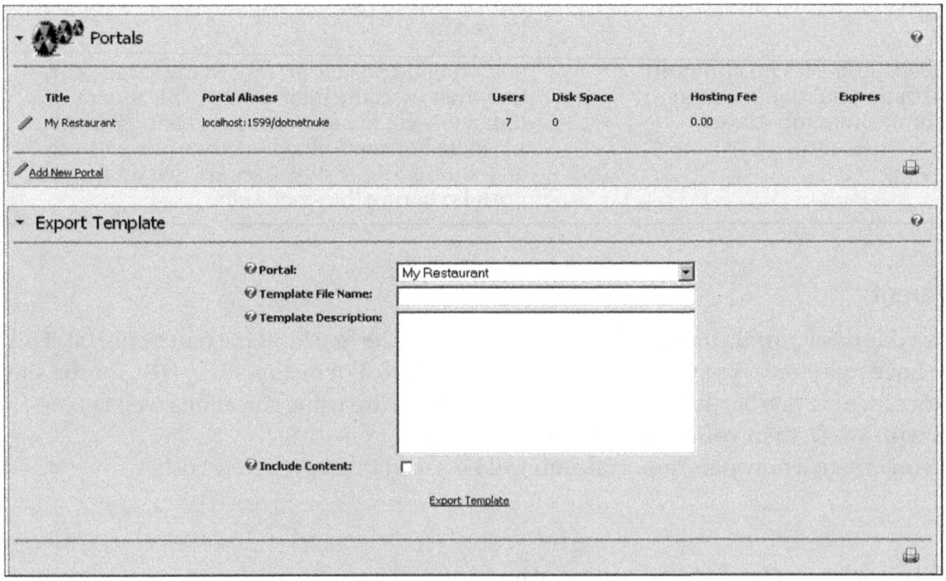

Figure 9-16. *The portal settings screen*

You can see that I have one portal, called My Restaurant, which is the main one. You also see a section to export a template. This section is used to make a portal template for use in the DNN wizard when creating a new site. You will not need to export a template.

Click the Add New Portal link. Fill in the page as shown in Figure 9-17.

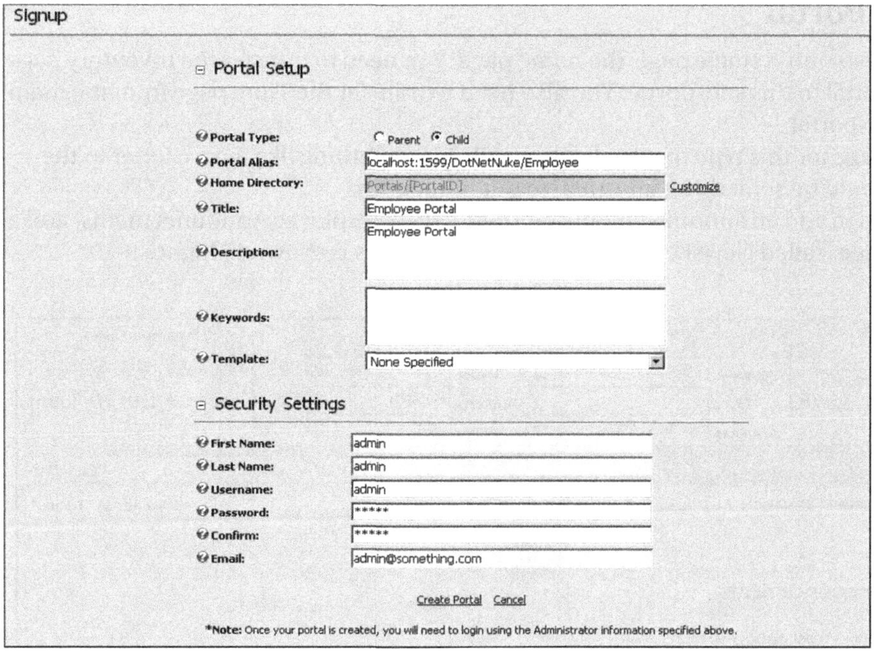

Figure 9-17. *Creating a new portal*

Make this a child portal and tack on "/Employee" at the end of the portal alias.

Make sure that you include the security settings. The username and password will be used as the administrator account for this portal.

Click Create Portal and . . . it chokes, because it needs a template file. OK, choose the portal template, retype your password, and try creating it again.

You may get a nasty looking error when DNN is done chugging. However, you can see the new portal by choosing Host ➤ Portals again. This is shown in Figure 9-18.

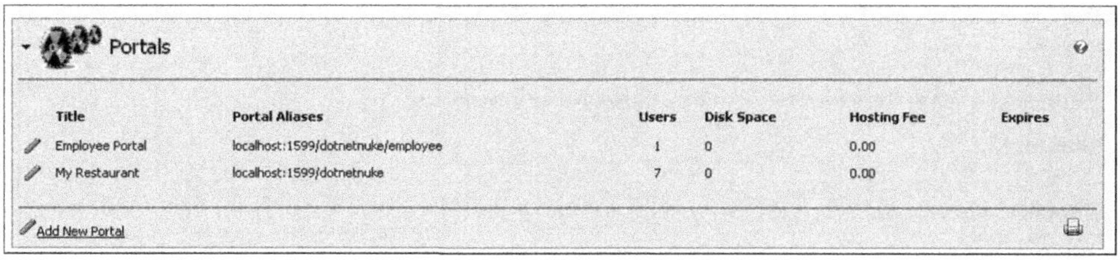

Figure 9-18. *A new employee portal is created.*

Click the new employee portal and you will be taken to the new website you just created. It will be a plain home page with nothing in the menu bar but Home, Admin, and Host. You can see here that you are still logged in as the host for this portal as well as the main one. You can now edit this portal. This is cool.

Editing the Portal

Your new portal has only a single page: the home page. You need to transfer the Inventory page from the main portal to this sub-portal. You also need to transfer the Time page from the main portal to this sub-portal.

The home page for this type of portal will usually be something like a newsletter to the employees. It should be something informative but innocuous.

You will need to add an announcements module, called Employee Announcements, and a text/HTML module, called NewsLetter, to the home page. This is shown in Figure 9-19.

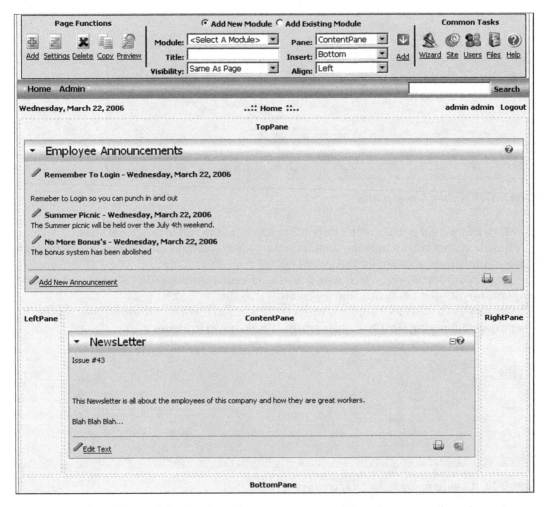

Figure 9-19. *The addition of the Employee Announcments and NewsLetter portals to the main page*

I set the login reminder announcement to not expire. I set the summer picnic announcement to expire on July 5.

This page is seen by all users who navigate to this page. Since there is no link to this portal on the main portal, the user must know the URL in order to get here.

Since this is a new portal, there will not be any Employee security role. This role is not carried over from the main portal.

Log in to the Employee portal as administrator (or host) and add the Employee security role as described earlier, in the "A New Role" section of this chapter.

Creating the Inventory Page

Unfortunately, you cannot copy a page from one portal to another. You can only copy a page from within the same portal. You will have to copy the Inventory and Time pages from the main portal in here by hand.

Create a new page, called Inventory, in the Employee portal. Make sure that its permissions are set for viewing by employees only.

Tip This is where Firefox and its tabbed windows come into play nicely. You can log into the main portal in one tab and the Employee portal in another tab. This way you can copy back and forth easily.

Add a new user-defined table module to the content pane of the Employee portal's Inventory page. Add the same content to this module that you have in the Inventory module of the main portal's Inventory page.

Make sure that the settings are the same. If you want, you can make different rows—whatever works for you.

Note A better way to display inventory would be to buy a data grid module (available from www.snowcovered.com) and display the inventory data directly from the database. If you really want to display data automatically, then I suggest you do this.

Creating the Time Page

Create a new page called Time in the Employee portal. Make sure that its permissions are set for viewing by employees only.

Add the TimePunch module to the content pane of this page. Since the TimePunch module is completely self-contained, there is no content to add. You are finished with the new portal.

Testing the New Portal

The users from one portal are not available in the new portal. Log in as the admin user and add an Employee user to the Employee portal. This is explained earlier in this chapter.

Log out of the portal, and you should see just the home page, as shown in Figure 9-20.

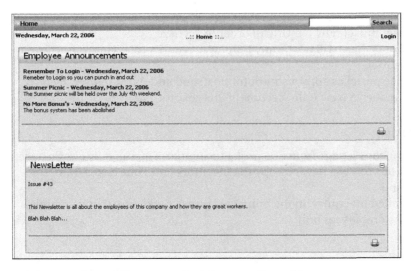

Figure 9-20. *The Employee portal with no one logged in*

Now log in as the newly created employee for this portal. You should be able to see the Inventory page and the Time page, as shown in Figure 9-21.

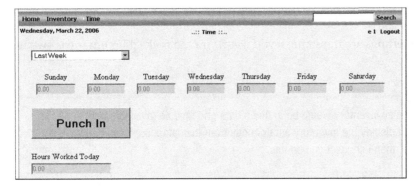

Figure 9-21. *The new portal, with the employee logged in*

The Time page should let you punch in and out of the system just as you were able to do in the main portal. If you looked at the database table, you would see that it has new rows, with different module IDs than what you saw when you punched in and out on the main portal. In fact, if you wanted, you could punch in and out in both portals, and the data would be kept separate. You need to do a little cleanup so that this isn't possible. Punching should only be done in the child portal.

Cleaning Up the Main Portal

Now that you've created the child Employee portal, it's time to get rid of any duplication in the main module. This means that you need to delete the Inventory and Time pages from the main module. You can do this by navigating to the page you want to delete, and clicking the Delete icon on the Page Functions bar. This is shown in Figure 9-22.

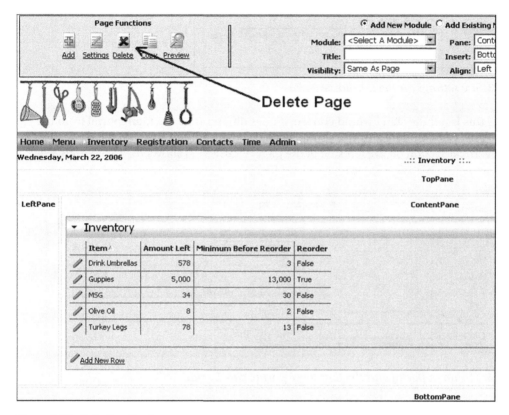

Figure 9-22. *Deleting the Inventory page*

Delete the Inventory page and the Time page.

The Look and Feel

One of the aspects I mentioned for using a DNN portal is that you can differentiate the look and feel of one portal from another. Right now, they both use the same skin. Not only do you want to differentiate the employee pages from the customer ones by using a different portal, but it would be nice to also have a different skin to differentiate between the portals.

Log into the Employee portal as administrator. In the Admin bar at the top of the page, click Site. Change the site skins as I have them in Figure 9-23.

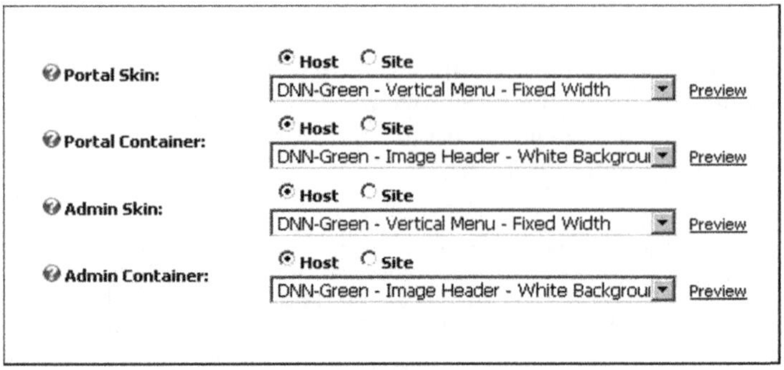

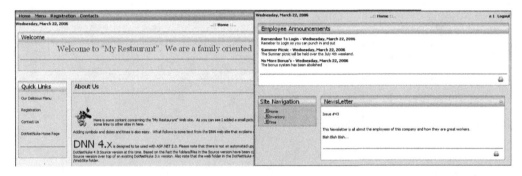

Figure 9-23. *Site settings for the Employee portal*

While this is not the skin I would choose, it does differentiate the main portal from the Employee one. Click Update and you should get a disgusting green site with the navigation links as a vertical section on the left side of the page. Figure 9-24 shows the two portals side by side.

Figure 9-24. *The main portal and the Employee portal, side by side*

Summary

This was a fun chapter. You started out with a single portal that had all the pages exposed to every casual browser.

This is not a good thing, so you learned how to create a new security role for the site and adjust the page settings so that they would only show to certain users. This made the Inventory and Time pages invisible to the casual browser and even to those who were registered users.

You learned that you must be logged in as administrator to give access to this new employee role and manage the roles for users individually. You also learned that you can auto-assign roles to registered users.

Once the roles were defined and page settings adjusted, you were able to log in as different users and see different pages.

The final thing you learned was how to separate the website functionality even more by creating a child portal. A child portal is one whose URL is the same as the parent's, but with the name of the child portal tacked onto the end. This allows you to have a single domain name that controls both internal and external websites.

The point of this whole book is to coach you along the way toward creating a web presence. So many companies have external and internal websites, and you now know how to create your own.

While restricting IP access is out of the scope of this book, I will mention that most companies' internal websites are restricted to a range of IP addresses specific to that company. This way, web users cannot get at the internal website unless they are on the company's intranet and have a valid IP address. This is accomplished with IIS management.

The next chapter will cover DNN security and finding a host for your new website. You will also load a new skin and container to change the look and feel of your website.

CHAPTER 10

■■■

DNN Hosting

Chapter 9 ended with you creating a new child portal that acted as your intranet. The child portal was not intended to be seen from outside your own private network.

What happens, though, if you are not hosting your own DNN website? Large companies with big IT budgets can host their own sites, but you probably will not be able to. Hosting your own site isn't so much difficult as it is time consuming and expensive, as far as equipment, knowledge, and bandwidth goes.

Since you will be hosting your site through a third party, you will not really have an intranet. Not to worry, though—the child portal idea still applies. There is no direct way to get to this child portal site without knowing it is there. Also, you will still need to log into the employee site to gain access.

This chapter covers how to get your website off your computer and onto an ISP's web hosting server. It also covers some other things to consider when creating your site. For instance, I have mentioned skinning plenty of times throughout this book. I will tell you how to download and enable a new skin, as well as what goes into one—in case you want to create your own skin.

Finally, I will cover security aspects of DNN.

Hosting

I have friends who host their own websites on their own computers at home. If you have the knowledge, you can do it as well. All you need is an IP address, and away you go. You do not even need a domain name.

Here is what I mean. A domain name is a friendly name like `www.something.com`. A domain name is unique and can have many extensions. Here are some of the extensions available:

- `.com`

- `.net`

- `.org`

- `.us`

- `.info`

- `.edu`

- `.name`

- `.co.uk`

- `.de`

- `.biz`

- `.tv`

- `.cc`

- `.bz`

There are many more, mostly to do with different countries. In the preceding list, `.de` is a domain name for all things German, and `.co.uk` is a domain name for websites in Great Britain. I am sure you recognize some of the other domain name extensions.

So, which one does everyone want? Once upon a time, we all wanted a domain name with the `.com` extension. The `.net` extension was a close second. This was because the general public didn't know many of the other domain extensions existed. Today, most people also know of `.org` and `.edu`, among others.

Unfortunately, since all domain names must be unique, and most domain names actually spell a word or phrase, a lot of the good ones are taken (for the well-known extensions).

A domain name is mapped to an IP address. IP addresses are also unique. However, no-one really cares what IP address they get. Most people who have websites do not even know what IP address they have.

The neat thing about browsers is that you can enter a domain name, if you know it, or an IP address that maps to that domain name. If you do not have a domain name, then you can just get an IP address, and away you go.

If you want to host your own site, you can get an IP address from your local cable or DSL company, and set up IIS to host your site. There are two reasons you should *not* do it, though:

- The cable home ISPs hate this. You can take up a lot of bandwidth hosting a site at home. All home Internet connections are bandwidth-limited on both the upload and download side. Even if you did host your own site, it may not be fast enough for anyone to use.

- It is technically demanding and requires that you know a lot more than just how to design a website.

I suggest you get your site hosted by an outside source. Fortunately, there is quite a bit of competition out there, and prices are very reasonable. Most of the time, you can get hosted with a domain name for a lot less than two hundred dollars a year.

What You Get from a Host

A company that hosts your site will provide you with the following things:

- *Guaranteed uptime*: Most boast 99.99-percent uptime. You are pretty much guaranteed that your site will never go down.

- *Constant backup*: This can be expensive to do yourself and can be even more expensive if you don't do it at all. Your host company will certainly back up all your stuff on a daily basis.

- *A mail server*: Many hosting sites give you multiple mailboxes to use.

- *Disk space*: Depending on what plan you take, most sites give you a certain amount of disk space storage, as well as a certain amount of e-mail storage.

- *Statistics*: Some plans give you statistics, such as hits and the like. Some plans make you pay for it.

- *Tech support*: All hosting companies have a person who can answer any question you may have about your website. Most get back to you almost immediately.

- *Scalability*: If you need to scale up to handle thousands of hits and downloads a day, most hosting companies have the capacity and equipment to handle it.

As far as hosting a DNN site goes, you also get some other things, one of which is free setup. I have seen hosting sites where you can sign up and request a person to install DNN 4.x for you. This is really a great feature. You end up with a good starting point and you can create your website right there on their server.

You may have noticed that, except for creating the TimePunch module, you did not use the features of ASP.NET or the IDE at all. In fact, if you have IIS running, rather than the debug web server that comes with VWD, you do not even have to load VWD to create your site.

Once the TimePunch module was created, you spent all your time within your site—using the DNN administrator capabilities to create it.

There is no reason that you cannot create a website directly on the host machine. This is really what DNN was created for.

Downloading Your Project

If you spent a lot of time creating your website on your machine at home, you do not necessarily want to recreate it on the host machine. You want to upload what you have and be done with it. Any good host will let you do this. In fact, any good host will *tell* you how to do this.

When you sign up for a hosting account, you will most likely be given access to some kind of interface to manage the files in your web space. This web space is a virtual root directory on their server. A virtual directory is an actual directory on some PC somewhere. IIS is told that this actual directory is now the virtual root of your website.

It could be that the host has a machine with many directories, each of which is mapped to another customer's virtual root of their website. IIS can handle many websites at once. If your site scales up to thousands of hits a day and needs tons of disk space, you may be assigned your own server or group of servers.

Here is a basic list of things you will need to do to upload your DNN site from your computer to a host computer and get it working. This list is general, but should give you a good idea that you can do it yourself.

Note If you used IIS as a web server for your site on your computer, your root would be `C:\Inetpub\wwwroot`. If you used the local web server, your root should just be `C:\`.

---

1. Make sure that the host can handle ASP.NET 2.0.

2. Edit the `Web.config` file. You will need to put in the correct database settings. These include the server name, database name, username, and password. Right now, you do not have the server name. This is because your database is on your machine with the ASP.NET system. On a hosting site, the database may be on a different machine. You get this account information from the host provider.

3. Upload all your DNN files to your root folder. The host will give you a way to do this, usually by FTP. In my case, the files would include everything in `C:\DotNetNuke` and all its subfolders. If you are using IIS on your local machine, then your files would reside in `C:\Inetpub\wwwroot\DotNetNuke`.

4. Open your browser and navigate to your domain name. When you get to your domain, DNN will set up your database objects when it first loads. As you have seen on your own machine, this can take several minutes.

5. Manage your site.

This list seems so simple and yet complicated at the same time. There are so few steps, but you really need to get them right.

Finding a Host

Finding someone to host your site is easy. If you search for "DNN Hosting," you'll find pages and pages of companies willing to host your site.

I suggest that you get a host who will install DNN for you and provide a level of support that you can feel comfortable with. Most say that they will answer any support ticket questions within an hour so. This is not too bad.

My own preference is to find a host who seems to specialize in hosting DNN sites. While anyone who has a Windows server, and can handle ASP.NET 2.0 and SQL Server, can host a DNN site, there is a lot more to it than just that. They should have a DNN expert on hand.

Installing a Skin

The skin that comes with the basic DNN install is the blue and white one you are familiar with. It is not very exciting.

As I have said before, there are a number of places where you can get new skins to give your website a unique look that matches your site content. One of them is www.snowcovered.com.

If you are courageous, you can create your own skin. I will show you how to do this in Chapter 11. For now, this section will show you how to install a new skin and activate it in your site.

You will test the skin in the My Restaurant registration page.

Uploading a New Skin

When you install your DNN site on another computer, you will have a folder called Install. If you look on your own computer, you will see a folder called C:\DotNetNuke\Install. This is shown in Figure 10-1.

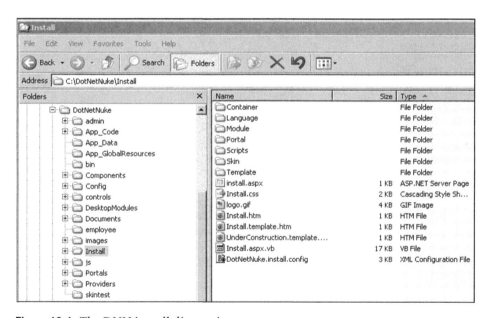

Figure 10-1. *The DNN install directories*

You can see here that there are subfolders for installing containers, skins, languages, and so on. If you were to buy a skin from somewhere like www.snowcovered.com, you would download the skin to C:\DotNetNuke\Install\Skin. From there, you would use DNN to actually install it.

I have provided a skin for you, called Flowers. This skin comes with a container as well. The skin controls the look and feel of the pages within the website, while the container controls the look and feel of the module itself.

I will show you how to install the Flowers skin here, and in the next chapter I will show you how to make the skin and container yourself.

Copy the `Flowers - Fixed Width.zip` skin to the `C:\DotNetNuke\Install\Skin` folder. Next, copy the `Flowers.zip` container to the `C:\DotNetNuke\Install\Container` folder.

The rest is incredibly simple. Make sure you are logged in as host. Navigate to Admin A Skins. You should get a web page like the one shown in Figure 10-2.

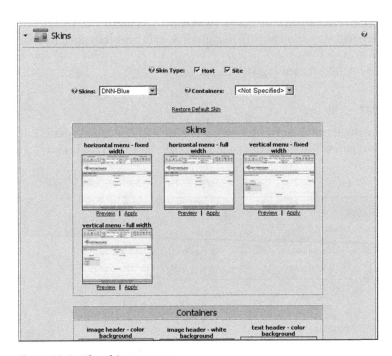

Figure 10-2. *The skin manager*

This is the skin manager screen. You can see here that I have chosen the DNN-Blue set of skins. This has four skins and four containers. The one I provided only has one skin and one container.

Scroll down to the bottom of this page and click Upload Skin. You should get the screen shown in Figure 10-3.

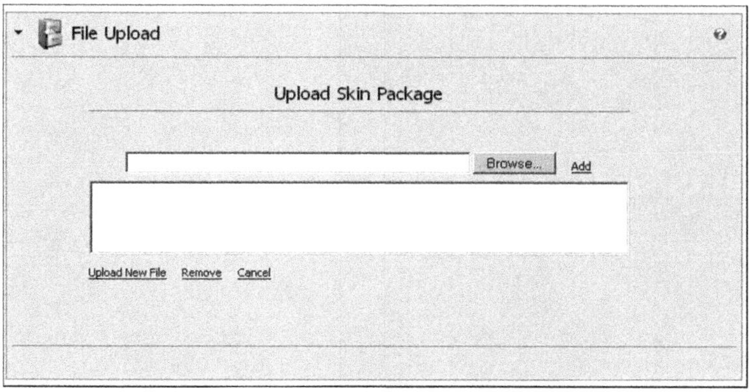

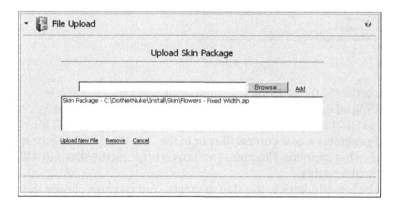

Figure 10-3. *Uploading a skin using the File Manager*

Use the Browse button to choose the skin you put in the Install folder. Once you've chosen it, click the Add link, and it will appear in the box, as shown in Figure 10-4.

Figure 10-4. *A new skin, ready for upload*

Click the Upload New File link, and the skin manager will churn a bit and install the skin for you. You will get a log file showing what happened. This is shown in Figure 10-5.

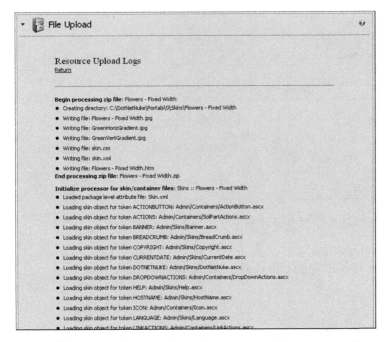

Figure 10-5. *A skin install log*

It is interesting to note what the log file is telling you. First of all, you can see that it is unzipping the skin file and finding all the files within. It then scans the `Flowers - Fixed Width.htm` file for all the possible DNN tokens. Once it completes the scan, it replaces all the tokens with DNN controls and generates a user control file out of the `.htm` file. This last part is not evident in this log, but that is what happens. Chapter 11 will cover creating the skin and will explain this process much more thoroughly.

Click Return, and you will be brought back to the skin manager. You can now choose the Flowers skin in the Skins drop-down list. If you do, you will get a screen like Figure 10-6.

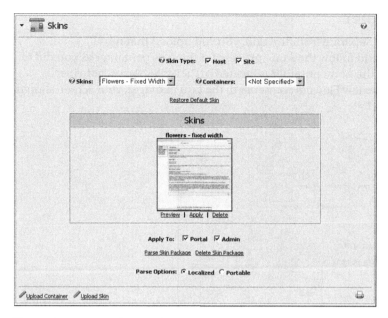

Figure 10-6. *A new skin, with picture*

I have included a picture of the new skin in action so you can see what it looks like before you choose it.

■**Note** This skin, unlike the DNN skins that come with the DNN install, only has two panes per page. If you take a closer look at Figure 10-10, you will see that the only pane visible to you is the content pane. The other pane is on the same line as the search bar. When testing this skin, make sure you test it on a page with only one module. Make sure that module is in the content pane. Nothing bad will happen otherwise, it is just that your other modules that were in the other panes will all be gathered in the single pane here.

Installing the Container

Since the Flowers container is separate from the skin, you will upload that next.

Click Upload Container, and follow the same process for the new container as you did for the new skin. Remember that the new container is located in `C:\DotNetNuke\Container`.

When you have chosen the new Flowers container in the skin manager, your screen should show a preview like Figure 10-7.

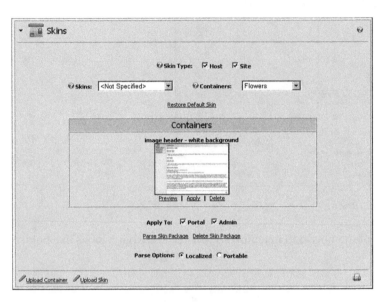

Figure 10-7. *Preview of the Flowers container*

While logged in as administrator or host, I want you to navigate to the registration page of the restaurant website. This page is shown in Figure 10-8.

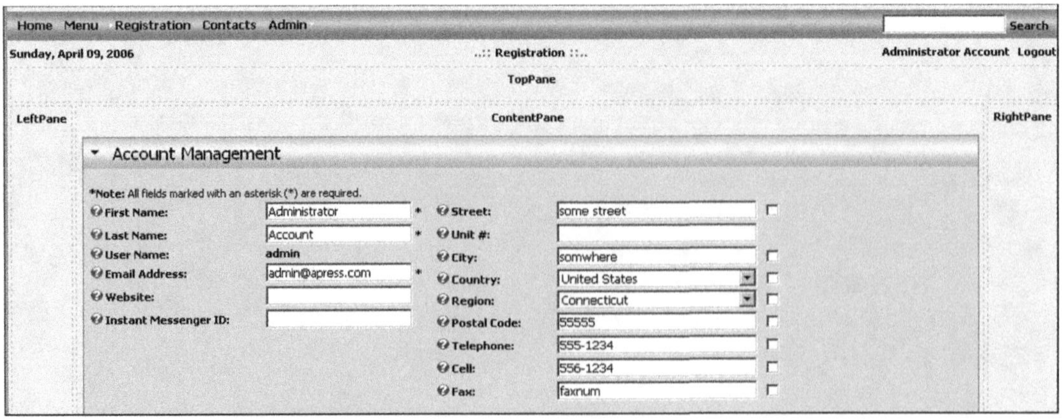

Figure 10-8. *The registration page*

This page only has one module, and it is inside the Content pane. This layout fits your new skin.

Click the Settings icon on the Page Functions icon bar at the top of the page. Scroll down the settings page and choose the Flowers skin and container. This is shown in Figure 10-9.

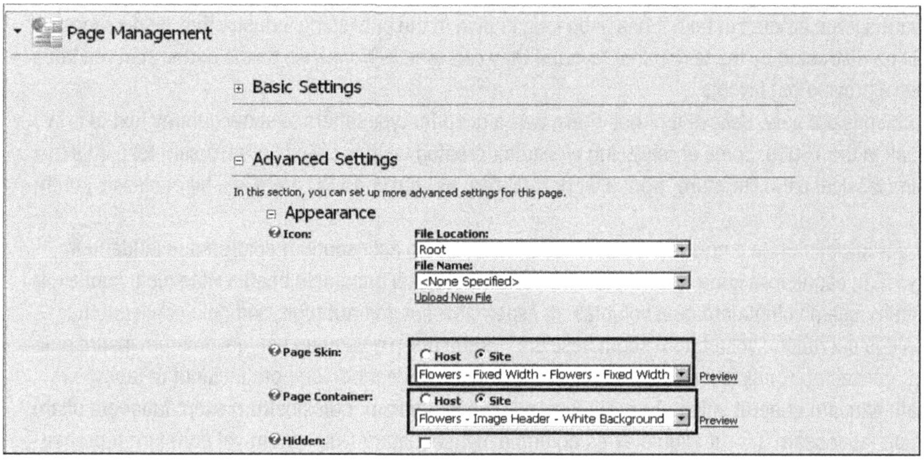

Figure 10-9. *Choosing the Flowers skin and container*

Note that you will need to check the Site radio button in order to find the new skin and container in the list.

Click the Update link at the bottom of the page, and your screen should change to the new skin and container. This is shown in Figure 10-10.

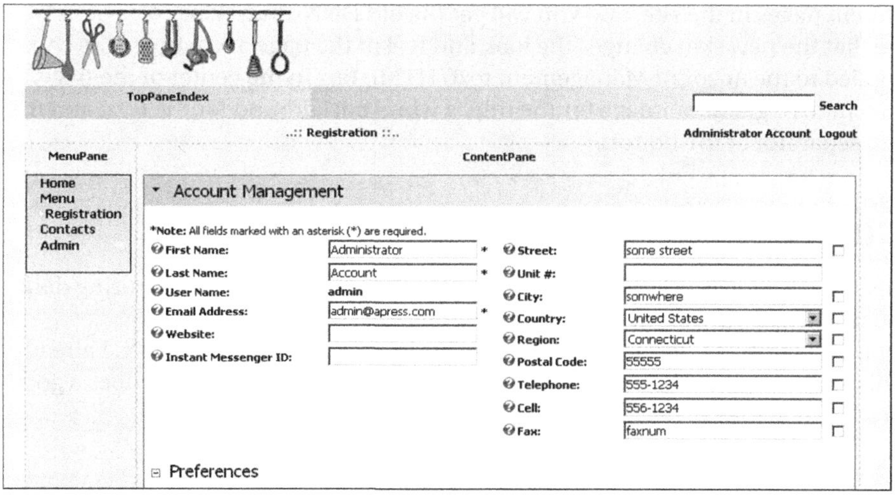

Figure 10-10. *The new skin, applied to a single page*

LOREM IPSUM TEXT

The quandary that you often have in putting together a demo screen is the text you use to fill up a page.

If you are creating a new page and wish to have some text boxes with some text in them, what do you do? You could just start typing random sentences, but that actually gets hard and tedious after a while, especially if you want a large amount of text. It has been long known in the publishing industry that readers looking at a layout will be distracted by the text in that layout if they can read it. Nonsense text is better than readable text when you're proving out layouts.

This problem is not new. Believe it or not, there was a need for typesetters to show dummy text to prove out layouts back in the 1500s. Some enterprising typesetter created what is called Lorem Ipsum text. This text has its roots in classical Latin literature, from a work by Cicero written in 45 BC. Here is a bit of classic Lorem Ipsum text:

"Sed ut perspiciatis unde omnis iste natus error sit voluptatem accusantium doloremque laudantium, totam rem aperiam, eaque ipsa quae ab illo inventore veritatis et quasi architecto beatae vitae dicta sunt explicabo. Nemo enim ipsam voluptatem quia voluptas sit aspernatur aut odit aut fugit, sed quia consequuntur magni dolores eos qui ratione voluptatem sequi nesciunt. Neque porro quisquam est, qui dolorem ipsum quia dolor sit amet, consectetur, adipisci velit, sed quia non numquam eius modi tempora incidunt ut labore et dolore magnam aliquam quaerat voluptatem. Ut enim ad minima veniam, quis nostrum exercitationem ullam corporis suscipit laboriosam, nisi ut aliquid ex ea commodi consequatur? Quis autem vel eum iure reprehenderit qui in ea voluptate velit esse quam nihil molestiae consequatur, vel illum qui dolorem eum fugiat quo voluptas nulla pariatur?"

(My spell-checker goes nuts on this text.) There are several websites that generate this text for you. Try www.lipsum.com.

The next time you want to demo a page, you can include some of this text very quickly.

Note that this new skin has the menu on the left-hand side and does not include the date. Navigate to different pages in the site, and you will get the old DNN-Blue skin.

You can see that the new skin changes the look and feel of the page as a whole. The container skin is applied to the Account Management text/HTML box in the center of the page. This container includes a gradient image for the title, a white background for the text, and the green line for the separator at the bottom.

DNN Security

Let's talk about security in DNN. There are two types of security: one concerns securing data from authorized users, and the other concerns preventing hacking.

The first type of security is addressed using the security roles provided by DNN. I already went through this extensively in Chapter 9 when I talked about permissions. DNN does a good and flexible job when it comes to this kind of security.

Unauthorized Break-Ins

The criminal hacker that gets at sensitive data is what we all hear about on the news. Some of these hacks are truly spectacular. Here is a short list of how hackers can compromise your system:

- Social hacking
- Brute force username and password hacking
- Application profiling
- SQL injection
- Entry point attacks
- Cross-site scripting
- Identity theft
- Unmanaged code hacking
- View state hacking

These security threats are addressed in greater detail in the following sections. Keep in mind, though, that this can never be an exhaustive list, as new hacks are being tried all the time.

Social Hacking

Remember Kevin Mitnick? He is probably the most famous hacker of all. He was caught and, of course, now make bunches of money as a security consultant.

Anyway, his favorite form of hacking is the easiest. He would call someone at a company and pretend to be someone who worked there who needed some information. Many times he was able to get people to give him usernames and passwords to sensitive data. This is called social hacking.

DNN cannot do anything about one of your employees giving out usernames and passwords, but you can. By the same token, you can also prevent people from putting their passwords on a Post-it note on their monitors. This is also a common way to get information.

Preventing social hacking is one major way to secure your system.

Brute Force Hacking

This is sometimes called dictionary hacking. What happens is that a hacker uses a program that tries to get into a site using a known username. The password he tries comes from a dictionary of passwords. In fact, an actual dictionary is often used. As long as there is no retries limit and no restrictions on passwords, a hacker is quite likely to find a password that is a valid word or phrase.

Unfortunately, DNN does not have password blacklists, forced password formats (such as length and mixture of characters and numbers), or password expirations. You can, however, buy modules that enable these things for you.

The best thing to do to defeat dictionary attacks is to have a policy in place that enforces a complicated password.

This brings up another point. When you installed DNN, the opening page told you to change the admin and host passwords. Make sure you do this. You should also change the admin and host usernames as well. This is not so apparent in DNN. Here is how to do it:

1. Log in as host.

2. Add a new user who has an administrator role.

3. Log in as the new administrator user you just created.

4. Go to the user management screen and delete the admin user.

You can do the same for the host user, only you need to add a new superuser account. Currently, there is no way to rename a user. There is a module that you can buy that lets you do this, though.

Application Profiling

If I was to navigate to a site and I saw some telltale signs that I was on a DNN portal, I could immediately try a few simple hacks. For instance, I could guess that the administrator username is Admin, and I could guess that the person who owns the site is lazy and that the administrator password is also Admin. I bet this would get me into a number of DNN sites.

Hackers often look for telltale signs of the software used to make a site. This is called application profiling. DNN has quite a few of these telltale signs. Fortunately, you can turn these off to prevent this kind of application profiling. The following list details some of the ways that you can make DNN more secure in this regard:

- The title bar can be changed so that it does not betray the DNN version.

- The source code comments can be eliminated so that when someone views the source in the browser they cannot tell it is DNN code. DNN has a liberal license that allows you to eliminate these comments.

- The DNN copyright message in the page footer can be turned off.

It does not take much effort to protect DNN from application profiling.

SQL Injection

This is nefarious indeed. In a program in which SQL queries are used, a hacker can insert or alter an existing database query. This is done by using quotes to break out of a select statement.

The classic example is when a login page uses something like `select * from logintable where username='admin' and password='password'`. A hacker can inject a quote and comment characters to create a new SQL statement. The new statement could read like this: `select * from logintable where username='admin' and password='%'';--password'`. The addition of the `';` closes the initial statement. The `--` act as comment characters.

This new SQL statement effectively gets the password from the login table, where the username is "admin."

You saw from creating the module that DNN tries not to use SQL statements directly. DNN uses stored procedures for all database access. This greatly reduces the possibility of hacking using SQL injection techniques.

Entry Point Attacks

Many websites use multiple pages. To the casual user, it looks like DNN uses multiple pages as well. After all, the restaurant website had a home page, a menu page, a contacts page, and so on. Each of these pages could be a point of entry for a hacker.

What most people don't realize, though, is that DNN only has a single page: the `default.aspx` page. What happens is that with a few exceptions, all the other pages that DNN shows for your website are virtual. They are made on the fly from user controls. This will become apparent to you in the next chapter when you create your skin from scratch.

The fewer the entry points, the fewer mistakes you will make, and the less opportunity hackers will have to get inside.

Cross-Site Scripting

This attack occurs when someone visits your guestbook or forum. The hacker can then submit something to the site and inject HTML tags with the submission. This website then executes this HTML code.

DNN has functions in the core modules that strip HTML tags when updating or adding to forum entries. These functions are global and are found in the core. You can use them yourself if you create a DNN module that accepts text input.

The best way to see how this is done is to read the code that comes with the DNN modules. The `Admin\Security\signin.ascx.vb` file is used to sign people into your website. It calls the following method:

```
objEventLogInfo.LogUserName = objSecurity.InputFilter(txtUsername.Text,
        PortalSecurity.FilterFlag.NoScripting Or
        PortalSecurity.FilterFlag.NoMarkup)
```

This method call strips HTML and script from the users' login names.

Identity Theft

This attack occurs when a hacker uses a cross-site scripting attack to steal cookies while in a public forum or discussion group. If a hacker steals a cookie, he can then log into the portal.

DNN does not store session state in disk-based cookies. It stores it in an in-memory encrypted cookie. Back when you created the DNN TimePunch module, you used the system session state to store your own session state. Since the system session state is encrypted, so was the session state objects you stored. DNN does a good job of preventing identity theft.

Unmanaged Code Hacking

DNN is written using ASP.NET. As such, it uses managed code. Managed code does not use pointers, and all data type errors are caught at compile time. Arrays are protected from bounds overflows. Buffer overruns (a common entry point for attack) cannot happen.

It is possible to call unmanaged code, but the DNN core does not do this. The DNN core, along with the .NET Framework, is very robust.

View State Hacking

As I have explained, one of the neat features of ASP.NET is the view state. A control will appear to maintain its contents during a round trip to the server.

View state is accomplished by using hidden fields on the form to contain the data for all the forms controls. This view state can be encrypted by using triple-DES encryption via an entry in the `machine.config` file.

ASP.NET also has something called a machine authentication check (MAC), which can be performed on the view state. This is enabled on the page with
`<%@ Page EnableViewStateMac="true"%>`.

The MAC encodes the view state with a hash code using the MD5 algorithm. On postback, ASP.NET checks the encoded view state to verify that it has not been tampered with. The MAC cannot prevent tampering, but it can notify you if the view state has been altered.

Secure Sockets Layer

The most common level of security that most Internet surfers know of is SSL. The Secure Sockets Layer (SSL) is something that all web users are familiar with. Anyone who has purchased anything on the Internet or provided sensitive data has seen the little lock icon at the bottom-right-hand corner of the page.

You can also recognize SSL in the URL. Instead of seeing `http://`, you will see `https://`. The *s* stands for *secure*.

How SSL Works

SSL is a cryptographic system that uses two keys to encrypt the data. One key is the public key known to everyone, and the other key is a private key known only to the recipient.

The public key is used to encrypt the data, and the private key is used to decrypt the data. Both of these keys are contained in an SSL certificate. The encryption is commonly 128-bit encryption. There are also 40-bit encryption certificates, but they are easily broken by hackers with the right tools and time. A 128-bit encryption algorithm is more than a trillion times a trillion times more difficult to break.

An SSL certificate is something that you buy from a company such as `www.verisign.com`. These companies are considered trusted sources of certificates, and VeriSign digitally signs the certificate you buy from them. This digital signature identifies you as a trusted source for anyone browsing to your site.

An SSL certificate is about $1,000.00 per year. You can also get a trial certificate if you like.

SSL and DNN

DNN does not work natively with SSL. You can secure the whole DNN site inside of IIS if you like, but securing individual pages is not so easy. There are modules that you can buy that enable the interaction between DNN and SSL. You can find these modules on www.snowcovered.com.

Most people who use SSL with DNN only secure the login and registration pages. However, if you use some kind of e-commerce on your site, then you will need to secure that as well.

If you need to secure your DNN site with SSL, I suggest you buy a module that does this for you.

The best way to test out any SSL module you buy is to get a trial certificate. You can then see if it covers the web pages you want, and if it is worth your money to buy it.

Summary

This chapter has covered a couple of things. First of all, it covered what happens when you want to go live with your new website.

While you can host a site from your home PC, it is not advisable. The money you have to pay for a domain name and hosting services is minimal compared to the effort and knowledge required to keep a website up and running 24-7.

I gave you suggestions on how to find a hosting site for your DNN project, and what to look for. There are quite a few DNN hosting sites out there.

Next, I covered how to install a new skin and container. This was fairly trivial. The skin and container I provide with this book are the ones that you will make yourself in the next chapter.

Then I covered a variety of security threats to DNN. DNN is based upon ASP.NET, which has quite a bit of security built in. The DNN core team is also very aware of possible hacking attacks, and has done everything it can to ameliorate this potential problem. On this score, DNN performs well.

These days, quite a few websites are gathering sensitive information from their users. If you want your site to do this, I suggest you look into getting an SSL certificate and a module that lets you use it on a page-by-page basis.

The next chapter covers how to make a new skin and container for DNN. You will find out that the skinning method DNN uses does not require any programming, and as such can be accomplished by graphic designers without any help from programmers.

CHAPTER 11

■ ■ ■

Creating a DNN Skin

Chapter 10 described how to install and work with a DNN skin and container. You took the supplied skin that comes with this book and installed it in a new web page you created to test this new skin.

This chapter will teach you how to create the skin you used in the last chapter.

When I was thinking about this chapter, I was torn between whether this would be out of the scope of this book. However, I think that as a programmer you can really benefit from doing this yourself. There is very little good information on creating your own skin, so I think this chapter is unique and valuable.

What Is a Skin?

A skin is the combination of the layout and the look and feel of a page. By look and feel, I am talking about the use of images, text, and colors.

DotNetNuke takes these skins and injects the content (modules) where it should go within the skin. This allows for the mixture of static layout with dynamic content.

How DNN Does Skins

A skin in DNN starts out with an HTML table that defines the page. This is pretty standard for creating a page. However, this layout does not actually become a page. It becomes an ASP.NET user control. The layout is created inside an .htm file and gets transformed by the DNN skinning engine to become an .ascx file.

When the user sees the results of the .htm file, he sees what looks like a complete web page. Within an .htm file, you can include tokens, which take the form [TOKEN]. There are many tokens that DNN recognizes, such as [LOGO] and [LANGUAGE].

These tokens are read by the skin parser and replaced with dynamic DNN user controls when the .htm file is turned into an .ascx file. Here is part of an .htm file that includes tokens (the HTML is incomplete):

```
<table class="containermaster_flower" cellspacing="0" cellpadding="5"
       align="center"
  border="0">
  <tr>
    <td class="containerrow1_flower">
      <table width="100%" border="0" cellpadding="0" cellspacing="0">
```

```
        <tr>
          <td valign="middle" nowrap>
            [ACTIONS]</td>
          <td valign="middle" nowrap>
            [ICON]</td>
          <td valign="middle" width="100%" nowrap>
             [TITLE]</td>
          <td valign="middle" nowrap>
            [VISIBILITY][ACTIONBUTTON:5]</td>
        </tr>
      </table>
    </td>
  </tr>
```

See the [ACTIONS], [ICON], [TITLE], [VISIBILITY], and [ACTIONBUTTON:5] tokens? Now here is the .ascx file after the DNN parser has done its magic:

```
<%@ Control language="vb" CodeBehind="~/admin/Containers/container.vb"
    AutoEventWireup="false" Explicit="True"
    Inherits="DotNetNuke.UI.Containers.Container" %>
<%@ Register TagPrefix="dnn" TagName="ACTIONS"
    Src="~/Admin/Containers/SolPartActions.ascx" %>
<%@ Register TagPrefix="dnn" TagName="ICON"
    Src="~/Admin/Containers/Icon.ascx"%>
<%@ Register TagPrefix="dnn" TagName="TITLE"
    Src="~/Admin/Containers/Title.ascx"%>
<%@ Register TagPrefix="dnn" TagName="VISIBILITY"
    Src="~/Admin/Containers/Visibility.ascx" %>
<%@ Register TagPrefix="dnn" TagName="ACTIONBUTTON5"
    Src="~/Admin/Containers/ActionButton.ascx" %>
<%@ Register TagPrefix="dnn" TagName="ACTIONBUTTON1"
    Src="~/Admin/Containers/ActionButton.ascx" %>
<%@ Register TagPrefix="dnn" TagName="ACTIONBUTTON2"
    Src="~/Admin/Containers/ActionButton.ascx" %>
<%@ Register TagPrefix="dnn" TagName="ACTIONBUTTON3"
    Src="~/Admin/Containers/ActionButton.ascx" %>
<%@ Register TagPrefix="dnn" TagName="ACTIONBUTTON4"
    Src="~/Admin/Containers/ActionButton.ascx" %>
<link href="<%= SkinPath %>../Container/container.css" rel="stylesheet"
    type="text/css" />
<table class="containermaster_flower" cellspacing="0" cellpadding="5"
    align="center"
  border="0">
  <tr>
    <td class="containerrow1_flower">
      <table width="100%" border="0" cellpadding="0" cellspacing="0">
```

```
    <tr>
      <td valign="middle" nowrap>
        <dnn:ACTIONS runat="server" id="dnnACTIONS" /></td>
      <td valign="middle" nowrap>
        <dnn:ICON runat="server" id="dnnICON" /></td>
      <td valign="middle" width="100%" nowrap>
         <dnn:TITLE runat="server" id="dnnTITLE" /></td>
      <td valign="middle" nowrap>
        <dnn:VISIBILITY runat="server" id="dnnVISIBILITY" />
        <dnn:ACTIONBUTTON5 runat="server" id="dnnACTIONBUTTON5"
              CommandName="ModuleHelp.Action" DisplayIcon="True"
              DisplayLink="False" /></td>
    </tr>
  </table>
</td>
</tr>
```

You can see from this code that the [ICON] token has been replaced with the code `<dnn:ICON runat="server" id="dnnICON" />`. This is true for the other tokens as well.

It is entirely possible (and is done in practice) to create the user control `.ascx` code and skip the `.htm` token code altogether. However, the `.htm` code is much easier to read and can be edited by people who do website layout with no coding capability. The `.ascx` file is harder to follow. I will explain this more as we get into the chapter.

DNN Tokens

Way back when you downloaded the DNN installer, you should have also downloaded the DNN help files. If not, I advise you to go to the DNN website and download them now. Included in these help files is a file called `DotNetNuke Skinning.pdf`. This file is a technical explanation of skinning. It also has a handy table of all the tokens you can use, and what their default values are. Following is the list of tokens available as of DNN 4.0.2. I will leave it to you to look up their usage.

- ACTIONBUTTON

- BANNER

- BREADCRUMB

- CONTENTPANE

- COPYRIGHT

- CURRENTDATE

- DOTNETNUKE

- DROPDOWNACTIONS

- HELP

- HOSTNAME

- ICON

- LANGUAGE

- LINKACTIONS

- LINKS

- LOGIN

- LOGO

- PRINTMODULE

- PRIVACY

- SEARCH

- SIGNIN

- SOLPARTACTIONS

- SOLPARTMENU

- TERMS

- TITLE

- TREEVIEWMENU

- USER

- VISIBILITY

The neat thing is that these tokens can be placed anywhere in the table you create. DNN takes care of the rest. These tokens make creating skins so much easier. Along with including these token in an .htm file, you can also include a special .xml file that defines attributes for the DNN controls that replace these tokens. I will cover this .xml file later in this chapter.

CSS Basics

While the .htm file table layout and the tokens represent the layout of the skin, it is the .css file that defines the look and feel.

Cascading style sheets (CSS) contains attributes for elements contained within an HTML table.

Here is a piece of HTML code using attributes in the tag itself:

```
<td bgcolor="fuchsia" width="100%">
  <hr color="#ffffff"/>
  <table width="100%" border="0" cellpadding="0" cellspacing="0">
    <tr>
      <td align="left" valign="middle" nowrap>
        [ACTIONBUTTON:1]</td>
```

```
    <td align="right" valign="middle" nowrap>
      [ACTIONBUTTON:2] [ACTIONBUTTON:3] [ACTIONBUTTON:4]</td>
  </tr>
</table>
</td>
```

Now here is the same piece of HTML code using a .css file:

```
<td class="containerrow2_flower" >
  <hr class="containermaster_flower"/>
  <table class="containermaster_flower>
    <tr>
      <td class="containermaster_flower2">
        [ACTIONBUTTON:1]</td>
      <td align="right" valign="middle" nowrap>
        [ACTIONBUTTON:2] [ACTIONBUTTON:3] [ACTIONBUTTON:4]</td>
    </tr>
  </table>
</td>
```

It is the same code, except that the second version calls out a class in some of the tags, rather than actual attributes.

Here is where the *cascading* part comes in. The table has a class of containermaster_flower. If the <td> tag within this table did not have a specific class applied to it, then the attributes of the class in the <table> tag would cascade down and be used in the <td> tag. As it is, this example has an overriding class of containermaster_flower2.

The other benefit of using a .css file is that all the attributes can be abstracted outside of the HTML code. It is easier to make a change to a single CSS class than to try to find all instances of an attribute being used inside many HTML pages.

CSS Contents

I have referred to CSS classes. A CSS class is a set of attributes whose name begins with a period. Here are three classes from the container.css file (which you'll create later in this chapter):

```
.containermaster_flower {
        width: 100%;
        background-color: #C7FFDC;
        border-right: #00A63E 1px solid;
        border-top: #00A63E 1px solid;
        border-left: #00A63E 1px solid;
        border-bottom: #00A63E 1px solid;
}
.containerrow1_flower {
        background-image: url(GreenHorizGradient.jpg);
        background-repeat: repeat-y;
        background-color: White;
}
.containerrow2_flower {
```

```
        background-color: #ffffff;
}
```

Inside the braces for each class, you have the list of attributes that get applied to that class. There are a ton of attributes that can go in a class. However, only a subset of these attributes can be applied to any particular HTML tag. It is perfectly fine to apply a CSS class to many different types of HTML tags. Only those that can be applied to a particular tag will be applied. The others will be ignored.

Later in this chapter, I will cover the .css files and CSS classes that you need.

Preparation

The skin that you'll be making will have a bunch of flowers as the logo. It will also have a horizontal gradient for title bars and a vertical gradient for the menu.

The menu will be placed vertically along the left side of the page, and there will only be a single pane: the content pane (DNN requires at least one content pane per skin, and it must be called contentpane).

You will be creating the skin and the container in a different folder than the DNN folder you are used to. It will end up being a completely new project within VWD.

Create a new folder on your machine somewhere, and call it Flowers. Within this folder, create two others called Skin and Container. The folder structure should look like Figure 11-1.

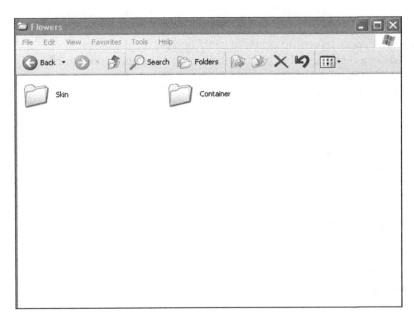

Figure 11-1. *Folder configuration for the Flowers skin*

You will be using an existing skin as a template. Create a folder named DNN-Blue inside both the Skin folder and the Container folder.

Using a Template

When I create a skin, I like to use a template to jump-start the process. It is much easier to change a skin then to create one from scratch.

The skin you will use as a template will be the DNN-Blue skin, which you should be familiar with. This is the default skin that was applied to your website upon installation.

My DNN installation directory is `C:\DotNetNuke`. Yours should be the same.

Open `C:\DotNetNuke\Portals\_default\Skins\DNN-Blue`. Copy the following files into the `Skin` folder you just created:

- `gradient_DKBlue.jpg`

- `Horizontal Menu - Fixed Width.ascx`

- `Horizontal Menu - Fixed Width.htm`

- `Horizontal Menu - Fixed Width.jpg`

- `skin.css`

The Skins Files

I will digress a little here and explain these files.

The `Horizontal Menu - Fixed Width.jpg` file is a picture of a sample page using this skin. This picture is used by the skin manager in DNN. Start up your DNN project and log in as administrator. Click Admin ➤ Skins to get the Skins settings page. Yours should look like Figure 11-2.

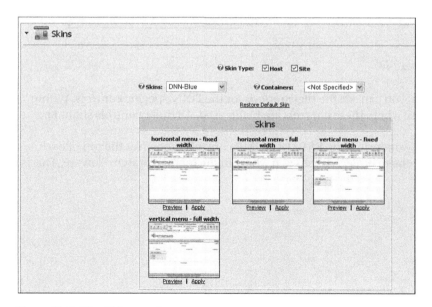

Figure 11-2. *The Skins settings page*

You see the pictures of the different skins that are available to you in here. You can even preview a skin if you like. While it is nice to include the Horizontal Menu - Fixed Width.jpg file, it is not necessary. I think, however, that you should include the picture.

The Horizontal Menu - Fixed Width.ascx file and the Horizontal Menu - Fixed Width.htm file are essentially the same.

If you open the .ascx file, you will see this code shown in Figure 11-3.

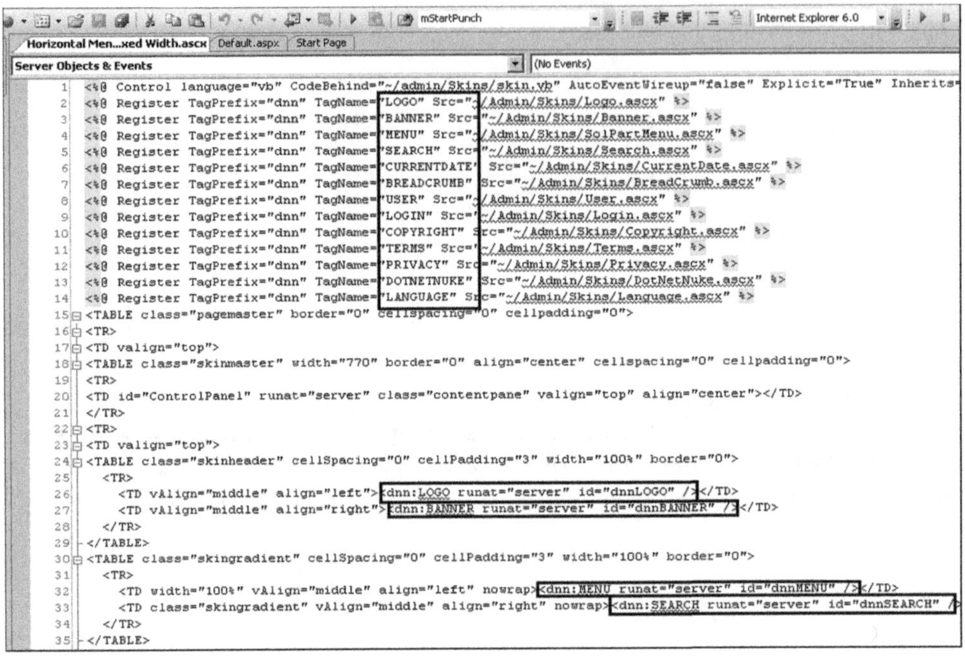

Figure 11-3. *The skin's .ascx file*

At the top of the file, you can see the registrations for the DNN-specific controls. Within the <TD> tags, you can see where these controls are being used. All these controls should be familiar to you.

Just in case you are wondering, the BREADCRUMB control is shown at the top of each page in the restaurant website project. It tells you where in the menu hierarchy you are. This is shown in Figure 11-4.

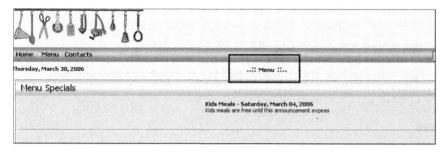

Figure 11-4. *The BREADCRUMB DNN control*

The `.htm` page in this list is exactly the same as the `.ascx` page, but without the controls. Instead, it has tokens to replace the controls. This is shown in Figure 11-5.

```
 9  <TD valign="top">
10  <TABLE class="skinheader" cellSpacing="0" cellPadding="3" width="100%" border="0">
11      <TR>
12          <TD vAlign="middle" align="left">[LOGO]</TD>
13          <TD vAlign="middle" align="right">[BANNER]</TD>
14      </TR>
15  </TABLE>
16  <TABLE class="skingradient" cellSpacing="0" cellPadding="3" width="100%" border="0">
17      <TR>
18          <TD width="100%" vAlign="middle" align="left" nowrap>[MENU]</TD>
19          <TD class="skingradient" vAlign="middle" align="right" nowrap>[SEARCH][LANGUAGE]</TD>
20      </TR>
21  </TABLE>
22  <TABLE cellSpacing="0" cellPadding="3" width="100%" border="0">
23      <TR>
24          <TD width="200" vAlign="top" align="left" nowrap>[CURRENTDATE]</TD>
25          <TD width="100%" vAlign="top" align="center"><B>..::</B> [BREADCRUMB]<B>::..</B></TD>
26          <TD width="200" vAlign="top" align="right" nowrap>[USER]  [LOGIN]</TD>
27      </TR>
28  </TABLE>
```

Figure 11-5. *The .htm file, showing tokens*

When DNN installs the skin, it takes this `.htm` file and creates a user control (the `.ascx` file), replacing the tokens with the DNN controls.

When you are making a skin, you can either make it directly by generating a control in VWD, or you can generate the `.htm` file and let DNN make the user control. Either one works, but there are two overarching reasons to make the `.htm` file:

- Editing the `.htm` file requires no programming whatsoever. This means that you can make a complete skin using nothing more than Microsoft Paint and Notepad if you like.

- The `.htm` file with the tokens is much easier to edit. It has less for you to remember and less for you to program.

Many people use Adobe's Dreamweaver and Fireworks programs to generate the fancy graphics and edit the .htm and .css files. Since these programs cost money, I like to use the VWD editor to create the skins. I use Microsoft Paint to do the graphics.

The last two files of interest here are the .css file and the .jpg file. While the .htm file contains the layout of the skin, the .css file contains the look and feel. The gradient file DKBlue.jpg is the graphics for the blue vertical gradient.

Viewing the Template

You will be using VWD to create the skin. In order to do that, you need to open a new instance of VWD and create a new website.

Choose File ➤ Open Web Site. Navigate to the Flowers folder, which contains your new skin and container. Mine is shown in Figure 11-6.

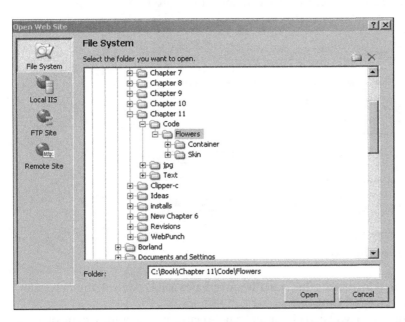

Figure 11-6. *Opening a new website based on the new skin folder*

Click Open, and the Solution Explorer should show the folder structure and files you just put in there (see Figure 11-7).

Figure 11-7. *The Solution Explorer, showing the skin folder structure*

Double-click the .htm file to open it in the IDE. When you see the source code for this file, click the Design button at the bottom-left of the IDE to see what the HTML code looks like in design mode. Your design view should look like Figure 11-8.

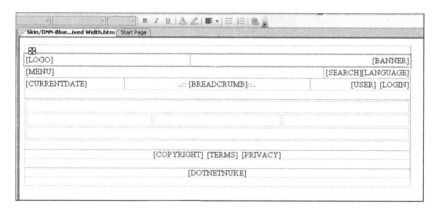

Figure 11-8. *Design view for the layout of the DNN-Blue skin*

Does this look familiar to you? It should. Figure 11-9 shows a blank contacts page in a DNN portal.

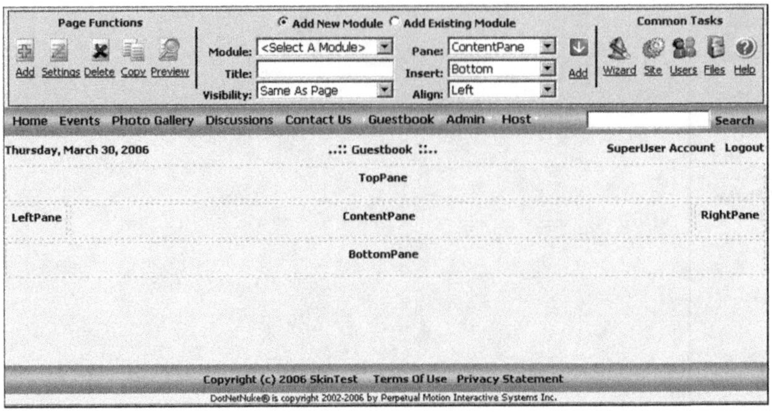

Figure 11-9. *A blank page based on the DNN-Blue skin*

You can see the tokens in Figure 11-8 and how they get translated to controls in Figure 11-9. You can also see the table cells in the center of Figure 11-8 between the BREADCRUMB and TERMS tokens. These table cells correspond to the placement of the panes in Figure 11-9.

Pretty cool, huh? But where is all the blue stuff and images shown in Figure 11-8? This picture only shows the layout. Remember I said that the look and feel is contained in the .css file.

VWD has a neat feature with which you can instantly overlay a .css file onto a layout template. In the Solution Explorer, click the skin.css file. Now drag it over and drop it on the design panel showing the layout. Make sure you drop it outside the table. You can tell because a blue box appears wherever your mouse is as you drag the .css file around the design page. You want the blue box to be the whole page. Figure 11-10 shows the result.

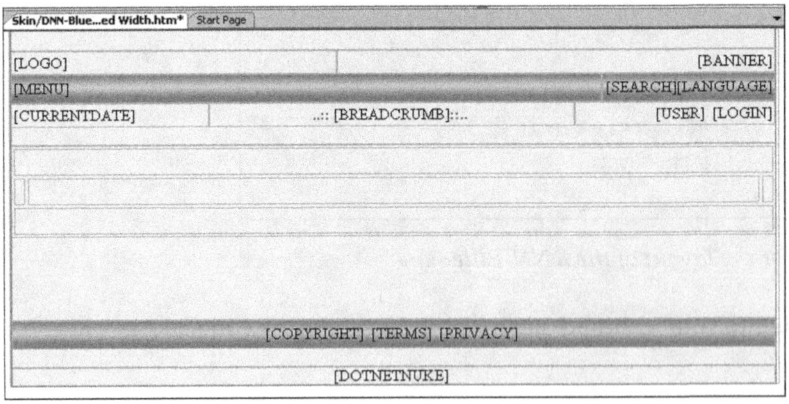

Figure 11-10. *CSS applied to the layout*

If you look at the source for this page, you will see a new line at the top of the page:

```
<link href="../../Skin/DNN-Blue/skin.css" rel="stylesheet" type="text/css" />
```

This line of code was added by the IDE to associate this style sheet to the layout.

Creating the Images

This new skin will contain three images: one is the logo, one is the horizontal gradient used in the copyright and title bars, and one is the vertical gradient used in the menu.

I created these gradients using Microsoft Paint. The vertical and horizontal images are shown in Figure 11-11.

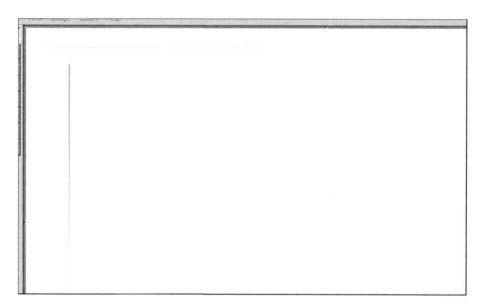

Figure 11-11. *The horizontal and vertical gradients*

First of all, these are two different files that I combined here to show you how they look. What do you notice? They are barely visible, the width of the vertical gradient is one pixel, and the height of the horizontal gradient is also one pixel.

I could have made these .jpg images to be the size I wanted, but that would have drastically increased the size of the file. Right now, these files are just 1 KB each.

When I reference these images in the .css file, I will use a CSS command to repeat the image to fill out the space. This is very fast and enables me to have a lightweight skin for download.

I have included these gradient images in the code with the book. Copy these images to the DNN-Blue folder, and your Solution Explorer should look like mine, shown in Figure 11-12. If you have your project open, you may need to refresh the Solution Explorer to see the new files.

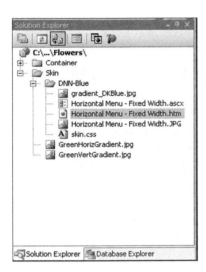

Figure 11-12. *The Solution Explorer, showing the gradient images*

There are a couple more files that need to be in this skins folder as well. Copy the skin.css file from the Skin\DNN-Blue folder to the Skin folder. Copy the Horizontal Menu - Fixed Width.htm file from the Skin\DNN-Blue folder to the Skin folder. Rename this .htm file Flowers - Fixed Width.htm. Your Solution Explorer should now look like Figure 11-13.

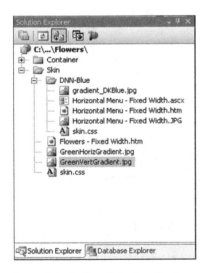

Figure 11-13. *The Solution Explorer with all files*

Open this new Flowers - Fixed Width.htm file, and drag the new skin.css file on top of it like you did before. Your screen should look like Figure 11-14.

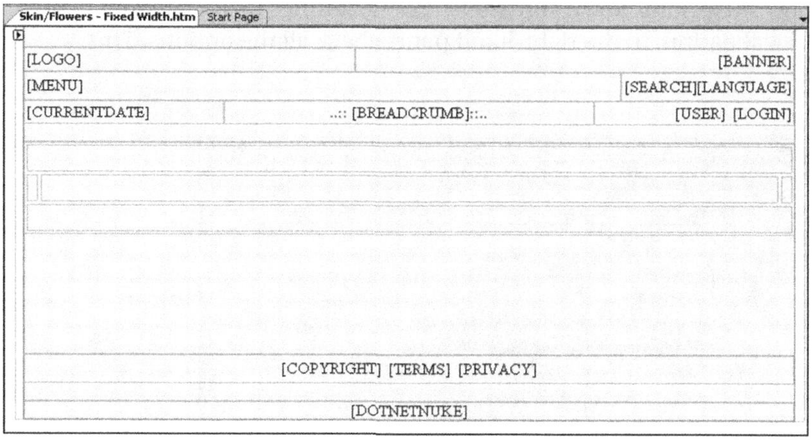

Figure 11-14. *The new skin, with CSS applied*

Now that you have the layout and the `.css` file associated, it is time to edit the `.htm` layout file.

Editing the Skin

Your final skin for this page will be simpler than this one. The layout will end up looking like Figure 11-15.

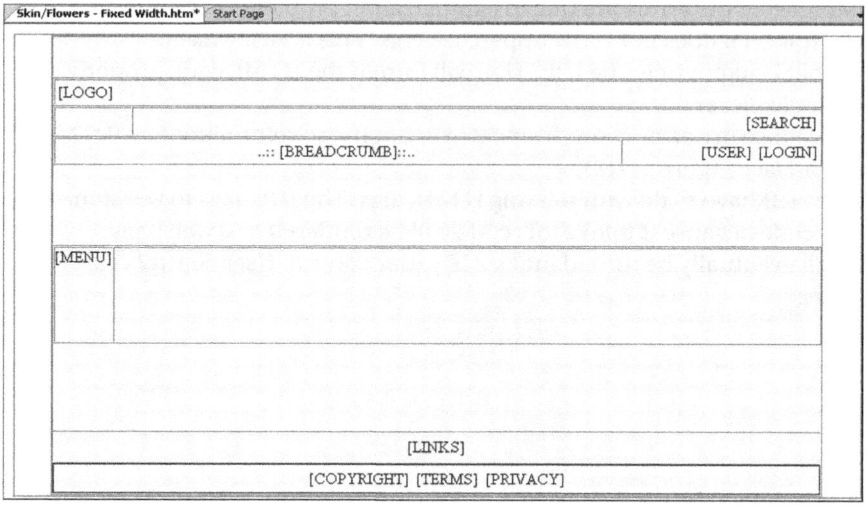

Figure 11-15. *Final layout of the new skin*

You will start by editing the source code for this layout. Click the source button to view the HTML code.

In the IDE, click Tools ➤ Options. Make sure the Show All Settings box is checked. Scroll down and click HTML ➤ Validation. In the right-hand pane, check all the options. This is shown in Figure 11-16.

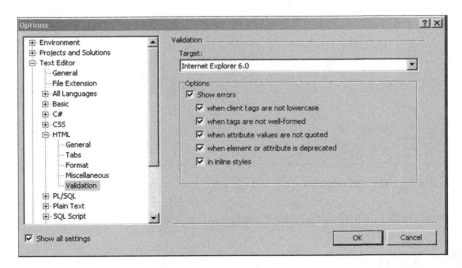

Figure 11-16. *Setting up HTML validation*

Click OK, and then click back on the source of the page. All of a sudden, you will see a ton of errors. I have 59 of them, as evidenced by Figure 11-17.

You can see that most of the errors are due to capitalization problems with Internet Explorer 6. Internet Explorer 6 does not allow uppercase tags. This is easily fixed.

Click Edit ➤ Format Document in the IDE. This will format the HTML code properly so that it works in Internet Explorer 6.

Not only did this reduce my error count from 59 to 3, but it also reformatted my HTML code to be easier to read (see Figure 11-18).

The errors that are left have to do with missing HTML tags. The IDE likes to see some surrounding tags for this code because it thinks this code will be rendered as a web page.

This .htm code will eventually be turned into a .NET user control. User controls cannot have the following tags:

- <HTML>

- <FORM>

- <BODY>

These tags will be supplied by the web page that the control is inserted into. These last three errors are fine.

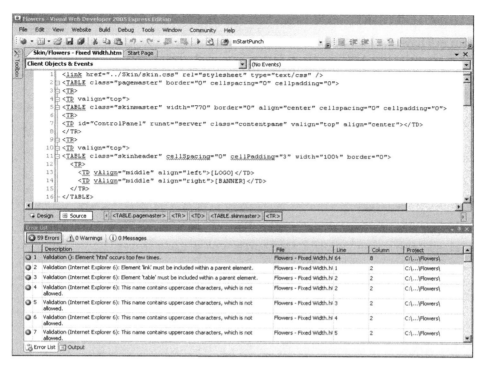

Figure 11-17. *HTML validation errors*

Figure 11-18. *Reformatted document with fewer errors*

Rearranging the Table

Your new layout will have the logo at the top, with the search box in the cell right next to it.
Below that, it will have the BREADCRUMB and user/login cells. Below this will be the menu
and another pane on the left with a content pane on the right side. At the bottom will be the
familiar copyright/terms/privacy bar.

You need to delete and rearrange some cells. Listing 11-1 shows the complete HTML code
for this new layout.

Listing 11-1. *The new skin layout code*

```
<link href="../Skin/skin.css" rel="stylesheet" type="text/css" />
<table class="pagemaster" border="1" cellspacing="0" cellpadding="0">
  <tr>
    <td valign="top">
      <table class="skinmaster" width="770" border="1" align="center"
          cellspacing="0" cellpadding="0">
        <tr>
          <td id="ControlPanel" runat="server" class="contentpane"
              valign="top" align="center">
          </td>
        </tr>
        <tr>
          <td valign="top">
            <table class="skinheader" cellspacing="0" cellpadding="3"
                width="100%" border="1">
              <tr>
                <td valign="middle" align="left">
                  [LOGO]</td>
              </tr>
            </table>
            <table class="skingradient" cellspacing="0" cellpadding="3"
                width="100%" border="1">
              <tr>
                <td class="toppaneindex" id="TopPaneIndex" runat="server"
                  valign="top" align="center"></td>
                <td class="skingradient" valign="middle" align="right" nowrap>
                  [SEARCH]</td>
              </tr>
            </table>
```

```
      <table cellspacing="0" cellpadding="3" width="100%" border="1">
        <tr>
          <td width="100%" valign="top" align="center">
            <b>..::</b> [BREADCRUMB]<b>::..</b></td>
          <td width="200" valign="top" align="right" nowrap>
            [USER]  [LOGIN]</td>
        </tr>
      </table>
    </td>
  </tr>
  <tr>
    <td valign="top" >
      <table cellspacing="0" cellpadding="0" width="100%" border="1">
        <tr >
          <td class="menupane" id="MenuPane" height="100px" runat="server"
              valign="top" align="left">[MENU]</td>
          <td class="contentpane" id="ContentPane" runat="server"
              valign="top" align="center"></td>
        </tr>
      </table>
    </td>
  </tr>
  <tr>
    <td align="center" valign="middle">[LINKS]</td>
  </tr>
  <tr>
    <td valign="middle" align="center">
      [COPYRIGHT]  [TERMS]  [PRIVACY]
    </td>
  </tr>
      </table>
    </td>
  </tr>
</table>
```

Since you have not changed any of the .css file classes, I am sure that this code will need tweaking pretty soon. However, it does give the layout you're looking for.

Adjusting the .css File

You will start with the menu. The DNN-Blue skin displays the menu horizontally. You want your menu to display vertically. The attributes for the DNN controls that replace the tokens are contained in an .xml file called skin.xml. Currently you do not have one, so you need to copy one from somewhere.

Copy the file C:\DotNetNuke\Portals_default\Skins\DNN-Blue\skin.xml into the skins folder you created for this project.

Refresh your Solution Explorer and double-click this file to open it. You will see XML code for the BREADCRUMB and TREEVIEW tokens. This is shown in Figure 11-19.

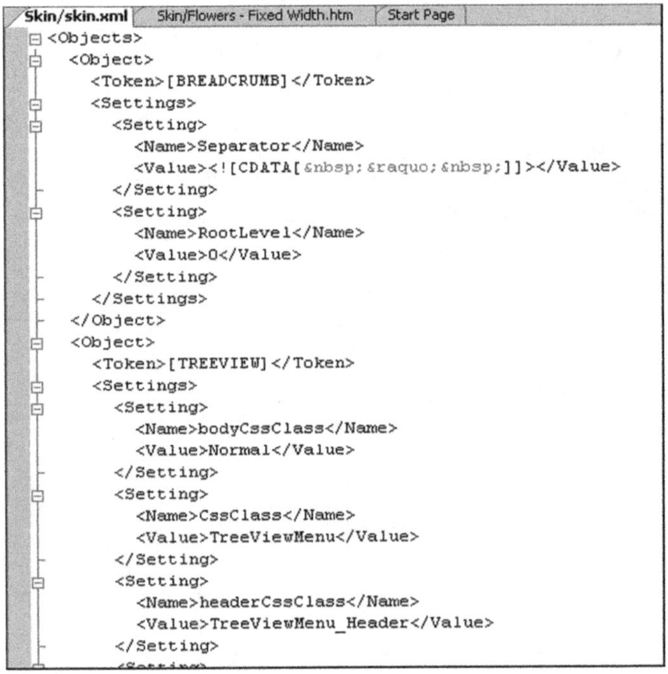

Figure 11-19. *The skin.xml file, showing attributes for the tokens*

The default .xml file that you just copied over does not have information for the MENU token, so you need to add an element for this.

Delete the TREEVIEW element from this .xml file, and add the following element (delete the <Object> and </Object> tags that surround the TREEVIEW element as well):

```
<Object>
  <Token>[MENU]</Token>
  <Settings>
    <Setting>
      <Name>display</Name>
      <Value>vertical</Value>
```

```
    </Setting>
  </Settings>
</Object>
```

Now you just have settings for the BREADCRUMB and MENU elements in this file. While it is not necessary to have this file (as evidenced by the lack of all the tokens in this one), you sometimes do need to override the default values. The default setting for the MENU token is horizontal.

Note The documentation that comes with DNN has a file called DotNetNuke Skinning.pdf. This document contains a table with all the tokens and all the settings that these tokens can have. Read it.

Now your skin.xml file contains the correct settings.

The skin.css file needs to change to reflect the images that you want to display and to get the colors correct. You will start at the beginning of the page and work your way down. Open the skin.css file in the IDE. It should look like Figure 11-20.

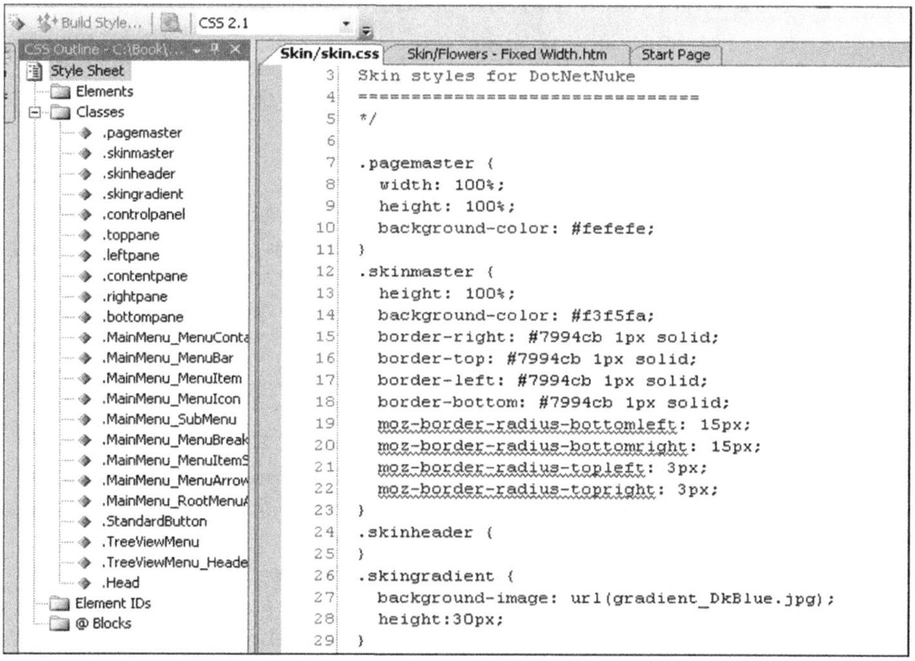

Figure 11-20. *The skin.css file*

To the left of the skin.css file is the CSS Outline pane, which you can use to navigate to the different classes in the .css file.

If you look at the .htm file, you will see that the main table that represents the whole page is using the class pagemaster. This is shown here:

```
<table class="pagemaster" border="1" cellspacing="0" cellpadding="0">
```

Tip You will notice that I have the border set to 1. I do this for every table in the file. This way I can see the outline of each cell in design mode. It makes it much easier to edit. I will set this value to 0 before I actually use it.

You'll make the background color a pale yellow. Change the background color for the pagemaster class to #ffff99.

The next table down in the .htm file represents everything that the user sees within the page. This table uses the skinmaster CSS class. I would like this color to be a different yellow. Change the skinmaster background color to #ffff33.

If you switch back to the page's design mode, you will see these CSS changes take effect. You will see the background of the whole page become a pale yellow, and the interior background of the page become a darker yellow. You have no use for the borders in this class, so delete them.

In case you were wondering, the borders that start with moz are specific to Mozilla browsers and are not standard. They are intended to give a rounded edge to the table.

Including the Image

The gradient image you're creating will be displayed in the rows that contain the search box and copyright. To do this, you'll change the skingradient class in the .css file. This class should look like the following:

```
.skingradient {
    background-image: url(GreenHorizGradient.jpg);
    background-repeat: repeat-y
}
```

This class uses the green horizontal gradient that I created, and is located in the Skin folder. Since this gradient is only 1 pixel high, you can use the background-repeat attribute of this class to make the gradient fill the whole row.

Save this file and edit the source for the .htm layout file. You will see that the table tag containing the SEARCH token already uses the skingradient class.

Scroll down to the cell that has the COPYRIGHT token, and include the skingradient class here. The code is shown following:

```
<tr>
  <td class="skingradient" valign="middle" align="center">
    [COPYRIGHT]  [TERMS]  [PRIVACY]
  </td>
</tr>
```

Now switch to the page's design mode, and you should see your changes in the layout, as shown in Figure 11-21.

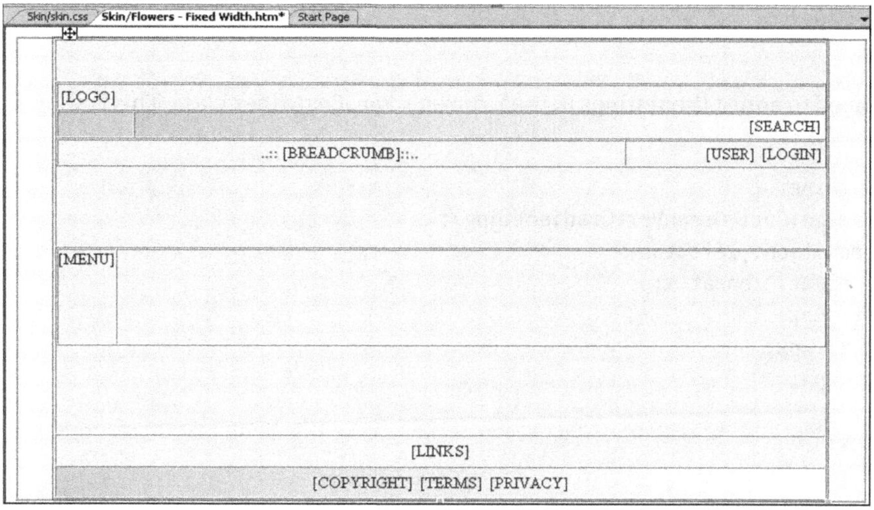

```
Skin/skin.css  Skin/Flowers - Fixed Width.htm*  Start Page

[LOGO]

                                                              [SEARCH]
                        ..:: [BREADCRUMB]::..                 [USER] [LOGIN]



[MENU]




                            [LINKS]
                    [COPYRIGHT] [TERMS] [PRIVACY]
```

Figure 11-21. *New colors and gradient images in the layout*

So far, so good. Next is the `controlpanel` class in the `.css` file. This class controls the background color of the control panel that you see when you log into the page as administrator or host. This panel is shown in Figure 11-22.

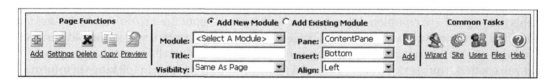

Figure 11-22. *The control panel*

Since baby blue is fine with me, I will leave this class alone. You will notice from Listing 11-1 that the cell containing the content pane uses the `contentpane` class. You will change this to use the `controlpanel` class. The code is as follows:

```
<tr>
  <td id="ControlPanel" runat="server" class="controlpanel"
      valign="top" align="center">
  </td>
</tr>
```

You do not have a left, right, top, or bottom pane anymore, so delete these classes from the `.css` file.

The source for the `.htm` file calls out a `menupane` class for the cell that contains the MENU token. You do not have the class in the `.css` file yet, so you need to make one.

Open the `skin.css` file and add the following code just above the `contentpane` class:

```
.menupane {
    padding-right: 4px;
    padding-top: 6px;
}
```

You will also need to adjust the settings in the `MainMenu_MenuContainer` class. This is shown following:

```
.MainMenu_MenuContainer {
    background-image: url(GreenVertGradient.jpg);
    background-position: left top;
    background-repeat: repeat-x;
    padding-left: 6px;
    padding-right: 4px;
    padding-top: 0px;
    width: 100%;
    height: 100px;
    border: 1px solid black;
}
```

You can see that I use the vertical gradient image and that I repeat it in the x direction to fill out the cell. Notice also that I have padding around the menu to keep the text from reaching the edge of the gradient image.

Testing the Skin

At this point, you have completed the skin (you still have the container to do), and it is time to test it. The first thing you have to do is package up the skin for export. If you are an old hand at working with .NET, you know that you can very easily create an install for a DLL or program that you created. You also know that you need a manifest file that contains all kinds of information about your program.

The guys at DotNetNuke decided against this. They decided to package skins and containers in a `.zip` file. Personally, I agree with this approach. It is very easy to implement and maintain.

Now you need to create a `.zip` file for your new skin.

Packaging the Skin

Open Windows Explorer and navigate to the `Flowers\Skin` folder. It should contain the files shown in Figure 11-23.

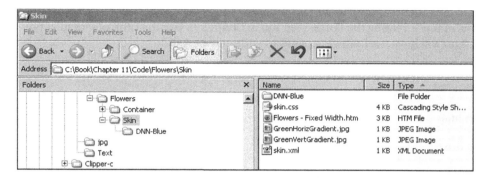

Figure 11-23. *The files contained in the Skin folder*

Select all the files in here except for the DNN-Blue folder, and right-click the Flowers - Fixed Width.htm file. Select Send To ➤ Compressed (zipped) Folder. This is shown in Figure 11-24.

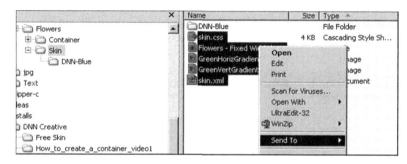

Figure 11-24. *Zipping up the files*

You should get a file called Flowers - Fixed Width.zip. That's it. Your skin is packaged. How easy was that?

Creating the Test Harness

In software, a test harness is a shell of a program that is used to test your code. In your case, you will test your code in a new portal.

You created the Employee portal in Chapter 9. You did this to separate the functionality of the website.

You need to create a new portal in the restaurant website called SkinTest. To do this, follow the instructions in the "Creating the Portal" section in Chapter 9. Use the Club or Organization Site template. You will have the following pages in your new portal:

- Home

- Events

- Photo Gallery

- Discussions

- Contact Us

- Guestbook

You will be uploading the skin into this new portal and testing it on the new pages in here.

Uploading the Skin

Now you need to upload the skin to DNN. Open your DNN SkinTest site, and log in as host.

Choose Admin ➤ Skins, and click the Upload link at the bottom of the page. Browse to your new skin package, and select the skin to upload. This is shown in Figure 11-25.

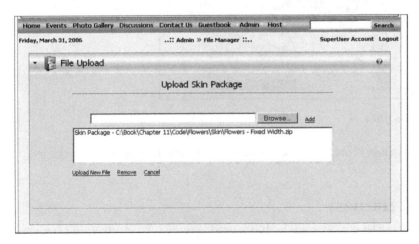

Figure 11-25. *Choosing a new skin to upload*

Click the Upload New File link, and DNN will upload the new skin, parse it, and install it. You will get a screen like Figure 11-26.

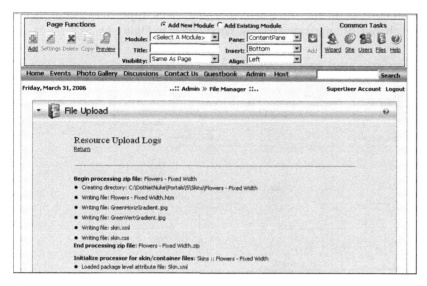

Figure 11-26. *Installing the new skin*

Scroll down this page to see all that the skin installer did for you. At the bottom, click the Return link, and you will be brought back to the skin manager page. Choose the Flowers - Fixed Width skin from the Skins drop-down menu, and you should see the screen shown in Figure 11-27.

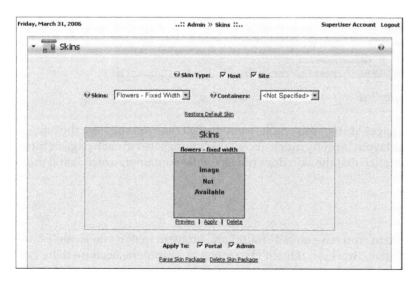

Figure 11-27. *The new skin installed*

Notice that you do not have an image. You will fix this later. Click Apply to see what happens. Your screen should change dramatically to show what I have in Figure 11-28.

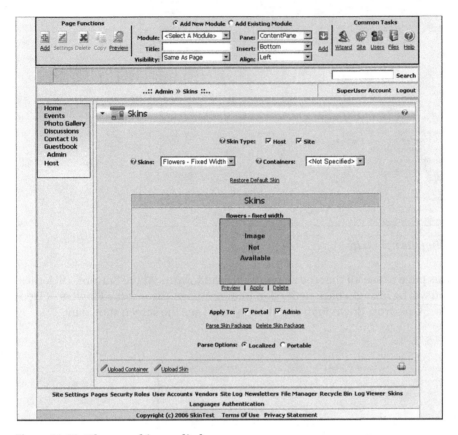

Figure 11-28. *The new skin applied*

Notice the lines in the page? Most of this results from the fact that you still have the border of all the tables set to 1. The layout is pretty much acceptable, though. Go to each page in turn, and see what it looks like. Notice that the skin does not affect the container, which is still the DNN-Blue default.

Skin Edit Cycle

OK. You have installed the skin. You have already found one problem in that you haven't turned off the table cell borders. However, this isn't too much of a problem, because there is a way to quickly edit the skin and just as quickly test it.

First of all, you need to find the folder where DNN put your skin. This skin is being tested in a portal, and is not available to other portals. I uploaded my skin to the site, not the host.

Open Windows Explorer and navigate to the C:\DotNetNuke\Portals folder. You will see the default portal, as well as some others that are named 0 through n. This is shown in Figure 11-29.

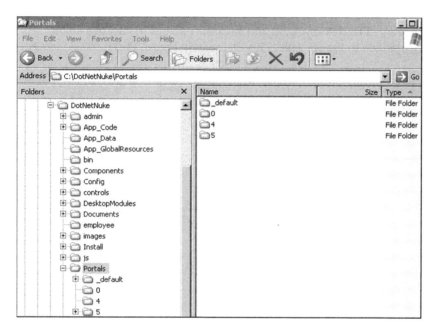

Figure 11-29. *DNN portals*

You may have a different portal setup than me. If you open each portal folder, you will see some other sub-folders. I found the Flowers skin in my portal 5. This is shown in Figure 11-30.

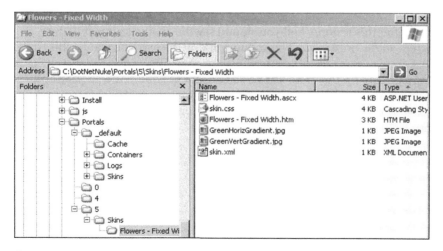

Figure 11-30. *Finding the skin*

Go back to the skin IDE and change the borders of all the tables to 0 in the .htm file. Save the file.

Now open the folder in which you are doing development on the skin, and copy the Flowers - Fixed Width.htm file to the DNN skins folder where DNN put this skin.

While you're logged into the test portal you made, click Admin ➤ Skins to get to the skin manager. Choose the Flowers - Fixed Width skin, and click the Parse Skin Package link to enable the change you just made to the .htm file. This is shown in Figure 11-31.

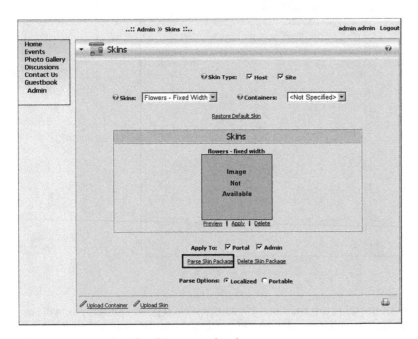

Figure 11-31. *Parsing the skin to get the changes*

Click the Home link after this is done, and you should see the changes appear in the page. You can do this repeatedly until you get your skin working the way you want—this is pretty quick.

How about adding a picture for this skin? Take a screenshot of your new web page and save it to the Flowers skin folder that you are developing with. Make sure that this screenshot is called Flowers - Fixed Width.jpg. Copy this file over to the portal skin folder and refresh the screen shown in Figure 11-31. It should now look like Figure 11-32.

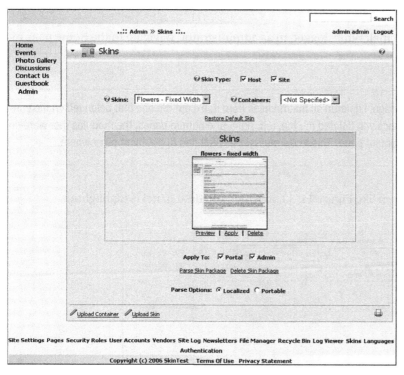

Figure 11-32. *The skin, with the preview image*

The preview image has the DNN-Blue container.

One Last Skin Change

If you log out of the site, you will see a gray bar at the top of the page where the administrative control panel goes. This is because you are using the wrong CSS class for the control panel.

Edit the .htm file again, and replace the code for the ControlPanel cell with the following:

```
<tr>
  <td id="ControlPanel" runat="server" class="contentpane"
        valign="top" align="center">
  </td>
</tr>
```

Now save this file and copy it to the portal skin folder. Reparse the skin package again and log out. The admin panel should not show anymore.

The Last Panel

You need to test the last panel. While logged in as administrator, navigate to the home page of this portal.

Note While on the home page, I deleted all the modules from it, except the one that belonged on the content pane. You will find that since you deleted the top, left, right, and bottom panes, the modules that were in those panes are now in the content pane. This looks messy, but DNN had to put them somewhere.

You should see a screen like Figure 11-33, in which the final panel is highlighted.

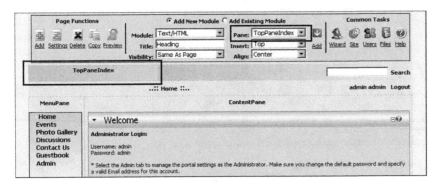

Figure 11-33. *TopPaneIndex needs to be filled.*

As administrator, you can see that you still need to insert a text/HTML module in the Top-PaneIndex pane.

Add a text/HTML module, and then add a single line of text to the module. Now log out. Your screen should look like Figure 11-34.

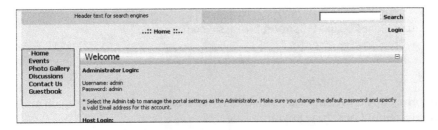

Figure 11-34. *A text/HTML module added to TopIndexPane*

Most search engines give weight to indexing pages based on words they find at the beginning of a page. Adding a spot at the top of your page where you can insert a phrase concerning your website will give you a better chance of rising up in the search engine hit results.

Other Skinning Tasks

You have finished the basics of creating and testing a new skin for DNN. However, there is much more that you can do. For instance, you have a LOGO token in the skin. I have supplied a logo for you, called logo.jpg. It is a picture of a bunch of flowers. Put this logo.jpg file in your Flowers\Skin working directory. Refresh your Solution Explorer so that it looks like Figure 11-35.

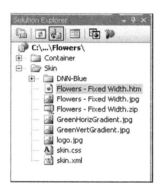

Figure 11-35. *Adding a logo to the skin folder*

Now copy this logo.jpg file to the skins folder you are working with for the SkinTest portal.

While logged in as administrator or host for this portal, click Admin ➤ Site Settings. Scroll down to the Logo setting, as shown in Figure 11-36.

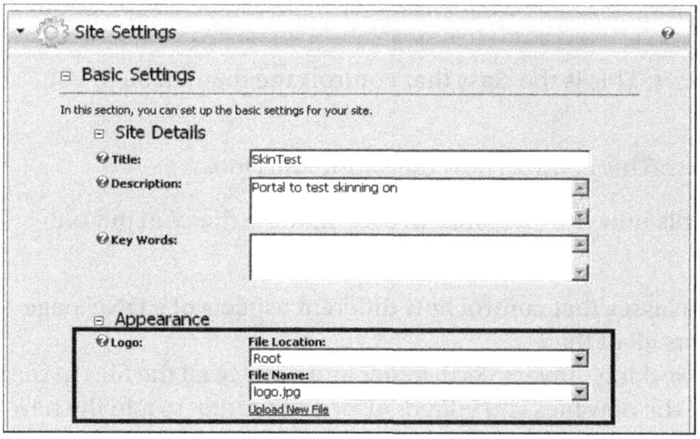

Figure 11-36. *Adding a logo*

Click the Upload New File link, and browse to the logo file you copied to the skin folder of this portal. Choose the `logo.jpg` file, upload it, and click the Update link at the bottom of the page. If you log out, your new page should look like Figure 11-37.

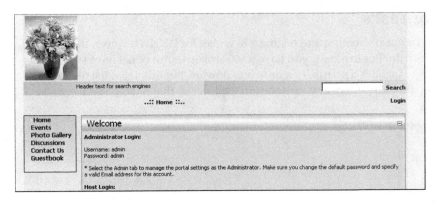

Figure 11-37. *The new skin showing the new logo*

Now, I admit this is not the best skin, and you couldn't sell it for a hill of beans. My intent, though, was simply to show you how to create a skin.

What Else Can Be Skinned?

I did not cover every aspect of skinning here. There are some other things that you should change when creating a professional skin. Here they are:

- *The* `MainMenu_MenuBar` *CSS class*: This controls the appearance of the horizontal menu bar.

- *The* `MainMenu_MenuItem` *CSS class*: This controls the appearance of the menu item when you hover over it.

- *The* `MainMenu_MenuIcon` *CSS class*: This is the class that controls the menu icon (if you have one).

- *The* `MainMenu_SubMenu` *CSS class*: This controls how the sub-menus look.

- *The* `Head` *CSS class*: This controls how the title looks in each module that you put on a page.

There are a bunch of other CSS classes that control how different aspects of a DNN page look. The DNN documentation covers all of this.

The last thing to do is go to the working `Flowers\Skin` folder and replace all the files in the `Flowers - Fixed Width.zip` file with the new files you edited. Also, don't forget to add the new files (`logo.jpg` and `Flowers - Fixed Width.jpg`) as well.

Creating a Container

Now, the last thing to do in a skinning operation is create a container to go with it. In your case, this will be easy.

When you started this chapter, I had you create skin and container folders within the Flowers folder you're using for developing this skin and container pair.

Within the Skin folder, you created a DNN-Blue folder and copied some files from the DNN-Blue skin into it to use as a template. I will have you do the same thing for the container.

Copying a Template

Open the Flowers\Container folder, and create a new folder within it called DNN-Blue. Open another Windows Explorer instance and navigate to C:\DotNetNuke\Portals\default\Containers\DNN-Blue. Copy the following to the DNN-Blue folder you just created:

- container.css

- container.xml

- gradient_LtBlue.jpg

- Image Header - White Background.ascx

- Image Header - White Background.htm

- Image Header - White Background.jpg

You should already know what these files are, as you've worked with their analogs when you created the skin. Figure 11-38 shows the Solution Explorer for your Flowers project (make sure you refresh the Solution Explorer in the IDE).

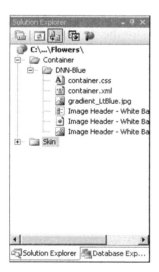

Figure 11-38. *The Solution Explorer, showing the DNN-Blue template files*

While you are in the Solution Explorer, copy the `Image Header - While Background.htm` file to the `Container` folder. Do the same for the `container.css` file.

Expand the `Skin` folder, and copy the `GreenHorizGradient.jpg` file to the `Container` folder. You can do all this by right-clicking the file and choosing Copy/Paste. Your Solution Explorer should look like Figure 11-39.

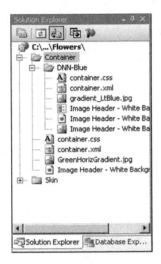

Figure 11-39. *The Solution Explorer, now with the correct files in the Container folder*

Make sure that formatting and validation are turned on in the IDE (see Figure 11-16). Open the `Image Header - White Background.htm` file (from the `Container` folder) in the IDE, and you will see the same capitalization issues you came across in the skin file. Click Edit ➤ Format Document in the IDE to fix these errors. You should now have about five errors left. This is shown in Figure 11-40.

You will need to fix the third and fifth error by adding the end tags for the `<br>` and `<hr>` tags. (Makes you wonder about the included skins, eh?) If you don't know how to do this, then now is a good time to look it up in the help.

The other errors occurred because VWD thinks that this will become a web page rather than a user control.

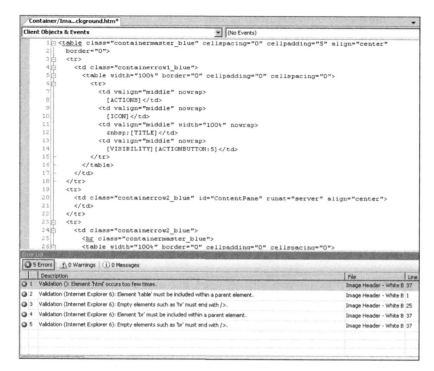

Figure 11-40. *Remaining errors after reformatting the document*

Click the Design tab for this page, and you will see what the container layout looks like. This is show in Figure 11-41.

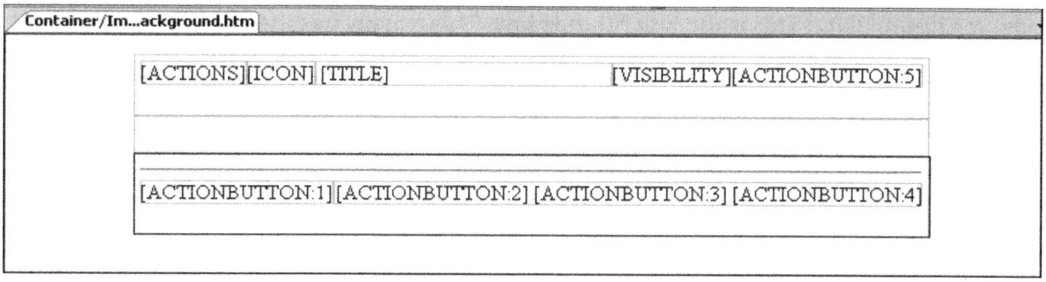

Figure 11-41. *The layout of the container*

As you did with the .css file for the skin, you need to associate the container.css file with this .htm file. While in design mode, drag the container.css file from the Solution Explorer and drop it on top of the design pane. Your design screen should now look like Figure 11-42.

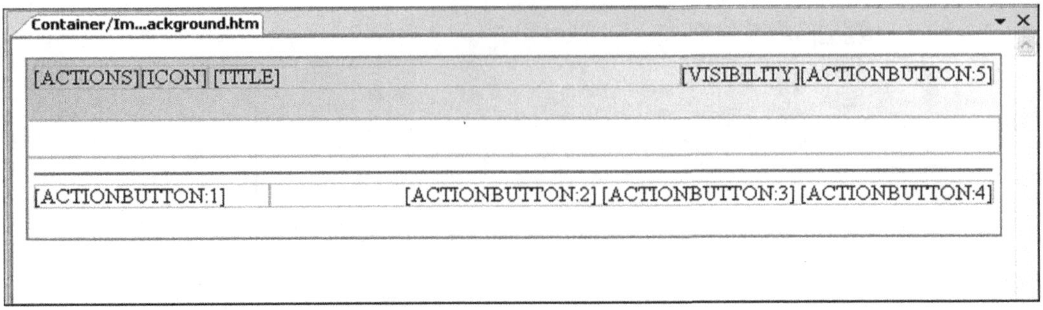

Figure 11-42. *The container.css file associated with the .htm file*

If you look at the source for the .htm file, you will see a new line at the top linking the container.css file with this .htm file.

The explanations for the tokens are as follows:

- ACTIONS: This is the drop-down menu that gets you the settings for the module.

- ICON: This allows you to place an icon next to the title.

- TITLE: This is the title of the module.

- VISIBILITY: This determines whether the module is visible.

- ACTIONBUTTON:5: This is the help icon.

- ACTIONBUTTON:1: This is the Edit Module link. This usually has the pencil icon next to it.

- ACTIONBUTTON:2: This is the XML icon that allows syndication in your module.

- ACTIONBUTTON:3: This is the Print Module icon.

- ACTIONBUTTON:4: This is the Edit Module Settings icon.

Editing the Template

Switch over to view the source of the .htm file. Change each of the class names to end in _flower rather than _blue. Listing 11-2 shows the new source code.

Listing 11-2. *The changed class names*

```
<link href="../Container/container.css" rel="stylesheet"
      type="text/css" />
<table class="containermaster_flower" cellspacing="0" cellpadding="5"
      align="center"
  border="0">
```

```
<tr>
  <td class="containerrow1_flower">
    <table width="100%" border="0" cellpadding="0" cellspacing="0">
      <tr>
        <td valign="middle" nowrap>
          [ACTIONS]</td>
        <td valign="middle" nowrap>
          [ICON]</td>
        <td valign="middle" width="100%" nowrap>
           [TITLE]</td>
        <td valign="middle" nowrap>
          [VISIBILITY][ACTIONBUTTON:5]</td>
      </tr>
    </table>
  </td>
</tr>
<tr>
  <td class="containerrow2_flower" id="ContentPane" runat="server"
      align="center">
  </td>
</tr>
<tr>
  <td class="containerrow2_flower">
    <hr class="containermaster_flower"/>
    <table width="100%" border="0" cellpadding="0" cellspacing="0">
      <tr>
        <td align="left" valign="middle" nowrap>
          [ACTIONBUTTON:1]</td>
        <td align="right" valign="middle" nowrap>
          [ACTIONBUTTON:2] [ACTIONBUTTON:3] [ACTIONBUTTON:4]</td>
      </tr>
    </table>
  </td>
</tr>
</table>
<br/>
```

Now that you have renamed the references to the classes, you need to rename the actual classes. Open the container.css file and rename the classes to be the same as the classes used in the .htm source. This container.css code is as follows:

```
.containermaster_flower {
    width: 100%;
    background-color: #dfe5f2;
    border-right: #7994cb 1px solid;
    border-top: #7994cb 1px solid;
    border-left: #7994cb 1px solid;
    border-bottom: #7994cb 1px solid;
```

```
      moz-border-radius-bottomleft: 15px;
      moz-border-radius-bottomright: 15px;
      moz-border-radius-topleft: 3px;
      moz-border-radius-topright: 3px;
}
.containerrow1_flower {
      background-image: url(gradient_LtBlue.jpg);
}
.containerrow2_flower {
      background-color: #ffffff;
}
```

As with the `skin.css` file, you have some attributes of the `containermaster_flower` class that begins with `moz`. You can delete these attributes, as they are specific to Mozilla browsers and you will not use them here. Mozilla will use the normal border attributes.

The main table for this container is divided into three rows. The first row contains the current blue header. The second row contains the actual module. The third row contains the horizontal rule and the bottom action tokens.

The top row will have the gradient as its image. Since this top row uses the `containerrow1_flower` class, you need to add a reference to the gradient image to this class.

The new `containerrow1_flower` class is shown here:

```
.containerrow1_flower {
      background-image: url(GreenHorizGradient.jpg);
      background-repeat: repeat-y;
      background-color: White;
}
```

The image is now the horizontal gradient, which repeats in the vertical (y) direction. I made the background color white so that the gradient will look OK in cases in which the header is longer than the gradient (and because the gradient ends in white).

Next, you'll change the background color of the container from a light blue to a light green. You're also going to change the container border to a green. The new `containermaster_flower` class is shown following:

```
.containermaster_flower {
      width: 100%;
      background-color: #C7FFDC;
      border-right: #00A63E 1px solid;
      border-top: #00A63E 1px solid;
      border-left: #00A63E 1px solid;
      border-bottom: #00A63E 1px solid;
}
```

The new container looks like Figure 11-43.

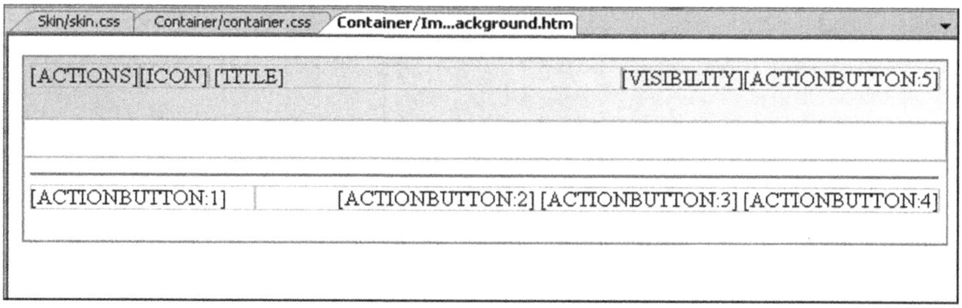

| Skin/skin.css | Container/container.css | Container/Im...ackground.htm | ▼ |

[ACTIONS][ICON] [TITLE]   [VISIBILITY][ACTIONBUTTON:5]

[ACTIONBUTTON:1]   [ACTIONBUTTON:2] [ACTIONBUTTON:3] [ACTIONBUTTON:4]

Figure 11-43. *The newly redesigned container*

The last thing you need to do is create a nice-looking picture of the container to be shown in the skin manager. However, you need to use it before you can create the image. Next, you will package it up and try it out.

Packaging the Container

Open Windows Explorer and navigate to the Flowers\Container working folder. Zip up all four files like you did with the skin files. Rename the zipped file Flowers.zip. This is shown in Figure 11-44.

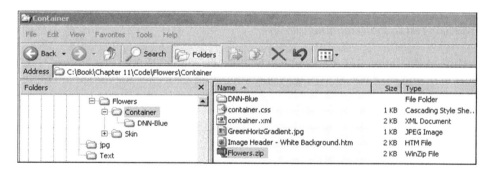

Figure 11-44. *The container package*

Now that you have the container all packaged up, you need to install it into your SkinTest portal.

Log into your SkinTest portal as host. Click Admin ➤ Skins. You should have the same page as shown in Figure 11-45.

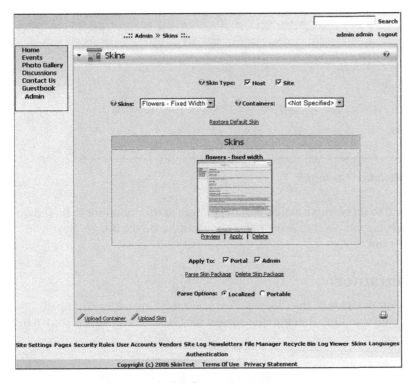

Figure 11-45. *The SkinTest upload container screen*

Click the Upload Container link, and you will be brought to the file manager screen. Use the Browse button to find your newly packaged container, and then click the Add link. This is shown in Figure 11-46.

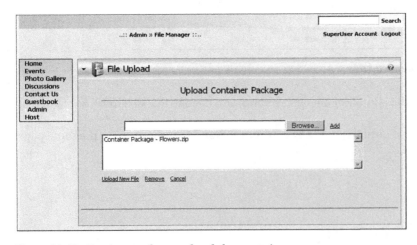

Figure 11-46. *Getting ready to upload the container*

Click the Upload New File link, and you should get a log file screen like Figure 11-47, show-ing you that the container upload was successful.

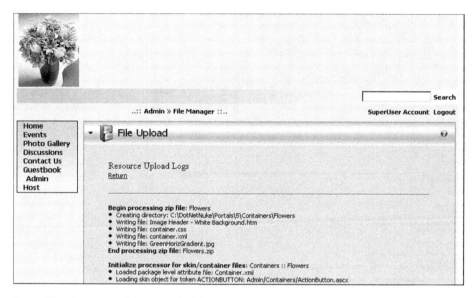

Figure 11-47. *Successful upload of the new container*

Click the Return link, and in the skins upload page, choose the Flowers container. You can see in Figure 11-48 that you do not have the image to see what it looks like yet.

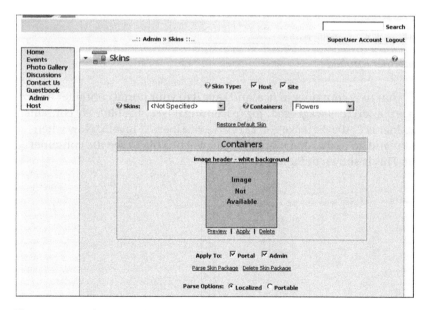

Figure 11-48. *Choosing the Flowers container*

Click the Apply link, and log out of the portal. You should be taken back to the portal's home page with the new container. This is shown in Figure 11-49.

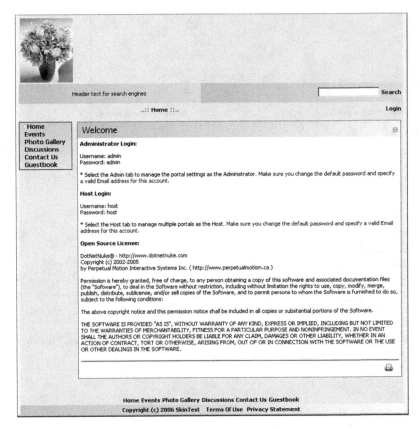

Figure 11-49. *The new container applied*

Take a screenshot of your new container in use, and save it to your portal container folder. Name the file `Image Header - White Background.jpg` (assuming it is a `.jpg` file). My container folder for this DNN container is `C:\DotNetNuke\Portals\5\Containers\Flowers`. Now when you log in as administrator and go to the skin manager, you will be able to see the container thumbnail on the screen. This is shown in Figure 11-50.

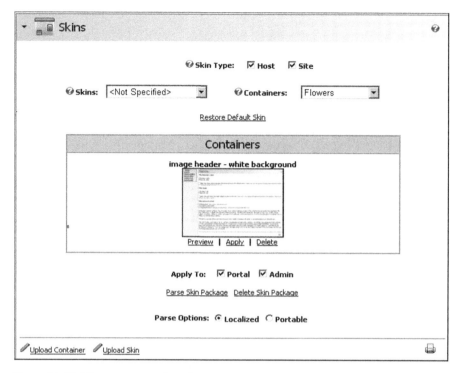

Figure 11-50. *The new container image*

If you want to distribute this container, do not forget to add the image to the container
.zip file.

Summary

How cool was that? You got to make your own skin and container. You found out that it was not
really all that hard, and in fact consisted almost entirely of look-and-feel design-oriented code.

There was no C# code in here, and if you did not have VWD as a designer, you could have
done the whole thing in a simple text editor.

DotNetNuke has enabled you to create a two-tiered presentation layer. The use of tokens
inside the skin and the ability of ASP.NET to compile user control code make for a fast load of
the skin for the user.

While this skin is not the prettiest or the most involved as far as images go, it does give you
the foundation to be able to create your own with confidence.

The next chapter will be rather advanced. It will cover topics such as JavaScript and Ajax
technologies to enable your website to be more efficient and faster.

CHAPTER 12

JavaScript and Ajax

This chapter deals with two aspects of website programming that can really propel your site to new heights.

So far in your ASP.NET programming, you have performed what is called server-side processing. If you remember, the TimePunch module used controls that all had attributes of `runat="server"`. Whenever an event occurred, that event was sent back to the server during a postback, and the event was processed using C# code.

This method of programming has two very important advantages. For one, it truly separates the code from the display. Second, by using the C# language, you are taking advantage of all the aspects that managed code has to offer. By this I mean that using C# allows you to have type safety, use IntelliSense, and use all kinds of neat objects, such as collections.

The one thing that server-side processing does not give you, however, is speed. Since the user does not care in the least how you programmed the website, speed is far more important than programmer efficiency.

To be truthful, speed has always been the most important factor. Let's look at the first component of speed: JavaScript.

JavaScript

JavaScript got its start in 1996 as a part of Netscape 2.0. Early JavaScript could crunch numbers well and could also modify forms.

Originally called LiveWire or LiveScript, the name was changed to JavaScript upon release to take advantage of the immense popularity of the Java programming language, which was also used for web programming. Many people think that JavaScript is Java or a subset of it. It is not Java. In fact, much of the syntax is different.

Later in 1996, JavaScript was submitted to Ecma for standardization. It then became known as ECMAScript. If you look in the .NET help, more often than not it refers to ECMAScript rather than JavaScript or JScript, which is Microsoft's version of ECMAScript.

What Can JavaScript Do?

JavaScript is often called the dynamic part of Dynamic HTML (DHTML). You know how you go to some sites and you run your mouse over a button and that button changes color or shape?

This is all done in JavaScript. What happens in a case like this is that an image is placed on the screen using an `<img>` tag. This tag is a valid HTML tag recognized by all browsers. An attribute is added to this tag denoting what happens during a mouseover event. This attribute will specify a JavaScript function to be called. This JavaScript function acts as the event handler, and the image is swapped out with a slightly different one.

This kind of thing is done all the time. You will do it a little later.

So what other things can JavaScript do for you?

- Handle HTML events

- Get access to any tag or control on the page and alter it

- Add attributes to any tag on the fly

- Create HTML code on the fly

- Perform mathematical functions and fill in fields

- Perform validation on text fields

- Create complicated objects and add them to the Document Object Model (DOM)

- Perform a postback

- Execute Ajax (Asynchronous JavaScript and XML) calls

- Perform drag-and-drop functions

These are just some of the things that I can think of off the top of my head. Once you learn how to use JavaScript, you can really make your websites pop.

JavaScript Syntax

As I said, many people think that JavaScript is a subset of Java. While it does look a bit like Java, the language is very different.

VB (before .NET) allowed you to create programs that had variables with no data type. Since VB had no way of knowing how you would use the variable, it automatically assigned it the type Variant. This type was big enough to hold any data type in VB.

JavaScript does the same sort of thing. In fact, you cannot define a data type for a JavaScript variable. Here is a small JavaScript function:

```
Function MultNums()
{
    var a;
    var b;

    a = 3;
    b = 4.5;
    a = a * b;
}
```

You can see that I declared variables a and b, but with no data type. I end up assigning an integer to a and a float to b. Then I save a float back into variable a. I can basically do anything I want with any variable I have.

This is drastically different from a similar C# function. A C# function would need to have the data types declared, and you would not be able to save a float value inside an Integer type.

You would need to cast it first, which would truncate the fractional part and could give you the wrong answer.

Here are some of the basics of JavaScript:

JavaScript functions can have arguments.

JavaScript functions can return values.

While the Ecma specification does not require semicolons at the end of *every* line, you should end every JavaScript line with a semicolon just to be sure your code does what you intend it to do. If you forget a semicolon here or there, your JavaScript code could behave differently than you expect.

JavaScript uses the same comments as Java or C#. You can comment out a line or part of a line with the double forward slash (//), or you can use the block comment, like this: `/* comment */`.

Normal scope rules apply to variables in JavaScript. Variables declared inside a function go out of scope when the function ends. Unlike in C# and Java, you can create global variables in JavaScript.

All JavaScript code on a page must be included inside `<script> </script>` tags.

Browsers recognize several scripting languages. You must declare that you are using JavaScript as opposed to VBScript, for instance. Most of the time this is done with a language attribute in the `<script>` tag.

JavaScript cannot access the variables in the code-behind page when running on the browser. However, it is possible to transfer values from the server to JavaScript before the page is sent to the browser.

The list of JavaScript features and when to use them can go on and on. The website `http://javascript.internet.com` has gobs of tutorials, code, and neat stuff on both JavaScript and Ajax. I suggest spending some time on this site and looking around at what you can do.

When to Use JavaScript in ASP.NET

You want to use JavaScript in ASP.NET when you need to do simple control validation and some DHTML work.

I know that ASP.NET has a Validate control, but this only validates your input after you are done. What happens if you want to prevent a certain input while the person is typing? You do not want to postback the whole page for every key that the user types.

The DHTML work I most often do is popping up message boxes and manipulating images.

Let's try a small example of a web page using JavaScript along with server-side controls.

A Small Example

This example will include several different ASP.NET server controls, as well as some HTML controls and images. JavaScript will be used extensively to make the page more dynamic.

This example is designed to give you a flavor of client-side programming vs. server-side programming. A full JavaScript tutorial is outside the scope of this book.

Start by creating a new website in VWD. Make sure that the location is File System and that the language is C#.

■**Note** Go to Tools ➤ Options ➤ HTML Designer, and change the CSS Positioning to No Positioning. From now on, you will be using tables to position controls and HTML tags.

While in design mode, drop an HTML table on the form (you will find this in the HTML group). This table is not a server control. You want to end up with a three-by-three-cell table on the form. Make the cells in the first two columns have a width of 33 percent, and make the cells in the last column have a width of 34 percent.

Make the cells in the top two rows have a height of 33 percent, and make the cells in the bottom row have a height of 34 percent. Figure 12-1 shows the design.

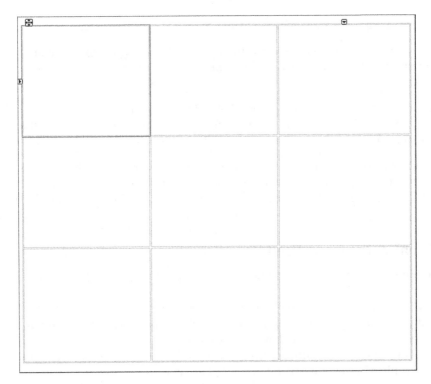

Figure 12-1. *A table with equally spaced rows*

You can select multiple cells at once and change common properties if you want to make things go faster.

Select all the cells in this table, and set the `align` property to `center` and the `valign` property to `middle`. This completes the setup of the table. Now you'll put some controls in the cells.

Server-Side Controls

You will start with the first row of cells. The controls in here will be from the toolbox, and they will be the standard server controls that ASP.NET provides. Add the following controls to the first cell in row one (since all the cells have center alignment, you will need to add the controls one at a time, and then press the Enter key to get to the next line before adding another control in the same cell):

- A label with the text "Server Text Box."

- A text box with an ID of `txtText`.

- A button with an ID of `cmdEnter` and the text "Enter."

The second cell in the first row needs these controls:

- A label with the text "Server Button."

- A button with an ID of `cmdChange` and the text "This Text."

The third cell in the first row needs these controls:

- A label with the text "Server List and Button."

- Two radio buttons with a `GroupName` of `rb`. Make the text for the first button read "Choose List 1," and make the text for the second button read "Choose List 2." Give the first radio button an ID of `rb1`, the second an ID of `rb2`. Change the `AutoPostBack` property of these radio buttons to `true`.

- A drop-down list with an ID of `lstList`.

The first row should look like Figure 12-2.

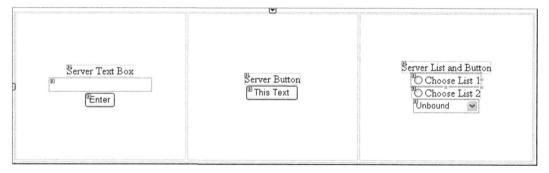

Figure 12-2. *The first row filled*

Now that you have these controls, you will need to add some code to them. Double-click the Enter button in the first cell of the first row. Double-click the "This Text" button in the second cell of the first row. Double-click the two radio buttons in the last cell of the first row. You should have four event handlers for these controls. Listing 12-1 shows the event handlers with the code for these controls. You will need to add the using System.Drawing directive to the top of your page first.

Listing 12-1. *Event handlers for the third cell's controls*

```
protected void cmdEnter_Click(object sender, EventArgs e)
{
  txtText.BackColor = Color.Red;
  txtText.ForeColor = Color.White;
}
protected void cmdChange_Click(object sender, EventArgs e)
{
  if (cmdChange.Text == "This Text")
    cmdChange.Text = "The Other Text";
  else
    cmdChange.Text = "This Text";
}
protected void rb1_CheckedChanged(object sender, EventArgs e)
{
  //Clear the list then add item according to this radio button
  lstList.Items.Clear();
  lstList.Items.Add("First 1 rb");
  lstList.Items.Add("First 2 rb");
  lstList.Items.Add("First 3 rb");
  lstList.Items.Add("First 4 rb");
  lstList.Items.Add("First 5 rb");
}
protected void rb2_CheckedChanged(object sender, EventArgs e)
{
  //Clear the list then add item according to this radio button
  lstList.Items.Clear();
  lstList.Items.Add("Second 1 rb");
  lstList.Items.Add("Second 2 rb");
  lstList.Items.Add("Second 3 rb");
  lstList.Items.Add("Second 4 rb");
  lstList.Items.Add("Second 5 rb");
}
```

You can see that the first cell's Enter button changes the text background and color. This is a common thing to do when validation of the text entry signifies an error.

The second button event handler changes the text in the button. You did this for the three time punch projects.

The last two radio button event handlers fill the drop-down list with different choices. This kind of thing is also common in web pages.

Compile and run the code. Click the second cell's button, and you will see the text change. The size of the button will also change to accommodate the text.

Type something in the first cell's text box, and press its button. The background color of the text box will change to red. If you click the radio buttons, you will see the list change values. This page is shown in Figure 12-3.

Figure 12-3. *Server-side controls*

This is all well and good—it all works, and the page seems to react instantly and appears to operate seamlessly.

Now it is time to see the downside of server-side controls. In the first cell of the second row, add an Image control. Make the width 250 pixels. This will clamp the image size to be within the cell.

I have supplied you with an image of some wild turkeys playing what appears to be slip-and-slide on my minivan. It was amazing to watch!

Anyway, this image is 600 KB in size. For the Image control, browse to this picture for the ImageUrl property. Your page should look like Figure 12-4.

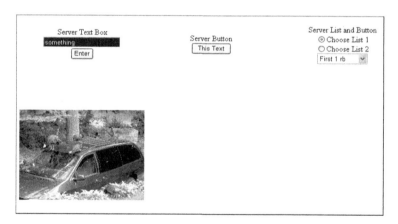

Figure 12-4. *Server-side controls, with an image*

Now I want you to click the second button and the radio buttons as well. You will see the page flicker as it rerenders the image every time you click something.

Note You will notice this flicker effect much more with Internet Explorer than with Firefox. However, even Firefox will bog down with a page that is very dense.

Now imagine a real estate page with many pictures and some server controls. How long would you wait for the whole page to render every time you clicked on it?

Speed Up with JavaScript

In the first cell of the third row, add a label with the text "Server Text Box." Below this, add a text box with an ID of txtClientText. Below this, add a button with an ID of cmdEnterClient and the text "Enter."

In the second cell of the third row, add a label with the text "JavaScript Highlighted Button." Below this label, add an Image control from the HTML section of the toolbox. This is really just a standard HTML <image> tag. Make the ID cmdImgButton.

I have given you three images that will be used in this control. They are as follows:

- btn_down.gif

- btn_hover.gif

- btn_normal.gif

In this Image control's src property, navigate to the btn_normal.gif file. This will show in the image. Your design page should now look like Figure 12-5.

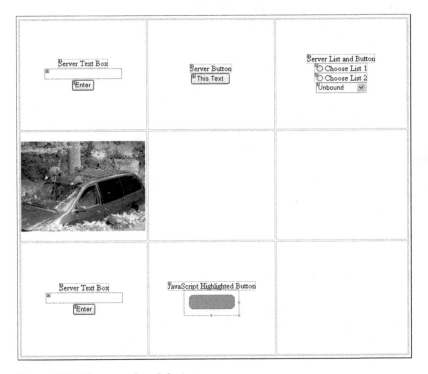

Figure 12-5. *The completed design page*

Now comes the cool JavaScript stuff. Listing 12-2 shows the HTML code for the last row of the table.

Listing 12-2. *The code for the last row of the HTML table*

```
<tr>
  <td align="center" height="34%" valign="middle" width="33%">
    <asp:Label ID="Label4" runat="server" Text="Server Text Box">
    </asp:Label>
    <asp:TextBox ID="txtClientText" runat="server"></asp:TextBox><br />
    <asp:Button ID="cmdEnterClient" runat="server" Text="Enter"
            OnClientClick="return ValidateClientText()" /></td>
  <td align="center" height="34%" valign="middle" width="33%">
    <asp:Label ID="Label5" runat="server"
          Text="JavaScript Highlighted Button">
    </asp:Label><br />
    <img id="cmdImgButton" src="btn_normal.GIF" style="cursor: pointer"
        onmousedown="cmdImgButton_Down()"
        onmouseup="cmdImgButton_Up()"
        onmouseover="cmdImgButton_Hover()"
        onmouseout="this.src='btn_normal.GIF'" /></td>
  <td align="center" height="34%" valign="middle" width="34%">
  </td>
</tr>
```

Notice the code for the first button. Here it is:

```
<asp:Button ID="cmdEnterClient" runat="server" Text="Enter"
        OnClientClick="return ValidateClientText()" /></td>
```

It calls out an event handler for the `OnClientClick` event. This is an event that ASP.NET gives you that fires before the server `onclick` event. Notice that it says `return ValidateClientText()`. If this JavaScript function returns `false`, then the server-side `onclick` event is aborted.

You would use this kind of event to do some validation before the server code takes over. There is no point in a server round trip if the user entered obviously wrong data. Here is the JavaScript function:

```
function ValidateClientText()
{
  // http://www.w3schools.com/css/default.asp
  //I can raise an alert in here
  //I can also set the background color and the font color
  //css: background-color
  //css: color
  //Must get element first
```

```
  alert("ValidateClientText");
  var txt = document.getElementById("txtClientText");
  txt.style.backgroundColor = "Red";
  txt.style.color = "White";

  //return false to prevent postback
  return false;
}
```

Notice that I declare a variable in here and get a reference to the text box by using the getElementById JavaScript command. I suggest you use this whenever referring to any control on an ASP.NET page. You can sometimes refer to the control directly, but sometimes not. Doing it this way always works.

This JavaScript function does the same thing as the server-side code did for the text box in the first row.

Listing 12-3 gives you the complete JavaScript code for this page. I put this section of code below the closing </html> tag.

Listing 12-3. *The complete Javascript code*

```
<script language="javascript">

function ValidateClientText()
{
  // http://www.w3schools.com/css/default.asp
  //I can raise an alert in here
  //I can also set the background color and the font color
  //css: background-color
  //css: color
  //Must get element first

  var txt = document.getElementById("txtClientText");
  txt.style.backgroundColor = "Red";
  txt.style.color = "White";

  //return false to prevent postback
  return false;
}

function cmdImgButon_Hover()
{
  var img = document.getElementById("cmdImgButton");
  img.src="btn_hover.GIF";
}
```

```
function cmdImgButon_Down()
{
  var img = document.getElementById("cmdImgButton");
  img.src="btn_down.GIF";
}

function cmdImgButon_Up()
{
  var img = document.getElementById("cmdImgButton");
  img.src="btn_normal.GIF";

}

</script>
```

Notice that all this code is wrapped inside `<script>` `</script>` tags. You will see the three JavaScript functions that change the image displayed for the button depending on the mouse actions.

Compile and run the code. Type something in the text box and click the Enter button. You will see the text box change with no flicker. Run the mouse over the center button image, and then click it. You will see that it changes color according to your mouse movements. Again, this is done with no server intervention and no flicker.

This kind of JavaScript programming really makes the page appear much faster. It also reduces the drain on the web server resources.

When you clicked the first button on the third row, you got a Windows message. While handy and easy to program, it is not friendly or pretty at all. I am going to show you a much better JavaScript alternative.

A JavaScript Window

When you first started working with HTML code in this book (the WebPunch project in Chapter 5), I had you change the HTML positioning option to absolute positioning. This is where each control is given a left and top position attribute, depending on where you placed it on the page. This allowed you to drag and drop controls on the designer as if you were building a Windows form.

Later in the TimePunch program for the DNN module (in Chapter 7), I had you place the controls programmatically within an HTML table. This allowed the controls to move relative to how the table was sized.

At the beginning of this example, I had you change the HTML positioning option to No Positioning. This allowed you to use the designer to place a table on the screen and drop controls within it.

There are occasions when you'll want to do a combination of both. One of those cases is when you want to make a visually pleasing message box to replace the Windows message box. Not only will this message box be nicer, but it will also allow you to gather input from the user and submit a page if necessary.

Flip over to the source pane in the IDE. Just between the ending `</div>` and `</form>` tags, enter the following HTML code:

```
<div id="popup" style="width: 400px; height: 200px;
            background-color: LightGreen; position: absolute; left: 200px;
            top: 200px; border: solid 2px red; visibility: hidden"
            align="center">
    <br />
    <br />
    <asp:Label ID="Label6"
                runat="server"
                Text="This is a friendler popup than the normal
                        'Alert' statement that windows gives you.">
    </asp:Label>
    <br />
    <asp:Label ID="Label7"
                runat="server"
                Text="Be aware though that this popup is not modal!">
    </asp:Label>
    <br />
    <br />
    <asp:Button ID="Button1"
                runat="server" Text="OK"
                OnClientClick="this.style.visibility='hidden'" />
    <br />
</div>
```

First of all, this `<div>` tag is outside of the table code. This means it is not in any cell. Next, you will notice that the `div` is positioned absolutely inside the `style` tag. The last thing to notice about this `<div>` tag is that its visibility starts out as hidden.

Inside this `<div>` tag, there are several controls that, when shown, make this tag look like a pop-up window.

The OK button inside this `div` uses some inline JavaScript code telling the `div` to disappear again.

Add one line of code to the `cmdImgButton_Up` event handler. Here is the event handler function, with the new code displayed in bold:

```
function cmdImgButon_Up()
{
  var img = document.getElementById("cmdImgButton");
  img.src="btn_normal.GIF";

  document.getElementById("popup").style.visibility="visible";
}
```

This line of code makes the `div` visible. Your pop-up window should now look like Figure 12-6.

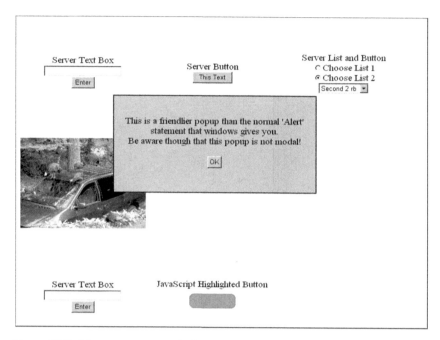

Figure 12-6. *A better pop-up window*

See how the div overlaps the underlying image? It really looks like a new window, when in fact it is not. Click the OK button in the pop-up window, and the window will disappear. Since this OK button is a server control, it will also do a postback to the server.

By the way, if you really plan to use div pop-ups like this, then I suggest that you learn how to make them modal. You should also thoroughly test them to see if they work in all the browsers you want them to, and if they cover over all the controls and other elements on the page. You do not want a pop-under window.

I have shown you some simple JavaScript that demonstrates that you can really make your website more dynamic with no extra load on the web server.

Debugging JavaScript

I bet you tried to set a breakpoint in the JavaScript somewhere. JavaScript cannot be debugged until the code is running. Since the JavaScript is most likely to be run on a different machine's browser than the server, there is no way to debug it using the IDE.

You can debug JavaScript, though, using the Microsoft Script Debugger. With this method, you can only debug JavaScript while in Internet Explorer. You cannot use this method inside Firefox. The Microsoft Script Debugger comes with Microsoft FrontPage or Microsoft Office 11.

■Note You can download an extension to Firefox that allows you to debug JavaScript running within Firefox. It is called Venkman and can be downloaded from www.mozilla.org. The following link provides a nice synopsis of the debugger: www.mozilla.org/projects/venkman/venkman-walkthrough.html.

Open Internet Explorer and click Tools ➤ Internet Options ➤ Advanced. Scroll down to Disable Script Debugging and uncheck this option. This is shown in Figure 12-7.

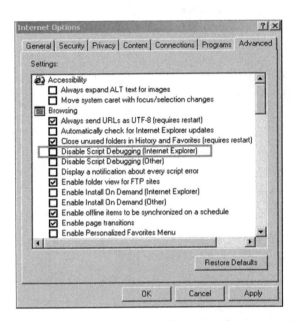

Figure 12-7. *Enabling script debugging for Internet Explorer*

Now that Internet Explorer is enabled for debugging, you can debug the JavaScript. Run your JavaScript project, and while in Internet Explorer, click View ➤ Script Debugger ➤ Open. Click Yes for the Microsoft Script Editor (MSE). MSE will open, and you will get a window telling you to step into a remote procedure call. This is shown in Figure 12-8.

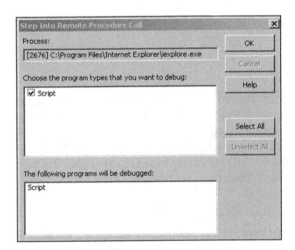

Figure 12-8. *Click OK to see the script.*

You should get what is shown in the two window panes in Figure 12-8. If you don't, you won't be able to view the script.

Scroll down to the `ValidateClientText` JavaScript function, and place a breakpoint as shown in Figure 12-9.

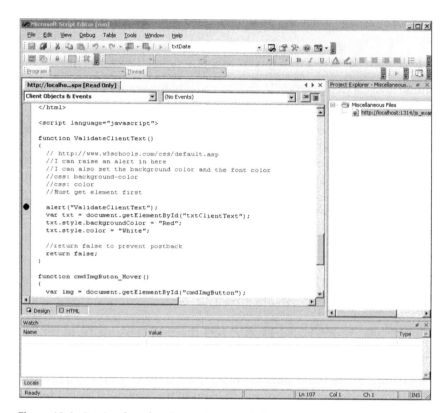

Figure 12-9. *Setting breakpoints in JavaScript*

If you click the bottom button, your code will stop at this point in the JavaScript code. From here, you can debug the code the same way that you can in the VWD IDE. This JavaScript debugging will save you tons of time.

The next thing you can use to really make your web pages pop is something called Ajax.

Ajax

As mentioned, Ajax stands for Asynchronous JavaScript and XML. (Truth be told, it does not have to be asynchronous, but the acronym is cool anyway.)

I love this technology. It is not new, but its potential has just recently been rediscovered. Ajax allows you to send and get information from a web server without having to post the whole page. I have been using it for a while now in both JSP and in ASP.NET 2.0. It really makes complicated pages run much faster, and eliminates any flicker associated with web pages. If you use Ajax with DHTML and JavaScript, then you can have a website that looks like a normal Windows Forms program.

Here is what you can do with Ajax:

- You can get information for a single text box on a web page and only change that text box. No need to refill any other field.

- You can send a simple static page to a client's browser and then fill the fields later. This makes for a faster-loading page. Once the page has loaded, you can use Ajax to update individual fields as needed.

- You can send information down to a web server without sending the whole page.

- A user can continue to use a web page while an Ajax call is being serviced by the web server; this is the asynchronous part.

I was initially concerned about including Ajax in this book. If you program Ajax all by yourself, it is very complicated. I have programmed Ajax from scratch in JSP, and it is not pretty. Most of the problems occur because Internet Explorer and Firefox implement Ajax differently.

However, I would say that in the last year, Ajax libraries have popped up that take the complicated nature of Ajax and abstract it away from the programmer.

ASP.NET 2.0 includes support for client callbacks. Client callbacks are ASP's nod to Ajax. Implementing callbacks is much easier than coding Ajax from scratch.

Note Microsoft is about to release the Atlas library somewhere around the middle of June 2006. Atlas is a complete Ajax library from Microsoft.

Ajax and JavaScript

Ajax relies heavily on JavaScript. Normally, if you were making an Ajax call, you would need to gather the parameters using a JavaScript function, and then make the Ajax call. Upon return, the browser would call another one of your JavaScript functions with the result of the call. This other JavaScript function would then be responsible for parsing the result and filling in the necessary fields on the form.

The *X* part of *Ajax* refers to XML. An Ajax call returns a string from the web server. This string can be of any length. If your Ajax call only needed a single field's value, then this simple string is fine. However, if your Ajax call needed to fill in several fields in a page, you would have a problem.

Ajax Limitations

The way to get around this multi-value return problem is to delimit the string on the server end, and parse it on the browser inside your JavaScript function. You can insert a non-printable character between each return value as you make up the string. Upon return, you would need to search this string and parse out the values.

The better way to do this is to create an XML document at the server with the key/value pairs of all the fields you want to update on the client. You would then serialize this XML document into a single string that gets passed back to the browser.

A big limitation, though, is that neither Internet Explorer nor Firefox handles XML natively. There are no JavaScript functions that can unwind an XML document and parse the XML element out of it. You need to code this by hand using extensive and complicated JavaScript code.

Fortunately, there are a bunch of XML JavaScript libraries on the Internet that will do the job for you. Quite a few of these are free.

So far, though, for all the Ajax I have used, I have only had a single instance in which I actually needed to pass back an XML string to the browser. I could always get away with a simple delimited string.

There is one other big problem with Ajax as it is implemented in Internet Explorer. Internet Explorer uses an ActiveX control to instantiate the XMLHttpRequest object necessary for Ajax to work. Disregarding the fact that ActiveX can be compromised, this control can be turned off by security-conscious IT personnel. If you turn off this control, the whole Ajax thing unravels and dies inside Internet Explorer.

While in Internet Explorer, choose Tools ➤ Internet Options, and click the Security tab. Click the Custom Level button, and then scroll down to the ActiveX settings. Figure 12-10 shows the setting responsible for unsafe ActiveX scripting.

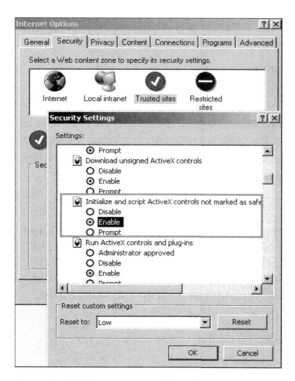

Figure 12-10. *Allowing unsafe scripting*

Disabling this security attribute will break Ajax in Internet Explorer when used over the Internet. It will not break it, however, when used on your own machine or in an intranet environment.

The way to get around this is to make the Ajax site a trusted site in Internet Explorer.

Firefox implements Ajax natively, and does not rely on ActiveX. Microsoft is changing the way it supports Ajax in Internet Explorer 7 to implement it natively, like Firefox.

ASP.NET and Ajax

Like I said, ASP.NET 2.0 handles Ajax for you by providing client callback functionality. In fact, this functionality is built directly into the ASP.NET 2.0 TreeView control. The Ajax comes into play when you use the "populate-on-demand" functionality of the TreeView control.

A Small Ajax Example

Start out with a new ASP.NET website project in C#. Mine is called AjaxExample. Add an HTML table whose attributes are as follows:

- Give the top two rows a height of 33 percent.

- Give the bottom row a height of 34 percent.

- Give the left two columns a width of 33 percent.

- Give the last column a width of 34 percent.

- Make each cell vertically align in the middle.

- Make each cell horizontally align in the center.

Note While I was investigating exactly how to do this callback thing, I found a small error in the ASP.NET help. The help and its example were completely wrong. The callback functionality was further refined after the help and help examples were generated, and the help never caught up. Perhaps it will have by the time you read this book, but as of writing, note that the help is wrong.

Essentially, start out the way you did with the JavaScript example. In the center cell, add an HTML Input button. Give it an ID and name of cmdFill, and make the text read "Fill List." Below this, add an HTML Select control. Give it a name and ID of lstList, and a size of 10. This is the number of values the list can contain before a scroll bar will be shown. Click the Style property, and in the Position window, make the width 50 percent. This is shown in Figure 12-11.

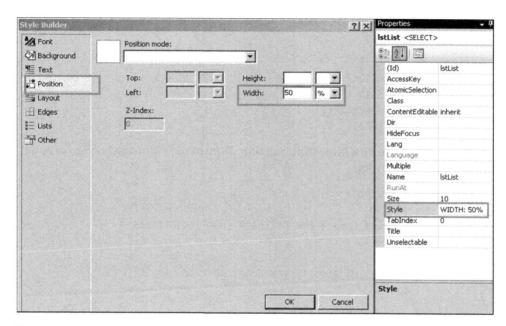

Figure 12-11. *Setting the style for the Select tag*

Your center cell should look like Figure 12-12.

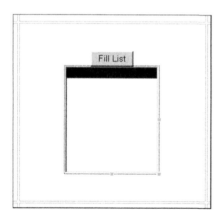

Figure 12-12. *The center cell, with a blank list*

Now comes the fun part. Flip over to the source and add an onclick event to the button. Here is the code:

```
<input id="cmdFill"
        type="button"
        value="Fill List"
        onclick="GetList()"
        name="cmdFill" />
```

The GetList function will be a JavaScript function. Type in the following JavaScript code just before the closing </head> tag:

```
<script language="javascript">

//This function gets called before the callback function happens
function OnBeforeCallback()
{
  //This function can be eliminated if you don't want to use it.
}

function CallServer(arg)
{
  //This is a little bit of HTML that replaces this
  //callbackStr variable with its C# string variable from the server.
  <%=CallbackStr%>
}

//This function gets called when the server has finished crunching code
//and sends back the answer
function CallbackResult(txt)
{
  var lst = document.getElementById("lstList");

  ClearOptions(lst);
  var info = txt.split("|");
  for(k=0; k<info.length; k++)
    AddToOptionList(lst, k, info[k]);
}

//This function gets called automatically if there is an error in the
//Ajax call.
function onError(message, context)
{
  alert("Ajax Error = " + message);
}
```

```
//This function gets called from pressing the button
function GetList()
{
  CallServer("Get List");
}

//This function clears a select list of all its options
function ClearOptions(OptionList)
{
  // Always clear an option list from the last entry to the first
  for (x = OptionList.length; x >= 0; x = x - 1)
  {
    OptionList[x] = null;
  }
}

//This function adds an option to the select list
function AddToOptionList(OptionList, OptionValue, OptionText)
{
  var LastOption;

  // Add option to the bottom of the list
  LastOption = OptionList.length;
  OptionList[LastOption] = new Option(OptionText, OptionValue);
}

</script>
```

The callback functionality lets you call a JavaScript function before the callback happens. You can call this function to validate controls or massage data, or you can do nothing at all in this function. I called this function OnBeforeCallback. You can call it anything you want. You will refer to it in the code-behind C# file. Microsoft likes to call this the "context." I think my name is better.

The CallServer JavaScript function actually makes the call. Again, I named this function myself. Notice the bit of code that reads <%=CallbackStr%>. This code is run on the server and substitutes the C# variable CallbackStr inside these brackets. As you will see later, this turns out to be a Microsoft JavaScript function call that does the actual callback.

The CallbackResult JavaScript function gets called automatically when the server is done processing your call. Note the txt argument. This is what the server returns to you. You will also note that in this function I am parsing the txt argument and filling in the Select control.

The GetList function will be called when the button is clicked. The ClearOptions and AddToOptionList functions handle the Select list tasks. (I told you there would be a lot of Java-Script involved here.)

Go to the C# code-behind page. Make sure your code matches the code that follows:

```csharp
public partial class _Default : System.Web.UI.Page, ICallbackEventHandler
{
  public string CallbackStr;
  public string CallBackReturnVal;

  protected void Page_Load(object sender, EventArgs e)
  {
    //This bit o' code gets translated and loaded into the client script
    CallbackStr = ClientScript.GetCallbackEventReference(this,
                                          "arg",
                                          "CallbackResult",
                                          "OnBeforeCallback",
                                          "onError",
                                          false);

  }

  #region callback functions

  //This function is required to handle the callback from the web page
  //It is invoked when the browser makes an Ajax request to the server
  public void RaiseCallbackEvent(string eventArgument)
  {
    for (int k = 0; k < 20; k++)
      CallBackReturnVal += "option" + k + "|";
  }

  //This function actually gives back the answer
  public string GetCallbackResult()
  {
    return CallBackReturnVal;
  }

  #endregion
}
```

In order to handle the callback functionality, you will need to make sure that your page inherits from the ICallbackEventHandler class. You will see this in the first line of this code.

You will need to code the RaiseCallbackEvent method and the GetCallbackResult method.

■**Note** If it were up to me, I would have renamed the RaiseCallbackEvent and GetCallbackResult methods "RespondToCallback" and "SendCallbackResult," respectively. I think this makes more sense according to what they actually do.

You can see that the `RaiseCallbackEvent` method creates a delimited string of list options. The `GetCallbackResult` method just returns them. You never call these methods directly. They are run as a result of the callback happening.

The last thing to talk about here is the `Page_Load` method. It sets a string (the one referred to in the ASP page as `<%=CallbackStr%>`) to the result of a `GetCallbackEventReference` method. The arguments of this method call are as follows:

- A reference to the current page.

- A string representing the argument; remember that in the JavaScript function `CallServer(arg)`, arg is the argument.

- A string whose value is the name of the JavaScript function that gets called when the server is done.

- A string whose value is the name of the JavaScript function to call before making the callback. This can be an empty string if you do not want to call a pre-callback function.

- A string whose value is the name of a JavaScript error function if something bad happens during the callback.

- A Boolean value that determines if the callback is synchronous or asynchronous. This call is asynchronous.

Now that you have the code set up, it is time to compile and run it. Before you do that, though, let's add some stuff to the other cells to make sure that Internet Explorer does not do a postback. Again, add an Image control to some of the other cells. Inside each image, refer to the turkey image I supplied. I have five of them on my page. This makes my page almost 3 MB in size. Any postback will take a long time to render the images.

Run your web page and click the button. Your screen should look like Figure 12-13.

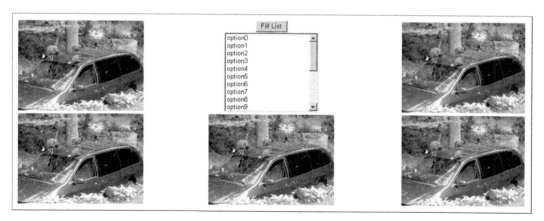

Figure 12-13. *The list is filled by callback.*

There should be no flicker when you click the button.

Right-click the web page and select View Source. Your `CallServer` JavaScript function should be like this:

```
function CallServer(arg)
{
  //This is a little bit of HTML that replaces this
  //callbackStr variable with its C# string variable from the server.
  WebForm_DoCallback('__Page',arg,CallbackResult,OnBeforeCallback,onError,false)
}
```

The `<%=CallbackStr%>` was replaced with the code in bold. You can of course enter this code directly in the ASP page. I think it is easier to understand, though, if you do it as shown in this example.

Summary

This chapter is pretty advanced. It has been all about increasing the performance and usability of your web pages.

You found out that that you can use JavaScript with the ASP server controls to bypass unnecessary postbacks to the web server. This allows you to add some DHTML to your page to make it stand out and be more responsive to the user.

The last thing I covered in this chapter was Ajax. Ajax is a technique that allows you to make asynchronous calls to the web server and get back results with no postback involved. While this involves a lot of JavaScript, the trade-off is often blazing speed in updating your web pages. If there is no rendering of the page when fields are updated, then there is no flicker, and the page will be more like a desktop application for the user.

The next chapter deals with what to look at if you want to take your web programming to the next level. Hopefully, this book will only be the starting point for your new website programming skills.

CHAPTER 13

∎∎∎

Next Steps and Suggestions

This book is essentially finished. No more projects. This chapter is about where you go from here.

This book was a short one when you consider the other huge tomes on web programming. However, I think it was just long enough. What follows are some ideas that you can use to further expand your knowledge.

I picked DotNetNuke as a web page development framework because it is easy to use and expand. It is very flexible in its methods of website personalization. It is also provides a sense of confidence in that it is quite secure.

While you can make perfectly good and slick web pages using VWD exclusively, the process would be very complicated and would require far more programming knowledge than this book assumes. It would also require a far larger book. DNN has abstracted that knowledge away from you to make it easy to develop web pages.

Of course, the fact that DNN and VWD are both free is a huge consideration as well.

ASP.NET Development

Some of you may be programmers who develop web pages and some may be web developers who dabble in programming. Either way, ASP.NET offers you a chance to really make your websites stand out.

Developers can leverage the visual development aspects of ASP.NET to get the look and feel of a web page going. Web developers can use client callbacks and the code-behind capabilities of ASP.NET to easily make the connection between the browser and the web server.

The thing is, with .NET, you no longer have to specify how the page information gets back to the server. Here is a typical start of an ASP.NET page:

```
<html xmlns="http://www.w3.org/1999/xhtml">
<head runat="server">
  <title>My Web Page</title>
</head>
<body>
  <form id="form1" runat="server">
```

POST AND GET

Other than Ajax, there are two ways to get information from a browser page to a web server. They are called GET and POST. Here are the differences.

With a GET, the information being sent is in the form of a querystring attached to the URL. A querystring is prefixed with a question mark. Here is an example of a GET: `http://mywebsite.com/topic.asp?FOOD_ID=1234`.

You can see that the page URL ends with a question mark, and the querystring is `FOOD_ID=1234`. This tells the web server to render a page with information pertaining to a `FOOD_ID` of `1234`.

Typically, a GET is reserved for getting data. A POST, on the other hand, is used for sending data back to the web server. A POST does not use the URL, but instead embeds all the page information inside the message.

A POST is encoded differently than a GET and is therefore handled differently when the message gets back to the server.

A GET can be bookmarked, but if a POST is bookmarked, you have no way of knowing if the information you have will be the same information you had when you bookmarked the site. Because a GET uses a querystring inside the URL, the bookmark will retain that querystring.

Note that there are only two attributes of the `<form>` tag. Now here is a typical start to a JSP page:

```
<html>
<head>
<title>Some page</title>
</head>
<body onload="loadFct()" onunload="unloadFct()" class="myclass">
<form autocomplete="off"
      action="<%= xSession.getServletPath() + "servlet" %>"
      id="mypage
      name=" mypage "
      method="post"
      enctype="application/x-www-form-urlencoded">
```

Note how the JSP HTML code requires a method type of post. It also includes the encoding type to be used when the page is posted.

While this difference may seem small, it is very nice that ASP.NET takes care of all this for you.

Another thing that ASP.NET helps with a great deal is *view state*. Normally, when you post a page back to the server, it sends the page back with new information. Even though most of this information existed in the fields before you posted the page, the web server must still gather this information and fill all the fields again when it renders the page.

ASP.NET uses view state. This is a method that is accomplished behind the scenes when you use ASP.NET server controls.

What happens is that the page saves all the information about all the fields on the page in a hidden tag. This tag and its contents are sent back to the web server, which refills all the fields on the page automatically when it renders the page.

You can see the VIEWSTATE field when you view the source on the page. You will do this in the next section.

Investigating ASP.NET

I have learned a lot over the years by looking at how other people create their web pages. I look at the visual and see what controls they are using and how the page is laid out. I also go under the covers whenever possible to see how it is all done.

A great learning experience when working with ASP.NET is to look at the code it produces. This is especially true if you are a JSP programmer or have written your own web pages by hand. Let's look at the example shown previously.

The HTML code for an ASP.NET page does not include any method of getting data back to the server. Nor does it include the name of the .aspx C# page that will handle the server requests from this page. You did see this information in the JSP code I showed you. If the mechanics of web pages require this information in the <form> tag, then where is it in the ASP.NET code?

Note that the <form> tag in the ASP code says runat="server". When the web server renders the page, this missing information gets injected into the HTML code before it gets sent to the browser. Let's prove it.

Open your JavaScript example project from the last chapter. (This was the one showing the turkeys mauling my minivan.)

Here is some of the ASP.NET code:

```
<html xmlns="http://www.w3.org/1999/xhtml">
<head runat="server">
  <title>Untitled Page</title>
</head>
<body>
  <form id="form1" runat="server">
    <div>
       <table style="width: 782px; height: 692px">
        <tr>
          <td align="center" height="33%" valign="middle" width="33%">
            <asp:Label ID="Label1" runat="server" Text="Server Text Box">
            </asp:Label><br />
            <asp:TextBox ID="txtText" runat="server"></asp:TextBox><br />
            <asp:Button ID="cmdEnter" runat="server" OnClick="cmdEnter_Click"
                        Text="Enter" /></td>
          <td align="center" height="33%" valign="middle" width="33%">
```

Run the code and browse the page in Internet Explorer. When the page appears, right-click it and scroll down the list of choices until you get to View Source. Click View Source, and your text editor will come up with the HTML code that the browser sees. Here is what ASP.NET did with the HTML code:

```
<html xmlns="http://www.w3.org/1999/xhtml">
<head><title>
    Untitled Page
</title></head>
<body>
<form name="form1" method="post" action="Default.aspx" id="form1">
<div>
<input type="hidden" name="__EVENTTARGET" id="__EVENTTARGET" value="" />
<input type="hidden" name="__EVENTARGUMENT" id="__EVENTARGUMENT" value="" />
<input type="hidden" name="__LASTFOCUS" id="__LASTFOCUS" value="" />
<input type="hidden" name="__VIEWSTATE" id="__VIEWSTATE"
        value="/wEPDwUKLTU1NDA1ODMyMWQYAQUeX19Db250cm9sc1JlcXVpcm
            VQb3N0QmFja0tleV9fFFgQFA3JiMQUDcmIxBQNyYjIFA3JiMjD
            Wr2rpwIPaoWbwN+T1IfbLU/gY" />
```

Look at the <form> tag. It now has a post method, and it calls out the server code (in the action attribute) that handles postbacks from this page. I have highlighted this code in bold.

Do you notice something else here that was not in the original HTML code in the IDE? It is the hidden VIEWSTATE tag. The value is hashed and encrypted. This tag contains all the information about all the fields on the form. You can imagine how long it can get in the case of a dense page.

This VIEWSTATE field is not the only hidden field you see. There are some others in here that are used to keep various forms of state.

The Server Controls

You can also use the View Source capability to figure out how the server controls work. Here is some of the ASP.NET code again:

```
<asp:Label ID="Label1" runat="server" Text="Server Text Box">
</asp:Label><br />
<asp:TextBox ID="txtText" runat="server"></asp:TextBox><br />
<asp:Button ID="cmdEnter" runat="server" OnClick="cmdEnter_Click"
                Text="Enter" /></td>
```

Here is the source that is sent to the browser:

```
<span id="Label1">Server Text Box</span><br />
<input name="txtText" type="text" id="txtText" /><br />
<input type="submit" name="cmdEnter" value="Enter" id="cmdEnter" /></td>
```

The asp:Label control is turned into a <span> tag. Using a <span>tag is a very common way to depict a label.

The text box is turned into an <input> tag whose type is text. This is also a very common way to represent text boxes on a web page.

The point I am trying to make here is that there are a finite number of HTML tags that can be used to represent controls. ASP.NET must conform to the HTML standards in order to run on all browsers. Therefore, ASP.NET server controls are always made up of common HTML tags used singly or in groups.

Most people who have programmed web pages by hand know all these tricks. ASP.NET does it all for you. It even injects custom JavaScript code when necessary to enhance a control.

I would suggest that if you really want to bring your web programming to the next level, then you should investigate how .NET does web pages. Perhaps you could invent your own server controls that enhance the existing ASP.NET server controls with your own custom JavaScript and HTML tags.

Other .NET Stuff

While you're enhancing your knowledge of how web pages work, here are some other things you may want to investigate:

- Go to www.quirksmode.com. You will find a wealth of HTML questions and answers including what works in which browsers. This is a very interesting site.

- Learn how to debug JavaScript fully. You saw that JavaScript can be debugged while running in Internet Explorer. You should also learn how to debug JavaScript running in Firefox.

- Learn the web page life cycle. Learn what gets rendered first, and where to put JavaScript in your page to make sure that you are referring to valid HTML tags.

There are lots of things to learn about HTML and ASP.NET. The more you know, the more you can do.

More Fun with DotNetNuke

Just as there are lots of things to learn about .NET, there is also a wealth of information to gain with DotNetNuke.

Do not just think of DNN as just a way to build websites. Don't forget that you have all the source code. You will find it very instructive to look through the source to find out how DNN does things. There are a lot of very smart people working on this product, and you can learn a lot from them.

Modules

I had you create a module for use in your DNN website in Chapters 7 and 8. This module was a little different from the usual fare in that it manipulates information you put in it. Quite a few modules out there are just created to present information in different ways. Many let you enter information such as blog modules; but again, they just present back the information that you entered.

Hopefully, you saw from the TimePunch module project that there are a lot of different things that you can do with modules. I suggest trying to write a few more.

While we're on the subject of modules, I also suggest that you learn how to package them and distribute them. Other programmers are selling modules—why not you?

Other DNN Tricks

One of the things that I put in the Flowers skin that I had you create was space for a module near the top of the page. The point of this space was to allow you to insert text that could be picked up by search crawlers.

Creating a great web page is only half the battle. You need to get people to see it. The way to do this is through search engines.

The search crawlers give precedence to information they find near the top of a page. They especially give preference to what is between the `<title>` `</title>` tags.

Do some research on the Web on how to get your page to rise up in the search rankings.

Blogs on Your DNN Site

One of the things that a search engine does when it finds a new site is index it, and then it comes back to it in a short while. If the site has not changed, then it waits longer before it reindexes the site. If your site doesn't change very often, then the search engine will begin to take a very long time before it comes back to your site.

There are millions of websites out there that must be indexed. Why spend time on yours if you will never change it?

I suggest that if it is at all appropriate, you should create a blog on your site. A blog changes all the time (provided you keep writing), which keeps your site fresh. A fresh site, of course, is visited more often by the search engines.

Reading the Documentation

When you installed DNN, you also downloaded the complete set of DNN documentation. This documentation includes help on not only how to create modules, skins, and so on; it also includes help on a rich set of API calls that DNN provides you. Here is a list of documents that I suggest you read:

- *DotNetNuke Client API Client Callback.pdf*: This document describes how DNN wraps the ASP.NET 2.0 client callback functionality. This wrapper allows you to use client callbacks in not only .NET 2.0, but also in .NET 1.1.

- *DotNetNuke Client API DragDrop.pdf*: This document describes how DNN containers can be dragged and dropped. You can use the information here to figure out how to include your own drag-and-drop functionality in the browser.

- *DotNetNuke Client API MinMax.pdf*: This document describes how DNN minimizes and maximizes the modules without using client callbacks. This document is very interesting, and the description and examples are very good.

- *DotNetNuke Client API.pdf*: This is the mother lode of documents for DNN. It describes the complete API and how the client and server talk to each other. The API can be used for creating modules, and it can also be extended.

- *DotNetNuke Localization.pdf*: DNN provides a way to localize your code for any culture; this document describes how this is accomplished.

Summary

All in all, DotNetNuke is a great way for you to establish a web presence. It doesn't require that you be an expert to create dynamic websites, and there's little you can't do with DNN if you take time to learn a bit more about it.

Considering that all the tools you need are free, and the websites you can create can be pretty slick, you can't lose.

I hope that you have found this book useful and interesting, and that you will expand your knowledge even further with the suggestions I've made in this chapter.

Index

Find it faster at http://superindex.apress.com

Find it faster at http://superindex.apress.com

forums.apress.com

FOR PROFESSIONALS BY PROFESSIONALS™

JOIN THE APRESS FORUMS AND BE PART OF OUR COMMUNITY. You'll find discussions that cover topics of interest to IT professionals, programmers, and enthusiasts just like you. If you post a query to one of our forums, you can expect that some of the best minds in the business—especially Apress authors, who all write with *The Expert's Voice*™—will chime in to help you. Why not aim to become one of our most valuable participants (MVPs) and win cool stuff? Here's a sampling of what you'll find:

DATABASES

Data drives everything.

Share information, exchange ideas, and discuss any database programming or administration issues.

INTERNET TECHNOLOGIES AND NETWORKING

Try living without plumbing (and eventually IPv6).

Talk about networking topics including protocols, design, administration, wireless, wired, storage, backup, certifications, trends, and new technologies.

JAVA

We've come a long way from the old Oak tree.

Hang out and discuss Java in whatever flavor you choose: J2SE, J2EE, J2ME, Jakarta, and so on.

MAC OS X

All about the Zen of OS X.

OS X is both the present and the future for Mac apps. Make suggestions, offer up ideas, or boast about your new hardware.

OPEN SOURCE

Source code is good; understanding (open) source is better.

Discuss open source technologies and related topics such as PHP, MySQL, Linux, Perl, Apache, Python, and more.

PROGRAMMING/BUSINESS

Unfortunately, it is.

Talk about the Apress line of books that cover software methodology, best practices, and how programmers interact with the "suits."

WEB DEVELOPMENT/DESIGN

Ugly doesn't cut it anymore, and CGI is absurd.

Help is in sight for your site. Find design solutions for your projects and get ideas for building an interactive Web site.

SECURITY

Lots of bad guys out there—the good guys need help.

Discuss computer and network security issues here. Just don't let anyone else know the answers!

TECHNOLOGY IN ACTION

Cool things. Fun things.

It's after hours. It's time to play. Whether you're into LEGO® MINDSTORMS™ or turning an old PC into a DVR, this is where technology turns into fun.

WINDOWS

No defenestration here.

Ask questions about all aspects of Windows programming, get help on Microsoft technologies covered in Apress books, or provide feedback on any Apress Windows book.

HOW TO PARTICIPATE:

Go to the Apress Forums site at **http://forums.apress.com/**.

Click the New User link.

You Need the Companion eBook

Your purchase of this book entitles you to buy the companion PDF-version eBook for only $10. Take the weightless companion with you anywhere.

We believe this Apress title will prove so indispensable that you'll want to carry it with you everywhere, which is why we are offering the companion eBook (in PDF format) for $10 to customers who purchase this book now. Convenient and fully searchable, the PDF version of any content-rich, page-heavy Apress book makes a valuable addition to your programming library. You can easily find and copy code—or perform examples by quickly toggling between instructions and the application. Even simultaneously tackling a donut, diet soda, and complex code becomes simplified with hands-free eBooks!

Once you purchase your book, getting the $10 companion eBook is simple:

❶ Visit **www.apress.com/promo/tendollars/**.

❷ Complete a basic registration form to receive a randomly generated question about this title.

❸ Answer the question correctly in 60 seconds, and you will receive a promotional code to redeem for the $10.00 eBook.

2560 Ninth Street • Suite 219 • Berkeley, CA 94710

eBookshop

Offer valid through 12/06.